Dynamic Supply Chain Alignment

To Jonathan Douglas Gattorna

Dynamic Supply Chain Alignment

A New Business Model for Peak Performance in Enterprise Supply Chains Across All Geographies

JOHN GATTORNA AND FRIENDS

GOWER

Published by
Gower Publishing Limited   Ashgate Publishing Company
Wey Court East   Suite 420
Union Road   101 Cherry Street
Farnham   Burlington,
Surrey, GU9 7PT   VT 05401-4405
England   USA

www.gowerpublishing.com

British Library Cataloguing in Publication Data
Gattorna, John.
  Dynamic supply chain alignment : a new business model for
  peak performance in enterprise supply chains across all
  geographies.
  1. Business logistics--Management.
  I. Title
  658.7-dc22

  ISBN: 978-0-566-08822-3

Library of Congress Cataloging-in-Publication Data
Gattorna, John.
  Dynamic supply chain alignment : a new business model for peak performance
in enterprise supply chains across all geographies / by John Gattorna and Friends.
    p. cm.
  Includes index.
  ISBN 978-0-566-08822-3
  1. Business logistics. 2. Delivery of goods--Management. I. Title.
  HD38.5.G376 2009
  658.7--dc22

                                                              2009003342
Reprinted 2009

Mixed Sources
Product group from well-managed
forests and other controlled sources
www.fsc.org Cert no. SA-COC-1565
© 1996 Forest Stewardship Council
FSC

Printed and bound in Great Britain by
MPG Books Group, UK

Contents

List of Figures

List of Tables

Acknowledgements

The genesis of this book lies in its forerunner, *Strategic Supply Chain Alignment* (Gower Publishing, 1998). Then, as now, Jonathan Norman, Publisher at Gower Publishing, has continued to encourage and motivate me to commit to paper my evolving thoughts about enterprise supply chains. A decade has passed, so there is plenty to write about as we follow the mantra 'learn-by-doing'. Also, the title this time has changed to emphasize the 'dynamic' rather than the 'strategic' characteristic. This is a natural progression as the world speeds up and markets become less predictable and more complex as a direct result. However, a decade later we also understand the underlying mechanisms at work much better, and this is helping to shape our response.

To all the authors who have joined me in this book, thank you. I owe you a debt of gratitude for the time, thought and effort you have all put into this book. Invariably these are all friends that I have made over the years in the global supply chain community; we have battled together to further our individual and joint understanding of this emergent field.

Special thanks are due to my two research assistants at the Macquarie (University) Graduate School of Management, Sydney: Kate Hughes and Maslada Nobhandhu. They have been very patient with me as I continued to deliver long lists of topics that I wanted them to find and research.

Finally, to Graciela Parker-Day, my Executive Assistant, who has shaped the text as it grew and developed all the diagrams, thanks for your continuing dedication; you can take a short holiday now before we start work on the next project!

John Gattorna
Sydney, Australia

Preface

Just like the world financial system, but for different reasons, corporations need a new business model for their enterprise supply chains going forward. The old conventions no longer work in this new world of volatile and increasingly unpredictable demand and supply. The enterprise needs to become more 'connected' to its own parts, as well as its partners up and down the chains it participates in. So too, we need to embrace new ways of looking at customers to gain deeper more insightful impressions of what they are telling us about the way they want to buy products and services. And then we need to convert these signals into corresponding action driven by the people in the business – leaders and staff alike – who are aligned to their customers' service expectations. This is the world of *dynamic* supply chain alignment where, increasingly, supply chains are the business.

Talk to different executives about supply chains these days, and you get as many different interpretations about scope, so let's put that one to bed right away. Supply chains (note the plural) pervade every enterprise on earth, and include all the activities, linkages, information exchanges and relationships along these 'chains' formed by parties who choose to work with each other, be they buyers or sellers, or indeed third-party service providers. The common goal of each and every 'chain' of parties is to move products and services ever closer to final consumption, more cost-effectively than the next competing chain.

But products and services don't just move through supply chains by themselves, adding value as if by accident! They move because humans make conscious decisions along the way. Some of these humans we call *customers* and they are downstream from a supplier or, indeed, at the end of the line if they are the ultimate end-user/consumer. They 'pull' products through the pipeline on demand. And yet modern firms know relatively little about the 'buying behaviour' of their customers/consumers. It's an unforgivable lapse, and one that will come back to haunt these firms in the difficult times that we face following the recent meltdown of financial services and subsequent recession in the real economy.

On the inside of the enterprise we have another category of humans in the form of employees, managements and boards, all making decisions at various levels which directly and indirectly impact on the way products and services are 'pushed' through the pipeline. Taken together, I estimate that 40–50 per cent of the activity in contemporary supply chains is driven by human behaviour, enabled, of course, by technology (another 40 per cent), and physical infrastructure (10 per cent). And yet we know so little about how this human behaviour plays out across enterprise supply chains except to observe the visible outcomes. What is missing from this picture?

A NEW WAY OF ORGANIZING OUR RESOURCES

In a world that grew up in relatively predictable operating environments over a long period after the Second World War, we fell into sloppy ways and became content with the functional silos that grew like Topsy in our businesses and across whole industries. These were slow and ponderous structures, but they seemed to do the job at the time. And they made managing people in large corporations relatively easy. But as we entered the new Millennium the world accelerated thanks to the Internet, but at the same time became increasingly unpredictable. Customers learned and became more demanding, seeking ever-faster response times. Our typical response was to look for technological solutions, underpinned by increasing process standardization. Something had to give, and it has. Companies that have pursued such an approach have found themselves seriously misaligned with their customers, and in many cases the short-term solution has been near-fatal and only saved by costly manual intervention. Sainsbury's, the UK retailer, is a prime example and an early victim of this cycle.

DYNAMIC ALIGNMENT: THE WAY TO GO

The concept of 'alignment' is simple to say, yet not so simple to implement, but leading-edge firms that are embracing alignment principles are reaching significantly higher levels of performance. In brief, in order to achieve sustained corporate performance, it is necessary to 'align' four vital facets of an enterprise's operation: an understanding of customers; the corresponding strategies to approach and satisfy these customers; the internal capability of the enterprise, where all the energy and resources reside; and the leadership style of the top management team. This is not a supply chain concept per se; rather, it is a whole-of-business concept. The connection we found was that, if you understand how to align businesses with their customers and suppliers, it will inform you how supply chains can be successfully configured and operated.

The breakthrough came after years of work in the field when we realized that, for any product or service category, there exists only a limited number of *dominant* buying behaviours among target customers – indeed, no more than three or four. By definition, this means that we can largely cover the market with a correspondingly small number of supply chain configurations, reverse-engineered back from the previously identified behavioural segments. Also, we found that these natural buying behaviours could change for short periods under new or different situations, and then later return to their original state. This provides the *dynamic* component of business and its supply chains, a phenomenon that has never previously been adequately addressed by enterprises.

THE FOUR GENERIC TYPES OF SUPPLY CHAIN

Continuous replenishment supply chains focus on the relationship with customers (and suppliers), and involve sharing information freely. Strategic Partnerships, long-term stability and mutual trust are all key components of this type of supply chain. Indeed, this type indicates the 'zone of collaboration' which is very distinctly restricted to those parties who have collaborative values and are committed to helping each other for mutual benefit.

The particular subculture that must be present to drive this type of supply chain is characterized by an organization design that involves a cluster of multidisciplinary personnel, with a bias for relationships, underpinned by standard processes that focus on relationships.

IT applications include Customer Relationship Management (CRM), Supplier Relationship Management (SRM) and Key Performance Indicators (KPIs) all of which are aimed at retaining loyal customers and suppliers. The leadership style for this type of supply chain is necessarily one of consensus and concern for other team members.

Lean supply chains focus on efficiency and lowest cost-to-serve. In order to achieve this outcome, high-volume, low-variety business is ideal, and products are made and distributed to forecast. Economies of scale are the order of the day, in what is mostly a predictable operating environment for essentially mature products and services. The subculture that underpins this type of supply chain is one that focuses on reducing the cost of core processes and aims for a high Delivery-In-Full-On-Time-Error-Free (DIFOTEF). Conformance to policy is the order of the day, and routine is not to be disturbed under any circumstances. The leadership style emphasizes stability and cost control. Good steady work, if that is what you like.

Agile supply chains are all about delivering a quick response to demanding customers, mostly by making to order using postponement techniques. This has to be the case because the operating environment is now quite unpredictable.

The organization is composed of clusters of multidisciplinary personnel who have a common goal of speed as they focus on specific customer segments. The leadership style is unrelenting in the quest to meet tough objectives, often in high-growth markets.

Fully flexible supply chains are designed to meet unplanned and unplannable demand. The subculture is essentially entrepreneurial and involves a small group of like-minded individuals seeking creative solutions, fast. The leadership is by inspiration, and always authentic.

However, it is rare to find the same type of supply chain on both the supply side and the demand side. The more usual situation is a combination. For example, the Spanish retailer, Zara, uses 'lean' supply chains to procure and import uncut fabric from low-cost source markets such as China, bringing it closer to its consumer markets. Indeed, it maintains a 'fabric bank' in Spain and surrounding countries, and about every three weeks it decides on designs for the next cycle, selects and cuts the fabric, manufactures the finished garments and distributes them to its stores across Europe and the Far East. This latter operation is very fast by clothing industry standards and is in effect an agile supply chain at work. Daewoo Shipping in Korea do something similar, but their product is a supertanker or ore carrier launched every 1½ days – a phenomenon of superb heavy engineering technique.

FROM DENIAL INTO THE LIGHT

The truth is that many senior management teams have been, and still are, in denial about the influence of human behaviour on the operational (and financial) performance of the firm and its constituent supply chains. Why? Because it is all a bit scary to contemplate. It means that the modern line executive has to get out of his/her functional ghetto and become more of a 'universal' manager, seeking to understand and mould the performance of all the functions inside the enterprise for the benefit of customers, suppliers and the enterprise itself. When more executives get to this stage of development the profits will flow more readily, and sustainability of performance will not be the big issue that it is today. The way forward is right there in front of us; but we must have the courage to throw off old ways and embrace the new.

Prelude:
Findings of Expert Panels
– Shades of Things to Come

John Gattorna

In February 2008 a major event in the Asia Pacific supply chain calendar was held in Melbourne – the 2008 Supply Chain Business Forum. The event was hosted by the Institute for Logistics and Supply Chain Management (ILSCM) at Victoria University, Melbourne and co-hosted by the Macquarie Graduate School of Management (MGSM), Sydney, under the direction of Dr John Gattorna who holds adjunct positions at both institutions.

The three-day event was organized around eight panels, each debating topics of great relevance to the wider business community. Attendance at the Forum was by invitation only, which meant that the 100 panelists and participants who attended were there because they were passionate about the topics on the agenda and wanted to contribute their knowledge and experience.

A 'Proceedings' document was prepared to record the outcomes of the various discussions, and Anna Game-Lopota, editor of *Logistics* magazine in Australia, agreed to draft short articles to capture the spirit and essence of each panel discussion. An adapted version of these articles follow, and are included here because they point the way to many of the topics that are covered in more detail later in this book. The original versions were also published as a series in *Logistics* magazine during 2008.

ENTER THE VALLEY, ASCEND THE MOUNTAIN[1]

Anna Game-Lopata

'Modern companies are overservicing some customers and underservicing others; but for the most part they don't know which is which', says John Gattorna at the 2008 Supply Chain Business Forum.

When Stuart Whiting joined DHL Express Taiwan as general manager he found an organization with no standard approach to understanding or aligning with its customers.[2]

'Companies traditionally look at customer segmentation from a transactional point of view,' Whiting explains. 'So the heaviest volume customers would be managed by the major account managers, and the lowest volume customers would be managed by the customer service department.'

'We knew instinctively this wasn't right,' he says.

Whiting told the 2008 Supply Chain Business Forum panel on aligning enterprise supply chains with customers, suppliers and 3PL providers that, while DHL was managing customer demand, processes weren't systematized.

'We had multiple behaviours and multiple responses within the organization,' he says. 'But we weren't optimized. We weren't providing the best of the organization or fully satisfying customer needs.'

Whiting realized that if DHL Taiwan wanted to be number one and continue to stay ahead of its competitors, it was absolutely critical that the team accept the need to change – a particularly difficult task given that he was the only English speaker in the Mandarin-speaking office.

'I was honest,' Whiting recalls. 'I said: "I don't know what we're going to be changing, but let's go into this with the view that we've got to change the status quo. If we can do that, it will mean our eyes are open as we're finding out what we need to achieve."'

Whiting took action, adopting supply chain thought-leader John Gattorna's model of 'Dynamic Alignment'.

Gattorna, whose initiative was behind the invitation-only Forum, and who was chair of the panel, argues that customers' buying behaviours aren't chaotic; rather, patterns are always discernible if you look hard enough.

> '*Modern companies are overservicing some customers and underservicing others; but for the most part they don't know which is which.*'

'Unless you start with a frame-of-reference, your operations strategy and everything you're doing in terms of transformation is really just guesswork,' he says. 'The only absolutely accurate frame of reference is a complete understanding of what customers want when they buy your products and services.'

Gattorna's Dynamic Alignment model, explained fully in his most recent book, *Living Supply Chains*,[3] deconstructs customer segmentation according to four main dominant buying behaviours and the associated customer service expectations. These behaviours are defined as 'collaborative', 'efficient', 'demanding' and 'innovative solutions'.

'Collaborative' behaviour relates to environments with stable, predictable patterns of demand, where mature, sometimes augmented, products are delivered regularly. Customers in this segment are loyal and forgiving, desiring a trusting collaborative partnership.

'Efficient' buying behaviour also relates to customers with regular or predictable demands, but it involves a more adversarial, transactional relationship.

'Demanding' customers require rapid responses to unpredictable supply-and-demand situations. They are price-aware, make commercial decisions based on pragmatism and prefer a more impersonal, outcome-oriented relationship.

The 'innovative solutions' customer looks for supplier-led developments and the delivery of new ideas, fast. He or she functions in high-risk conditions where demand is extremely volatile, requiring speed, change, innovative solutions and individual decision-making. This customer will pay no matter what the price.

Although the patterns are consistent, Gattorna says that organizations can't set up their supply chains on the assumption that customers will always buy products the same way – even staples like milk or petrol.

'What you need to do is set up three or four supply chain configurations involving different combinations of standard processes, and hard-wire them into your business. Then, if a loyal customer suddenly has a disaster and wants you to turn inside-out to solve the problem, you've got the capability already embedded. You can then revert to the original, low-cost lean supply chain when the crisis subsides.'

Gattorna sees supply chains as 'living systems', driven by human beings – customers, suppliers and third parties. The key to Dynamic Alignment is the process of successfully matching internal business subcultures and leadership styles with the specific ways in which customers like to buy products and services.

'Once you understand the buying patterns for any product or service, then it's not difficult to reverse engineer the organizational design, processes, Key Performance Indicators (KPIs) and incentives, internal communications – all the things you need to use to shape the subcultures within your business that drive the different "conveyor belts" towards customers,' he explains.

But the proof is in the pudding. It took Stuart Whiting eight months of intensive customer interviews and market research to really understand the dynamics of DHL's Taiwan marketplace, including customers' behaviours and the most appropriate strategies to address their needs.

'We've seen a significant increase in profitability from our most important collaborative customer segment,' Whiting says. 'By systematizing our response, we also opened up a whole new hitherto untouched customer segment.'

'Looking at our customer satisfaction responses in that very short period of time, we saw a 15 per cent increase across what we call "first-choice KPIs". These are the attributes that make DHL the first choice – the qualities that make a customer call 1800 DHL before calling any of our competitors.'

'The process of developing a systematized model of dominant customer behaviours has also reduced our cost-to-serve from 2.9 to 2.5 per cent of revenue,' Whiting adds. 'With an optimized model, I can see we're becoming sharper with the new focus. Previously we had the mentality of "one-size-fits-all" at the lowest possible unit cost to DHL. But the new approach allows us to respond to four dominant customer behaviours in the marketplace and ensures we deliver the appropriate agile or flexible responses in line with particular customer demands.'

Whiting says that understanding customers and the marketplace is the hardest thing for a company to do.

'If you haven't yet developed that critical understanding, you have no business playing with your supply chain,' he asserts.

At the New Zealand-based dairy cooperative Fonterra, customer segmentation enabled the misalignment of objectives and processes to be identified.

'With segmentation complete, we intended to meet the requirements of our customers in a phased approach,' says general manager and panelist Nigel Jones.[4]

However, when data depicting what customers wanted Fonterra to deliver was compared with what the company planned to supply and what was actually delivered, the differences were marked.

'Our objectives were defined to drive performance at the business unit level and not across the end-to-end supply chain,' Jones explains. 'This ended up causing one business unit's set of objectives to impact the performance of the others.'

'In addition, our production planning and manufacturing scheduling processes weren't adequately linked. We were left with a situation where there wasn't enough time to correct supply plans when deviations arose, which affected the downstream supply chain.'

'Once you understand the buying patterns for any product or service, then it's not difficult to reverse engineer the organizational design, processes, Key Performance Indicators (KPIs) and incentives, internal communications.'

'Despite our good intentions, visibility was very limited – both in relation to customer requirements and off-take across the supply chain, and impacted negatively on operational performance. Often the wrong assumptions were being made for packing and shipping processes.'

With no mechanisms in place to stabilize the 'must do' part of the business, constant replanning of supply was required, and this increased costs.

Once the alignment of Fonterra's objectives was achieved, the organization was able to collect better information to drive planning and improve plan stability.

'Visibility of production schedules and material availability dates finally began to increase', Jones says, 'along with increased compliance to plan and a decrease in rework.'

Panelists agree that it's essential to incorporate strong leadership into the process of developing an organization's internal cultural capability.

For panelist and managing director of Perth-based company Distinctive Building Products, Brett Rice, the process of understanding customers, recognizing internal culture and reforming the associated attitudes and belief systems was a journey that took two years at his former company, Boral Panel Board (WA), during which a drop in revenue had to be endured.

'In WA, the demand for labour is very intense,' Rice says. 'With a high level of staff churn it's difficult to instil strong values around culture and process.'

'Misalignments were exacerbated by the salespeople's tendency to shy away from customers who needed better service, and overservice those who were stable. Once we had segmented our customers, we needed to align what we knew about them with the way we executed internally. It was time to enter the valley and ascend the mountain.'

'We approached this by embedding the values we were promoting into every meeting and regularly reviewing our alignment strategies with customers. We stay close to all our teams and customers, and make a point of investing heavily in development and training, including attending graduations.'

As a result of its focus on customer processes and culture, Boral Panel Board (WA) achieved an increase in sales volumes of 52 per cent over three years.

'Revenues increased by 53 per cent and operating profit by 350 per cent,' Rice proudly says. 'There was an enormous improvement in our ability to meet demand as cultural reform took effect. As our track record grew, so did customer expectations, which also invigorated our performance.'

According to DHL's Stuart Whiting, everybody in the organization should be a leader.

'It doesn't matter whether you're a driver, customer service manager, salesperson or the boss of an organization; you've got to behave like a leader in your area of influence.'

'One of the things I promote heavily is making sure that every employee understands the strategy we are pursuing in the marketplace. This allows them to adopt the mannerisms of leadership and make their own particular contribution.'

'Our team therefore knows what we've done as an organization to align to customers' buying behaviours, they know all of the attributes that make DHL different to the competition, and as a result the whole organization is genuinely a lot more customer-centric.'

GLASS WALL[5]

Anna Game-Lopata

Not all business is good business in the outsourcing relationship, the 2008 Supply Chain Business Forum finds. Leading supply chain solutions provider Linfox Logistics has reduced its customers from 300 to 104 since 2002, while increasing profits by 200 per cent.

CEO Michael Byrne told the 2008 Supply Chain Business Forum panel on the critical contribution of 3PLs that his company's strategy has been viewed as high risk and therefore controversial.[6]

'Linfox Logistics is asset-heavy, while others are stripping assets,' he explains. 'More importantly, we spend a lot of time thinking about customers. We see customers as unique – as business partners.'

'We have no standard offering. Customers want to be valued, they want attention and they're smarter and better informed than in the past. We need to keep up with them and be robust with them,' he says.

Byrne, whose company sponsored the invitation-only Forum, says he doesn't think that 3PLs look after their customers very well.

'For a strategic partnership to succeed, execution needs to be near perfect,' Byrne says. 'Since such strategic relationships require enormous effort and time, it makes commercial sense to have fewer customers.'

'More importantly, we spend a lot of time thinking about customers. We see customers as unique – as business partners.'

According to panel chair, Professor Martin Christopher of the UK's Cranfield School of Management, the rapid change from a supplier-driven market to one of mass customization has increased the need to harness the skills and capabilities of others.

'Because skills are of strategic importance to business the trend is irrevocably moving towards virtual arrangements and the sharing, rather than ownership, of data,' he says.

'Most businesses are not prepared to pass over control, and are not yet ready to change the structure of their business,' Christopher maintains. 'A certain level of discomfort with this change is also inevitable because most businesses are still primarily transactional rather than strategic in their relationships with providers.'

With 15 years' experience in the area of outsourcing contract law, panelist Jeremy Clarke, principal lawyer with the UK firm LLC Law points out that, in an environment where many brand organizations outsource close to 100 per cent of their activities, the concern over control should now be 'old hat'.[7]

'In such a partnership, information has to be disclosed in order for the provider to understand the user's business,' Clarke says. 'We need to actually embrace a policy of opening ourselves up to appropriate organizations who offer the opportunity to improve our business overall, and that is a matter of trust.'

'It's also a matter of careful selection, employing the right kind of protections, controls, due diligence and appropriate contract provisions to make sure that issues don't arise. If a provider can't demonstrate the right approach to safeguarding confidential business information, the user shouldn't even be talking to that provider,' he says.

According to panelist Connor O'Malley, Group Executive of Logistics and Planning for National Foods Australia, strategic conversations can't take place unless a 3PL exhibits near-perfect operational execution. The fact that true partnerships remain problematic and 25 per cent of organizations are still unhappy with their logistics provider seems to add weight to this view.

Jeremy Clarke argues that 3PLs are often expected to garner all the core information about a user organization and somehow pull out a 'white rabbit' solution under impossible circumstances.

'Contracts are often rudimentary and not particularly well thought through,' he explains. 'They tend to be too lengthy in the areas that are less important and pretty thin in the areas that are very important, like Service-Level Agreements (SLAs) and KPIs.'

'If you haven't got a very clear understanding of your own business, the provider organization in turn will have a distorted view, too. This will produce a standard kind of contract where non-standard issues might be the most critical, even at the heart of why a company might be outsourcing in the first place. That's simply a recipe for an inappropriate contract.'

'Each of the parties must make sure that it has a framework or structure in place governing the relationship which is straightforward, does the job, provides appropriate protection, gives a fair balance of risk and reward, and is hopefully long term. Otherwise, you're continually reinventing the wheel over very short periods of time.'

'Early termination is a major problem and a headache. In essence we've got two organizations. One of them is buying and one of them is selling. Each party needs to fully understand the other's business, the way it operates, its culture and objectives. Undertaking this process is the key to successful outsourcing, but it's a complex task. It takes some work. It doesn't fly off the page, you've got to drill in, and invest a minimum of three months up-front. And then at the end of three months you can more accurately decide whether you have the right fit.'

Panelists agree that large contracts should be a facilitator for leveraging the business, rather than an excuse to hide behind a problem. Users must understand their outsourced activity and proactively manage service or manufacturing partners to ensure that they continue to do the best job possible or risk losing their competitive position in the market.

On the other hand, Jeremy Clarke questions whether 3PLs should wait to achieve operational excellence before embracing strategic relationships.

'Engaging in a collaborative framework and improving your buy-and-sell contracts will help organizations better understand their business,' he says. 'It's almost like a self-fulfilling prophecy. Wisely chosen organizations with whom you're engaged will make an immediate contribution to improved efficiency.'

Clarke says that 3PL relationships of the future will be underpinned by contracts refined to include more KPIs and service levels, as well as provisions to review and refresh these periodically.

'Such contracts are the basis for providing services on the ground, whether they're warehousing or transport or other value adding services,' he says. 'Rather than shoehorning strategies for improving the business into these arrangements, some companies are developing new structures where the buy–sell agreement is overlaid with a collaborative framework. This needn't be a complicated legal document, but one that can transition from the initial two or three years to a longer period, such as five or ten years. Inviting your service provider to take a more proactive role in terms of the future development of your business takes place at a different level and requires multiparty involvement.'

> *'We need to actually embrace a policy of opening ourselves up to appropriate organizations who offer the opportunity to improve our business overall, and that is a matter of trust.'*

'Modern-day business moves very quickly, and the driver is fast change,' Clarke warns. 'If businesses put contracts in the bottom drawer, and fail to measure their business performance in a meaningful way, they'll be unable to function effectively in the long run. That's why I say look at contracts and keep those KPIs alive, fresh and relevant.'

Connor O'Malley believes that it's up to the customer to determine the extent of a relationship with a provider. 'Common myths include the notion that 3PLs don't add value, that they don't understand their customer and that they're more focused on increasing their own margins than reducing a customer's costs,' he points out. 'Whatever the level of the relationship, values must align. The customer's value proposition must be clearly defined for both parties.'

'Inevitably there will be a wall between providers and their customers,' O'Malley says. 'In the worst scenario it's a brick wall; in the best, it's a glass wall. It's up to the customer to let their 3PLs in.'

BETTER THAN A CURE[8]

Anna Game-Lopata

Supply chain risk keeps CFOs awake at night, yet they commonly say that they don't have the time or budget to deal with it, according to Vinod Singhal of Georgia Tech in the US.[9]

Supply chain disruptions are becoming more frequent. According to a recent Accenture survey of 151 industry executives in the US, 73 per cent had experienced significant disruptions in the last five years.[10] Despite this, further research by Aberdeen Group reveals that less than half these companies have systems in place to manage and respond to disruptions.

Professor Vinod Singhal, chair of a panel exploring the financial impact of supply chain disruptions at the 2008 Supply Chain Business Forum, believes that executives have too many risks to manage, so it's a question of where to focus limited resources. Singhal told the invitation-only Forum, an initiative of international supply chain expert John Gattorna, that while terrorist attacks, natural disasters and other highly publicized supply chain disruptions generate discussion and concern, the industry still doesn't really know where to direct its energies. 'Most executives can see the value proposition of improving efficiencies and reducing costs,' Singhal says, 'but they have a hard time getting a handle on the economic consequences of supply chain disruptions. This may prevent them from making investments and changes that could mitigate the risk of disruptions.'

By way of example, Singhal points to the 2007 product recalls at Mattel. 'The company wouldn't have expected its Chinese suppliers to be using lead paint,' he says. 'Similarly, Airbus wasn't able to predict development woes which caused delays to the delivery of its A380.'

'Supply chain risk keeps CFOs awake at night, yet they commonly say they don't have the time or budget to deal with it.'

Vinod Singhal is the author of the most comprehensive and detailed analysis published to date on the long-term performance effects of supply chain disruptions. Based on a study of 800 large public firms in the US, Singhal finds that supply chain disruptions result in stock prices between 33 and 40 per cent lower than their benchmarks over a three-year period. This starts one year before, and ends two years after the disruption has been announced.[11]

'Essentially, companies don't run straight to the market when they have a problem,' Singhal says. 'They wait for the right moment and in the meantime try and fix it. When a company announces the supply chain disruption to the capital markets, there's an instant negative response and, on average, we see a 7 per cent drop in share price for each of the 800 companies. More interestingly, about six months before the announcement we see a 12–13 per cent underperformance in the share price.'

'In the six months before an announcement, the stock market may not know the reason for the problem, but negative effects can already be felt,' Singhal says. 'These bring the stock price down. After making an announcement, the company might put mechanisms in place to recover, but the competition starts to take advantage of the situation and we see another drop to about a 10 per cent underperformance in the following year.'

Disruptions also increase risks to the brand. 'What we found is that volatility following a disruption increases by about 21 per cent over a two-year period,' Singhal says. 'This means the stock market perceives the company to be very risky – one that's failing to manage its supply chain and make money.'

Singhal describes a 13.5 per cent hike in share price volatility in the year after the disruption compared to volatility in the year before the disruption. Not surprisingly, his research finds that disruptions have a significant effect on profitability. 'After adjusting for industry and economic effects, the average impact of disruptions is a 107 per cent drop in operating income, 7 per cent lower sales growth and an 11 per cent growth in costs,' he says. 'Companies that were making a lot of money before the disruption are making losses by the time they deal with it,' he adds. 'Profitability drops firstly because the disruption means customers are not getting the product. Sales drop off by about 7 per cent, quite a big number for most companies. Secondly, the disruption increases costs by about 10 per cent because, along with fixed costs, the company has to take action to recover from the disruption. Overall, this amounts to a 107 per cent drop in profitability.'

'The mindset for many companies is to source low-cost products from China, for example, but they need to understand this involves risk.'

Panelist Professor Martin Christopher of the UK's Cranfield School of Management says that trends exacerbating supply chain risk include leaner, more complex global supply chains, the centralization of production, reductions in the supplier base and outsourcing. 'Supply chain efficiency isn't just about speed,' he says, 'but about agility, or the ability to move from one speed to another. However, a conflict arises for lean companies because the key to agility is capacity. While it's not seen as desirable to have idle inventory, there may be a role for some slack in the supply chain to mitigate the risk of disruption.'

'It's true that everyone is facing cost pressures and building in slack capacity can be expensive,' concurs Vinod Singhal, 'but there are certain critical nodes in the supply chain where building a buffer could prove an essential strategy. These are the points in the supply chain at which a breakdown will cause devastation.'

'Using single sourcing, for example, has been very popular in the last ten years but it can cause supply chain stress,' Singhal adds. 'If you have a single source supplier that fails to perform you're in trouble.'

'Companies need to develop a healthier culture for supply chain risk management as opposed to financial risk.'

Mitigating supply chain risk is essentially about prevention, rather than cure. Panelist David Bird, director of PriceWaterhouseCoopers' Risk Advisory Division says that mitigating risk requires companies to develop and monitor long-term processes which lower risk without impacting operational efficiency.

'Companies should scan the environment for opportunities to reduce risk without major investment,' he says. 'They should frequently question the cost–benefit ratio of certain strategies, such as buying insurance to transfer risk.'

Vinod Singhal argues that the problem with transferring risk is that it's difficult to quantify exposure.

'With automobiles or property damage, for example, you can price the risk very well,' he says. 'Not so for risks relating to the structure of the supply chain. It's true that insurance companies are getting more active in supply chain risk management, but I'm not sure they'll be prepared to cover economic impacts that are consistently difficult to quantify.'

Singhal maintains that there's no escaping the fact that mitigating risk requires an arduous process of assessing the primary sources of risk your company might be facing.

'The mindset for many companies is to source low-cost products from China, for example, but they need to understand this involves risk. So the first step in any mitigation strategy is to understand what's happening in the supply chain. Companies can't be expected to deal with every kind of risk, but once you have some kind of risk 'map' then you can start to put counterstrategies in place.'

Panelists agree that developing a risk management culture at the highest level is essential to prevent and respond to supply chain disruption. 'People don't pay much attention to risk management on the supply chain side,'

Vinod Singhal observes. 'There's an unwritten code of failing to give credit for fixing problems that never happen. Managing the supply chain well is simply expected. Companies need to develop a healthier culture for supply chain risk management as opposed to financial risk. This must start at the C-level. Once management understands the risk, investments can be made to develop the required capabilities to deal with that risk.'

Singhal cites Wal-Mart as a case in point; the company deploys a dedicated group to monitor risk related to weather alone, such as hurricanes or snow storms. 'That's a commitment Wal-Mart's top management has made,' Singhal says. 'Company people have a clear understanding that it's a very important aspect of the business. The second thing with respect to culture is that people who see potential risks should be willing to communicate it up the ladder. Often when there's a risk, people don't want to talk about it. So you really have to build a culture where people are very open, even when it's bad news. Without a rigorous approach to risk mitigation and management, any investment made to reach high performance levels could be wasted. Once you create value you need to take action to preserve it. You might make a lot of money, but if you lose it all, what's the point?'

QUANTUM LEAP FORWARD[12]

Anna Game-Lopata

Inspired by world ranked supply chain management companies, including Li & Fung of China, Arshiya International is a supply chain management company with a difference.

President Paul Bradley told the 2008 Supply Chain Business Forum that the Mumbai stock exchange listed multinational is set to take India and the Middle East by storm.[13]

The two-year old company already has a market cap exceeding US$350 million. Bradley, who has worked closely with Li & Fung's Dr Victor Fung, told the panel investigating new supply chain business models that he had been approached by another transformational thought leader, Ajay Mittal, from one of India's top business families, to help build a new supply chain model for India. Mittal, Arshiya's chairman and managing director, was faced with a challenge.

'India is about to rise and the market potential in the Middle East is also growing,' Bradley says. 'In four and a half years, 10 per cent of consumer purchasing in India will take place in retail malls, 800 of which are currently under construction. That will make India the fifth largest retail market globally, equating to more than US$124 billion in consumer spending.'

Rather than incrementally improving logistics in India, Bradley says that he and Mittal searched the world for the most radical ideas and how they could be integrated. As an example of the results, Bradley says that Arshiya is now 'inside' four separate Indian retailers, including a major group which has outsourced its supply chain to the company.

'Our new 4PL entity is offering Indian CEOs and Presidents the opportunity to have a strike team of supply chain professionals from the Arshiya International fully analyze their business, including mapping current processes and product distribution patterns across their entire networks,' he says. 'After gaining full access to company data for a month, including all its costs, salaries, product portfolio, manufacturing, interest rates, logistics, forecasts, minimum order quantities – everything, – we provide the ideas to completely redesign the customer's supply chain. And we do it for free. But if we can show that we've achieved savings and efficiencies by the end of that month, our customers agree to cede supply chain control to us on a long-term basis, typically three to five years.'

'If we exceed certain KPIs, customers give us a special bonus each year,' Bradley adds. 'If we can find new ways to save money, a client will share part of it with us for the first year. This is a completely new concept for India.'

'Our clients have very visionary CEOs at the helm who are embracing new approaches to achieve competitive advantage,' he continues. 'They provide us with information a traditional logistics company would never usually have access to. There are no hidden spreads, but we charge a management fee which is allocated against our senior management cost, where the real knowledge lies.'

With the exception of a few companies such as Arshiya, the new business models are not being created on a very wide scale. To date, for example, the 4PL model described by Paul Bradley is still largely misunderstood within the logistics industry, both in India and elsewhere. These days, the term usually denotes a kind of 'super 3PL' which manages other providers and offers a wide variety of 'value-added' services. Internationally recognized supply chain expert and panel chair John Gattorna, whose initiative was behind the invitation-only Forum was one of a team from Andersen Consultants (now Accenture) that shaped the initial 4PL concept in the mid-1990s. He says that it was intended to do away with inflexible contracts, replacing them with a more collaborative, equity-based relationship.

'You can't "tender" for a 4PL according to our original concept,' Gattorna emphasizes. 'Companies that choose to develop a 4PL based on contractual relationships find it difficult to function, because if difficulties arise, finger-pointing begins rather than focusing on finding a solution.'

According to Gattorna, the true 4PL, or Joint Services Company (JSC) as he prefers to call it these days, is a joint venture between a group of organizations that bring complementary 'capabilities' to the table, initiated by two or more companies as the lead owners and, ultimately, controllers of the business. These enterprises might be competitors or have dissimilar markets, but they must have a compatible culture and shared vision.

These businesses form a consortium or joint venture where 3PLs continue to provide the physical assets such as warehousing and transport, but the 4PL manages them. It is, in effect, a non-asset owning management company.

> *'Our clients have very visionary CEOs... They provide us with information a traditional logistics company would never usually have access to.'*

'As well as 3PLs, junior equity partners in the consortium might include consultants and finance companies,' Gattorna explains. 'But every stakeholder has to bring some capability to the party.'

Along with equity in the management company, the relationship requires a 'prenuptial' exit agreement, stating how long the parties must commit before choosing to roll over or buy back capabilities according to an agreed formula. Such an agreement would also contain incentives and rewards to encourage a strong working relationship. Companies place key staff in the new vehicle – personnel who bring strong business acumen, experience and know-how to ensure its proper functioning.

Gattorna believes that, once the new company is working properly, the parties involved can make returns on their capabilities and assets, along with fees and dividends according to their equity holding. In an ideal case, companies would allow the vehicle to manage their assets and infrastructure until such time as they wished to buy back their capabilities.

The fundamental reasoning behind such a structure is to allow companies to acquire instant capabilities and scale quickly. If capabilities are well chosen, including shared infrastructure and assets, companies could substantially cut costs and improve the bottom line through increased volumes. However, it's not difficult to see why the idea hasn't been more broadly embraced. One only has to witness the rapid consolidation in the logistics industry to realize that most prefer the perceived control achieved via acquisitions and mergers compared to the more nebulous benefits of mutual risk and shared reward. The joint services company structure is yet to surface in Australia, and worldwide examples are still few and far between.

Early attempts at the 4PL structure managed to absorb elements of the concept, but ultimately fell down in various ways. Gattorna highlights Connect 2020, a subsidiary of UK water utility Thames Water, which manages procurement and logistics services for Thames Water in the UK. It was formed as a joint venture with Andersen Consulting (now Accenture) in 1995, and the plan was to add other utilities in following years. Although the consortium still continues it has been unable to attract other utilities because they feared that value would be extracted from them for little benefit in return. Despite this, Connect 2020 has achieved a 10 per cent supply chain cost reduction, a 40 per cent reduction in inventory, a 70 per cent reduction in back-orders, and an increase in customer service levels to over 97 per cent. This is a quantum performance improvement!

Another example is the 1994 joint venture between US-based agricultural machinery company New Holland and Accenture in an 80–20 structure in their Italian operation. Although it was later bought back by New Holland, this was not before the company had made US\$67 million savings in its first seven years, along with a 20 per cent inventory reduction, a 65 per cent increase in operational efficiency, a more than 90 per cent improvement in order fulfilment accuracy and 15 per cent freight savings.

'The dozen or so 4PLs that I've seen around the world over the last decade, including GE Medical Systems, Ford España in Spain, AT&T Wireless and others, are prototypes that we've learned a lot from,' Gattorna says. 'Now is the time to take the model to a new level and a new scale.'

One of the sticking points in the development of the original 4PL (and, later, JSC) was the perceived inability for equity partners to easily move in and out of the arrangement. Gattorna points to the Virtual Network Consortia (VNC), a similar model that presents a solution to this problem.

'Rather than strict equity arrangements, VNC stakeholders form a loose alliance,' Gattorna says. 'They can join and leave the consortium as appropriate, forming a plug-and-play arrangement. In most other respects, the VNC is similar to a JSC. Both models focus on acquiring the capabilities needed at a particular point in time to do a particular job. They provide a particular supply chain solution at speed and at scale.'

'Both utilize highly connected processes across companies and shared investments and incentives, however, in a VNC, everything can be unwound if desired by the major stakeholders,' he adds.

The VNC model seems a good fit for Arshiya. Of the company's structure, Paul Bradley says the answer was to create a 'value chain umbrella' with many different participating companies.

'A partner company can enter any part of the enterprise, but imagine the power when you connect them all,' he enthuses. 'Arshiya is also affiliated with two US multi-billion-dollar companies, with more strategic alliances likely to evolve. We can take the best global practices and networks, yet drive the company as an Indian multinational.'

Under the 'umbrella', Arshiya customers can access product distribution capacity across India, FTWZ infrastructure and rail networks, global shipping services (air and ocean), project logistics services, standalone IT and 4PL supply chain capabilities that can adapt to changing requirements in any market.

Unlike any other 4PL, Arshiya owns its own IT network and intellectual property through Singapore-based company Cyberlog.

'Arshiya might have ten different warehouses in India with completely different operators, but customers can go online using the Cyberlog system and see the product on rack three, level two of a particular warehouse with full visibility,' Bradley explains. 'We're a single point of contact. The IT system links several warehouses yet they're all different companies. We interface to SAP and INTRA but we have no licence restrictions. With hundreds of programmers, we can design new IT systems any time we want and our costs are controlled.'

While Arshiya grows its business in India and the Middle East, Australian panelist Brett Higgins of AMP has identified an opportunity to transform the local tourism industry, using a variation of the VNC model.

'There's no single source of truth for tourism supplier information,' Higgins says. 'Despite the plethora of choices, customers can't easily plan, select and purchase travel goods or services.'

Higgins's idea, to be developed within his own travel services company, XYZ Travel, is to build collaborative supplier relationships locally and go to market nationally.

19

'Suppliers of transport, accommodation, attractions, and tour operators need to be streamlined so that wholesale information is more easily accessible to retailers, including those online,' he says. 'Capabilities need to be assembled to achieve rapid development and expedited entrance to the marketplace.'

In order to achieve this, Higgins says that XYZ Travel will need to establish the right operational culture and consider the key management levers.

'Strong brand awareness and distribution through travel agent shop fronts can be achieved through strategic alliances with airlines and other resource partners,' he maintains. 'However, visionary leadership, high business acumen, corporate intellectual property and an effective supply chain target operating model will be essential.'

'I'll be looking for accelerated business advancement, an instant distribution channel and an innovative flexible business culture,' he adds. 'Such a business will require an industry solution focus and needs to deliver high customer satisfaction. High partner commitment will be incentivized through equity in the business, but clear assessment criteria and a process for selecting strategic partners will need to be developed. This must include detailed capability requirements with a fair return for each, and provision for the entry and exit of partners.'

'John Gattorna argues that regulatory restrictions are no longer an excuse to avoid pushing the boundaries in search of new business models.'

It's difficult to imagine businesses in the current international business climate forming such alliances without the desire to guard perceived competitive advantages. General Manager of Supply Chain Strategy and Procurement for the Fonterra Dairy Cooperative Group and panelist Nigel Jones reflects this view.

He says that, while Fonterra appreciates the need to find the right business model to improve performance going forward, the company is hesitant to deliver increased control of its intellectual property (IP) to third parties along the supply chain.

'Seasonal fluctuations in dairy production, low visibility, underutilization, a small talent pool and an inability to justify investment is causing costs that lower the international competitiveness of New Zealand exporters and importers,' Jones says. 'At Fonterra we're faced with the problem of finding a way to deliver value while still retaining our IP. We see a further complexity arising in that if we were to outsource our IP, we may lose the value that our volumes provide. Until now, Fonterra has been unable to find a 3PL partner that can get its head around all the issues involved.'

Jones also observes that it's hard for Australian companies to know where to draw the line in terms of what can be done without breaking the Trade Practices Act, especially in relation to working with competitors.

According to principal lawyer, Australian Competition and Consumer Commission (ACCC), and panelist Alexandra Merrett, it's often (though not always) possible to structure a collaborative venture or new business model in a way that achieves the desired objectives without contravening the Trade Practices Act.

'The ACCC would counsel parties considering collaborating with their competitors or attempting new business models to first seek advice from lawyers with competition expertise,' she warns. 'This is a very technical area of law. Rather than approaching lawyers with a structure already in mind, it can be preferable to explain to your legal team exactly what you are trying to achieve and leave it to them to consider ways in which you can do it.'

Merrett says that it's is also worthwhile remembering that, even where particular outcomes look as though they may contravene the Trade Practices Act, there are special 'exemptions' available.

'The most likely form of exemption relevant to collaborative arrangements between competitors or possibly new business models, would be an authorization, which is only available upon application to the ACCC and requires demonstration of sufficient "public benefit" arising from the arrangement to outweigh any competitive detriment,' she explains. 'Obtaining authorization can be time-consuming and expensive, but – depending upon the scope of the collaboration or new business model – definitely worth it, particularly when compared to the very high penalties that apply to contraventions of the Act.'

'The bottom line, though, is that this is a very complicated area of law, so parties need to be prepared to spend money on good legal advice,' Merrett says. 'Getting it wrong can be extremely expensive, not to mention bad for a company's reputation.'

Despite this, John Gattorna argues that regulatory restrictions are no longer an excuse to avoid pushing the boundaries in search of new business models.

'A pressing factor for change is that operational excellence has a diminishing returns effect,' he says. 'After a period of time, the elements combining to drive performance such as transportation and warehouse management yield lesser profit – even with continuing, or greater investment. Dynamic alignment enables a rejigging of what you do internally to face up to your market better. But even having done this there's still a limit to how far you can go by way of improvement.

'There are many opportunities for consortia to pool huge volume across industries. In countries such as Australia and New Zealand, it may be the only way we can build scale to compete with the bigger companies overseas.'

While Gattorna admits that the idea requires a leap of faith from a CEO willing to break the mould, he argues that, if a company were to build an entity such as a VNC, it would potentially be looking at a 30–40 per cent net improvement in operating performance after set-up costs.

'In conjunction with realignment initiatives at the enterprise level, industry leaders must seek new multi-enterprise execution models that deliver change at speed and scale,' he says. 'While it may take increasing pressure on the bottom line before companies are willing to change, we've gone as far as we can with operational excellence. We now need a quantum leap in another direction to move forward.'

NEW MANTRA[14]

Anna Game-Lopata

In 2007, despite unprecedented demand, export losses due to coal chain capacity constraints were in excess of $2 billion per annum in New South Wales alone. General Manager of Xstrata Rail and Ports, and panelist Anthony Pitt told the 2008 Supply Chain Business Forum panel on achieving requisite collaboration that the resulting vessel queues cost the Hunter Valley and Goonyella coal chains more than $700 million per annum.

'The delivery of new rail and port infrastructure continues to be a constraint to realizing full export potential across Australia's coal chains,' Pitt told the invitation-only forum, an initiative of internationally recognized supply chain expert John Gattorna. 'Our industry in the Hunter Valley has only managed an 8 per cent growth despite more than $500 million in new infrastructure. Compare this with a growth of 75 per cent in thermal coal exports achieved by Indonesia in the last four years.'

Remarkable, by contrast, is the success of the Hunter Valley Coal Chain Logistics Team (HVCCLT) in achieving productivity gains using existing infrastructure. The first of its kind in Australia, HVCCLT is a collaborative organization responsible for the daily planning of all Hunter Valley coal industry exports. Created as a trial in 2003, the Logistics Team was set up by Pacific National (PN) and Port Waratah Coal Services (PWCS) as a response to increasing demand from the industry to improve capacity.

Former HVCCLT General Manager Anthony Pitt says that the expectation from inception was to deliver significant capacity by running coal chain operations as a system rather than as a series of component parts as was previously the practice.

'The short-term goal of increasing throughput has been realized, along with the longer-term objective of providing investment planning advice to the industry,' he says. About 90 per cent of the Logistics Team's resources are put towards improving system capacity.

'The HVCCLT presided over a spectacular 20 per cent increase in productivity from existing infrastructure,' Pitt says. 'The vast bulk of that benefit is generated through its cooperative model, which enables latent capacity to be unlocked through greater coordination of activities like maintenance programmes at the track and ports.'

'In terms of the longer-term initiative, the HVCCLT advisory service directly contributes to the efficiency of members' capital expenditure across the entire system,' Pitt enthuses. 'Members are modifying and even adding new infrastructure initiatives in the knowledge that those changes are in the interests of the coal chain as a whole. The team has also helped prevent investment in infrastructure that might otherwise be underutilized.'

On a handshake, PWCS and PN agreed to co-locate their planning teams to enable more effective communication and the generation of new ideas about how to increase system capacity. Joined by Newcastle Port Corporation, the trial was expanded and formalized in 2005 as a joint venture with stated objectives and governance.

HVCCLT members now include PN and QRNational as the train operators, Australia Rail Track Corporation and Rail Infrastructure Corporation as the track owners, PWCS as the operator of cargo assembly and ship-loading services, and Newcastle Port Corporation which manages the vessel movements.

23

The functioning of the HVCCLT collaborative system completely relies on the voluntary participation of its members. However, as Anthony Pitt explains, the truly cooperative venture does not legally compel any of the group to cooperate in daily planning or to comply with associated instructions.

'I won't say that it was without its challenges,' Pitt admits, 'but everyone quickly came to the conclusion that it was the only sensible way to operate the coal chain. The profit generated from this approach to planning was immediate.'

Despite strong pressure on member organizations resulting from bullish growth forecasts from the industry, Anthony Pitt is confident the collaborative model provided by the HVCCLT will prevail.

'In the current marketplace, where the demand for coal out of Newcastle is exceptionally high, the need for more capacity certainly creates an environment with the potential for tensions and competition,' he says. 'But I think the success of the model has been the glue that's kept the team together, and is leading to greater cooperation into the future.'

'On a handshake, PWCS and PN agreed to co-locate their planning teams to enable more effective communication and the generation of new ideas.'

So successful is the HVCCLT model that it has been widely recognized and recommended to other supply chains by the Prime Minister's infrastructure taskforce.

What, then, is behind the wider failure of stakeholders to manage the rapidly growing infrastructure capacity challenge?

According to Anthony Pitt, the 'common objective' ingredient, essential to the success of collaboration, is missing.

'This is mainly caused by the fragmented ownership structure of coal chain stakeholders', he says, 'which creates a misalignment of agendas.'

He explains, 'On one end of the scale, industry-owned coal-loading terminals such as Port Waratah Coal Services and the Newcastle Coal Infrastructure Group (NCIG) are the only entities in the coal chain investing ahead of demand. Their shareholder and customer incentives are perfectly aligned, but they have no long-term contracts to underpin investment.'

'Where partners find their subcultures are not a natural "fit", one partner, often the supplier, needs to adapt to mirror the other, usually the customer, for a collaborative relationship to be sustainable.'

'The lack of long-term contracts for track and port means future demand is invisible,' Pitt says. 'It also means infrastructure providers are forced to second-guess the industry. Since each infrastructure provider holds its own view of demand, making investment decisions is extremely difficult.'

'On the other end of the scale, ARTC, the government-owned rail infrastructure provider is focused on the Weighted Average Cost of Capital (WACC) and stranded asset risk,' Pitt maintains. 'Apart from political risk, the ARTC is unlikely to face any significant consequence from non-investment.

'Meanwhile, the train companies are functioning in a highly competitive market. They invest based on contracts with customers, but, often, the contracts aren't linked to what the coal chain can deliver as a system. For example, in 2007, 112Mt of contracts were sold in a system that can only manage a maximum of 95Mt.'

In addition to aligning objectives, principal of Carpenter Ellis and panel chair Deborah Ellis says that achieving requisite collaboration requires the parties involved to have, or develop, appropriate subcultures and the capability to sustain them.

Based on John Gattorna's theory of the four generic basic types of organizational cultures and the various combinations of these that are possible,[15] Ellis shows that, upon an initial assessment, the subcultures of the PWCS and PN diverge from other stakeholders in the coal chain.

'PWCS and PN share alignment with each other, sitting in between the "hierarchical" and the "rational" cultural types, while the Port of Newcastle, ARTC and Queensland Rail exhibit a purely "hierarchical" organizational culture,' she says. 'Of the four types, both the "hierarchical" and "group" subcultures have an internal focus. However, while the "group" subculture thrives on synergy and teamwork with the aim of achieving cohesion, the "hierarchical" subculture is motivated by systems, measurement and control. It seeks ordered outcomes.

'The "rational" and "entrepreneurial" subcultures share an external focus, but the "rational" subculture is motivated by action, objectives and energy to achieve results, while the "entrepreneurial" subculture is more focused on innovation and flexibility to achieve growth, Collaborative groupings ultimately need to reflect the dominant buying logics of their customers.

'Where partners find their subcultures are not a natural "fit", one partner, often the supplier, needs to adapt to mirror the other, usually the customer, for a collaborative relationship to be sustainable.'

'To make matters more complex, aligned subcultures might not always mean a perfect fit,' Ellis adds. 'In the case of PWCS and PN, where the subcultures sit between "hierarchical" and "rational", the relationship may only succeed with a results-oriented and dynamic collaborative model.'

Essentially, Ellis argues, establishing a collaborative relationship requires strong leadership to pull the partnership together initially, as was the case for the HVCCLT, when PWCS and PN agreed to take the first steps.

'Once the opportunity has been identified and a direction agreed, effective leadership is 90 per cent of the ingredients required to enable the implementation of a collaborative arrangement,' Ellis says. 'Process and systems become far more important as the relationship is being embedded and institutionalized, with leadership becoming only 15 per cent of the ingredients required to keep the partnership flourishing.'

Panelist Professor Ivan Su of Soochow University in Taiwan points to another kind of collaborative model, successful because of the consistent leadership contributed by Japanese exporter and supply chain company ITOCHU Corporation.

'With a business philosophy of customer satisfaction and joint growth with stakeholders and the general public, ITOCHU has expanded its thriving Family Mart business into Taiwan, Thailand, Korea and more recently China,' he says.

According to Professor Su, the success of ITOCHU's Family Mart chain can partly be attributed to a clear understanding of market demands for 24-hour convenience shopping and having a successful home market business and supply chain.

'For ITOCHU, collaborative efforts have always been underpinned by persistently developing local knowledge and the right model for Asian business development,' he says. 'Cultural alignment and leadership is reinforced by rotating company executives and the frequent exchange of key operational personnel in the supply chain. This ensures the transfer of the right business experience and knowledge to the regional firms under one central orchestrating mechanism.'

Importantly, another factor in ITOCHU's collaborative success is its approach to fostering local motivation and loyalty through providing regional Family Mart stores and their service providers with an equity position in the business.

'While ITOCHU Corporation holds 61 per cent of its rapidly growing Taiwan-based Family Mart business (now the second largest CVS in Taiwan), Taisun, along with other local firms, holds the other 20 per cent,' Professor Su explains. 'Family Mart Taiwan's service provider, the Taiwan Distribution Company (TDC), established in 1989, is 50 per cent owned by Family Mart Taiwan and 20 per cent by ITOCHU Company and other local firms.'

John Gattorna says: 'the new mantra for Australian business should be "to compete in the market, but cooperate in the supply chain".'
'Once we psychologically step across the line to that stage of maturity we'll very quickly rise in world standings."

Despite the obvious benefits of collaboration, panelists agree that the concerns Australian organizations have about losing competitive advantage through opening themselves up to deeper partnerships is impeding development.

John Gattorna argues that the energy and thought that has gone into competitive analysis has been excessive, taking the collective eye away from the execution of strategy.

'This area of darkness inside the business has to be opened up by people who aren't afraid of what they might find,' he says. 'Rather than being distracted by competitors, we need to concentrate on the forces within, develop appropriate subcultures and communications and genetically re-engineer our businesses internally.'

Gattorna also believes that businesses have misunderstood the role of collaboration.

'We still have this view in Australia and elsewhere that collaboration will fix everything,' he says. 'As we move from "lean" manufacturing to "lean" supply chains, people need to choose those partners with which they really want a long-term mutually beneficial relationship. For the rest of your customers, you simply use another formula.'

According to Arshiya International president and panelist Paul Bradley, collaboration means admitting that there are ways to improve your business beyond what you can do yourself.

'Organizations need to build relationships the Asian way, with trust, shared visions and even with competitors,' he says. 'They then need to set up rules of engagement, which is always done at the top.'

Bradley argues that smart businesses use technology to keep control.

'You use your ideas and human talent to drive the competitive advantage,' he says. 'If you have the courage, there are ways you can collaborate that are of mutual benefit on fixed assets and fixed structure.'

By way of example, Bradley points to his Indian-based company Arshiya, which is building free trade warehousing zone parks at major ports across India, and will be open to both customers and competitors to enable aggregation.

'Instead of competing, imagine smaller, mid-sized warehouses leasing space out to retail competitors,' he enthuses. 'Being neutral, Arshiya will put in its own, fully-owned IT system and people to manage the warehouse and protect confidentiality. The warehouses, which are currently losing money due to excess capacity, will gain the business we bring in for them. It's genuine collaboration. It's a win–win model.'

'The question is,' Bradley adds, 'do we want a fixed logistics structure for moving products between A and B, and holding information within, or do we want to build dynamic supply chain models that can shift and adapt continuously as the market inevitably changes?

'As cost of capital changes, as labour changes, as currency fluctuates, we increasingly need dynamic supply chain models with full, transparent control of product flow. It's no longer theory; it's done by companies that collaborate.'

In terms of the coal chain, this amounts to a projected 50 per cent growth in export volumes over the next five years.

The predicament also rings true for other industries.

'The new mantra for Australian business should be "to compete in the market, but cooperate in the supply chain",' John Gattorna says. 'Once we psychologically step across the line to that stage of maturity we'll very quickly rise in world standings.'

SECRET SAUCE[16]

Anna Game-Lopata

In 50 years, the Costa Group, Australia's largest private wholesaler/distributor and exporter of fresh produce, hasn't suffered a single industrial dispute.

Managing director and panelist Simon Costa told the 2008 Supply Chain Business Forum panel on leadership, vision and innovation that, while staff turnover in the sector can be as high as 30 per cent, Costa remains below 1 per cent.

'Productivity and service levels are high in any week,' he says, 'with staff consistently averaging 0–3 errors per million cartons.'

Costa believes that the key to achieving supply chain execution excellence is a reversal in the traditional 'systems, process, people' model.

'There's a fundamental difference in the way we run our business,' he told the invitation-only Forum, an initiative of international supply chain expert John Gattorna. 'Through our Character First programme, we focus on developing the right people. Systems and process follow. The resulting service levels have prompted our current growth into grocery, freezer, dairy and meat distribution.'

Visitors to Costa sites often find it difficult to believe that a performance above industry standards has been produced without financial incentives.

'Our staff receive normal hourly rates of pay,' Costa says. 'It's all about feeling part of a team that's really achieving results. At the end of the day, people work for money, but pride in doing a good job comes equal first or close second.'

So important is the Costa Group philosophy of Character First that it has become a company campaign. Every month employees across the business stop work for almost an hour to talk about character. Qualities such as dependability are discussed in relation to life and the workplace. People who've benefited the company by demonstrating a particular trait are recognized and awarded.

'There were managers who questioned the cost of stopping work each month, because they couldn't predict the savings,' Costa says. 'The costs of inefficiencies and rework simply fell away. Once the culture was right, profit took care of itself. But without leaders living it out front, Character First could never have taken hold.'

Current research bears this out, according to panel chair and emeritus professor at Macquarie Graduate School of Management, Roger Collins.

'The most successful companies are those where senior leaders communicate with their people at least 30 times a year, be it face-to-face or through videoconferencing,' he says. 'They talk to staff about the purpose of their organization. "Why do we exist? And furthermore, what are our goals and what's our strategy? How are we going to achieve those goals?" And finally, as Simon Costa suggests, they discuss the values that guide company behaviour.'

'Senior-level management must also communicate performance,' Collins adds. 'For example, how are we going against our objectives? What's the gap?'

While the role of corporate leadership in setting the context within a business is essential, Collins maintains that it isn't enough in itself.

29

'I think we've now reached a turning point in our understanding of leadership,' he says. 'More organizations are moving away from the concept of leadership as an individual contribution. They're now thinking of it as collective behaviour – or "distributed leadership".'

According to Roger Collins, distributed leadership functions at two further levels, beyond corporate management.

'"Local or direct" leadership occurs at middle management level with managers who have responsibility for staff who touch either suppliers or customers in the supply chain,' Collins explains. 'At the local level, we know that the role of the leader is more productive if managers pay attention to what staff members do right rather than what they do wrong. They've got to find ways of giving positive feedback at least three times more frequently than negative feedback if they're going to win the hearts and minds of their people and create high engagement. Staff engagement creates the third level of distributed leadership – that of self-leadership. This is where staff engagement at all levels of the organization allows for decision-making that's consistent with where the organization's going.'

'Engaged employees not only talk about their organization in a positive way, opening opportunities for future talent attraction, but they're also less likely to leave. In terms of turnover, we find people are more likely to leave a job if their manager's no good, not because their job isn't challenging. Finally, engaged employees will give you more than you ask; they'll go over and above what's expected of them in their work.'

'Essentially, distributed leadership starts with senior leaders who then engage local leaders in a way that leads to self-leadership. It's about having employees that don't require supervision or direction because it's clear to them what they have to do, and they have the engagement and the commitment to be willing to do it.'

Clearly, recruitment forms a major component of this process. Roger Collins says that it's critical to hire people whose values are aligned to those of the organization. The Costa Group takes this philosophy further.

'Management literature often says "People are the company's most important asset, look after your people",' Simon Costa says. 'That's wrong. It's the right people who are essential to a business. The wrong people will bring you undone every time.'

'We believe there's nothing about the industry that can't be taught,' he explains. 'As interviewers we're the slowest in the world, incorporating numerous character-based questions. Whatever it costs, we get it back – with the right employees who don't leave.'

Panelists recognize that a very intimate link exists between strong leadership and the innovation required for global competitive advantage. Former Macquarie Graduate School of Management dean and panelist Roy Green[17] argues that knowledge creation and diffusion are at the core of economic activity.

'Innovation is a complex, non-linear process with multiple sources,' Green says. 'However, recent data shows that investment in research and education is a key driver of scientific output internationally – an area where, historically, Australia has been found wanting.

'We're seeing a reversal of the decades-long deterioration in Australia's terms of trade, but for how long? Currently in Australia a paltry 4 per cent of GDP is invested into higher education, research and development. Compare this with over 6 per cent in Finland and close to 7 per cent in Denmark.'

'At the end of the day, people work for money, but pride in doing a good job comes equal first or close second.'

As it is a country increasingly losing its manufacturing base, Green believes that it's pertinent to compare Australia's corporate and governing mindset with that of Ireland, which has turned a similar predicament into an advantage.

'Ireland currently has the largest global percentage of high technology industry exports,' he says. 'At close to 60 per cent this is higher than the US and the OECD. Australia, by contrast, has less than 20 per cent high technology exports.'

What is causing this gap? Roy Green quotes the Irish National Development Plan of 2000 as a clue: 'There is a strong link between investment in the research and innovation base of the economy and sustained economic growth. The accumulation of "'knowledge capital'" will facilitate the evolution of the knowledge-based economy.'

He continues, 'It's also clear that developing the knowledge required for innovation requires successful partnerships through strong leadership which evolves through structured collaboration, networking, spillovers, and diffusion within and between organizations. According to research by Ecotec, the top critical success factors for global innovation include networking, innovative technology and human capital respectively.'

Green describes high-performance management and work systems as 'clusters of effectiveness attributes' which release creativity.

'While our institutions are essential components of global innovation and economic performance, technological adaptation and workplace learning depend on human capital and organizational effectiveness which Australia is yet to fully develop.'

Panelist Dina Oelefsen, Principal of Leadership Development (SA), concurs, pointing to still prevalent misalignments within our institutions as a major cause of cost, uncertainty, reluctance to make capital investments and, ultimately, as an inhibitor of innovation.

'Where relationships are weakening and there's increasing conflict between teams, it's a sure sign of gaps in the leadership,' she says. 'Misalignment occurs in two main forms. Where structural incompatibility exists, slow decision-making, double messages and communication breakdowns contribute to diffuse work levels and red tape.'

'Where values are incompatible, power imbalances, lack of transparency and perceived hoarding of value can result in a lack of trust which erodes effective functioning and the ability to be innovative.'

Roger Collins believes the 'ground up' approach, common in supply chain businesses, sometimes works against them.

'Organizations go through many stages of growth from start-up to maturity,' he says. 'Sometimes you need different leaders at different stages in the life cycle of the company. The very person who starts the company may not be the best person to grow it or manage it in difficult times.'

An extension of this idea is that supply chain leaders are failing to delegate tasks they once performed to make room for strategic thinking.

'Anxieties rise when we move outside our comfort zone or areas of competency, and no one wants to look stupid,' Dina Oelefsen says. 'Leaders need to stop meddling and focus on thinking long-term, and rewarding contribution rather than output, and contracting clearly to empower their people both inside and outside the organization.'

Like Roy Green, Roger Collins argues that successful supply chains require the kind of collaboration and coordination that can't be achieved without high levels of trust and communication.

'I think too often we assume that somebody who's good in one industry will be good in another but the evidence suggests that's not the case,' he says. 'Unless a chief executive understands the unique demands of good supply chain management, they probably won't make it work.'

But what are the hallmark qualities of leadership? Is there a secret sauce?

'We tend to think of attributes like intelligence and personality as critical to strong leadership, but this doesn't stand up under the research,' Roger Collins says. 'The qualities that are cited most frequently are authenticity and humility.'

'People really want to know if their leader is genuine,' Collins explains. 'They ask themselves "Does this person do what they say? Are they fair dinkum?" And if they're not humble, the risk is that they'll eventually destroy themselves.'

Panelists agree that successful leaders realize that supply chains are built around people and interpersonal relationships, rather than computer systems, trucks, trains, boats and planes.

'Supply chains are very vulnerable because they're so complex and systemic,' Roger Collins says. 'Under these conditions, success comes from the day-to-day consistent commitment of people working together in the interests of the customer. You don't achieve that sort of behaviour from management; team work comes from leadership and that's the difference. Management will help you plan and control things, but leadership engages the hearts and minds of your people.'

Says Simon Costa: 'My sense of pride in the Costa Group has nothing to do with turnover or growth. When I visit company sites, the number of people who want to thank me and talk about opportunities provided by our business is incredibly encouraging.'

THE PRICE OF LIFE – TO DO NOTHING IS NO LONGER AN OPTION[18]

Anna Game-Lopata

The 2008 Supply Chain Business Forum finds that humanitarian logistics is undervalued and underresourced, with only a handful of aid organizations prioritizing the creation of high-performing logistics and supply chain operations.[19] Three-year-old Pascaline lives in a village in Rwanda. She was diagnosed with Type 1 diabetes when she was 12 months old, and spent a year in hospital. She is now cared for by a local health centre, but, without the supply chain providing her with insulin and monitoring, she will die. President of the International Diabetes Federation, Professor Martin Silink, told the 2008 Supply Chain Business Forum that diabetes is becoming an epidemic, with global cases expected to hit 380 million in 2025. This is up from 246 million in 2007.

The worldwide cost of diabetes in 2007 was US$232 billion. In 2025 it's predicted to reach US$302 billion. With 70 per cent of cases in developing countries, Silink told the invitation-only panel addressing the rise of the humanitarian supply chain, that diabetes is more than ever a disease of poverty.

Despite this, over 70 per cent of the world's diabetes-related health-care costs are spent in the more advantaged nations.

'In many developing countries the most common acute complication of diabetes in childhood is death,' Silink says. 'These deaths are all preventable. To do nothing is no longer an option.'

According to international humanitarian logistics consultant and panelist Michael Whiting, the Indian Ocean tsunami of December 2004 proved beyond doubt that logistics is a vital component of humanitarian aid.

'Every year 250 million people are affected by natural disasters and a further 45 million people by the devastating effects of armed conflict,' Whiting says. 'The twenty-first century has brought with it earthquakes, tsunamis and volcanic eruptions and the indications are that disasters are happening more frequently and often several at once.

'Humanitarian logistics fails to attract the required level of funding and support to provide adequate relief efforts around the world.'

'In general however, humanitarian organizations are probably about 15 years behind their private sector counterparts, who realized the importance of a efficient supply chain a long time ago, particularly given the increasing opportunities to "go global".'

The challenge facing both commerce and humanitarian agencies is identifying, recruiting, training and retaining logistics personnel of the right calibre.

'For most agencies, high employee turnover rates, fragmented technology, poorly-defined manual processes and lack of institutional learning over time result in relief operations that are not as efficient or effective as they could be,' Whiting admits. 'The bottom line is that relief to the vulnerable is then either delayed or delivered with reduced effectiveness.'

Whiting believes that, as a result of its perceived lack of importance, humanitarian logisticians in many organizations do not have the competence required to handle complex emergency situations.

'Humanitarian logistics fails to attract the required level of funding and support to provide adequate relief efforts around the world,' he says. 'In some organizations, such as IFRC, WVI, UNHCR, UNICEF and WFP, there are several excellent, formally trained logisticians who happen to work with organizations that offer them job security, good pay and recognition. But this is not the norm.'

'All too often, humanitarian operators have no option but to work with essential staff only, offering, in most cases, employment packages that fail to attract suitably qualified staff to support services roles. They are forced to work without any rolling stock and the information management systems they desire.'

Whiting points to the focus on short-term direct relief as a pattern that discourages investment in the very systems and processes needed to reduce expenses and make relief more efficient in the long run.

'This often results in logistics and other support services not having adequate funding for strategic preparedness and infrastructure investment such as information systems,' he says. 'In this context donors are the problem. The fact is that donors generally do not fund planning activities, they fund programmes. This situation shows signs of changing, but the change is slow. Until donors are prepared to contribute funds to logistics contingency planning and infrastructure there will be little change.'

Whiting argues that improvements to logistics and supply chain management performance will enable the significant savings required to fund logistics infrastructure improvements, which in turn will enable further efficiencies.

'It is an accepted fact that in emergencies, supply chain costs can represent up to 35–45 per cent of the total cost of operations,' he explains. 'Compared to this, normative state operations are of the order of 15–20 per cent, with indications in 2007 that the average cost in Europe came closer to 10 per cent of the total cost of operations. This represents a spread of between 20–25 per cent of the total cost of humanitarian logistics operations.'

In 2005 an estimated US$18 billion was raised by the international community and public donations for humanitarian assistance against an estimated US$10 billion raised in 2000. Allowing for the Iraq/Afghanistan (2003) and Indian Ocean tsunami (2004–05) spikes, humanitarian aid levels reveal a steady upward trend.

'Judicious use of best-practice and cutting-edge supply chain management practices presents a potential cost saving by closing the gap between emergency response supply chain costs and normative-state supply chain costs,' Whiting says. 'The margin of 20–25 per cent inefficiency on humanitarian aid of US$7 billion represents US$1.4–1.75 billion per annum.'

'A determined drive to achieve even a 1 per cent saving across the board would yield between US$140 and US$175 million per annum; figures that should galvanize the most jaundiced donor or aid agency official.'

'Diabetes is becoming an epidemic, with global cases expected to hit 380 million in 2025. This is up from 246 million in 2007.'

World Vision is one aid organization that in 2006, served more than 100 million people in 97 nations, including 3 million children. A respected Non-Government Organization (NGO), World Vision raised US$2.1 billion in cash and goods for its work in that year

World Vision director of Global Supply Chain Management and panelist Gerard de Villiers agrees that the lack of supply chain management skills within the organization presents a considerable challenge.

'In 2006, World Vision's tsunami response was definitely hampered by inadequate supply chain management expertise at all levels,' he says. 'The organization needs to develop better supply chain structures with defined roles and responsibilities.'

'Problems were also caused by communication difficulties and lack of visibility,' he adds. 'The lack of a non-food item tracking system led to the adoption of the commodity tracking system with less than ideal results. Inadequate understanding of WV policies resulted in some inappropriate procurement decisions and a failure to take advantage of outsourcing opportunities.'

Despite this, de Villiers points to successful partnerships with local merchants and air and sea freight carriers that ensured supplies were available, at fixed prices.

'Having supply chain management expertise on the ground was a big positive,' he says. 'The establishment of a central warehouse helped ease local supply chain delivery issues, enabling us to make good use of food commodities, gifts in kind, and non-food items.'

De Villiers asserts that the involvement of numerous parties in emergency response poses one of the most significant challenges to the coordination and efficiency of aid, and the experience of Logistics Recruitment's group managing director and panel chair Kim Winter attests to this observation. Winter, who took it upon himself to play an active role in the private-sector response to the 2004 tsunami, has been recognized by the UN and the Sri Lankan government for teaming up with DHL, Dexion and Toll Holdings to deploy a team of logistics specialists during the Columbo airport heavy-lift operation, which enabled essential supplies to reach victims of the disaster.

Although he approached the project with hard-edged capability, Winter says that humanitarian supply chain management comes down to either saving lives or counting bodies.

'I contacted 42 NGOs to offer my services in recruiting logistics and supply chain expertise to the region,' he says. 'Not one of them responded.'

Winter was eventually contacted by the World Economic Forum Disaster Recovery Team who asked him to lead Australia's tsunami response. He has recently been invited to represent the Australian supply chain sector to establish enhanced protocols for best-practice operations during sudden-onset humanitarian disasters.

Michael Whiting argues that collaboration and coordination has improved since the tsunami crisis and the subsequent recovery and rehabilitation programme. Implementation of the findings of the Humanitarian Response Review (HRR) in August 2005 led to the introduction of a new approach: the 'cluster' concept, much like that suggested by John Gattorna in Chapter 9 of this book for private-sector supply chains.

In the 'cluster' concept, individuals from a variety of organizations work together as a group to share information rather than functioning as 'silos' through their organizations alone.

'The very introduction of the clusters at field and headquarters level has brought about closer coordination and collaboration between UN agencies themselves, between UN agencies and NGOs, and between NGOs,' Whiting says.

'In 2005, recently published studies revealed that between 48 and 58 per cent of all known humanitarian funding flowed through NGOs,' he continues. 'However, the HRR, from which the cluster concept evolved, is still seen by many as a creature of the UN. 'Cooperation between organizations in a meaningful way exists and is increasing, but, without the substantial buy-in of a larger number of NGOs and intergovernment organizations, the effectiveness of the cluster approach will be limited.'

'A major issue that arises again and again is the seeming inability of the humanitarian world to learn from past experience,' Whiting goes on to observe. 'The intensity of relief efforts, high staff turnover (as much as 80 per cent during the response to the 2004 Indian Ocean tsunami) and the crisis-oriented nature of disaster response creates an environment in which there is endemically a lack of institutional learning.'

'Post-crisis, aid workers are immediately assigned to the next mission, leaving no time to reflect or focus on possible improvement. There's also a reluctance to collaborate and share information, which results in the inability to systematically learn from mistakes from one disaster to the next.'

While there's no silver bullet, panelists believe that dynamic alignment is an essential first step to bring about an improvement in the delivery of appropriate and timely humanitarian aid.

'Dynamic alignment is vital to aid effectiveness,' Whiting says. 'Beneficiaries, the United Nations, NGOs, development and implementing partners, together with other stakeholders, must embrace the same humanitarian relief principles and objectives and agree to work together to effectively assist in emergency and humanitarian disasters.'

SUSTAINING GAIA[20]

Anna Game-Lopata

The earth's capacity to sustain the activity of people is shrinking fast.

Associate director of sustainability for the Portland Group and chair of a panel examining the essence of sustainability Mark Reynolds told the 2008 Supply Chain Business Forum that by using a simple resource accounting tool[21] it's possible to ascertain that, in 1985, our ecological footprint, or the land and water area we use for resources and waste disposal, exceeded the capacity of the biosphere for the first time

In 2008 the human population is now consuming 25 per cent more than what the earth's long-term biocapacity can give. By 2030 this figure will reach 50 per cent.

'Biocapacity is expected to decline further as we overload or exhaust some resources,' Reynolds says. 'For example, our dependence on fossil fuels has grown ninefold since 1960, with rich countries having the greatest footprint.'

'The earth's capacity to sustain the activity of people is shrinking fast.'

'Cheap energy has enabled the tremendous growth in goods and services we have enjoyed for the last half-century, but as we're all aware, the situation has been changing for some time. As developing nations achieve greater economic prosperity, the challenge will grow exponentially, given the sheer number of people in those countries.'

Reynolds told the invitation-only Forum, an initiative of internationally recognized supply chain thought-leader expert John Gattorna, that 90 per cent of the human ecological footprint is made up of supply chains delivering food, goods and services.

'Goods and services include everything we buy – cars, TVs, toys, furniture, haircuts, holidays, concerts,' he explains. 'Supply chains are therefore powerful vehicles to drive sustainability.'

Supply chain director for George Weston Foods and panelist Maurice Sinclair says that consumer demand for processed food is a significant contributor to Greenhouse Gas emissions (GHG).

'The growth of processed food production incurs longer travel distances, changed chemical states, extra packaging and higher water content,' he says. 'By default it impacts on GHG greater than products consumed in a natural state.'

By way of example, Sinclair points to the production of a can of baked beans, which has a supply chain extending back to the iron ore mined and procured to produce the steel cans, the forests and paper mills used for the labels and, of course, to the farming of the beans.

'It also involves the logistics operations between the manufacturers who package the beans and retailers who sell them,' Sinclair says.

'In addition, it's pertinent to remember Australia is expected to generally receive less rain than it has done in the past,' he reasons. 'The dispersal of that rain will impact on our sheep and wheat belt and other major food producing regions.'

'Achieving sustainability in the supply chain is not simple,' he adds. 'There are many areas to consider. However this should not dissuade us from moving towards a greener supply chain environment.'

Panelists agree that sustainability is a system condition; it must be considered through the end-to-end supply chain, and collaboration is necessary in order for it to flourish.

Link Strategy Principal Alice Woodhead has completed several collaborative projects with producers aiming to reduce the carbon output of their operations. The Sugar Link Project is a significant example.[22]

'The project aimed to help develop a shared vision for a sustainable sugar supply chain in NSW,' Woodhead says. 'With the burning of sugar cane viewed as dangerous and negative for the environment, the strategy of the project was to develop some new processes, systems and technologies for "green harvesting".'

She points out that the Sugar Link Project also attempted to build an understanding of collaborative initiatives towards a sustainable sugar supply chain which includes consumers, their communities and the environment as stakeholders.

'From an initial position of producing a huge carbon output to becoming energy-positive, the process took five years, including the development of new systems and the associated training,' she says. 'Being a fairly insular cooperative, it also took some time for the farmers to develop an understanding with the community about what they were seeking to achieve.'

'In the sugar industry, management of supply chains is changing considerably in response to the often-difficult market environment,' Woodhead explains. 'Market forces present real challenges to wholesalers and retailers but are exceptionally problematic for primary producers who often lack the knowledge to manage these new and dynamic relationships. Food manufacturers and retailers increasingly demand consistent quality and on-time products from their suppliers.'

'In recent years, considerable emphasis has been placed on rationalizing the economic value chain to reduce excess costs and increase efficiency.'

'Manufacturers and retailers have responded to the marketing opportunity with product-label claims such as "animal friendly" and "organic". However, the credibility of these products depends on the ethical values of the chain partners and the verification of the claims through the entire supply chain.'

For many companies, which in the past have had an exclusive focus on providing economic value for shareholders, these consumer demands are driving new business strategies and changing relationships among chain partners.

'Ultimately, the Sugar Link Project achieved a commitment from stakeholders to sustainable farming practices, including waste water management, best-practice guidelines for farm management and "green harvesting" through collaboration and increased transparency,' Woodhead explains. 'It resulted in the ethical branding retailers were looking for to cater to the concerns of an increasingly influential breed of consumer.'

Along with improvements in practices, the Sugar Link Project developed a target and reporting system to ensure the continuation of the process. While the achievements of the Sugar Link Project represent the efforts of just a few, the tide is turning in Australia. The country' largest polluters, classified as companies that emit more than 125 kilo tonnes of GHG and produce or consume 500 terrajoules of energy will soon be required to report under a new legislative framework.

'Supply chains are therefore powerful vehicles to drive sustainability.'

The National Greenhouse and Energy Reporting (NGER) Act 2007, along with subordinate legislation, the NGER Regulations, the Emissions and Energy Methodologies Instrument and the External Audit Instrument, demand mandatory reporting for any corporation that emits GHG and produces or consumes energy at a specific activity level.

'The NGER System Regulations Policy Paper, released early in 2008 proposes to phase reporting in over three years from July 2008,' Maurice Sinclair says. 'Corporations will report within legislated industry sectors as a precursor to an Emission trading scheme.'

Initial compliance will come at a cost in the short term. 'At the end of the day mandatory reporting will be incorporated as a business cost,' Sinclair says, 'while companies ascertain their base position. Once they've measured their actual output there will be all sorts of opportunities to reduce GHG and energy consumption, which should result in significant commercial benefits along the way.'

'The process will force businesses to look at better ways to rationalize and create more efficiency across their supply chains,' he adds. 'For example, companies might focus on distribution, particularly into difficult to serve and high cost-to-serve markets.'

'It could involve shared reverse logistics in terms of crate returns, pallet returns and other handling devices and materials that require reverse logistics collaborative operations. Collaborative efforts, essential to achieving sustainability, might result in the redesign or creation of more efficient rolling stock such as low-profile trailers, mezzanine trailers to allow for the elimination of shipping waste or looking to reduce the amount of drag and wear by close coupled trailers.'

41

'Investigating alternative energy sources or hybrid fuel systems to reduce the significance of the fossil fuel base is another growing area, along with the use of multi-temperature vehicles to increase shipping efficiency and to reduce the number of vehicles on the road.'

'Companies might also attempt to reduce the amount of airfreight where possible, and increase sea freight.'

'Shipping is more CO_2 efficient when measured on a per unit basis, and space on the ship can be used as a warehouse with stock holding time calculated in,' Sinclair adds.

According to Sinclair, waste is one of the most significant contributors to GHG.

'If we can reduce the global waste in the food industry, which is estimated to be as high as 20 per cent, this equates to a reduction in GHG emissions of about 4–5 billion litres of fuel and as many as 5 million tonnes of emission annually,' he says. 'In the George Weston Foods business, for example, 15 per cent product returns is considered the industry average. That means at best we expend 115 per cent of effort to get 85 per cent efficiency.'

'This is an industry norm globally. Can you imagine the excess packaging, wasted finished goods, reduced production efficiency, excess marketing effort, increased transport in and out of the plants, and so on? Essentially, better demand planning will lead to reductions in stored inventory and ultimately waste.'

Despite the opportunities, Sinclair calculates that only about 5 per cent of companies actually know what they're in for.

'The beauty of the legislation is that it's mandatory,' he says. 'In the same way as GST reporting is now part of everyday life, the requirement for NGER compliance will drive daily business activity. The need to generate sustainability as added value to the business will also grow as strong leadership embeds it throughout the organization.'

But what is the first step for companies wishing to comply?

'In reality the first step towards creating a sustainable supply chain is to actually know what your carbon footprint is so that you have a base measure going forward,' Sinclair explains. 'Understanding the commercial impact will come once you know your footprint. Whereas a year ago you might never have heard of measuring carbon footprint, three companies have already achieved it, including Fonterra, McDonald's and DHL. George Weston Foods is employing an environmental manager and developing a working group to look and address our greenhouse gas emissions and future compliance activity.'

'I know of at least half a dozen other companies with whom I directly liaise that are looking at the same principles. I think we've moved beyond lip service now. This legislation has been the best thing that's happened to our planet for many years.'

Without dynamic alignment of supply chains, however, it's not possible to accurately measure your carbon output.

'John Gattorna's "dynamic alignment" model is a way to ensure the often conflicting goals of commercial success and socio-environmental responsibility can be reconciled and achieved,' says Maurice Sinclair. 'By looking at the behaviour along supply chains it's easier to match and design the interrelationships in a more harmonious way, to reduce waste and improve efficiency.'

'I would say that other than measuring your output, companies need to understand their strategy; the different buying and selling behaviours of their customers and suppliers, and then create the appropriate supply models through their chains. That will impact on the amount of inventory held, how it's procured, where it's held, how it's held, and the speed through the chain. Once alignment is understood, you can go about measuring your current footprint against the climate model and start making improvements within that context.'

While there is clearly a growing concern for the environment, as evidenced by the significant call from clients to investigate sustainability and compliance within Mark Reynold's business in 2007, Maurice Sinclair says that there will still be those who'll need to be forced to comply, 'kicking and screaming', rather than being proactive.

Senior research analyst of sustainable funds for AMP Capital Investors and panelist Dr Ian Woods believes that businesses must think carefully about the impact on brand and reputation, and ultimately cost, of this attitude.

'A recent AMP Capital Investors analysis finds 77 per cent of the value of the typical Australian company is made up of intangibles,' Woods says. 'Successful risk management and supply chain relationships and management can represent an important part of company value.'

'Whereas a year ago you might never have heard of measuring carbon footprint, three companies have already achieved it, including Fonterra, McDonald's and DHL.'

43

'Consumers now look for signs of certification and assurance, such as quality, safety and environmental management systems,' he explains. 'These might include an organization's general approach such as a "green lead", the use of biofuels, or product stewardship. It might equally include a specific sector chain of custody initiatives such as the Forest Stewardship Council Certification, the Waste Electrical and Electronic Equipment Directive or the National Packaging Covenant.'

Alice Woodhead sees emergent thinking within organizations looking to engage with social and environmental auditing, transparency, equitable distribution of wealth and knowledge and corporate responsibility.

'The change has come about in part because of the need to connect with the "conscientious consumer",' she observes. 'Finding a common language between competing needs and agendas within the supply chain is the next challenge.'

Maurice Sinclair maintains that there's a huge opportunity for Australia to use its wealth and technology to restructure its economy with a view to staying prosperous while using energy more cleverly and reducing waste and land use.

'The big dilemma facing developed nations is that, on one hand, we need to maintain the noble goal of sustaining Gaia or looking after Mother Earth and, on the other, we have to make sure that our companies are commercially viable,' he says. 'Otherwise the effort required will be severely short changed by rationalists whose sole focus is shareholder wealth.'

'Those that do position themselves early with the muscle, mass and collaboration skills will obviously be in the strongest position to maximize the opportunities as early adopters by incorporating the culture of sustainability as value into their business.'

NOTES

1 Panel #1: Aligning enterprise supply chains with customers, suppliers, and third party providers.
2 See Chapter 16 for a more detailed case analysis.
3 J.L. Gattorna, *Living Supply Chains*, FT Prentice Hall, Harlow, 2006.
4 Refer to Chapters 12 and 17 for more details of the experience at Fonterra, New Zealand.
5 Panel #2: The critical contribution 3PLs can potentially make to overall corporate performance.
6 See also Chapter 23 for a more detailed discussion on 3PLs.
7 Ibid.
8 Panel #3: The impact of supply chain disruptions on corporate operational and financial performance.
9 'Supply chain disruptions result in lengthy recovery times, affect customer service and profitability', Accenture Study, New York, October 2006.
10 K.B. Hendricks and V.R. Singhal (2003), 'The effect of supply chain glitches on shareholder value', *Journal of Operations Management*, 21, pp. 501–522.
11 See Chapter 22 for more detail on supply chain disruptions.
12 Panel #4: Supply chain business models of the future.
13 See Chapter 27 for more detail on the Arshiya business model.
14 Panel #5: Achieving 'requisite' collaboration in enterprise supply chains.
15 J.L. Gattorna, *Living Supply Chains*, FT Prentice Hall, London, 2006.
16 Panel #6: Leadership, Vision, and innovation: supply chains in enterprise-leading roles.
17 Effective from October 2008, Professor Roy Green is Dean, Faculty of Business, University of Technology, Sydney.
18 Panel #7: Rise of the 'humanitarian' supply chain phenomenon in a troubled world.
19 See also Chapters 5, 6 and 7 for a more detailed treatment of 'humanitarian logistics/supply chains'.
20 Panel #8: The essence of 'sustainability' in contemporary supply chains.
21 See also Chapters 20 and 21.
22 *Towards a Sustainable Sugar Supply Chain*, Department of Agriculture, Fisheries and Forestry, Bureau of Rural Services, Australian Government, 2006.

1 People Powering Enterprise Supply Chains[1]

John Gattorna

L et's cut to the chase and stop dancing around the issues that pervade
contemporary supply chains. People, and people alone, are at the centre
of every enterprise supply chain that exists in the world today. On the
outside we call these people 'customers' or 'clients', and on the inside we
have boards, management and employees running the business. That's a lot
of involved people! But where are the Human Resource Management (HRM)
professionals? Aren't they supposed to advise and assist top management to
shape all this 'people power' on the inside of organizations so that we can
better satisfy customers and produce a correspondingly improved bottom
line? Of course there is no 'bottom line' if there is no 'top line', a fact that is
sometimes lost on managers with a one-dimensional focus on costs.

It seems to me, as I travel the world and engage with major corporations,
that the number of HRM professionals is increasing, but their impact is
getting less. I see no evidence that they have mastered the complexity that
disparate human behaviour brings to organizations, and, by extension,
supply chains. Quite to the contrary, I observe a reversion to type, where they
preoccupy themselves with activities that they mostly feel comfortable with
– for example, personnel administration, car policies, recruitment, wages
and award payments, health and safety, superannuation, and other routine
matters.

A MORE ENLIGHTENED VIEW OF CONTEMPORARY SUPPLY CHAINS

Supply chains permeate every type of enterprise, whether commercial or
not-for-profit; they pervade our lives and are the 'pathways' through which
products and services move as they gather value (and cost) en route to the
end-user/consumer. Along the way there are lots of processes, activities and
relationships involved, enabled by technology and infrastructure. But the
latter are only enablers, not the main game. I think we have forgotten this
reality as we progressively became smitten by advancing technology, and in

turn this has sidetracked many organizations away from the only focus that is important – customers. This reality is particularly true of enterprises that have been through the rigours of implementing an Enterprise Resource Planning (ERP) system. But it should not necessarily be the case.

The truth is that most organizations have not reached an acceptable level of understanding of their customers' dominant buying behaviours, because they haven't really been thinking in these terms, although few, if any, will admit it. I see very few enterprises in my travels that genuinely understand and have an in-depth knowledge of their customers. Even those that do appear to quarantine that knowledge in functional silos such as Marketing or Sales, which then leaves the back-of-shop operational staff largely in the dark, and second-guessing customer requirements. Hey, if we would only admit to ourselves that the real enemy is on the *outside* of the organization, not on the inside, we would be much better off! The real villains are marketing and sales personnel who are not doing enough to translate their sometimes intimate knowledge through to other parts of the enterprise. But we will leave that particular argument for later.

> *'The number of human resource management (HRM) professionals is increasing, but their impact is getting less.'*

ALIGNING THE ENTERPRISE AROUND CUSTOMERS

There is only one fail-safe frame of reference when designing and operating contemporary supply chains – the customer and the customer situation. This is the starting-point for all subsequent action. If you don't think this way, you are either guessing or kidding yourself! Once you fully understand the behavioural structure of your marketplace it is possible to 'reverse engineer' the configuration of your supply chains back through the organization to actual operations on the ground. And, because there is always more than one type of dominant buying behaviour evident in any product/service-market situation, it follows that there is likely to be more than one type of supply chain. Indeed, I have consistently found empirical evidence to suggest three to four generic types of supply chains, and/or variations of these, in different mixes, depending on the product, service or country. Briefly, these are as follows:

1. *continuous replenishment* supply chains to service the 'collaborative' segment;

2. *lean* supply chains to service the 'efficiency' segment;

3. *agile* supply chains to service the 'demanding' segment; and

4. *fully flexible* supply chains to service the 'innovative solutions seeking' segment.

And as customers move away from their natural or preferred buying behaviours there is a good chance that they will move, either temporarily or permanently, to one of the other three buying states listed above. In some large organizations it is possible to discern more than one buying behaviour present. So, any response must have a *dynamic* capability; this is not duck-shooting where you have a single response and endeavour to infinitely adapt your response as customers move across your sights. That approach is cost-prohibitive because of the myriad exceptions involved, and it is very wearing on the people inside the business.

Once you pin down the structure of your marketplace, it is possible to develop a corresponding range of responses that align with the different customer buying behaviours you have identified. This becomes a *packaging* exercise where you mix and match recipes of attributes such as price, brand, speed and/or consistency of delivery, relationships, degree of innovation and more. The same basic product or service can be delivered in many different ways to suit the same or different customers. All well and good, but the problems are only just starting. The devil is in the detail of implementing the supply chain configurations to deliver these *intended* strategies, rather than their formulation, and that is where people play major roles, front and centre. They can either make things happen, or resist simply because they want to. This is an insidious form of resistance because it is difficult to identify and measure in real time, and often the effects only become apparent after significant time has elapsed. And by then it is usually too late to recover.

THE KEY TO SUCCESSFUL EXECUTION IS PEOPLE

The *dynamic alignment* concept requires that four levels of human endeavour be aligned – *marketplace*, *response(s)* to customer demands, internal *cultural capability* and *leadership style* – all held together primarily with leadership, organization structures, processes and technology. The biggest problems occur at the interface between intended responses (strategies) and the internal cultural capability of the enterprise. Indeed, 40–60 per cent of written plans are never delivered on the ground, and the reason for this is the dislocation that occurs at the strategy–cultural capability interface. It is not due to competitor activity as many would have us believe. The root cause of non-performance is much closer to home – that is, inside the enterprise itself, a type of 'Trojan Horse'. My question therefore is as follows: what have HRM professionals been doing to understand and address these issues for, and on behalf of, CEOs? Where is the research to better inform practice? In short, where have they been when we needed them most? Are they not the custodians of the corporate culture? How have they advised top management in the quest to reduce obvious 'misalignments', particularly at this crucial interface? The answers to all these questions are pretty negative, and, worst of all, there is little or no respite in sight. Organizations continue to operate much as they have done for decades, and educational institutions are teaching the same old stuff to their students, the next generation of managers. It's a vicious circle that we must break out of sooner rather than later. That time is getting close for many organizations – otherwise they won't survive.

THE FOUR GENERIC SUPPLY CHAIN ALIGNMENT CONFIGURATIONS

Each of the four generic supply chain types listed above look different at each level of the alignment framework. They have to be in order to focus on a particular dominant buying behaviour. Each of these unique configurations is depicted in Figures 1.1–1.4.

48

For the purposes of this discussion we will focus on the forces at work at the cultural capability level, because it is here that the human action inside the enterprise plays out, mostly hidden from view. This is also where the 'forces of darkness' lurk, leading to gross organizational ineffectiveness. It is also right here that we need HRM professionals to be focusing their attention and providing technical advice and support to senior management. The following attributes that shape and create subcultures are the ones we want them to focus their attention and energies on.

1. *Organization design.* Other than 'leadership style' itself, this is the most powerful force for shaping subcultures because it constrains the way in which people work, just like a straitjacket. Unfortunately, it is also

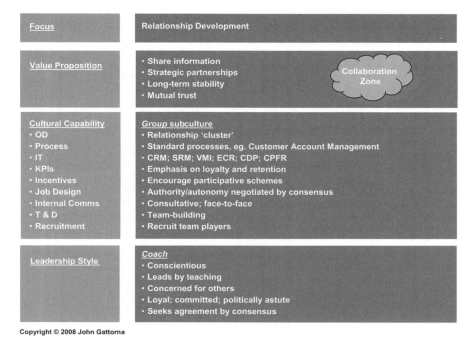

Copyright © 2008 John Gattorna

Figure 1.1   Continuous replenishment supply chains

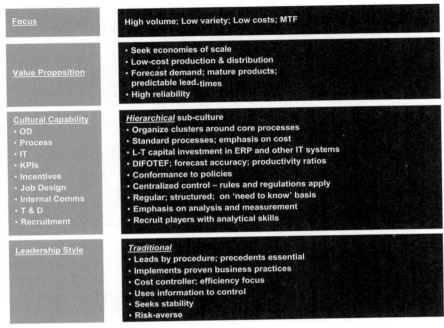

Focus	High volume; Low variety; Low costs; MTF
Value Proposition	• Seek economies of scale • Low-cost production & distribution • Forecast demand; mature products; predictable lead-times • High reliability
Cultural Capability • OD • Process • IT • KPIs • Incentives • Job Design • Internal Comms • T & D • Recruitment	*Hierarchical* sub-culture • Organize clusters around core processes • Standard processes; emphasis on cost • L-T capital investment in ERP and other IT systems • DIFOTEF; forecast accuracy; productivity ratios • Conformance to policies • Centralized control – rules and regulations apply • Regular; structured; on 'need to know' basis • Emphasis on analysis and measurement • Recruit players with analytical skills
Leadership Style	*Traditional* • Leads by procedure; precedents essential • Implements proven business practices • Cost controller; efficiency focus • Uses information to control • Seeks stability • Risk-averse

Figure 1.2   Lean supply chains

the area that has seen the least progress in theory over the last several decades. Organizational designers have been unable (or unwilling) to come up with anything better than the traditional functional silos, and variations of this, such as matrix structures. Functional silos served us well in the relatively slow-moving world of the 1950s, 1960s and 1970s, but have become progressively more misaligned with the way customers want to buy over the last two decades. It seems we will never rid ourselves of this format, and maybe we won't have to. More about that point shortly.

Matrix organization structures were introduced to overcome the weakness highlighted above in functional silos, but have generally not been effective, and will not get any more effective from here on. The problem is the internal conflicts generated at each intersection between a customer-focused account manager and the all-powerful vertical functions that hold the budgets. No joy there.

In my view there is a way forward that allows us to engage and align with customers more effectively in a fast-moving operating environment. I called this organizational format a 'cluster'. The idea is to build groups or clusters of multidisciplinary personnel that faithfully replicate both the competences required to service a particular customer segment, as well as embedding the required mindset bias. For example, where we have a continuous replenishment supply chain aligned with a collaborative segment of customers, it is important to embed a 'relationship' mindset or subculture and support this with the appropriate processes and technology, as discussed below.

In this way, we can keep the conventional functional silos in place, but with a different raison d'être. They become the repository of specialist skills and competences, and the 'force generator' from which the new clusters draw personnel of all disciplines for short- or long-term assignment to particular clusters.

Likewise, clusters for each of the other three types of supply chain can be configured with the appropriate mix of disciplines and mindsets. Surely this is an area where HRM professionals can play a major role, working with functional and cluster heads to engineer the required configurations. More details on how to design and operate 'clusters' follow in Chapter 9.

2. *Positioning people in appropriate roles* – that is, square 'pegs' in square holes. This is where the fine-tuning begins. Personnel are closely reviewed in terms of their technical skills and mindsets, using such techniques as the Myers Briggs Type Indicator (MBTI) for the latter, to ensure that they 'fit' any roles they are appointed to. We are talking about nuances here, but they count tremendously towards organizational effectiveness at the aggregate level. The days of wiping out whole layers of management are gone. Looking back, that was born of ignorance and heavy-handedness.

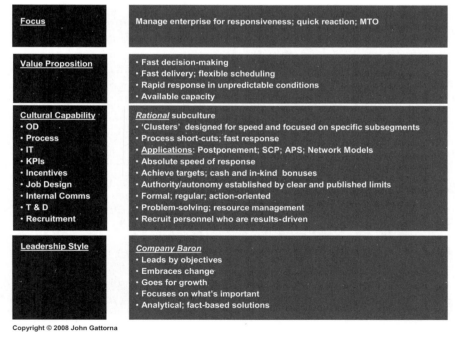

Focus	Manage enterprise for responsiveness; quick reaction; MTO
Value Proposition	• Fast decision-making • Fast delivery; flexible scheduling • Rapid response in unpredictable conditions • Available capacity
Cultural Capability • OD • Process • IT • KPIs • Incentives • Job Design • Internal Comms • T & D • Recruitment	*Rational* subculture • 'Clusters' designed for speed and focused on specific subsegments • Process short-cuts; fast response • Applications: Postponement; SCP; APS; Network Models • Absolute speed of response • Achieve targets; cash and in-kind bonuses • Authority/autonomy established by clear and published limits • Formal; regular; action-oriented • Problem-solving; resource management • Recruit personnel who are results-driven
Leadership Style	*Company Baron* • Leads by objectives • Embraces change • Goes for growth • Focuses on what's important • Analytical; fact-based solutions

Figure 1.3   Agile supply chains

3. *Process re-engineering.* There are no mysteries here, but the key is to ensure that the primary processes which align with each supply chain type or pathway are in place. They become standard and are invoked by the cluster as required.

4. *Information technology and systems.* These simply mimic and institutionalize the processes already established through enlightened re-engineering. The problem to date has been that organizations have been throwing the full gambit of systems technology at every type of customer situation, without discrimination, looking in vain for the 'silver bullet'. However, there is no such thing in supply chain management. What we need is an underpinning ERP system to provide one version of the truth, and then interface this with different combinations of IT applications. So, for example, the main application servicing the collaborative customer segment might be a Customer Relationship Management (CRM) system. It will help us manage the loyal high-value customers in the way they expect, where relationships and trust are paramount. More about this vital dimension later in this chapter.

5. *Key Performance Indicators (KPIs).* This is an area of management that seriously impacts on performance, yet is so badly understood. People will do what's inspected, not what's expected. So you have to use this principle in framing the KPIs unique to each type of supply chain. Out with the so-called 'balanced scorecard', and in with a few very carefully selected KPIs, purposefully designed to

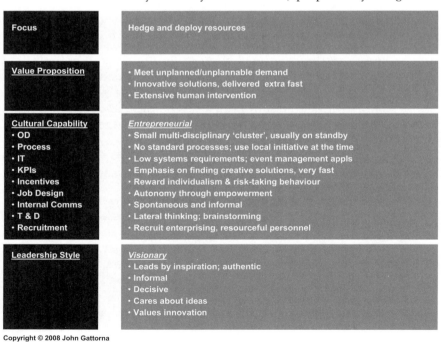

Copyright © 2008 John Gattorna

Figure 1.4   Fully flexible supply chains

faithfully signal what management wants people in the firm to do. More about this in following pages of this chapter and Chapter 14.

6.   *Incentives*. These are the mirror image of the KPIs, selected especially for particular situations. It's a matter of 'horses for courses'. What are the most appropriate incentives for personnel who are themselves steeped in relationship-building and maintenance. Is it cash? Or is it something in kind that will further motivate them? Again, over to the HRM professionals to figure this out. That's what they are paid to do!

7.   *Internal communications*. Different subcultures have different communication styles. The trick is to embed the style that best aligns with the subculture you are trying to shape. In the case of the organizational cluster driving the continuous replenishment supply chain, this is likely to be very inclusive, with actions only being taken after a consensus is reached. To be fair, this can sometimes be a slow drawn-out process but, then again, when you are servicing this type of relationship-focused customer, time is on your side. Nothing changes fast. Everything is a result of a lot of thoughtful consideration. So the cluster is just reflecting that trait.

8.   *Training and development*. Here we expect that HRM professionals will design and conduct a Personal Development Programme (PDP) for each and every individual executive. Gone are the days of spending big on mass training initiatives. This was wasteful at best and a dereliction of duty at worst.

9.   *Recruitment*. This parameter represents a very powerful force for 'genetically engineering' selected subcultures in an organization, to reflect the external market structure. Thankfully, I have met a number of recruitment firms recently that 'get it' and are actively engaged in delivering individuals to enterprises that meet technical, experiential and mindset parameters. Logistics Recruitment[2] is one such organization, Russell Reynolds is another, and their efforts are to be applauded. What we need from the internal HRM professionals is engagement in this vital enterprise-building process.

10. *Leadership style*. Finally there is the overarching influence of leadership style that is perhaps as important in shaping subcultures in enterprises as organization design. Here again, there are plenty of sophisticated tools available to HRM professionals to measure and monitor management and leadership styles, but you also have to know what to do with this data. HRM professionals can assist management by helping and advising in the formation of the various clusters and, in particular, which individual executive is appropriate for the particular leadership role being considered.

TECHNOLOGY IS A WONDERFUL THING

Indeed, technology is a wonderful thing when it comes to operating supply chains. The convergence of the Internet and the simultaneous development of a myriad software packages in the early 1990s was the breakthrough we had been waiting for. This broke the stalemate we had been caught in for the entire previous decade, as companies struggled to improve internal cross-functional integration. Up until that point, efforts to improve integration had largely been stymied by internal cultural forces bent on resisting change, and problems with the compatibility of various available technologies. All that changed sometime in the 1990s, and, if anything, the balance swung too far the other way as companies raced to meet the dreaded Y2K deadline of 1 January 2000.

That said, there is still too much emphasis on technology as the likely 'silver bullet' which is going to solve all the problems of underperforming corporate supply chains; this will never be the case. Nevertheless, too many enterprises are throwing every type of system at their supply chains, with little thought as to what designs do and don't work. Too often, large system implementations are justified on the basis of false premises – for example, inventory reduction and increased stock-turns – when they should be seen as a strategic investment and foundation for other systems.

My work in the field with many companies over the years reveals that the specific configuration of the technology we should apply inside a particular business depends largely on the structure of the market being served and the corresponding behavioural segmentation. This in turn informs what processes are most appropriate for each major segment, and the technology that underpins these processes simply follows.

Those readers who are familiar with my recent book, *Living Supply Chains*[3] will know that I have concluded, from many observations made in the field, that there are up to four main types of customer buying behaviour evident across many product/service categories, and this immediately equates to four corresponding generic types of supply chain, as indicated earlier. If this is true, and we believe it is, then each of those supply chains inside the company will require different treatment along several dimensions. And all four of these generic supply chains are likely to coexist. Indeed, the way we organize ourselves internally is simply a mirror image of the way our marketplace is structured in terms of customer buying behaviour. It stands to reason, therefore, that each type of supply chain will require a different technology recipe to achieve close alignment with the corresponding segment, and such is the case.

> *'There is still too much emphasis on technology as the likely "silver bullet" which is going to solve all the problems of underperforming corporate supply chains.'*

'REQUISITE' TECHNOLOGY

Like so many other things in life, there are patterns that work and those that don't work, and the same is true of technology applications. So, while an enterprise will surely benefit from discarding all its old legacy systems and replacing them with a single ERP system, that is only part of the story. What goes on top of this ERP is what matters. This argument is best amplified by the analogy of renovating an old house or a bathroom or kitchen at home. You can spend a lot of money on the new wiring and plumbing that goes in behind the walls, unseen. But you don't get the value from all this investment until you apply all the fittings – the taps, basins, toilet pans, electrical switches, light fittings and so on. The same holds true for technology, as depicted in Figure 1.5 which features the Oracle Suite by way of example.

Each supply chain type has a different technology emphasis. So back to our original theme which requires us to mix and match the applications that sit on top of the ERP, like 'pimples on a pumpkin'.

1. *Continuous replenishment supply chains.* This is the genuine 'collaborative' zone, and here the primary, indeed only emphasis, is on keeping the relationship going with our most loyal customers. There may only be 20 or so of them, but they could easily represent 60–80 per cent of our revenue and 80 per cent of our profitability.

   The customer account management process is key in this situation and should be underpinned by a suite of applications such as:

   • Customer Relationship Management (CRM);

   • Vendor Managed Inventory (VMI);

   • Collaborative, Planning, Forecasting and Replenishment (CPFR);

   and likewise on the supply side where relationships with strategic suppliers are critical – that is:

   • Supplier Relationship Management (SRM).

2. *Lean supply chains.* In this situation the emphasis moves away from loyalty and retention of loyal customers to a simple focus on efficiency and lowest cost-to-serve.

   All the processes will be standard, and the approach is to build clusters of personnel around specific processes, so that they become absolutely routine and low-cost. More about this in Chapter 9.

   The primary technology is the ERP system, supplemented by a network optimization modelling tool which is interfaced directly to the ERP. Other execution systems such as a Labour Management System (LMS) for scheduling the workforce will help drive costs down, and a Radio Frequency Identification (RFID) system will be invaluable in keeping track of stock and triggering replenishment protocols.

Using the Oracle Suite as an example

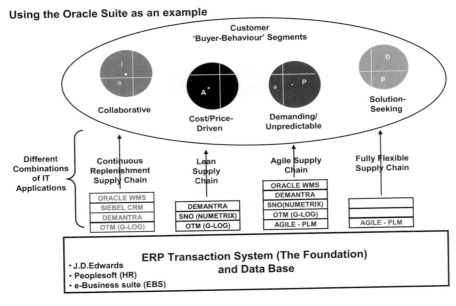

Copyright © 2008 John Gattorna

Figure 1.5   'Requisite' technology for supply chains

3.   *Agile supply chains*. Here the emphasis changes to absolute speed of response, even if that costs more! The name of the game when serving highly demanding customers in an unpredictable environment is to have the capacity already available – it's too late to scramble for capacity when demanding customers come calling, and, of course, they never give you a forecast in advance!

The trick is to reduce the number of processes to a minimum and use your technology to quickly run viable scenarios to fulfil the demands. Likewise with suppliers where you are pushing them for an emergency order that was not in the original forecast.

Most companies that develop agile capabilities use a range of tools and techniques – for example,

- Postponement: build an inventory of raw materials and/or components; or

- Build standard modules that can be quickly assembled into unique configurations;

- Supply Chain Planning (SCP);

- Advanced Planning and Scheduling (APS); and

- Customer Account Profitability (CAP); and, above all

- A network optimization modelling tool to assist decision-making.

4. *Fully flexible supply chains.* This is a 'catch-all' supply chain configuration that uses a high degree of human intervention, and potentially any and all systems as required, to produce an innovative solution in quick time for the customer, who at this stage doesn't care about the price. The situation is hurting them so much that they just want a solution, and very often it is only the supplier who has a chance of finding a solution in such a short timeframe. This type of supply chain uses whatever it takes to get a satisfactory result for the customer, and the technology can be sophisticated or basic.

In the end, typical situations involving a string of supply chain partners will require participants to mix and match different combinations of supply-side and demand-side technology point applications as described above. So a company such as Zara in the fashion industry might use *lean* techniques on the supply side, build a raw materials bank close to its consumer markets, and use postponement protocols to respond quickly to the fickle consumer fashion market on the demand side. Of course, the key on the demand side is to have the *capacity* to respond to unexpected surges in demand, in production, and downstream through to the store. Ultimately, knowing where to deploy what technologies is one of the vital keys to success in any marketplace.

OUT WITH 'BALANCED' SCORECARDS IN SUPPLY CHAINS, AND IN WITH 'BIASED' KPIs

There is nothing wrong with measuring aspects of your organization's performance, because after all we know from bitter experience that 'people do what's inspected, not what's expected'! But how far do you go in collecting data and analysing the myriad pivotal points in an organization? There is certainly no shortage of material on this point, and in the vanguard is the work of Kaplan and Norton (1992).[4] Their early work in particular was very comprehensive – perhaps too comprehensive. Why do I say that? Because on many occasions I have witnessed company executives bogged down in the detail, slavishly collecting data according to a long checklist, but have seen little evidence that this data, once collected, was fully analyzed and used in appropriate ways to increase performance. The hype may say otherwise, but this is the reality. Examine your own conscience on this point.

To be fair, the Kaplan and Norton 'balanced scorecard' incorporated both internal and external perspectives, and sought to cover both financial and non-financial measures, but it brought with it many critical weaknesses both in concept and operational use. Not the least of these were the difficulty of using it as a comparative tool between business units and the lack of a mechanism to aggregate measures for management across several business units in a conglomerate. In many ways it was a good idea that was primarily useful in translating an organization's strategic objectives into a coherent set of performance measures, no more, no less. [5]

More recent work by the same authors has attempted to overcome some of these weaknesses, but the fatal flaw is that they continue to treat the subject of performance measurement as an inanimate process rather than what it actually is: one of several levers potentially available to shape internal culture in the enterprise, which in turn shapes and drives visible behaviour.

SHIFTING THE FOCUS

We need to look at this issue of performance measurement and management in an entirely different way, and the first clue as to how this might be done comes with the realization that enterprises are really an aggregation of supply chains (or pathways) running through them, from source(s) of raw materials, components, packaging and sub-assemblies, along a myriad links to nodes in the network where value-creating activities are performed, and on downstream to customers and ultimately end-users/consumers. Along these pathways information and finances are exchanged and important human relationships are formed and managed. It is these human relationships that power supply chains and therefore the business overall. Technology and infrastructure are simply the enablers, albeit essential ingredients to success.

Referring to Figure 1.6, we will now consider each of the four generic supply chain types as they are influenced by KPIs. The essential point is that we should select and use a few KPIs with each type of supply chain, and the emphasis will, by definition, be different in each case. Gone are the general

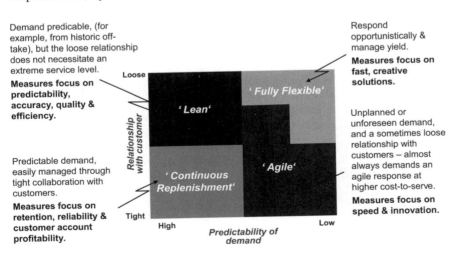

Figure 1.6   **Performance measures: the four generic supply chains**

Source: Adapted from Figure 2.3 in J.L. Gattorna, *Living Supply Chains*, FT Prentice Hall, London, 2006.

measures that can't be traced back and connected to specific facets of performance.

Continuous Replenishment Supply Chains – Where Relationships Matter Most

Here we are measuring such factors as: length of customer relationships; the degree of information being shared both ways; and the percentage that we, as a supplier, represent of a particular customer's spend in a particular product category. The focus is clearly on service reliability and retention of the relationship over the long term. Nothing less is acceptable, and yet how often do we see these valuable customers ignored and eventually lost forever, because they never come back no matter how much effort we pour, albeit belatedly, into the cause?.

To engage customers of the collaborative type in this way we need to create a 'relationship' subculture inside the business, which goes well beyond most commentators' process approach towards the subject of performance measurement and management.

Lean Supply Chains – Where the Focus is on Efficiency and Lowest Cost-to-Serve

In this type of supply chain we are bent on delivering a low-cost predictable service to customers who otherwise don't care for extras. In terms of measures, those that come to the fore are forecast accuracy, Delivery-In-Full-On-Time (DIFOT); cost per unit; and selected productivity ratios. Nothing else matters much. So inside our organization we need to encourage a 'cost-controlling' subculture that puts conformance to policy right up there in lights. This is not a place for mavericks.

Agile Supply Chains – Where Quick Response is Paramount

The emphasis in this type of supply chain moves from reliability to time sensitivity. How long does it take us to respond to the customer's request, even though we did not know it was coming? This is the world of unpredictability, and surviving and thriving requires wholly different capabilities. We measure time to respond and we measure the capacity of the supply chain at vital points along the pathway to our customers. It is more a case of optimizing our resources than maximizing utilization, because, by definition, servicing customers in this mode means that we need to design in redundancy, and that costs money, which customers must be prepared to pay for at some point.

The corresponding subculture is 'aggressively customer-focused' and bent on speed. This is not a place for long-drawn-out processes or consensus-seeking. This is a place for action.

Fully Flexible Supply Chains – Where Nothing is Impossible

This type of supply chain is designed to respond to the unplannable event and is therefore hard on resource usage. We are not bothered about cost, or utilization, or even relationships in this type of supply chain – only getting an acceptable result for the customer, fast, very fast. We see elements of this type in emergency or humanitarian operations, in breakdown situations and in military operations.

'The "one-size-fits-all" philosophy is dead forever, and with it goes all the general approaches to performance measurement and management.'

The subculture inside the organization is very much 'can-do', and everything and anyone who can assist in getting the desired result is drawn into the effort. There are little or no concerns about cost because a 'no-fix' means even greater cost. Creativity and innovation are key characteristics in this type of supply chain.

'BIASED' RATHER THAN 'BALANCED'

So that's where the preference for a 'biased' approach comes from – simply from recognizing that particular buying behaviours exhibited by customers at the end of supply chains requires differential – sometimes radically different – treatment to other situations. The 'one-size-fits-all' philosophy is dead forever, and with it goes all the general approaches to performance measurement and management. We must know and understand our marketplace and reverse engineer the appropriate selection of KPIs back from there. And to ensure they are executed we need to have in place an organization design, processes and other factors that shape the equivalent subculture; otherwise people will simply do what they prefer to do, rather than what we want them to do, and, as a consequence the 'misalignment' between our strategies on paper and our actions on the ground will become ever wider.

SOME EVIDENCE TO REFLECT ON

At the Smart'07 Conference in Sydney in June 2007 I addressed an audience of some 300 people on the topic of 'Living Supply Chains' and what this meant for designing and operating contemporary high-performance supply chains. At the end of my address I asked the audience six questions. The results are indicated below. If this audience is typical, which I think it is, we have a lot of work to do on our enterprise supply chains. The questions and answers were as follows:

Q1: Has your company/enterprise attempted to design/operate its supply chain network along 'alignment' principles? **Yes: 33%; No 67%**

Q2: Has your company/enterprise used behavioural segmentation of customers to inform the design/operation of its supply chains? **Yes 21%; No 79%**

Q3: Has your company consciously attempted to shape various subcultures to execute the different types of supply chains (pathways) that are running through the business? **Yes: 32%; No 68%**

Q4: Does top management in your company treat logistics/supply chain management as a specialist 'function' or as an integral part of the business? **Yes: 69%; No 31%**

Q5: Do you think top management in your company understands the role culture plays in powering corporate supply chains? **Yes 38%; No 62%**

Q6: If no, are they in denial? **Yes 77%; No 23%**

Perhaps you might like to answer the same questions yourself to get a reading on how far you are on or off the pace.

ALIGNMENT INSIGHTS

- *Humans and their behaviour is what propels supply chains; ignore that fact at your peril.*

- *Of all the factors that shape human behaviour on the ground, the two most powerful are 'leadership' and organization design. We shall have more to say about both in the following chapters.*

- *Technology, used in innovative and enlightened ways, is a wonderful enabler when it comes to operating supply chains; treat it with due care and don't have unrealistic expectations of its capability.*

- *Move away from 'balanced scorecards' to 'biased scorecards' and you will see immediate improvements in performance.*

NOTES

1   Adapted from articles in *Supply Chain Asia*, November–December 2007; January/February 2008; and May/June 2008.

2   Logistics Recruitment, a Sydney-based global recruitment network, with offices in ten countries. Logistics Recruitment has recently launched the world's first global careers site for supply chain and logistics professionals. Refer to: http://www.SupplyChainJobz.com.

3   J.L. Gattorna, *Living Supply Chains*, FT Prentice Hall, Harlow, 2006.

4   R.S. Kaplan and D.P. Norton, 'The Balanced Scorecard: Measures That Drive Performance', *Harvard Business Review* (January–February 1992), pp. 71–79.

5   R.S. Kaplan and D.P. Norton, *Alignment: Using the Balanced Scorecard to Create Corporate Synergies*, Harvard Business School Press, Boston, 2006.

2 'Requisite' Collaboration in Enterprise Supply Chains[1]

John Gattorna

'Collaboration' is one of those concepts that is overused and overworked in the supply chain vernacular. The reality is that for any product (or service) category in a given market, it is very unlikely that more than 25 per cent of customers at best will have truly *collaborative* buying values. By this I mean that they genuinely seek close relationships with their key suppliers; tend to single-source; are brand-loyal; will share information freely; are price-tolerant; and, above all, are forgiving in the way they tolerate failures in supply. In other words, they have the perfect customer profile. Yet what do many suppliers do? They ignore these sometimes suffering customers as they relentlessly pursue other more demanding customers who have none of the virtues listed above. Worse still, suppliers take advantage of their loyal customers by using them to cross-subsidize their more costly efforts in servicing demanding customers.

DEBUNKING SOME OF THE MYTHS

In the early years of 'lean' manufacturing, as introduced and practised by Japanese manufacturers, it was taken for granted that suppliers would collaborate in the systematic joint effort to eradicate cost, rather than just move it up and down the chain. This was a given, and all the parties to these selective arrangements benefited. However, as globalization took hold and supply chains became longer and more complex, something was lost in the translation. Today, while there are still supply chains in which the parties collaborate, there are also many other supply chains in which this is not the case. Indeed, various generic types of supply chains coexist in parallel to provide different supply experiences for customers in the same market. In my book, *Living Supply Chains*,[2] I make the distinction between those market situations where customers are genuinely collaborative and those where they are not. Why? Because you have to recognize which is which and deliver different 'value propositions' via different network configurations. We are now operating in a world where fine nuances make the difference between success and failure, operationally and financially, and you ignore this reality at your peril. To avoid confusion, I have labelled those supply chains where true collaboration exists as 'continuous replenishment'.

TRULY 'COLLABORATIVE' SUPPLY CHAIN CONFIGURATIONS

The cultural value that is treasured above all others in a truly 'collaborative' supply chain is *trust*, which in turn leads to close working relationships for mutual gain. Information is shared freely; long-term stability in the relationship is actively sought, and strategic partnerships are forged for mutual benefit. This is the much sought-after 'collaborative zone' as depicted in Figure 1.1 in the previous chapter (p. 48), and it is a condition that inevitably takes time and patience to develop and nurture.

'Suppliers take advantage of their loyal customers by using them to cross-subsidize their more costly efforts in servicing demanding customers.'

However, it is also a condition that depends almost wholly on the 'alignment' of cultures between buyers and suppliers in the chain, rather than anything more tangible. This is the part where many executives are either out of their depth or simply in denial about. Why? Because they either don't understand or don't want to delve into this abyss where all the 'forces of darkness' exist *in their own organizations*. I have always said that this is the area we should be focusing on, rather than getting carried away with Porter's competitive analysis. In reality there has been an unhealthy preoccupation with competitors and monitoring competition over the last few decades, often to the point of paranoia, and this has distracted executives from looking more deeply at the internal cultural capability of their own enterprises, where progress and greater understanding is going to bring greater returns for the time, effort and money invested. We will not be able to go to the next level of supply chain performance until this mountain is climbed and conquered.

THE UNIQUE SUBCULTURE OF 'COLLABORATION'

The key is to identify which customers have truly collaborative values and treat them as a separate segment to the others in your customer base. Unilever's former CEO, Anthony Burgmans got it right when he said, in effect, that *you should only collaborate with those customers and (suppliers) who genuinely want to collaborate.*[3] For the rest, do whatever you have to do, but don't waste your time trying to be collaborative – it is too wasteful of resources and goes to the heart of my observation that too many suppliers are overservicing some customers and underservicing others, and have no idea which is which!

So how do we shape the appropriate internal culture to drive continuous replenishment supply chains towards those customers who genuinely seek a collaborative relationship? It involves a unique combination of standard resources, as follows:

- Set up a series of multidisciplinary account 'clusters' that dedicate all their attention to specific clients, or groups of clients, who are clearly collaborative in both spirit and action.

- Select personnel for these teams such that the *net* bias in each team is one of empathy for customers and stability of the relationship.

- Put standard customer account management processes in place.

- Underpin these processes with selected technologies such as Customer Relationship Management (CRM), Vendor Managed Inventory (VMI) and other customer-friendly point applications. This is the right place to use such systems, but be warned that they are not as effective in other situations where customers do not display genuine collaborative values.

- Develop two or three Key Performance Indicators (KPIs) that will help you keep key customers' (or suppliers') relationships on track: for example, length of time the customer has been buying from you; the share of the customer's wallet in a particular product category. Other KPIs such as forecast accuracy and Delivery-In-Full-On-Time-Error-Free (DIFOTEF) are simply taken for granted in this type of relationship.

- Ensure that incentives for internal staff focus on schemes that encourage participation and sharing within the serving team – there is little place for individual egos in this subculture.

- Make job designs consistent with the incentives and involve a lot of discussion and consensus – fortunately there is always time available for a lengthy process with this type of customer because they don't like quick action and surprises.

- Ensure that there is a lot of personal face-to-face communications within the account clusters.

- Focus most of the training on team-building.

- Carefully select the personnel recruited to account clusters on the basis of the 'Feeling' (or F) dimension in their Myer Briggs Type Indicator (MBTI).

- Use a leadership style in the account clusters that is typically quite traditional in that everything is done by the book and stability of the relationship is regarded as paramount.

63

In other words, the internal clusters that service collaborative customers, across all disciplines, have to ideally reflect the same values as the customers that they serve.

'REQUISITE' COLLABORATION: A MORE ACCURATE DESCRIPTOR

So 'collaboration' is a condition that is definitely not for everyone. I prefer to think in terms of 'requisite' collaboration – that is, collaborating as much or as little as a particular customer wants or deserves. In this way you avoid a lot of costly overservicing. Once you have identified the truly collaborative customers in your marketplace you can take a minimalist approach to contracts and focus more on non-binding Memoranda of Understanding (MoUs) that provide guidance for engaging each other, but ultimately always rely on trust. And it works. Research I led in the Asia–Pacific region in 2003 clearly showed an inverse correlation between the performances of 3PLs in situations where they were locked into rigid and complex contractual arrangements.[4]

'Not every buyer–seller combination is ready for a collaborative relationship.'

As we move beyond traditional buyer–seller relationships and 3PL-style supplier relationships to more complex new supply chain business models (such as 4PLs), it is going to be vital that the partners selected to join supply chain consortiums and joint ventures are culturally aligned from the outset.

A TECHNIQUE TO CONSOLIDATE COLLABORATIVE RELATIONSHIPS

One technique that I have developed over the years to help foster collaborative relationships is 'strategic partnering'. This is a process I have written about at length in *Living Supply Chains*,[5] and involves developing enduring corporate relationships based on understanding and shared knowledge. The process takes its name from developing and maintaining a strategic 'fit' between the goals, capabilities and market opportunities of both buyer and seller organizations involved in a particular situation. *The two parties commit to a unique, but not necessarily exclusive, relationship that is key to success, and it works!*

ALIGNMENT INSIGHTS

- *Not every buyer–seller combination is ready for a collaborative relationship. Remember Burgmans' words: only collaborate with those who want to collaborate.*

- *Where you do choose to collaborate, you need a special type of supply chain configuration – the continuous replenishment supply chain.*

- *The new mantra for business, even in hostile competitive situations, should be to 'compete in the market, but cooperate in the supply chain'. This is a best-of-both-worlds strategy.*

NOTES

1 Adapted from an article, 'Collaboration in supply chains – the myth and the reality' in *Supply Chain Asia*, (March/April 2008), pp. 16–17.

2 J.L. Gattorna, *Living Supply Chains*, FT Prentice Hall, Harlow, 2006.

3 Anthony Burgmans, speaking at the 6th ECR Conference, Edinburgh, 2001.

4 'Characteristics, strategies, and trends for 3PL/4PL in Australia', Alpha Research Consortium, for the Logistics Association of Australia, 2003.

5 See Appendix 5C, 'Strategic partnering' technique, in J.L. Gattorna, *Living Supply Chains, op. cit.*, pp. 308–312.

3 Building Relationships that Create Value

Richard Wilding and Andrew Humphries

INTRODUCTION

It is well acknowledged that aligning supply chains requires technical competence focusing on the 'technical' aspects of the supply chain – for example, inventory management, scheduling, warehouse management and so on. However, a critical, often unremarked requirement is the relational competence of the members of the supply chain. Continuous replenishment supply chains are all about 'relationships' as Martin Christopher explains: 'Supply Chain Management is the management of upstream and downstream *relationships*, with customers, suppliers, and key stakeholders in order to increase value and reduce cost for all members of the supply chain.'[1] As a result, technical supply chain competency is now perceived only as a 'qualifier' and relational competence is seen as the 'winner'. Despite this, however, it is noticeable that organizations spend too little time considering the relational aspect of the supply chain.

In this chapter we explore the nature of supply chain relationships and the importance of managing them proactively to gain competitive advantage. In addition, we will describe the Supply Chain Collaboration Index (SCCI) which is used to build customer/supplier cohesion, identify problems that undermine teamwork and provide metrics for performance measurement, monitoring and continuous improvement.

COLLABORATION AND PARTNERSHIPS IN SUPPLY CHAINS

Collaboration in supply chains means 'working together to bring resources into a required relationship to achieve effective operations in harmony with the strategies and objectives of the parties involved thus resulting in mutual benefits'.[2] The word 'collaboration' generates many emotions; in certain parts of Europe, for example, 'collaboration' is viewed as a negative concept due to wartime experiences of collaborators, whereas in the US it is seen as a positive, enterprising term. The term 'partnership' is sometimes used to describe relationships; however, this is viewed negatively within certain sectors of the US due to legislation that stops 'partnerships' on account of their perceived anti-competitive nature.

> *'It is noticeable that organizations spend too little time considering the relational aspect of the supply chain.'*

In summary, whatever word is used may provoke an emotional response, but in this case we are discussing business relationships that generate a win–win outcome, benefiting both parties. Collaboration is the action of working with someone to produce or create something that neither organization could otherwise do alone. Not all commercial relationships are like this, and many transactional contracts are long-lived and successful. Therefore, careful judgement is needed in deciding which to devote scarce management attention to (this is, after all, matching changing customer needs and desires with different supply chain strategies).[3] But, in today's highly competitive world, 'strategic partnering' is becoming much more common than you think, and many apparently 'market-style' contracts have the potential to benefit from better teamwork.

FROM FUNCTIONS TO PROCESSES

The way we traditionally structure our businesses and organizations can result in an environment where collaboration is difficult to create and maintain. Generally, for large organizations we have specialist departments that are managed independently – for example, marketing, production and logistics. Command-and-control structures are put in place, headed up by a functional director. However, when we consider what a business does in order to fulfil a customer order, every department becomes involved. Businesses undertake processes, and processes are rarely performed in a single function within an organization, so, how departments work with each other to manage the process and, furthermore, to align to specific customers is critical to the organization's success. This is a subject that we will revisit in Chapter 9.

A typical supply chain, which includes all the organizations involved in supplying a product or a service, is essentially an entire process, from the extraction of raw materials to ultimate disposal. This means that the supply chain encompasses all the processes involved in planning, purchasing, making, delivering and perhaps returning and recycling the product after use. For this process to work effectively, individuals and organizations must work together and collaborate.

Everything we do within the supply chain should be focused on enhancing relationships, so any investment in IT should enhance relationships. This may be from the perspective of lowering costs and then passing on any net benefits to a customer, which in turn enhances the relationship. In order to manage, we need data, so to manage relationships we need data on *how* the relationship is performing – and the techniques described in this chapter demonstrate one approach to doing this. For effective supply chain management, collaboration is therefore a key success factor.

CREATING 'WIN–WIN' RELATIONSHIPS

To create a win–win relationships there are two key factors that must be developed. The first behaviour is C³ behaviour – a combination of **C**ooperation, **C**oordination and **C**ollaboration, and the second is trust. It has been recognized that, for successful collaborative relationships to thrive, trust and C³ behaviour are indispensable ingredients. C³ behaviour is seen as being essential for maintaining a successful business partnership, especially when it is linked with commitment to the achievement of shared, realistic goals. There is generally an evolution that needs to take place. Cooperation is initially required, often in the form of short–duration, low-risk working, which then builds to coordinated activity requiring longer commitment and greater working together. And, finally, collaboration is achieved when both parties jointly plan and define operations and strategy. This is very similar to any personal relationship. Initially, you may go on a short, low-risk 'date' – for example, a trip to the cinema. This may then progress to both parties spending more time together, coordinating their activities, and, finally, marriage may occur where both parties collaborate!

Trust is a cornerstone of business-to-business relationships. There appears to be a consensus that trust integrates micro-level psychological processes and group dynamics with macro-level institutional arrangements or, put more simply, that it encapsulates dispositions, decisions, behaviours, social networks and institutions. Trust enables cooperative behaviour, promotes improved relationships, reduces harmful conflict and allows effective response in a crisis. Trust requires risk (a perceived probability of loss), uncertainty (over the intentions of the other party), interdependence (where the interests of one party cannot be achieved without reliance on the other) and choice (alternative options are available) as essential conditions. Others see trust as being 'caused' (for example, by previous good experience, institutional reputation and commitment) and as affecting factors such as openness, reliability and honesty. A more general assessment suggests a combination of all these elements in a richer interaction between parties, which sometimes requires a leap in faith to achieve, but resulting in the creation of a reservoir of goodwill and the incentive to go the extra mile.

'In order to manage, we need data, so to manage relationships we need data on how the relationship is performing.'

In conclusion, there is little doubt that repeated cycles of exchange, risk-taking and successful fulfilment of expectations strengthen the willingness of parties to rely on each other and, as a result, expand the relationship, in effect producing a virtuous circle that can be developed and promoted. The alternative, untrustworthiness, may precipitate a downward spiral of conflict, leading to diminished operations or failure. It has been found that, over time, trust supported by credible actions is likely to establish a virtuous circle of ever-improving business-to-business relationship performance. Three generic levels of contribution of trust and C^3 behaviour in a business relationship have been identified:

1. *Win–lose or lose–win*: defensiveness, protectiveness, legalistic language, contracts that attempt to cover all the bases and are full of qualifiers and escape clauses, and where the atmosphere promotes further reasons to defend and protect;

2. *Compromise*: mutual respect and confrontation avoidance, polite but not emphatic communication, creativity suppressed;

3. *Win–win*: synergy, high trust and sincerity, producing solutions better than the sum of the contributions and participants enjoying a creative enterprise.

The correlation between these factors is shown in Figure 3.1.

If organizations work together (cooperate) on small projects, trust is developed, which enables organizations to feel comfortable about working more closely together (coordinating) in other areas and then finally having the confidence, as high levels of trust are developed, to 'collaborate' and jointly plan both strategy and operations. Furthermore, research has found that when high levels of trust and C^3 behaviour are present, a spiral of success is generated as shown in Figure 3.2. It is then possible to measure how well

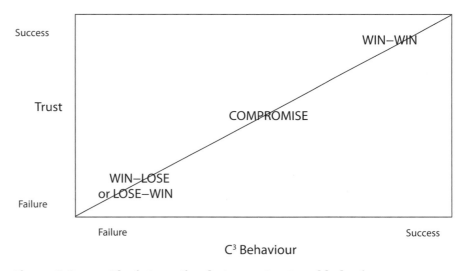

Figure 3.1   The interaction between trust and behaviour

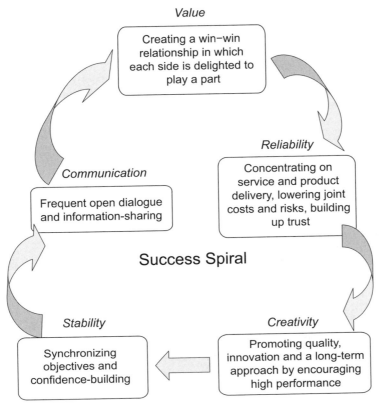

Value

Creating a win–win relationship in which each side is delighted to play a part

Reliability

Concentrating on service and product delivery, lowering joint costs and risks, building up trust

Communication

Frequent open dialogue and information-sharing

Success Spiral

Stability

Synchronizing objectives and confidence-building

Creativity

Promoting quality, innovation and a long-term approach by encouraging high performance

Figure 3.2   The supply chain relationship spiral of success

a relationship performs on each of the five dimensions within the 'spiral of success'. By doing this, organizations can then develop approaches towards collaborating more effectively.

In the following section we describe a methodology that can help organizations enter this spiral of success and achieve the benefits of supply chain collaboration. Although there are other analytical tools available, for the purposes of this discussion we will focus on one technique, the Supply Chain Collaboration Index (SCCI) that has proved particularly effective in helping organizations gain advantage from their commercial relationships.

THE SUPPLY CHAIN COLLABORATING INDEX (SCCI)

What is the Supply Chain Collaboration Index (SCCI)? The SCCI is a method of analyzing and diagnosing collaborative business relationships, both *between* organizations or *within* a single organization. The purpose of the analysis is to identify opportunities for improvement. The SCCI uses a scientifically designed methodology that provides an objective, independent performance evaluation of collaborative relationships.

As a diagnostic tool, it reveals important relationship efficiency issues and allows improvement targets to be set. It can be used as a strategic relationship portfolio management tool to understand the performance characteristics of an organization's operating divisions, of a consortium of organizations working to a single aim, and between an organization and a number of customers or suppliers. Two types of report can be generated: a high-level 'Barometer' that offers 'a quick look' at a relationship's performance and an in-depth diagnostic, known as the 'Partnership', which produces enough detail to allow a change programme to be initiated. The SCCI has been used in a large number of public and commercial organizations, including defence, rail, construction, automotive, manufacturing, retail, agriculture, and the food and drinks industry.

What are the Benefits of Using the SCCI?

The SCCI produces a clear understanding of the complex interactions between organizations. It allows managers to identify good and bad practice areas so that they can be strategically managed. The in-depth diagnostics pinpoint and benchmark key performance issues, thereby allowing negative and costly trends to be reversed. The recommendations specify the joint business improvement measures needed to reduce the time to get change programmes underway. The process mobilizes joint support for change by removing emotion and concentrating on problem-solving. It allows the strategic high ground to be taken to strengthen relationships so that fire-fighting becomes unnecessary. This encourages a focus on continuous improvement in effectiveness and the meeting of standards so that partners can concentrate on long-term value for money rather than short-term satisfaction with the contract 'small print'.

When is the SCCI Used?

The occasions when the SCCI might be used to improve relationship performance are many and varied, but cover a spectrum from 'rescuing' problem supply chain relationships through to a partnership-building exercise prior to a deeper business involvement. The SCCI will energize and sustain an ongoing business improvement programme and establish the baseline for improvement initiatives at individual relationship and portfolio levels. It will measure progress regularly over time as a governance initiative and can be used to satisfy stakeholders such as bankers, group HQ and possibly a government agency looking for proof of collaborative performance.

What Does the SCCI Measure?

The SCCI measures perspectives from both sides of the collaborative relationship on the five key relationship performance drivers:

1. Creativity – promoting quality, innovation and a long-term approach by encouraging high performance;

2. Stability – synchronizing objectives and investments in people and infrastructure that build confidence;

3. Communication – partaking in frequent open dialogue and information-sharing;

4. Reliability – concentrating on service and product delivery, lowering joint costs and risks, building up trust;

5. Value – creating a win–win relationship in which each side gains equally and is delighted to play a part.

In addition, information on seven further crucial relationship characteristics is provided:

1. Long-term orientation – promoting continuity and joint gains;

2. Interdependence – encouraging joint responsibility;

3. C^3 behaviour – collaboration, cooperation, coordination;

4. Trust – creating goodwill and the incentive to go the extra mile;

5. Commitment – a belief that maximum effort should be expended to maintain the partnership;

6. Adaptation – willingness to adapt products, processes, goals and values to sustain the relationship;

7. Personal relationships – generating trust and openness by personal interaction.

How is the SCCI Applied?

The SCCI is conducted through a series of short, online questionnaires and interviews with knowledgeable people. The results are given in a business-friendly format and clearly identify problem issues; and opportunities to enhance good practice are specified, together with courses of remedial action. The SCCI process takes a minimum of five weeks. The main stages, with estimated timings, are shown in Table 3.1.

What are the Outcomes?

Two types of report can be produced. A Barometer gives a succinct view of the effectiveness of a relationship. It can be used in a number of situations, but usually it provides an introductory performance benchmark where one has not been done before, a means of assessing the performance of a group of relationships such as a portfolio of suppliers/customers or a series of 'linkages' in a supply chain, and a regular monitoring exercise. It is often used as a confidence measure to decide whether more intensive investigation is needed or not.

Table 3.1   **Stages of the SCCI process**

Stage	Description	Estimate Time
1. Appoint Relationship Manager	• On each side, a senior executive who is very knowledgeable about the relationship is appointed to sponsor the exercise in his/her organization.	Week 1
2. Collect Company Data	• Details of the type and size of the businesses • Details about the complexity and length of relationship.	Week 1
3. Planning Meeting	• Attended by both relationship managers and SCCI staff • Agree SCCI project milestones.	Week 1
4. Apply Questionnaire	• Online 15 minute questionnaire checks key performance measures • Completed by as many people as possible involved in the relationship • Anyone from the shopfloor all the way to senior management gets involved.	Week 2–3
5. Prepare and Present Initial Report (High-level Barometer)	• Prepare report describing the key characteristics of the relationship (based on the results of the questionnaires) • Benchmark results against a large sample of measure supply chain relationships.	End of Week 3
6. Conduct and Analyze Interviews	• Present the results • Interview nominated staff – usually 2 per company • No longer than 1 hour, usually by phone • Analyze interviews.	Week 4–5
7. Prepare Final Report (In-depth Partnership Diagnostic)	• Prepare final report synthesizing the findings from both the questionnaire and interviews • Report highlights areas of improvement and suggests actions required to enhance collaboration in the relationship.	End of Week 5
8. Conduct Company Workshops	• Results disseminated within the organizations through workshops • Workshops are led by the organization relationship managers, but may be supported by a consultant.	Therafter

The in-depth Partnership diagnostic assessment provides both a performance benchmark and a statement of the effectiveness of the relationship. It is particularly adept at demystifying a complex, operational relationship and, by allowing personnel to 'see the wood for the trees', allows them to concentrate objectively on those actions that will affect the bottom line. As a joint process involving the knowledgeable people in each organization, it concentrates minds in an unemotive manner on improvement and invariably generates the detailed recommendations needed to initiate a change programme with little further study.

Having honed the organization into focusing on effective customer service, the SCCI provides the quick, efficient tools to build, improve and sustain the key supply chain relationships that deliver value to all who take part in them. Our case study describes how two electronics industry players did just this.

Case Study: Adapt, Learn and Prosper

The customer is a UK-based non-destructive testing electronic equipment manufacturer with global interests. The supplier is a UK logistics company providing electronic parts and specialist kitting services. Their relationship was ten years old and valued at £2 million per annum. The two companies had grown up together and following acquisitions the respective managing directors had decided to step back and appoint new managing directors of their core businesses. They also planned to collaborate on a major new product development initiative. An SCCI partnering review would provide a performance benchmark and an inventory of management issues that would give the new managing directors a clear view of what they were taking over. Both group managing directors believed that this relationship was very successful and, in the initial brief, could think of no problems to mention. However, as can be seen in the Traffic Light report in Figure 3.3, the SCCI assessment revealed that all was not well. The customer (centre column) was generally fairly satisfied, but the supplier (right-hand column) had reservations. From Figure 3.3 it is possible to see at a glance some serious differences of opinion and issues between the parties.

Main Measures	Joint	Customer	Supplier
Overall	73	79	66
Creativity	81	92	71
Stability	71	86	56
Communication	62	74	50
Reliability	67	63	70
Value	82	79	86
Additional Characteristics			
Long-term Orientation		72	72
Interdependence		100	50
C3 Behaviour		77	48
Trust		100	33
Commitment		92	75
Adaptation		69	74
Personal Relationships		100	44

- **Creativity:** promoting quality, innovation and a long-term approach by encouraging high performance
- **Stability:** synchronisation of objectives and confidence-building
- **Communication:** frequent open dialogue and information-sharing
- **Reliability:** concentrating on service and product delivery, lowering joint costs and risks, building up trust
- **Value:** creating a win-win relationship in which each side is delighted to be a part
- **Long-term Orientation:** encouraging stability, continuity, predictability and long-term joint gains
- **Interdependence:** loss in autonomy is compensated through the expected gains
- **C3 Behaviour:** Collaboration, Co-operation, Co-ordination, joint resourcing to achieve effective operations
- **Trust:** richer interaction between parties to create goodwill and the incentive to go the extra mile.
- **Commitment:** the relationship is so important that it warrants maximum effort to maintain it
- **Adaptation:** willingness to adapt products, procedures, inventory, management, attitudes, values and goals to the needs of the relationship
- **Personal Relationships:** generating trust and openness through personal interaction

Key:
	Bandings		See Cluster Definitions
Green	0-49	Red	Poor
Amber	50-59	Amber	Moderate 2b
Red	60-74	Amber/Green	Moderate 2a
	75-100	Green	Good

Figure 3.3   SCCI Traffic Light report

The two charts in Figure 3.4 contrast the customer and supplier in the five key relationship performance measures. As well as the grumbling blacks of dissatisfaction, note the high levels of white 'don't knows' on the supplier side in the lower chart. The high levels of 'insufficient knowledge' point to both poor internal communications on the supplier side and a lack of communication about the customer's intentions.

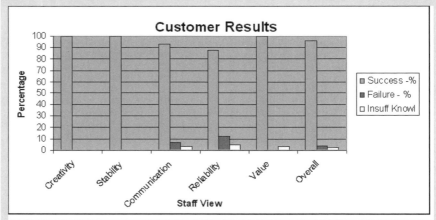

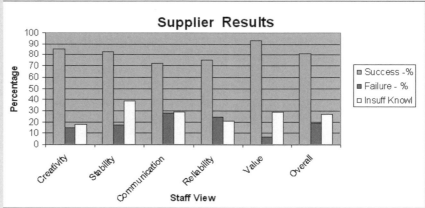

Figure 3.4   **Happy customer/grumbling supplier**

Figure 3.5 is a 'drill-down' into the operational effectiveness key performance measure. The contrasting patterns of black in the two charts indicate that the logistics supplier was keen to see precision in ordering, forecasting and performance, whereas the engineering customer resented being bound by 'red tape'.

This was a classic case where, over time, informal working arrangements had become a liability and the customer had failed to capitalize on the growing skills and capabilities offered by the supplier. The main issues were as follows:

- no formal or informal contract

- no common performance measures, quality standards or monitoring systems

- informal processes – for example, 'no notice' orders for stock, poor forecasting.

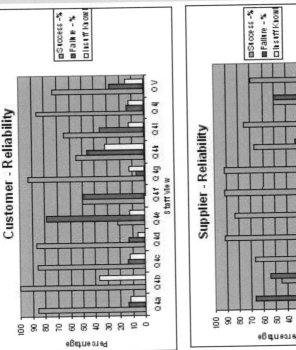

Reliability – concentrating on service and product delivery

a The quality of the contract outputs ie. spares/repairs/services, consistent product quality, fulfilled on-time orders, is entirely satisfactory.

b The quality of service delivery ie. delivery times, billing, payment, administration, delivery, is entirely satisfactory.

c The relationship is characterised by a continually improving product quality ethos.

d Problems are solved in a joint, open, constructive manner.

e Such is the goodwill in the relationship, the other party would willingly put himself/herself out to adapt to our changing requirements.

f We trust the other party to act in our best interests.

g The responsibility for making sure the relationship works is shared jointly.

h The other party provides us with useful cost reduction and quality improvement ideas.

i The other party is always totally open and honest with us.

j The other party always does what he says he will do.

Figure 3.5   **Comparing detailed customer/supplier performance**

The main outcome of the SCCI assessment was the opening of both organizations' eyes to the quite serious issues that had accumulated over time and which were preventing the partners from cooperating as effectively as they might. The detailed outcomes resulting from the assessment were as follows:

- regular, joint planning meetings held to define production schedules

- a joint product reliability action that immediately saved £50k per year on in-house testing

- supplier involvement in new product design, bringing lower cost, improved design reliability, better asset availability and more functionality as well as shortening time-to-market from five years to one

- customer-updated MIS with new, integrated system to improve asset control, marketing and materiel requirements forecasting

- over three years customer revenue up 38.5 per cent; supplier revenue up 100 per cent.

'We are now concentrating on solving the issues rather than shouting at each other.'

A CHECKLIST FOR MANAGING DYNAMICALLY ALIGNED COLLABORATIVE SUPPLY CHAIN RELATIONSHIPS

Effective, flexible, continuously improving supply chain relationships must be managed proactively; this is not something that can be left to the sales department as a secondary activity. Each partner (or account manager where an organization has been structured to face different customer groups) needs to appoint a relationship manager who has the authority to champion the needs of the relationship across the departments within his own firm and who is empowered to agree the collaboration tactics and solve relationship problems with his opposite number. A regular review meeting of the relationship managers and the appropriate senior managers from each firm must be held to do the following:

- Review performance targets in last period and issue statistics.

- Review work/orders in progress.

- Review forecasted sales and orders in next period.

- Consider and solve problems.

- Actively seek out and initiate process improvements.

- Review future plans (including new products) and initiate preparation.

- Examine and discuss industry and technology updates.

- Identify policy issues to refer to senior management.

- Involve other supply chain partners.

- Prepare joint communications, information and team-building events for the collaborating firms.

The relationship managers will also take on the role of identifying the opportunities for their organization to learn from their partner and of ensuring that they bring this to the attention of their senior decision-makers. Establishing a professional relationship management focus in an organization will accumulate appropriate skills and knowledge that will improve its ability to partner successfully and 'grow' this reputation in the market.[4]

Competition will no longer be between individual organizations but between the supply chains they are part of. The 'relational competence' of supply chain members is a critical factor in maintaining competitive advantage and should be seen as the 'winning' strategy. Collaborative supply chain relationships invariably represent the investment of significant time, money, infrastructure, IT and know-how. Moreover, such is their impact on business returns that they will strongly influence the organization's shareholder value, its competitive position, its reputation and its ability to team up with successful alliance partners. For these compelling reasons the SCCI relationship assessment tools and similar approaches should be used to regularly measure relationship performance and allow targets to be set to drive continuous improvement.

ALIGNMENT INSIGHTS

- *If supply chain management is about the 'management' of relationships, organizations need to measure relationships. As Lord Kelvin commented, 'If you cannot measure it, you cannot improve it'.[5] So learn to measure relationships in order to improve them.*

- *Measuring performance and correctly managing collaborative supply chain relationships will ensure that the aligned firm maximizes the value that its customers achieve in the short and longer term.*

- *Supply chain relationships may be functioning and generating average returns, with managers monitoring time, cost and quality. Unless the wider aspects of the partnership, including infrastructure and people, innovation, communications, operations and value capture are measured and managed proactively, premium returns will not be possible.*

NOTES

1   M. Christopher, *Logistics and Supply Chain Management: Creating Value-added Networks*, 3rd edition, FT Prentice Hall, London, 2005, p. 5.

2   R. Wilding and A.S. Humphries, 'Understanding collaborative supply chain relationships through the application of the Williamson Organisational Failure Framework', *International Journal of Physical Distribution & Logistics Management*, Vol. 36, No. 4 (2006), 309–329, p. 312.

3   J.R. Stock and D. Lambert, *Strategic Logistics Management*, McGraw-Hill, New York, 2001.

4   J.H. Dyer, P. Kale and H. Singh, 'How to make strategic alliances work', *MIT Sloan Management Review*, 2001, Vol. 42, No. 4 (Summer 2001), pp. 37–43.

5   Lord W.T. Kelvin, 'Electrical units of measurement', *Popular Lectures and Addresses*, Vol. 1 (3 May).

4 *Lean* and *Agile* Supply Chains

John Gattorna

Are lean supply chains the answer to everything? In a word, quite definitely 'no'! But judging by the way the lean concept is being pursued in many enterprises you would think so. Indeed, a lot of published material on lean as applied to supply chains is at best confused and misleading at worst – which has led to unreasonable and unfulfilled expectations. We have seen it all before – people in hot pursuit of the 'silver bullet' often missing the subtleties.

There is no doubt that the application of lean principles brings with it the elimination of waste in materials, processes, time and information. But sometimes this is achieved at the expense of agility and flexibility. Taken to extremes, lean can make a logistics network brittle and prone to failure because of the lack of embedded resilience.

The problem is that the original lean manufacturing principles, as espoused by Japanese automotive manufacturers, does not translate well into the wider supply chain operating environment, where volatility in contemporary markets often requires quite the opposite – more, rather than less, capacity, some of which is redundant part of the time and therefore potentially inefficient.

The original lean concept as applied in the largely controlled manufacturing space implied a relatively predictable marketplace on the demand side and a high level of collaboration with suppliers on the supply side, in a joint effort to reduce waste and take cost out of the total system. Unfortunately, these conditions, while they still exist today in some markets, are far less prevalent than in the 1980s.

What we now know about customers on the demand side is that they display a range of *dominant buying behaviours*, and this has to be matched by a corresponding set of responses from the immediate suppliers; this is embodied in my proprietary concept of *dynamic alignment*, already introduced in previous chapters. In brief, this concept, which applies on

a whole-of-enterprise basis, requires that supplying companies hard-wire
at least three or four different responses
into their business if they are to have
a chance of aligning with the majority
(approximately 80 per cent) of their
customers. Lean is just one of a number of
possible responses.

'We have seen it all before
– people in hot pursuit of
the "silver bullet" often
missing the subtleties.'

On the demand side, my work in many different markets with a myriad
product categories has revealed that not all customers are, or even want
to be, collaborative in their dealings with suppliers. Some customers are
straight-out adversarial; others are demanding and require a quick response;
and still others throw caution to the wind in desperate situations and expect
their suppliers to come up with innovative solutions in times of crises. And
customers can occasionally change their preferred behaviours for short
periods. So a one-dimensional response such as lean is not going to suffice
any more; *multiple* responses have to be prepared and delivered side-by-side,
as the market requires. Much the same applies on the supply side, where
suppliers are now customers of processors further upstream in the supply
chain.

So the lean supply chain variant of the original lean manufacturing
concept is more about seeking low cost-to-serve by ensuring that customers
downstream are not overserviced and resources are not wasted in the
process. Remember: *most, if not all, enterprises are overservicing some of their
customers and underservicing others – and the problem is they don't know which is
which*!

In lean supply chains as I define them, low cost is achieved, often in quite
adversarial circumstances, by doing the basics well – no more, no less.
The more 'collaborative' style of supply chain (which I have termed the
continuous replenishment supply chain) is something different again. Here,
customers (on the demand side) freely and willingly share information, get
involved in joint initiatives and generally seek a long-term stable relationship
with a few key suppliers.

But, in the classic lean supply chain, customers are not so willing to share, so
suppliers have to produce their own forecasts based on historical experience
– which works okay in predictable market conditions, but is a disaster in
volatile markets! And yet we see many enterprises pursuing ever more
accurate product forecasts in these volatile markets when what they should
be doing is focusing on forecasting future *capacity* requirements. Classic
lean supply chains are all about 'push', based on forecasts, whereas more
collaborative practices allow continuous replenishment supply chains to be a
combination of 'push' and 'pull'. On the supply side there is more likely to be
collaboration, especially if the balance of power balance favours the customer.

Look at the situation that suppliers to Wal-Mart face; they hardly have a choice, but is this genuine collaboration based on their values, or simply a type of forced collaboration?

For genuine lean supply chains, the value proposition to customers on the demand side is one of providing a standard, consistently reliable, low-cost service, one which customers can always bank on. They *know* what to expect, and plan accordingly. The primary focus of suppliers facing this situation is on reliable, efficient operations, producing products and services in high volume and low variety, to forecast. The key is scale if synergies in production and logistics are to be realized. That is all the good news. Now for the complications.

The parameters involved in designing and operating lean supply chains, as I have defined them, come at the cost of reduced agility. Agile supply chains, which are necessary in more unpredictable market conditions, require excess capacity on standby in order to be in a position to respond quickly. This is the world of Make-to-Order (MTO) or Assemble-to-Order (ATO) compared to the Make-to-Forecast (MTF) world where lean supply chains flourish. See Figures 4.1 and 4.2 which describe the differing internal and external conditions for lean versus agile supply chain configurations.

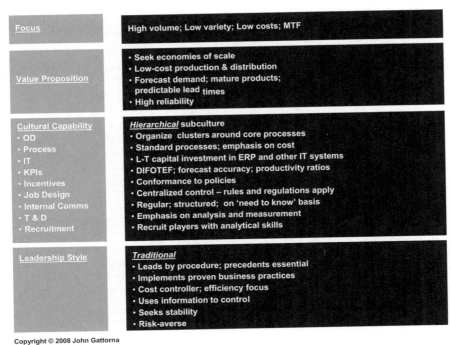

Focus	High volume; Low variety; Low costs; MTF
Value Proposition	• Seek economies of scale • Low-cost production & distribution • Forecast demand; mature products; predictable lead times • High reliability
Cultural Capability • OD • Process • IT • KPIs • Incentives • Job Design • Internal Comms • T & D • Recruitment	*Hierarchical* subculture • Organize clusters around core processes • Standard processes; emphasis on cost • L-T capital investment in ERP and other IT systems • DIFOTEF; forecast accuracy; productivity ratios • Conformance to policies • Centralized control – rules and regulations apply • Regular; structured; on 'need to know' basis • Emphasis on analysis and measurement • Recruit players with analytical skills
Leadership Style	*Traditional* • Leads by procedure; precedents essential • Implements proven business practices • Cost controller; efficiency focus • Uses information to control • Seeks stability • Risk-averse

Figure 4.1   Lean supply chains

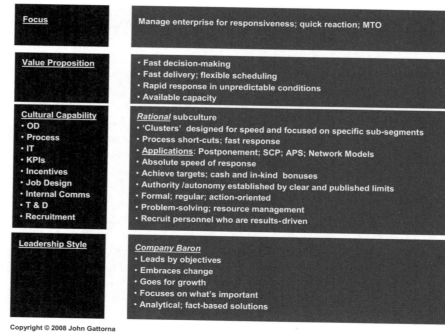

Focus	Manage enterprise for responsiveness; quick reaction; MTO
Value Proposition	• Fast decision-making • Fast delivery; flexible scheduling • Rapid response in unpredictable conditions • Available capacity
Cultural Capability • OD • Process • IT • KPIs • Incentives • Job Design • Internal Comms • T & D • Recruitment	*Rational* subculture • 'Clusters' designed for speed and focused on specific sub-segments • Process short-cuts; fast response • <u>Applications</u>: Postponement; SCP; APS; Network Models • Absolute speed of response • Achieve targets; cash and in-kind bonuses • Authority /autonomy established by clear and published limits • Formal; regular; action-oriented • Problem-solving; resource management • Recruit personnel who are results-driven
Leadership Style	*Company Baron* • Leads by objectives • Embraces change • Goes for growth • Focuses on what's important • Analytical; fact-based solutions

Copyright © 2008 John Gattorna

Figure 4.2   Agile supply chains

ALIGNMENT INSIGHTS

- *So what have we learnt? Lean supply chains are more complex than their more conventional manufacturing counterparts. And taken alone, lean supply chains are unlikely to be sufficient to service a company's disparate range of customers who, between them, may exhibit up to three or four different dominant buying behaviours, only one of which will be adequately served by a lean configuration. Hence the concept of multiple supply chain alignment, where supply chains of different configurations operate either in parallel or in various combinations to cover the range of customer buying behaviours evident in a given market.*

- *So how far do you go with implementing lean principles? Only a review of your marketplace can answer this question. Look at how the market is structured in terms of the relative sizes of the behavioural segments present, and this will inform you how much emphasis you need to put on lean principles inside the enterprise. Go lean where it is appropriate, but recognize that other pathways to customers are very likely to be required, in parallel or in series, and, above all, in synchronization.*

5 The Evolution of Fully Flexible Supply Chains

Kate Hughes

In *Living Supply Chains* (2006), Kate Hughes, with John Gattorna, developed the notion of two categories of 'dynamic' flexibility in contemporary supply chains – the 'business event' and the 'emergency response or humanitarian' fully flexible supply chains. This chapter will focus on the latter type and follow its evolution through the typical supply chain activities found in a humanitarian response effort.

SUPPLY CHAIN 'TYPES' IN HUMANITARIAN AID

Humanitarian supply chains are possibly the most complex type of supply chain. They are formed in response to unforeseeable and unplanned events that range from small localized natural disasters through to catastrophic events affecting large regions and populations. Natural disasters include events such as mudslides, earthquakes, tsunamis, cyclones and the like or longer–term more insidious problems such as drought, soil salination and deforestation that prevent the production of sustainable sources of food and disrupt everyday life for communities, towns and cities.

These supply chains are also formed in response to the outcome of intensive short- or long-term political dissent that dislocates normal business activities and destroys dwellings, resulting in the mass evacuation of people from their communities. Often a natural disaster precipitates the need for humanitarian aid, and this is then further affected by political issues – although the aid may be required as a result of political issues only. Tragically, many humanitarian supply chains become very long-term aid 'solutions' that span years or even decades, examples being Darfur in the Sudan and many areas of Afghanistan.

One step to facilitate the effectiveness of humanitarian supply chains is to identify the phases within the life of this type of supply chain in order to eventually model the stages and improve the processes of the enterprises providing the aid. One limitation of models is that, at best, they will only approximate reality, and there will always be exceptions and complications.

However, an improved understanding of the various activities and processes in humanitarian supply chains will help governments, the military, businesses and aid agencies in their decision-making so as to provide maximum benefit to the aid recipients. The ultimate aim for each humanitarian supply response is for it to be dismantled over time as business and community activities are re-established. Examples of this are the areas of Thailand that were affected by the Asian tsunami of December 2004, and in New Orleans after Hurricane Katrina the following year.

OVERVIEW OF THE 'PHASES' IN HUMANITARIAN SUPPLY CHAINS

Research in operations and supply chain analysis has tended to focus on identifying *one type* of supply chain that will adequately capture the characteristics of humanitarian supply chains. Unfortunately, due to the evolutionary nature of this supply chain, no single description will suffice. All humanitarian supply chains pass through a series of phases which are manifested as different supply chain types. The progression is from the initial agile response to fully flexible solutions and, in the best-case situations, this will move on to the rebuilding of businesses and communities with a range of lean, collaborative and agile supply chains as everyday activities are re-established. Thus, humanitarian supply chains are very difficult to model due to their complex and constantly changing nature.

Humanitarian supply chains also differ from most other supply chains in that the requirements of aid beneficiaries evolve over their lifetime: in the full supply chain cycle they will make a transition from being survivors at the outset to recipients and, later, to participants and customers. This evolution is the reason for the need to dynamically align activities, processes, stakeholders and the organizational design of participant groups. A lack of alignment with the end-consumer and the complexity of re-creating communities out of the tattered ruins of a region devastated by a natural disaster (or in political turmoil) creates situations where humanitarian supply chains degrade into permanent aid situations. Humanitarian supply chains can become 'stuck' in the agile response or fully flexible phase or even cycle around the rebuilding and restoration phases due to a variety of reasons such as: the lack of supplies and skills necessary for re-establishing communities and trade; lack of land; lack of sustainable sources of food, supplies and permanent dwellings; lack of community leadership and ownership; or ongoing political turmoil that disrupts or destroys rebuilding efforts.

Since the majority of activities performed within humanitarian supply chains are outsourced there is a need to have a larger coordinating group to oversee activities. This is not always possible in all situations. One prominent group includes the United Nations Joint Logistics Council (UNJLC) that was formed with the mandate to act as a logistics platform for coordinating aid in these situations. However, as the emergency situation is usually located in a context in which there are a number of cultural barriers (language, customs, local and political issues) and is on unfamiliar territory, often accompanied by mass destruction of the area, the coordination

'The ultimate aim for each humanitarian supply response is for it to be dismantled over time as business and community activities are re-established.'

of aid is extremely difficult – which can increase tensions and complexities in a critical situation.[1] More often, a national government and/or the military will decide to coordinate the aid response rather than allow the UNJLC to take the lead. This will have varying degrees of success, depending on their experience and political agendas, and the results can vary from the relative success of the response in the Sichuan Province in China after the earthquake of May 2008 to the a tragic example of Myanmar after Cyclone Nargis that occurred ten days earlier.

During the existence of these supply chains, often spanning many months, years or even decades, there are four identifiable and sequential phases. These tend to merge one into another over time and can even coexist in parallel in the same relief effort because not all response activities are implemented at the same time – or at the same rate – in all affected locations. This is primarily due to differences in the level of access to affected areas, the variation in the extent of the devastation, government restrictions to 'sensitive areas',[2] political unrest by independent groups (such as in areas of Africa), difficulty of access in some geographies, and the amount of aid provided over time compared to the level of aid actually required.

There is a prequel phase to the humanitarian supply chain that can reinforce and support the effectiveness of the aid response. Increased focus on emergency response preparation, aid identification, stockpiling of goods in strategic locations around the world and securing services ahead of time through Memorandums of Understanding (MoUs) for the provision of aid have all been identified as a critical part of the aid network. Lately, a number of countries and organizations – (for example, FEMA in the US, the UN, the Red Cross and Red Crescent Societies and some of the other larger international aid agencies – have been working together to prepare for catastrophic events. This has been achieved through scenario planning, setting up sense-and-response mechanisms (such as a tsunami warning system around the Pacific Ocean), stockpiling goods in various locations around the world (to enable faster response times to events *when* they happen), setting up agreements between governments and agencies for responsive actions and demarcating Incident Command Systems (ICS).

The phases in the humanitarian supply chain are: the emergency response (agile supply chains); survival (fully flexible supply chains) and rebuilding and restoration (when a series of coexisting, lean, collaborative and agile supply chains develop as the community is re-established). No phase is self-contained, nor is each completely distinctive across time and space. The activities tend to blend and meld into each other, with different parts of the aid response in different parts of a region often being at differing stages. However, there are clear trends within the humanitarian supply chain, and understanding these allows the activities of the aid providers (governments, military, agencies and businesses) to be dynamically aligned in order to ensure that the right supplies and services are provided *as needed* by aid recipients. Figure 5.1 depicts the various phases.

Prequel: Before Catastrophic Events

There is a growing demand by governments, aid agencies, corporations and the global community to plan (hedge and deploy) for events that require humanitarian aid. The aim is to improve the speed of response, reduce the loss of life and to try to mitigate the long-term impact of catastrophic events. Although the specific details of 'when, where, and what event' is unknown, efforts are being made to create stockpiles of products that will provide the basic necessities of life. The provision of supplies in this format will provide the 'excess capacity' required for a quick response typical of agile supply chains.

Some capabilities of these predominately service supply chains also include the identification of often highly trained personnel who can respond at short notice to an event. The building up of services is being pursued by a number of organizations (for example, the Fritz Institute and Red R) through the training and certifying aid workers. Many governments around the world have reserves in their defence forces who are employed full-time in businesses, but are 'on call' when situations require their help. There are also reserve groups of civilians who have trained in volunteer organizations such as the State Emergency Services (SES) and the Bushfire Brigade in Australia, whose skills can be used, as required, for humanitarian responses (international or domestic). Companies in specific business areas such as medical services and logistics have also identified skilled employees who can be released on short- or medium-term agreements to help in aid situations. In fact there is an increasing recognition of the necessity of skilled logisticians and supply chain experts for the successful implementation of humanitarian response efforts. Finally, many governments and aid agencies are establishing memorandums of understanding to improve their collaboration in emergency humanitarian aid situations.

'There is a growing demand by governments, aid agencies, corporations and the global community to plan (hedge and deploy) for events that require humanitarian aid.'

This 'stockpiling' of goods and services is, in effect, 'capacity building' for potential aid situations, yet involves lean and collaborative supply chain activities. These are the basic ingredients (goods and services) required for the agile supply chains that will facilitate and improve the response time if and when an event occurs. Other activities, such as building

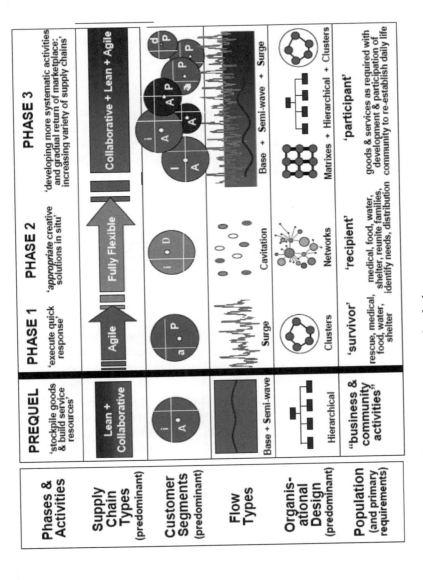

Figure 5.1   Simplified model of humanitarian supply chains

sense-and-response systems and scenario planning, are expensive, but these hedge-and-deploy activities improve the agility of the system, especially in the initial phase when speed is extremely important in order to save as many lives as possible. Although the initial event will still have a major impact and cause widespread disruption, improving the speed of supply chain response will have a ripple effect across all the phases of the supply chain. This can possibly mitigate the magnitude of the secondary impact of the event where often the loss of life due to disease and the shortage of food, clean water and other critical supplies is even greater than the deaths caused by the initial event.

Phase One: Emergency Response

The initial phase in humanitarian supply chains is triggered by an event, whether natural or political or a combination of both. The extent and impact of the damage could be geographically localized due to a one-off event, or ongoing in the case of a series of natural disturbances (such as volcanic activity, floods and earthquakes), or political unrest and military conflict. In accurate, but dramatic, terms the level of aid provided in response to the situation becomes the difference between life and death for many of those most affected. The initial immediate response to an emergency is the provision of aid in the form of skilled and trained personnel: medical teams; search and rescue teams; and experienced senior advisors from the United Nations, the military, government(s) and the larger NGOs to assess the damage and the level of aid required. This rapid mobilization of groups is an agile supply chain response.

The goods and services provided at this stage are often the minimal requirements for survival – the most basic provisions, including medicines, clean water, emergency rations and shelter. The survivors often require rescue and removal from immediate danger in order to prevent further injury or loss of life. The groups involved are usually the national government (and often other national governments), the military, large non-governmental organizations with specific training (for example, search and rescue teams with dogs and electronic listening devices) and the media. Most of these groups are sourced outside the area and are highly trained, with the skills and systems in place that enable them to respond quickly to an event. The result is an *agile* supply chain aligned to the requirements of the situation.

The humanitarian response often takes place under circumstances in which there is little or no infrastructure, piecemeal information, unreliable or irregular communication systems and limited IT support as a consequence of either the infrastructure having been damaged by the event or the area being underdeveloped. The emphasis in this phase is for aid workers to 'do something' such as provide medical services to reduce further loss of life, prevent or minimize the spread of disease, and identify and record people who are alive, injured, missing or dead. This is especially challenging when trying to record the details of the elderly, the very young and those who are infirm, dead or missing. Usually, foreign governments prioritize their efforts to evacuating their citizens and any other non-residents. The situation is not contained, but chaotic, the main focus being to try to find and rescue as many survivors as possible in the first few hours and days. The emergency relief effort is supported by experts in trauma and emergency medical aid, along with the provision of basic edible food and clean water sources for survival, and emergency shelter, bedding and clothing. At this early stage the media is usually heavily involved, although their input tapers off as time goes on. This phase extends from a few days to approximately the first week or two immediately following the event, with the end-consumer being a survivor who takes whatever is provided to stay alive and reach a safe haven.

Decision-making at this stage is usually centralized, with the national government extending the initial invitation for aid and assistance to other nations. Initially, aid agencies make most decisions external to the site, but leadership and responsibility is rapidly transferred to those 'on location', who are able to determine the best action considering conditions on the ground. The organization structure rapidly changes from a hierarchical to a cluster-based system on-site. Some groups specifically trained for these activities include the US Marines, various divisions of the UN, the International Red Cross and Red Crescent Societies, and other volunteer organizations such as Médecins Sans Frontières International (Doctors without Borders).

Phase Two: Survival

The emergency phase of humanitarian supply chains rapidly makes a transition from an agile response to seeking creative solutions as the extent of the impact of the event on survivors, communities and businesses, as well as the degree of damage, becomes understood and acknowledged. This can occur almost in parallel with the emergency phase. This is a situation of extreme supply chain disruption. The systems and activities within the original community are often completely wiped out, and the humanitarian supply chain has to be developed 'from almost nothing', relying heavily on resources supplied from outside the affected area in order to distribute medical aid and provide the basic necessities for life. This is the realm of the *fully flexible* supply chain in which the distribution of goods and services is not straightforward, and ongoing *in situ* decisions are required to sustain the flow of aid.

One of the first activities in the aid effort is to set up more established communication links and complete assessment reports on the scope of the event. This is often undertaken by external groups such as the media, the military, governments and so on, which often struggle to complete this task due to the extent of the destruction. The more fundamental activities include distributing food, clean water, clothing and bedding, and setting up temporary shelters, all of which are strongly linked to planning the extent of the aid required in the immediate future. In addition to these essential activities, the groups supplying aid are pressured by survivors, people outside the area and foreign governments to record missing persons and to identify as far as possible babies, children, the injured and those that died in the event, as well as the living. This information often helps reunite families, re-establish communities and provide a semblance of hope. However, this additional administrative burden on the groups supplying aid occurs within the context of needing to find daily solutions to almost insurmountable problems created by the aftermath of the chaos of the event coupled with the unpredictable response of donors, aid groups and governments.

'The appropriate systems and infrastructure that formerly provided these necessities are often absent or badly damaged, and the people with the skills to support them are often traumatized, missing, dead or have fled the region.'

This phase is primarily aimed at developing systems and unique solutions that will allow the effective delivery of ongoing medical aid for the injured or ill in the region, along with the provision of preventive medicine such as vaccines and medicines to curtail secondary infections and widespread disease, and the setting up of sanitation solutions, and often rudimentary schooling, in the later stages. The key to this response is to 'learn and adapt' in order to provide, as far as possible, the best aid available to survivors. The agencies working in this situation need to be entrepreneurial, self-sufficient organizational clusters that are basically well-connected networks of people and groups with the ability to make decisions in real time, on-site. The majority of end-consumers in this phase of the humanitarian supply chain tend to be passive recipients of aid, although this changes as time progresses.

This survival phase can be as short as two to six months or extend indefinitely if the level and type of aid – and compounding social and physical conditions – are not sufficiently adequate to help the recipients become participants in the activities and move to a semblance of self-sufficiency that approaches pre-disaster conditions. This stasis will be perpetuated if political and/or military activity in the area continues to cause ongoing disruptions that prevent the re-establishment of communities and business. In this phase, the humanitarian supply chain involves coordinating groups overseeing outsourced activities provided by third parties (that may or may not be skilled) in a solution configured uniquely to the particular disaster relief situation. These groups will develop *appropriate*, but often crude, processes following decentralized decision-making that occurs on-site and are capable of unique and creative solutions in response to extreme and ongoing evolving events

The aim of this phase is initially to establish more permanent systems and infrastructure that support the basics for the survival of those affected by the event (the requirements of this phase are not unique – water, shelter and the like); but the appropriate systems and infrastructure that formerly provided these necessities are often absent or badly damaged, and the people with the skills to support them are often traumatized, missing, dead or have fled the region. Basics such as distribution networks for fundamental goods and services, including the location of the central distribution centres, need to be re-established on a reliable and permanent basis. This requires support for a unique combination of social and cultural issues that can impact on the survivor's perception of the supplies provided (for example, dietary restrictions, religious taboos) and of the aid workers themselves (for example, in some societies women must not talk to, or have contact with, males outside their family). In addition, the scale of the event, the type and provision of products and services, the survivor groups that are present, the nationality or race of the aid workers and the supporting activities all need to be taken into account. Experience has shown that, although the form of the implementation and systems will be unique to each and every situation, what is actually required by the survivors remains fairly consistent.

There will always be some redundancy in this supply chain; groups may duplicate activities, or may even to greater or lesser extent undermine each others' activities as visions and agendas clash with the limited resources available. At times even government requirements can cut across the normal mandated activities – for example, in Afghanistan the UNJLC was required to issue new currency for the government (which was outside its mandated activities) at the same time as creating reliable food and clothing distribution networks.

Phase Three: Rebuilding and Restoration

Activities and processes within the humanitarian response will become more stable as the communities affected by the event(s) stabilize and re-establish. The requirement for urgent and creative solutions reduces in this phase as the fully flexible supply chain is superseded by an array of supply chain types that evolve out of the more routine and standardized activities developed within the aid situation. The re-establishment of more typical activities relating to community, culture, religion and businesses in the affected area help shift the humanitarian aid out of the chaotic reactionary phase of survival into the rebuilding and restoration phase. In this phase the survivors have become more collaborative in aid distribution and increasingly more self-sufficient. Over time – and in some areas and with some groups – the community will return to a state that matches its previous expression. However, this will be determined by both the extent of the damage caused by the event and the response of the survivors to the 'new ways of doing things' brought to the community by the aid workers. These can have a profound impact on both the likelihood of full restoration of an area and its subsequent expression.

This phase of the humanitarian supply chain is more stable and often less complex than the previous stage, and is characterized by a declining need for fully flexible solutions and the emergence of more typical *collaborative, lean and agile* supply chains all re-forming in a marketplace economy. This phase emerges from the previous one and will usually involve years of recovery work with ongoing involvement of international NGOs and smaller grassroots aid groups from the local community. The aim is to re-establish a semblance of community and to move *with* the participants through this phase to a level of independence with maximum involvement and empowerment. Often, refugee camps or temporary accommodation that shelter large groups need to be depopulated, with people moving into more natural community groupings and permanent accommodation, and then back to employment as sustainable and appropriate business networks are re-established. In fact, the aim of any humanitarian supply chain is that it is ultimately dismantled and businesses and community activities re-established.

'In reality, the humanitarian supply chain actually consists of a series of supply chains all with the same purpose.'

A NEW UNDERSTANDING

It is important to note that the timelines for each of the phases in humanitarian supply chains are determined by a complex combination of factors, including: the extent of the damage; the scale of the humanitarian response; infrastructure and access to the area; the level of economic development in the surrounding areas and their response; the number of people affected; the resilience of the survivors; and the survivors' motivation to re-establish what was lost. Furthermore, the timelines for each phase will be greatly extended if there are ensuing events or ongoing political unrest.

Over time, each humanitarian supply chain should be completely superseded by the re-establishment of sustainable communities. Understanding the phases in humanitarian supply chains has important implications for aid providers. The *dynamic* alignment of the different stages of the processes and activities with the requirements of the aid recipients provides the potential for the aid effort to be most effective. The more distinctive features of each phase can then be catered for by selecting activities that will most help the recipient and improve the agency's accountability to their donors.

The processes, activities, coordination systems and parameters can be determined using heuristics for identifying the phases. Although these are networks of supply chains rather than only one supply chain there are certain activities that take place within each stage. In reality, the humanitarian supply chain actually consists of a series of supply chains all with the same purpose – to rescue and prevent further loss of life, then to sustain life, and finally to rebuild communities.

ALIGNMENT INSIGHTS

- *Supply chain solutions are not simple – you need to identify customer behaviour and determine the way in which the environment modifies this behaviour. In complex situations such as humanitarian responses, this is critical for successful outcomes.*

- *Understanding the phases in humanitarian supply chains provides the information required for the appropriate provision of goods and services – at the right time – in a manner that will facilitate (rather than hinder) the ongoing progression of the response effort.*

- *Humanitarian supply chains are 'extreme supply chains' that require skilled and adaptable participants who are able to 'cope' with high levels of uncertainty and constantly changing operating environments.*

NOTES

1   A recent example of this occurred in the US with the coordination of recovery after Hurricane Ike in Texas.

2   Such as seen with the response in Bandeh Aceh, Indonesia, after the 2004 Asian tsunami, due to the long-term armed conflict between the Indonesian military and the Acehnese separatists.

6 Humanitarian Supply Chains in Action

Kim Winter

A s we have seen from the previous chapter, humanitarian supply chains are deployed to respond to sudden-onset disasters and are established to supply essential aid in situations of longer-term humanitarian need across the globe. While the admirable efforts of humanitarian and other contributing organizations (government, non-government organizations, UN agencies, charities, religious, political and private sector organizations) are widely acclaimed and acknowledged for their vital and often lifesaving work, visible failures in response to recent large disasters have shaken the confidence of supporters, donors and the general public alike

In some cases, the failures are the result of simple mistakes. In others, they are the result of fraud or non-performance, but, in the majority of cases, failure to maximize outcomes are the direct result of the failure of organizations to collaborate, understand the value of, and initiate the *dynamic* alignment of available resources within and between contributing organizations

ALIGNMENT FAILURE IS FREQUENT

In Sri Lanka and Indonesia after the Asian tsunami, hundreds of organizations of one form or another responded with offers to provide vital humanitarian support, save lives and assist in essential recovery operations. Nonetheless there were significant cases of misdirected and uncoordinated logistics efforts within and between contributing organizations. This has caused confusion, delays in delivering aid through the hubs, supplies being channelled to the wrong locations and, in many cases, failures to deploy aid to critical locations in a timely manner resulting in needless suffering and some avoidable fatalities.

In the US, the Red Cross came under intense scrutiny after a series of mishaps, including fraud,[1] a poor response to Hurricane Katrina victims, and FDA concerns over its handling of blood.[2]

All of this has led traditional donors – individuals and governmental organizations alike – to express disappointment in the operational performance of humanitarian organizations and in the humanitarian sector as a whole. At the same time, a new class of donors – corporations – has been frustrated in its attempts to work with humanitarian organizations, to get involved and make a difference.[3] The question facing humanitarian executives is how to restore confidence – particularly, the confidence of large-scale governmental donors who work with them as long-term partners and provide the bulk of the funding.[4]

'There were significant cases of misdirected and uncoordinated logistics efforts within and between contributing organizations.'

CHARACTERISTICS OF HUMANITARIAN SUPPLY CHAINS

Humanitarian supply chains typically create a bridge between the world's wealthiest countries, where most of the funding originates, and the world's poorest, where most (but not all) of the world's disasters occur. Large governmental donors exert a strong influence over the sector, as they provide the bulk of the funding for major relief and development activities. Prominent among these donors are the US and the European Union, whose contributions historically represent around 33 per cent and 10 per cent of total humanitarian aid respectively.[5] Between 1990 and 1998 more than 94 per cent of the world's major natural disasters and more than 97 per cent of deaths caused by natural disasters occurred in developing countries. These countries shouldered two-thirds of the economic losses during that period.[6]

HUMANITARIAN SUPPLY CHAINS VERSUS ENTERPRISE SUPPLY CHAINS?

The humanitarian context differs from the commercial context in two important ways. First, humanitarian organizations must at all times act in accordance with the principles of humanity, neutrality and impartiality. This means that they will prevent and alleviate suffering wherever found; will not influence the outcome of a conflict with their intervention; and will not favour one group of beneficiaries over another.[7] Second, since humanitarian 'consumers' (the direct beneficiaries) lack voice, there is no direct market mechanism to punish (or reward) ineffective (effective) organizations. While donors, like stockholders, do care about the effectiveness of the organizations to which they entrust their money, they receive limited feedback about the effectiveness of their partners' work.[8]

Humanitarian supply chains deal with perhaps the most challenging requirements of any; they must be 'multiple, global, dynamic and temporary'.[9] They must also respond and adapt rapidly to the unfolding chaos under extremely difficult conditions in the aftermath of a disaster. Businesses seeking to improve their responsiveness to emergencies could learn from the activities of humanitarian supply chains.[10]

Apart from these strengths, underinvestment in, and lack of appreciation of, logistics over time has led to a gap in capability vis-à-vis the more commercial enterprise supply chains.[11] This gap may be characterized in the following five 'pain points':[12]

1. lack of recognition of the importance of logistics;

2. lack of professional staff, accompanied by a high staff turnover in the field;

3. ineffective leveraging of technology;

4. lack of institutional learning;

5. limited collaboration (dynamic alignment) among humanitarian organizations.[13]

UN TAKES LEAD ON 'ALIGNMENT'

After the 2004 Asian tsunami, the Inter-Agency Standing Committee of the UN reorganized its main agencies and the large NGOs into 'clusters' to improve coordination, avoid competition (and possibly bidding up) for services throughout the supply chain, and to improve the level of collaboration between agencies with similar goals. So far, the 'cluster' model has been applied to nine areas, as follows:

1. Logistics: chaired by the World Food Programme (WFP);

2. Telecommunications: chaired by the Office for the Coordination of Humanitarian Affairs (OCHA);

3. Shelter: chaired by the UN Refugee Agency (UNHCR);

4. Health: chaired by the World Health Organization (WHO);

5. Nutrition: chaired by the United Nations Children's Fund (UNICEF);

6. Water, Sanitation, and Hygiene: chaired by UNICEF;

7. Early Recovery: chaired by the United Nations Development Programme (UNDP);

8. Camp Coordination and Camp Management: chaired by the UNHCR and the International Organization for Migration;

9. Protection: chaired by UNHCR.

The World Food Programme (WFP) was chosen to chair the Logistics cluster because it already has some excellent logisticians who are familiar with moving large quantities of food and materials around the world. However, not all relief logistics is food-related, and non-food logistics is different in two main respects – the products are not as homogenous and more air transport is employed, requiring additional skills and resources.

LESSONS FROM MYANMAR

The 'cluster' concept was deployed in-theatre for the first time in the 2008 Myanmar Cyclone Nargis crisis. According to senior private-sector humanitarian logistics specialists in Myanmar, from a logistics point of view, it was a mixed success. The greatest success was the fact that the model seemed to work and delivered a good result with no massive bottlenecks. The Control Tower (information centre) managed the information and communications processes well and allocated resources equitably. However, it was disappointing that some of the agencies that participated in the cluster meetings between 2004 and 2007 did not participate in the process and continued to act independently,

'Making do with substandard services and resources for financial or other reasons is no longer good enough.'

From a logistics perspective, horizontal *dynamic* alignment is the future.[14] However, there is still a far from an effective and efficient system in place in this respect. Much more work has to be done to convince the major NGOs to, first, contribute to, and use, the system and, second, improve the overall alignment of communications, training and operations modelling so that, when emergencies occur, each agency knows exactly what is required of them.

There is a growing view that, with some professional quantitative and qualitative analyses, a more efficient system will evolve with the dual emphasis of speed and efficiency. Utilizing private companies to effect the horizontal shared services would certainly improve efficiency. However, in future operations this means that the WFP has to take control, acting more transparently and decisively, and demonstrating strong and effective leadership. Furthermore, the designated leader needs to allocate roles quickly on a best-in-class basis – aligning the most suitable resource with the particular operational requirement in hand. Making do with substandard services and resources for financial or other reasons is no longer good enough.

HUMAN RESOURCES AT THE UN

Many organizations in the humanitarian world look to the UN for quality leadership in supply chain environments. While it is true to say that the UN possesses many highly qualified and experienced supply chain specialists across its range of agencies, is also true to say that there is a constant pool of senior high–quality, private-sector talent available and prepared to work for or with UN agencies, often on a *pro bono* basis. However, these personnel often become discouraged by UN recruitment processes. Something must be done about this flaw in the system. In the case of the Asian tsunami, many senior-level voluntary personnel deployed themselves to the region and attempted to make themselves available, *pro bono* to UN and other humanitarian agencies, only to be rebuffed due to the inability of these organizations to handle and process the available expertise. In the days following the Asian tsunami, hundreds of Australian private-sector companies and experienced/ trained personnel volunteered resources to a range of agencies in that country with little or no uptake. There has historically existed a widespread non-alignment within and between humanitarian organizations in terms of matching specialist skills and personnel with situational requirements. This systemic failure often results in many organizations deploying inappropriate personnel, late, into environments to count bodies, rather than count and assist survivors.

Criticism is often levelled at humanitarian organizations on the grounds that they operate their recruitment and deployment strategy and process on a 'who you know' rather than 'what you know' basis, with little leverage of best–standard, private-sector systems and expertise, which is often available free-of-charge to humanitarian organizations. While the essential leadership role of the UN is well acknowledged in humanitarian environments, there is also a widely held view that much of the UN administration is in need of a radical overhaul. Such is the case with the UN NY Recruitment Outreach and Career Development Field Personnel Division, Department of Field Support. The division was recently approached by a specialist private-sector supply chain executive recruitment organization which has interfaced with a number of humanitarian organizations, including the UN within disaster zones and possesses a solid understanding of skill-sets, deployment requirements and operational priorities. The recruitment organization attempted to engage the UN division as part of its global corporate responsibility mandate, with the offer, *pro bono*, to deploy one of the world's best-practice recruitment process technology and management resources to improve recruitment. The briefing meeting was terminated within 15 minutes by UN Division Chief who advised that the UN did not have a mandate to take advantage of, or align with, the private sector in regard to HR matters! What a pity.

In 2006 a UN resolution was passed to reform UN human resources management policies, mandating wide-ranging improvements in UN human resources, and a number of articles have since been produced, highlighting resistance within the UN to proceed with these reforms. Such is the resistance to cultural change in this vital agency.

ALIGNMENT WITH GOVERNMENT AGENCIES

Usually, the first organizations to enter a sudden-onset disaster area are local and international defence/military response units which are highly trained and equipped to save lives and restore essential services, fast. One of the great opportunities for humanitarian supply chains is for the organizations that follow initial government agencies into the theatre, to link up with them and create a platform of humanitarian relief that is aligned with professional/established needs analysis and clear requirements and actions, rather than the range of assessments and responses that usually develop from various other organizations. In many cases, often because of political and/or financial mandates, these specialized units are extracted from the disaster environments before adequate transition of projects can take place, leaving NGOs, charities and/or private-sector volunteer organizations to maintain continuity in humanitarian support. British and Australian government defence forces were very active in the aftermath of the Asian tsunami and are examples of government defence/military organizations recently initiating collaboration and alignment with humanitarian and private-sector organizations.

MILITARY AND PRIVATE SECTOR: PAKISTAN EARTHQUAKE 2005

In Pakistan after the Kashmir earthquake, a new alignment/consolidation concept was pioneered. Private-sector companies were running a temporary warehouse (*pro bono*) specifically for 'unsolicited goods'. This category can be defined as bilateral aid shipments with no designated consignee. The other type can be classified as 'NGO material', which is consigned to a specific NGO that has to clear the goods, much like any commercial shipment. About 9,000 tonnes of unsolicited relief items from 160 aircraft came into Islamabad over a three-week period. Goods were sorted by commodity: blankets, mattresses, tarpaulins, food, personal items like toothbrushes and soap and medical items, as well as heavier items such as generators, pumps and family-sized tents.

A sergeant from the US Marines, Chris Holst, visited the warehouse after a week or so and asked if we had any ideas to solve a problem they were having. While flying up to Kashmir in their Chinook helicopters, the Marines were finding isolated families on hillsides appealing for help. The ground was too uneven to land, so the Marines tried throwing items out of the helicopters. This didn't work as the items would normally break, even when contained in cardboard boxes. The solution was to create a 'speedball'. Using an express freight shipping bag made of woven polypropylene of 25–30kg capacity as the outer container, the freight team made up a 'family survival kit' from items in the warehouse, packed in a creative way. The first items into the bag were the soft goods – a mattress folded into a U-shape and two or three blankets with some clothes. In the middle went a bucket that had been pre-filled with food items, and items such as candles, matches, a cooking pot, mugs, soap – anything that was in the warehouse and considered useful, except liquids. Then, finally, on top would be another blanket or a small tent. The bag was then loosely closed with rope through the eyelets so that, on impact, the air could escape. The volunteers made 6,000 of these bags in ten days by setting up a production line and using downtime from the normal warehousing operation.

> *'After a while, the speedballs were rarely thrown out of helicopters and instead became the main method of moving aid up to the affected areas.'*

The effect was to create a 'family' survival kit of assorted shelter, health and food items that could sustain a small group for ten days or so. The 'speedballs' were extremely popular with different groups for a variety of reasons. First, they didn't split on impact when thrown from a height of 35m (100ft); in fact they bounced and rolled – hence the name 'speedball'. Second, the troops that had to load and unload the helicopters preferred them to boxes as the bag is as much as one man can reasonably carry, thus speeding up the time on the ground and enabling them to make more trips. Third, the humanitarians liked the idea that unsolicited goods were actually getting to beneficiaries quickly and effectively without going through military hands, and the distribution was equitable – no one got more than one bag. After a while, the speedballs were rarely thrown out of helicopters and instead became the main method of moving aid up to the affected areas, since, once the aircraft had landed, the bags could be quickly offloaded and fairly distributed amongst the waiting throng. It avoided mini-riots and major scrums. Lastly, quick research showed that the beneficiaries preferred them as well. A Pakistani airforce officer travelling with the Chinooks advised that the crowds waiting for the helicopters would shout excitedly when they saw red bags rather than hundreds of boxes.

In Myanmar, the UNHCR repeated the concept, albeit in a modified form. In the common warehouse in Yangon, the UN refugee agency had a variety of items – kitchen sets in boxes of four, mosquito nets in bales of 50, plastic sheeting in bundles of six and blankets in bales of 20. Using the same type of bags, donated by a private-sector express freight company (which happened to be running the common warehouse) the HCR representative created a 'shelter kit' comprising one kitchen set, two mosquito nets, blankets and plastic sheeting. She also added some locally procured items like soap and could have added food items such as noodles or rice had they been available. These kits were then taken down to the delta by barge and truck for easy distribution. From a logistics point of view there is always an optimum location to do the kitting where labour, time and space are available and where onward transport costs are not increased so much as to negate the benefit. In this case, Yangon warehouse was the ideal place in this emergency, as super-kitting (making a big kit from smaller kits) outside Burma would have increased transport costs and the delta hubs were too small and understaffed.

Finally there is a security advantage to this type of kitting. Putting commodities into kits changes their value. To a beneficiary, perceived value is increased as you don't have to acquire each component in a separate transaction. On the other hand, from a 'wholesaler's' point of view the value is decreased as goods can't be resold easily, thus effectively making goods less attractive to potential hijackers.

KEY PERFORMANCE INDICATORS

In business, 'if you can't measure it, you can't manage it' is a common saying, and this certainly applies to humanitarian logistics. NGOs tend to undervalue analysis as a way of improvement and take a very short-term operational view. 'Just get the job done' is the mantra, rather than spending time and resources planning, communicating, measuring and constantly striving to improve alignment/collaboration and outcomes during sudden-onset disasters.

A 'control tower' approach should improve measurement as plenty of data is centrally available for analysis. This should create more accountability and then alignment between organizations, resulting in less waste and significantly improved humanitarian supply chain outcomes.

GRASPING DYNAMIC ALIGNMENT WITH SMALL HANDS

An example of understanding and leveraging the benefits of the dynamic alignment model was initiated when, in 2005, a sole community elder cared for over 100 young children orphaned by HIV/AIDS. He made contact with a logistics company that happened to be working in his area, the world's largest slum – Kibera, Nairobi, Kenya. Kibera has often been referred to as a disaster area in its own right, a sprawling squatter camp of a million people in four square miles, established 20 years ago to cope with Sudanese refugees fleeing across the border from conflict in their homeland. Kibera has continued to expand in an area five kilometres from downtown Nairobi that the government or humanitarian agencies have failed to address.

Three short years later Josiah Munyutu is now headmaster of the largest school in Kibera, with 17 teachers plus cooks and security staff, providing 850 orphaned children with education, food, sanitation and medical care. The rapidly expanding community-based school is the centre for a range of sustainable projects supported through the not-for-profit Oasis Africa Australia[15] that he inspired in collaboration with a range of supporting organizations such as Feed the Children, local NGO Practical Action, Kenya Boy Scouts, and a range of Australia- and New Zealand-based private-sector companies.

The key to the school's success is an operating model based on supply chain principles and significant dynamic alignment with other organizations. Josiah has skilfully engaged essential stakeholders, secured investment, and identified and aligned stakeholder expectations. All parties effectively monitor outcomes, measured in part by the number of children delivered into the government secondary school system. The Kibera community school project and Oasis Africa Australia are actively aligning with increasing numbers of similarly focused organizations inside the Kibera slum, within Kenya, and internationally to coordinate resources and supply chains for the mutual benefit of all stakeholders, most importantly the orphaned children they serve.

ALIGNMENT INSIGHTS

- *Humanitarian organizations, government, NGOs, UN agencies, charities, religious, political and private-sector businesses all contribute essential resources during sudden-onset and longer-term disasters where humanitarian supply chains are required. These organizations are led and operated by hundreds of thousands of dedicated professionals and volunteers, the vast majority committed to the highest of humanitarian ideals and many making the ultimate sacrifice in their desire to help their fellow man. With successive natural disasters in recent years, however, failure by organizations to align expertise and capacity internally and externally has often resulted in less than satisfactory outcomes, including needless victim casualties.*

- *If you belong to an organization that participates in humanitarian supply chains, take an interest in and enquire how your organization's supply chain operates and is aligned internally and externally to deliver mandated outcomes, and whether a review process is in place to evaluate supply chain performance. Ask what supply chain planning is in place to respond to future sudden-onset disasters or provide satisfactory support in ongoing projects. Take action to initiate awareness and change at whatever level is required to improve alignment.*

- *If you are a donor, sponsor or in any other way support a humanitarian organization, ask how the organization's supply chain operates and is aligned internally and externally to deliver mandated outcomes. Enquire about past supply chain outcomes and whether a review process is in place to evaluate supply chain performance. Ask what supply chain planning is in place to respond to future sudden-onset disasters or provide satisfactory support in ongoing projects. Your interest can be a force for positive change, and your actions will apply pressure to ensure that the humanitarian supply chain performance that most organizations are mandated to deliver – but too often fail to deliver – is improved.*

NOTES

1   J.L. Salmon, 'Fraud alleged at Red Cross call centres', _Washington Post_, 27 December 2005.
2   S. Strom, 'Red Cross chief steps down; interim successor is named', _New York Times_, 13 December 2005.
3   A. Thomas and L.R. Kopczak, 'Life- saving supply chains and the path forward' in H.L. Lee and C-Y. Lee (eds), _Building Supply Chain Excellence in Emerging Economies_, Springer, New York, 2006.
4   L.R. Kopczak and M.E. Johnson, 'Rebuilding confidence: trust, control and information technology in humanitarian supply chains', 2007, http://www.ists.dartmouth.edu/library/347.pdf.
5   Thomas and Kopczak, 'Life-saving supply chains', _op. cit._
6   World Bank, _Attacking Poverty_, World Development Report 2000/2001, World Bank, Washington DC, 170.
7   IFRC, 'Promoting the fundamental principles and humanitarian values', 2007, http://www.ifrc.org/what/values (accessed 15 January 2007).
8   Kopczak and Johnson, 'Rebuilding confidence', _op. cit._
9   L.N. Van Wassenhove, 'Humanitarian aid logistics: supply chain management in high gear', _Journal of the Operational Research Society_, Vol. 57, No. 5 (2006), pp. 475–489, see p. 480.
10 Ibid.
11 Thomas and Kopczak, 'Life-saving supply chains', _op. cit._; Van Wassenhove, 'Humanitarian aid logistics', _op. cit._
12 Thomas and Kopczak, 'Life-saving supply chains', _op. cit._
13 Kopczak and Johnson, 'Rebuilding confidence', _op. cit._
14 This includes such activities as air charters; airport handling; initial ground transport; temporary warehousing; kitting; onward transport; sub-hub warehousing and final distribution.
15 See http://www.oasisafrica.net.

7 Enhanced Civil–Military Collaboration in Humanitarian Supply Chains

Michael Whiting

When a sudden-onset natural disaster strikes, the affected nation has the primary responsibility to initiate, organize, coordinate and implement disaster response within its territory. However, if the scale of the disaster is beyond the response capacity of local emergency management authorities, the affected state may request assistance from the United Nations (UN) and International and National Non-Government Organizations (INGOs and NGOs), among others.

Sudden-onset natural disasters are difficult to respond to because they are just 'what it says on the tin' – they are sudden and unexpected. Few nations and still fewer UN agencies, INGOs and NGOs can be continuously staffed and equipped to adequately respond to sudden-onset emergencies. The UN and NGO communities need time to mount a response, and time is the critical factor. At such times, heavy airlift is frequently at a premium. In sudden-onset natural disasters time can mean the difference between saving lives and counting bodies.

Generally, the only organizations that are appropriately staffed, equipped and have the means to deliver are the military. While the military are for the most part ready, willing and able to be on the front line of disaster relief, civilian aid organizations are often reluctant to relinquish control.

There is a clear and present need for the realignment of thinking between the military and the humanitarian communities. Such aligned thinking should also be reinforced by a mechanism of coordination and cooperation which is designed to flexibly meet the needs of both the military and the humanitarian community in a dynamic way – enter *dynamic* alignment.

In the last four years three sudden-onset emergencies have occurred in which military disaster relief was used: the Indian Ocean tsunami of 2004, the South Asia earthquake of 2005 and Cyclone Nargis in 2008. Each of these disasters elicited a quite different military response.

DOCTRINE

In the early 1990s, when the break-up of the former state of Yugoslavia was being played out, little existed in the way of doctrine that covered civil–military coordination in either the military or the humanitarian communities. In the intervening years much guidance and instruction has been laid out, but still a culture of distrust persists which can sometimes work to the disadvantage of those who are most vulnerable after a disaster has struck.

Traditionally, in complex emergencies there has been a distinction between the military and the non-military domain: an approach built upon the principles of international humanitarian law that makes a distinction between combatants and non-combatants, protecting the latter from armed attack. The subject of civil–military coordination is complex. In recent history, military assets have become increasingly involved in operations other than war, including the provision of relief and services to the vulnerable. The nature of modern complex emergencies is changing, and the humanitarian community has faced increased operational challenges, as well as greater risks and threats for their workers in the field – the death of aid workers in Afghanistan, Dafur, Kenya and Somalia in 2008 evidences this.[1] Practical realities on the ground have gradually necessitated various forms of civil–military coordination for humanitarian operations.

These developments, together with cases of military interventions claimed to be for 'humanitarian' purposes, have led to an erosion of the separation between the humanitarian and the military space[2] and have therefore threatened to blur the fundamental distinction between these two domains. It also raises significant concerns associated with the application of humanitarian principles and policies, as well as operational issues. These developments necessitate increased communication, coordination and understanding between humanitarian actors and require improved knowledge of each other's mandates, capacities and limitations.

The humanitarian community therefore felt it necessary to examine the wide-ranging issues arising from civil–military relations and to come up with a reference paper that extended beyond the individual guidelines that had previously existed.[3] In this chapter we focus on military assistance in the provision of relief.

BACKGROUND

Humanitarian and military actors have fundamentally different institutional thinking and cultures, characterized by the distinct chain-of-command and clear organizational structures of the military vis-à-vis the corresponding diversity in the humanitarian community. The two groups have different mandates, objectives, working methods and even vocabularies. It is important that humanitarian actors are aware of the varied reasons and motivations for the military to undertake actions that can encroach on the humanitarian space. On the other hand, it is equally important for military actors to understand the complex network of international NGOs that work with national and international staff and local partners. Humanitarian action is also largely dependent on acceptance by the parties to the conflict. Most of the local actors engaged in humanitarian work are present on the ground long before the arrival of international personnel and will continue their work after their departure. Susceptibility towards local sensitivities and adherence to the actuality and perception of impartiality and independence are therefore pivotal assets of any humanitarian operation, and this should be made known to the military.

Within the context of civil–military relations there are a number of situations where some level of coordination between the humanitarian and military actors may become necessary. Civil–military *coordination* is a shared responsibility of the humanitarian and military actors, and it may take place in various levels of intensity and form. Where cooperation between the humanitarian and military actors is not appropriate, opportune or possible, or if there are no common goals to pursue, then these actors merely operate side-by-side. Such a relationship may be best described as one of *coexistence*, in which case civil–military coordination should focus on minimizing competition and conflict in order to enable the different actors to work in the same geographical area with minimum disruption to each other's activities. When there is a common goal and agreed strategy, and all parties accept the need to work together, *cooperation* may become possible, and *coordination* can then focus on improving understanding, and through understanding and meaningful dialogue improvement in the effectiveness and efficiency of the combined efforts to serve humanitarian objectives can be achieved. The dynamics of this relationship is in many ways similar to the interorganizational networks promoted in supply chain risk management where aligning strategy and relationship type is pivotal to achieving a positive outcome. In supply chain risk management, different relationship management approaches are appropriate and have the potential to deliver different types of performance. The *dynamic alignment* of need and capability against a background of enlightened understanding of the capabilities and limitations of the various participants is essential. Such a relationship can be considered a collaborative relationship which requires the high involvement of both parties.

> *'It is equally important for military actors to understand the complex network of international NGOs that work with national and international staff and local partners.'*

In the humanitarian context it is important to maintain a clear separation between the roles of the military and humanitarian actors, by distinguishing their respective spheres of competence and responsibility: a classic situation best served by *alignment*. This approach is implicit in, and builds on, the principles of international humanitarian law, and is crucial to maintaining the independence of humanitarian action. The need for the humanitarians to maintain an actual and perceived distance from the military is especially important with regard to belligerent forces or representatives of an occupying power.[4] Any coordination with a party to an armed conflict must proceed with extreme caution, care and sensitivity, given that the actual or perceived affiliation with a belligerent might lead to the loss of neutrality and impartiality of the humanitarian organization, which could in turn negatively affect the security of beneficiaries and humanitarian staff, as well as jeopardizing the whole humanitarian operation in a conflict zone. Thus, cooperation – the closer form of coordination – with belligerent forces should in principle not take place, unless in extreme and exceptional circumstances, and only as a last resort.

However, the emphasis on distinction should not be interpreted as a suggestion of non-coordination between humanitarian and military actors. The particular situation on the ground and the nature of the military operation in a given situation will play a determining factor on the type of coordination that may take place. Possible features of civil–military coordination include the sharing of certain information, a careful division of tasks and, when feasible and appropriate, collaborative planning – *alignment* in its purest form.

A *dynamic alignment* between humanitarian and military actors is therefore necessary where, guided by core doctrine agreed by participants, the detailed roles and the alignment of respective roles will vary according to the situation on the ground.

The military often have the capability to help secure an enabling environment on the ground in which humanitarian activities can take place in relative safety. The military may also have practical means to offer in the delivery of assistance, such as rapid deployment of large numbers of personnel, equipment, logistics and supplies. However, humanitarian expertise – including beneficiary identification, needs assessment, vulnerability assessment, impartial and neutral distribution of relief aid, and monitoring and evaluation – will remain essential to an effective and successful humanitarian operation.

The nature of the relationship between one or a group of humanitarian organization(s) and the military, as well as the conduct of these actors in this relationship, may also have an effect on other humanitarian agencies working in the same area and beyond, possibly affecting the perception of humanitarian action in general. For example, the use of armed escorts by one humanitarian organization may negatively influence the perception of neutrality and impartiality of other humanitarian organizations in the same area. Coordination amongst humanitarian actors, preferably leading to a common approach to civil–military relations in a given complex emergency, is therefore desirable.

All humanitarian action, including civil–military coordination for humanitarian purposes in complex emergencies, must be in accordance with the overriding core principles of *humanity*, *neutrality* and *impartiality*. These are cardinal humanitarian principles which should be followed; there are also other important doctrines and concepts that must be respected when planning or undertaking civil–military coordination, and these are described in more detail in the following pages.

> **'The independence of humanitarian action and decision-making must be preserved at all times at both the operational and policy levels.'**

CIVILIAN-MILITARY DISTINCTION IN HUMANITARIAN ACTION

At all times, a clear distinction must be maintained between combatants and non-combatants – that is, between those actively engaged in hostilities and civilians and others who do not or no longer directly participate in an armed conflict (including the sick, wounded, prisoners of war and demobilized ex-combatants). International humanitarian law protects non-combatants by providing immunity from attack. Thus, humanitarian workers must never present themselves or their work as part of a military operation, and military personnel must refrain from presenting themselves as civilian humanitarian workers.

OPERATIONAL INDEPENDENCE OF HUMANITARIAN ACTION

In any civil–military coordination humanitarian actors must retain the lead role in undertaking and directing humanitarian activities. The independence of humanitarian action and decision-making must be preserved at all times at both the operational and policy levels. Humanitarian organizations must not implement tasks on behalf of the military nor represent or implement their policies. Basic requisites such as freedom of movement for humanitarian staff, freedom to conduct independent assessments, freedom to select staff, freedom to identify beneficiaries of assistance based on their needs, or free flow of communications between humanitarian agencies as well as with the media, must not be impeded.

SECURITY OF HUMANITARIAN PERSONNEL

Any perception that humanitarian actors may have become affiliated with the military forces within a specific situation could have a negative impact on the security of humanitarian staff and their ability to access vulnerable populations. However, humanitarian actors operating within an emergency situation must identify the most expeditious, effective and secure approach to ensure the delivery of vital assistance to vulnerable target populations. This approach must be balanced against the primary concern for ensuring staff safety, and therein a consideration of any real or perceived affiliation with the military. The decision to seek military-based security for humanitarian workers should be viewed as a last-resort option when other staff security mechanisms are unavailable, inadequate or inappropriate.

ESTABLISHMENT OF LIAISON ARRANGEMENTS

Liaison arrangements and clear lines of communication should be established between the military forces and the humanitarian community at the earliest possible stage and at all relevant levels in order to guarantee the timely and regular exchange of certain information before and during military operations. However, these activities should be conducted with caution. Either mentioning or concealing to the public the existence of direct communications between the humanitarian and military actors could result in suspicion and/or incorrect conclusions regarding the nature of the communications. Due to its possible impact on the perception of humanitarian operations, at times, it may be reasonable not to disseminate or publicize the liaison arrangements between the humanitarian community and the military. Obviously, such a decision has to be balanced with the need to ensure accountability, transparency and openness towards the local population and beneficiaries.

There are a number of initiatives within the UN system that focus on preparing humanitarian personnel on civil–military issues and practical liaison arrangements in complex emergencies. This includes the UN CMCoord induction courses, organized by the UN Office for the Coordination of Humanitarian Aid's (OCHA's) Military and Civil Defence Unit (MCDU). This unit also conducts predeployment training and workshops tailored to a particular content and mission.

In addition to UN CMCoord Officers deployed by OCHA, UN agencies may deploy Military Liaison Officers (MLOs) to focus on specific sectoral and operational civil–military issues and the UN Department of Peace Keeping Operations (DPKO) may deploy Civil–Military Liaison Officers (CMLOs). The UN Joint Logistics Centre (UNJLC), an inter-agency facility, also provides, when established, an effective and practical civil–military coordination function on an operational logistics level. However, many of the roles of UNJLC have been subsumed by the Logistics Cluster, and some gaps exist; one such gap is civil–military coordination at this vital coal-face level.

USE OF MILITARY ASSETS FOR HUMANITARIAN OPERATIONS

The use of military assets in support of humanitarian operations should be exceptional and only on a last-resort basis. It is recognized, however, that where civilian/humanitarian capacities are not adequate or cannot be obtained in a timely manner to meet urgent humanitarian needs, military and civil defence assets, including military aircraft, may be deployed in accordance with the *Guidelines on the Use of Military and Civil Defence Assets to Support United Nations Humanitarian Activities in Complex Emergencies* ('MCDA Guidelines') of March 2003.[5] In addition to the principle of 'last resort',[6] key criteria in the MCDA Guidelines include: (1) *unique capability* – no appropriate alternative civilian resources exist; (2) *timeliness* – the urgency of the task at hand demands immediate action; (3) *clear humanitarian direction* – civilian control over the use of military assets; (4) *time-limited* – the use of military assets to support humanitarian activities is clearly limited in time and scale.

As a matter of principle, the military and civil defence assets of belligerent forces or of units that find themselves actively engaged in combat *shall not* be used to support humanitarian activities.[7] While there are ongoing hostilities, it will be necessary to distinguish between operations in-theatre and those outside. In-theatre, the use of military assets for humanitarian purposes should generally not be undertaken. Only under extreme and exceptional circumstances would it be appropriate to consider the use, in-theatre, of military assets of the parties engaged in combat operations. Specifically, this situation may occur when a highly vulnerable population cannot be assisted or accessed by any other means. Outside the theatre of operations, military assets of the parties engaged in combat operations may be used in accordance with the above-mentioned principles and guidelines. However, preference should first be given to military assets of parties not engaged in combat operations.

Any humanitarian operation using military assets must retain its civilian nature and character. While military assets will remain under military control, the operation as a whole must remain under the overall authority and control of the responsible humanitarian organization. Military and civil defence assets that have been placed under the control of the humanitarian agencies and deployed on a full-time basis purely for humanitarian purposes must be visibly identified in a manner that clearly differentiates them from military assets being used for military purposes.

JOINT CIVIL–MILITARY RELIEF OPERATIONS

Any operations undertaken jointly by humanitarian agencies and military forces may have a negative impact on the perception of the humanitarian agencies' impartiality and neutrality and hence affect their ability to operate effectively throughout a complex emergency. Therefore, any joint civil–military cooperation should be determined by a thorough assessment of the actual needs on the ground and a review of civilian humanitarian capacities to respond to them in a timely manner. To the extent that joint operations with the military cannot be avoided, they may be employed only as a means of last resort and must adhere to the principles provided in the above-mentioned 'MCDA Guidelines'.

One must be aware that the military have different objectives, interests, schedules and priorities from the humanitarian community. Relief operations rendered by military forces could be conditional and could cease when the mission of the military forces changes, the unit moves, or if the assisted population becomes uncooperative. Such action by the military can also be conducted based primarily on the needs and goals of the force and its mission, rather than the needs of the local population.

SEPARATE MILITARY OPERATIONS FOR RELIEF PURPOSES

'Any operations undertaken jointly by humanitarian agencies and military forces may have a negative impact on the perception of the humanitarian agencies' impartiality and neutrality.'

Relief operations carried out by military forces, even when the intention is purely 'humanitarian,' may jeopardize or seriously undermine the overall humanitarian efforts by non-military actors. The other parties to the conflict and the beneficiaries may neither be willing nor able to differentiate between assistance provided by the military and assistance provided by humanitarian agencies. This could have serious consequences for the ability to access certain areas and for the safety of humanitarian staff, not to mention the long-term damage to the standing of humanitarian agencies in the region and in other crisis areas if humanitarian assistance is perceived as being selective and/or partial. Assistance provided by the military is susceptible to political influence and/or objectives, and the criteria used in selecting the beneficiaries and determining their needs may differ from those held by humanitarian organizations.

For these reasons, military forces should be strongly discouraged from playing the role of the humanitarian aid-providers. Their role in relation to humanitarian actors should be limited to helping create a secure operating environment that enables humanitarian action. If need be, diplomatic efforts should be used to explain and reiterate to political and military authorities the concern of the humanitarian community in this regard.

However, there may be extreme and exceptional circumstances that require relief operations to be undertaken by the military as a last resort. This might be the case when the military are the only actors on the ground or the humanitarians lack the capacity and/or resources to respond to critical needs of civilians.

THE PSYCHOLOGY OF COLLABORATION

For any alignment to work effectively we need to understand in-depth what inevitable risks this will bring to the various parties. These risks will be business-related or of an interpersonal nature. To collaborate implies that people commit to work together in a more intimate and transparent manner and the upside is easy to discuss and prove. The risks involved are harder to discuss, especially the risks regarding relationships.

Risk is the cognitive and rational side of the coin. The emotional side is fear and anxiety. When parties work with the intention to create collaborative relationships, they are most likely to put forward good news and good spirits (very much like couples do when they court). The required levels of trust and intimacy are not yet embedded to encourage them to discuss uncomfortable topics that expose their vulnerable side. It is therefore important to provide a process that can pre-empt the fears and risks which would not be expressed if left to the natural flow of relationship-building.

We can accurately anticipate what it is that people are likely to fear or feel threatened by once they embark on a process of collaboration. A few are listed below:

- *Loss of flexibility and full control over decisions.* When people commit to collaboration, they need to actively consider and include the other parties' needs and interest. Decision-making is therefore more complicated.

- *Loss of identity.* Collaborating may mean that the way of working changes to such degree that it promises to change who people are and what they stand for. A chain of organizations may even work under a whole new name and brand.

- *Loss of exposure as an individual entity.* Working with other stakeholders may mean that the competiton for donor investment becomes tougher, rather than more secure.

- *Increased inefficiency.* Becoming part of a greater whole may mean increased inefficiencies due to the size of collective operations. More policies, more signatures needed and more time required to get things done may seem inevitable.

Emphasis must be placed on, and time invested in, dialogue so that these (and other) fears can be addressed to facilitate a process in which practical ways of overcoming them can be identified.

Certain conditions are required to be able to connect parties on this level at such an early stage of the collaboration process. Specific circumstances and prerequisites exist.

To commit to anything material, significant and long-term (whether it is committing to having a robust, honest conversation about fears that will inhibit meaningful alignment or committing to working together in alignment) people need deep levels of trust. Few people trust implicitly. Most people take significant time to develop trust. Whilst the concept of dynamic alignment makes sense, it is only heartfelt need and goodwill that will deliver the logic. Not the logic itself.

Furthermore, it is unlikely that people will ultimately trust an institution. They may think they do, but trust can only develop among people – directly between individuals. To develop trust among these parties, the process design must provide an opportunity for people to connect and understand each other. It needs to be personal and authentic. Superficial and mechanistic 'get to know each other' exercises will fail to deliver the required connection. Real understanding between parties facilitates an emotional commitment that is worth much more than signatures on a contract.

When alignment work must take place among large institutions, a fair question and a massive challenge is how to facilitate trust among people within them. A process by which the representatives and leaders of these organizations can connect and engage on a personal level with adequate depth must be in place before they can truly take risks together. In brief, the makers and breakers of dynamic alignment would be the leaders of the various stakeholders. The type of leader needed in such circumstances is very specific – a collaborative leader. Their individual value system must be aligned with the notion of alignment.

The process of creating trust needs to focus on four core elements that drive trust in a relationship. Mayer, Davis and Schoorman's model of trust is a powerful one to guide conversation in order to establish a code of conduct that will deliver on these elements.[8] See Figure 7.1 for a pictorial representation.

To design such a trust-building process in which people can openly address risks and fears requires professionals who really understand complex psychological group processes and who can create a safe, constructive space for people to build relationships and new ways of working together.

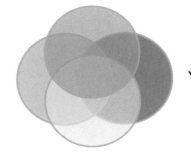

Competence
You are able to do what you promise

Commitment
You do what you say

Clear Communication
You say what you mean

Consideration
Take others' interest into account

Figure 7.1   Trust

Source: R.C. Mayer, J.H. Davis and F.D. Schoorman, 'An integrative model of organizational trust', *Academy of Management Review*, Vol. 20 (1995), pp. 709–743.

Regardless of how well the process is designed, contained and implemented, *realistic expectations* about how rapidly a collaborative relationship can be established and maintained are crucial. It takes time to move from being relative strangers to making a well-oiled integrated effort, and the parties involved need to be continuously reminded to be realistic in their expectations.

CASES OF COORDINATION IN ACTION

The Indian Ocean Tsunami

The sheer scale of the Indian Ocean Tsunami of 2004, in terms of both the geographical area covered and the number of killed, injured and displaced put the provision of humanitarian aid under greater stresses than ever before.[9] When the request for assistance was not met at the local level, it was then forwarded to the regional level, to the Combined Coordination Centre (CCC) in Thailand, to which liaison officers from participating forces were deployed. Coordination between all military forces and the humanitarian community was facilitated by the UN civil military coordination officers deployed by OCHA in support of the various UN humanitarian coordinators and other NGOs.

The CCC was embedded in the US-led Combined Support Force 536 (CSF 536), which was established at the Royal Thai Naval Base at U-Tapao. The CSF 536 was the III Marine Expeditionary Force commanded by US Lieutenant General Robert Blackman, which maintains a forward presence in Japan and Asia. Liaison officers from 12 countries: Australia, Austria, China, France, Germany, India, Japan, South Korea, Malaysia, New Zealand, Pakistan and Singapore were attached to the CCC. While a combined support force would typically operate under the command of one officer, the CSF 536 did not. It was a cooperative arrangement with all the countries represented reporting back to their national capitals.[10]

During the emergency phase of the response to the Indian Ocean tsunami the US alone made available 60 helicopters, which flew more than 2,200 missions, and fixed-wing aircraft, mostly C-130 and C-17 cargo aircraft, which flew over 1,300 missions, transporting supplies and equipment into and throughout the disaster area. The military support provided involved engineering, logistics and medical support from more than 24 nations.

In Indonesia, the national emergency response was led in the emergency phase by the Tsunami Relief Brigade based at Banda Aceh Airport under the command of Major General Bambang Darmono. Coordination of the military relief effort in Indonesia was effective because there was a clear chain of command led by the affected nation, and there was no blurring of the edges around what was military and what was humanitarian space. Daily briefings throughout the three-month emergency phase enabled best use to be made of the various assets on hand – there was effective dynamic alignment. Daily briefings enabled the stakeholders to adjust their response to their capacity and the needs of the vulnerable. Civil–military coordination was a principal enabler in the emergency phase of this relief effort.

The South Asian Earthquake

The magnitude 7.6 earthquake that struck northern Pakistan and India on 8 October 2005, was the world's third-deadliest natural disaster of the past 25 years, surpassed only by the 2004 Asian tsunami and the 1991 cyclone in Bangladesh. An estimated 74,650 people lost their lives – a higher death toll than the average annual loss to all natural and man-made disasters combined during the 1990s, excluding armed conflicts.

In addition to those who died, more than 76,000 people were injured, 2.8 million were left homeless, and 2.3 million had insecure access to food and other essentials. Furthermore, the affected population was spread over 30,000 km^2 in impoverished, mountainous and difficult-to-reach areas. Once the bitterly cold winter set in, it became clear that the earthquake would continue taking its toll for months to come. Humanitarian agencies found themselves working in a highly politicized international and domestic environment. Despite the importance of maintaining a depoliticized 'humanitarian space', the presence of humanitarian agencies played into many of the political fault-lines of contemporary Pakistan.[11]

The earthquake caused substantial damage and loss of life across Pakistan's North West Frontier Province and Pakistan-administered Kashmir. International humanitarian agencies found themselves working with, and at the invitation of, the military-led government of Pakistan. Overall coordination of the relief effort lay with the military-led Federal Relief Commission Rehabilitation Authority (ERRA). International military assistance in the form of logistical airlift, medical and engineering support was provided at the direct invitation of the president of Pakistan. The international military and the humanitarian agencies worked in a unique geographic and political environment. The development of close cooperation and dialogue between humanitarian actors, government officials, donors, national militaries and regional and international militaries was essential.[12]

Cyclone Nargis

Cyclone Nargis made landfall in Myanmar on 2 May 2008 affecting 2.4 million people and killing between 63,000 and 101,000 with a further 220,000 missing. As previously mentioned, it was the national government that was responsible for the disaster response in the first instance. The circumstances surrounding the response to Cyclone Nargis were complicated by the fact that the government of Myanmar was a reclusive one and, at the onset of the emergency, was in a state of denial. Great mistrust existed between the sovereign state and the humanitarian community.

The US and French navies had vessels in the region on exercise. These vessels could have provided immediate emergency relief in terms of helicopter support and much-needed relief supplies. Initially, the military government of Myanmar refused all foreign assistance. The intervention of the UN Secretary-General, and the Association of South East Asia Nations (ASEAN) was necessary before humanitarian aid workers were permitted entry into Myanmar and the flow of humanitarian supplies could commence in earnest.

Early on, the US military mounted more than 40 flights of emergency relief supplies from U-Tapao in Thailand to Yangon. Notwithstanding the fact that the government of Myanmar was a military government, and many of the state-owned and other institutions were run by retired military officers, the UN regional and country officials and the other humanitarian agencies put no priority on civil–military coordination. The development of dialogue between the authorities and humanitarian personnel at field level gradually led to a building of trust which enabled humanitarian aid to be more effectively distributed to the vulnerable.

It is possible that civil–military coordination could have more quickly facilitated the delivery of aid to the vulnerable survivors of the cyclone.

WORK-IN-PROGRESS

Humanitarian aid is programme-driven. Humanitarian logistics came of age during the relief effort that followed the Indian Ocean tsunami of 2004,[13] but more than four years on humanitarian logistics remains largely underresourced and is still considered by some as little more than a necessary evil. Donors, beneficiaries and the media are more closely monitoring the speed and efficiently with which relief organizations respond in times of disaster. Unfortunately, disaster relief is, and will continue to be, a 'growth market'. Both natural and man-made disasters are expected to increase by fivefold over the next 50 years due to environmental degradation, rapid urbanization and the spread of diseases such as HIV/AIDS, antibiotic-resistant tuberculosis and diabetes in the developing world.[14] There is therefore increasing demand (more disasters), and steadily rising costs (fuel and shortage of food).

Whilst humanitarian funding continues to rise in dollar terms, the rate of growth is slowing down – humanitarian assistance grew at a much higher average annual rate during 2000–2003 than it did during 2004–2006.[15]

One of the most cost-efficient and timely ways in which the speed and quality of delivery could be assured, and risks to the humanitarian supply chain in times of disaster mitigated, would be through an improvement in civil–military coordination. It should be improved to a point where everything that the military can offer humanitarian logistics can be utilized without compromising humanitarian principles. Real and meaningful dialogue is needed, predicated by willingness by the stakeholders to fully understand, appreciate and respect one another's positions while genuinely striving to find that illusive alignment that would be the catalyst required to change the current 'love–hate' relationship that prevails between them.

ALIGNMENT INSIGHTS

- *Much can be achieved to further improve civil–military co-ordination in the humanitarian arena by the adoption of the principles of dynamic alignment, where differences in culture, doctrine and organization can be confronted and understood by the stakeholders.*

- *Complex collaborative relationships demand alignment of the expectations and capabilities of the stakeholders to make them work.*

- *Supply chain integration and collaborative partnerships have a positive effect on supply chain performance in commercial logistics. Alignment of expectations in civil–military coordination will foster similar successful integration and collaboration in humanitarian logistics.*

ACKNOWLEDGEMENTS

For logistics to work effectively there needs to be a culture of teamwork. I have been fortunate that, in the humanitarian emergencies in which I have been operationally engaged, this culture has prevailed. I have learned much, and what I have learned is reflected above. I have also learned much from those whom I have met and talked with at the various forums and conventions held since 2004 in an attempt to improve the state of humanitarian logistics. It is a mistake sometimes to single out any one person or group of persons, but one person has helped me grasp some fundamental truths about the psychology of collaboration, a key to coordination and cooperation, and that is Dina Oelofsen. Without grasping this nettle, dynamic alignment is an impossible dream.

John Gattorna has been a first-class mentor, a steadfast supporter of humanitarian logistics, and has frequently allowed me to stand on my soap box to advocate the importance of logistics in the humanitarian endeavour.

NOTES

1   In the recent past, military support and/or protection for certain humanitarian operations has been provided in various complex emergencies, including (but not limited to) Iraq, Afghanistan, Côte d'Ivoire, Eritrea, Liberia, Northern Uganda, Sierra Leone, the Indian Ocean tsunami, and the South Asian earthquake.

2   For an explanation of 'humanitarian space' or 'humanitarian operating environment', see paragraph 3 of the *Guidelines on the Use of Military*

and Civil Defence Assets to Support United Nations Humanitarian Activities* in Complex Emergencies* of March 2003, http://ochaonline.un.org/mcdu/guidelines.

3   *Civil–Military Relationship in Complex Emergencies* – an Inter-Agency Standing Committee Reference Paper, UNHCR Refworld, 28 June 2004, http://www.unhcr.org/refworld/docid/4289ea8c4.html.

4   As an example of principles and practical considerations, including specifics on permissible and impermissible action when interacting with an occupying power, see the *General Guidance for Interaction Between United Nations Personnel and Military and Civilian Representatives of the Occupying Power in Iraq* of 8 May 2003, http://ochaonline.un.org/mcda/guidelines.

5   For the full text of the MCDA Guidelines, see http://ochaonline.un.org/mcdu/guidelines.

6   *Last resort* is defined as follows: 'Military assets should be requested only where there is no comparable civilian alternative and only the use of military assets can meet a critical humanitarian need. The military asset must therefore be unique in capability and availability.' (See paragraph 7 of the MCDA Guidelines, *op.cit.*).

7   See paragraph 25 of the MCDA Guidelines, *op. cit.*

8   Amy Kates and Jay R. Galbraithe, *Designing Your Organization*, Jossey-Bass, San Francisco, 2007.

9   John Mangan, Chandra Lalwani and Tim Butcher (eds), *Global Logistics and Supply Chain Management*, John Wiley & Sons Ltd, Chichester, 2008.

10   'Welcome Relief', *Janes Defence Weekly*, 18 May 2005.

11   T. Bamforth and J.H. Qureshi, 'Political complexities of humanitarian intervention in the Pakistan earthquake', *Journal of Humanitarian Assistance*, 16 January 2007.

12   At: http://ochaonline.un.org/roap.

13   G. Heaslip, 'Humanitarian aid supply chains' in John Mangan et al., *Global Logistics and Supply Chain Management*, *op. cit.*

14   A.S. Thomas and L.R. Kopczak, 'From logistics to supply chain management', Fritz Institute, San Francisco, 2005, www.fritzinstitute.org/PDFs/WhitePaper/FromLogisticsto.pdf.

15   Abby Stoddard and Katherine Haver Centre on International Cooperation, New York University and Adele Harmer Humanitarian Policy Group, Overseas Development Institute, 'Operational Consequences of Reform Project', Working Paper Humanitarian Financing Reform, Humanitarian Policy Group, June 2007.

8 Revisiting and Refining Lee's 'Triple-A Supply Chain'[1]

John Gattorna

Hau Lee's highly acclaimed seminal article[2] on 'The Triple-A Supply Chain' has now been out in the domain for five years, during which time our understanding of how supply chains function has increased exponentially. So it's high time we revisited the ideas in that article and added some refinements.

Lee gives many interesting examples to support his definitions of each of the 'As' – Agility, Adaptability and Alignment – but while these are quite descriptive, there remains some lingering questions about exactly what is going on under the surface. Indeed, Lee himself admits as much in the last paragraph of his article when he muses that '…what they [firms] need is a fresh attitude and a culture to get their supply chains to deliver Triple-A performance'.[3] He is right, of course, and in this extension to Lee's article I will endeavour to introduce that missing ingredient – the cultural perspective. Without it, I'm afraid the story remains purely descriptive and, as such, lacks explanatory power.

> *'Over 40 per cent of strategies written into business plans fail to be implemented, and it's all due to a "misalignment" between those strategies and the "values" of the people inside the organization.'*

By better understanding what is going on inside the human dimension of supply chains, it becomes possible to move from a purely reactive to a more predictive level. In other words, if you know what subcultures are in place and underpinning various supply chain strategies, you are in a better position to predict what the likely outcomes will be in the implementation phase. Unfortunately, in my experience, over 40 per cent of strategies written into business plans fail to be implemented, and it's all due to a 'misalignment' between those strategies and the 'values' of the people inside the organization and the partner organizations in the chain. They tend to do what they 'prefer' to do.

Lee posits that '… only those companies that build Agile, Adaptable, and Aligned supply chains get ahead of the competition'.[4] I agree with him. But

I think we need to explore and refine his definitions of these three 'As' to understand why this might be so.

REDEFINING THE THREE KEY PROPERTIES

Agility is becoming increasingly critical in today's volatile markets. But you pay a price for it. You can't be agile and cost-efficient coincidentally – something has to give. In truth, you will find customers in your markets that want one or the other or, at times, both responses. If the latter, you have to try to understand which they want more. To give an agile response at lowest cost-to-serve is, in effect, rewarding customers who are often behaving badly. In order to help find a way to resolve the seemingly endless (and sometimes conflicting) demands of customers, I developed the concept of '*dynamic supply chain alignment*'. This involves looking at supply chain design and operation from the perspective of the customer's *dominant buying behaviour.*[5] By segmenting markets for a wide range of product/service categories, I observed patterns which can be used to reverse engineer the equivalent supply chain configurations. Specifically, I seldom found more than three or four dominant buying behaviours present in any market for any product, which means that a small number of supply chain types is capable of covering up to 80 per cent of the market – no more, no less. And, although customers had a preferred way of working (based on their deep-rooted values), situations can still arise that cause them to change their behaviour (but not their values) for short periods – which then requires different supply chain solutions. See my broader concept depicted in Figure 8.1.

As we have seen in earlier chapters, in order to 'align' with the four main behavioural segments identified in my fieldwork, there are four discrete types of supply chain configurations – *continuous replenishment, lean, agile* and *fully flexible.*

1. *Agile and lean* For those customers who genuinely seek lowest-cost product (acquisition and fulfilment), lean is the solution for them. By definition, we are generally dealing with a relatively predictable market environment – a risk-averse customer with a transactional mindset – so there is a lot of emphasis on making and fulfilling to forecast, creating scale and using process improvement techniques such as Six Sigma to lower costs along the chain. Cost-efficiency is the dominant value shared by both customers and the supplying organization in this type of operating environment. More importantly, the underpinning subculture essential to successfully execute a low-cost solution for the customer is one that demands removal of all waste and involves routine processes, backed up by a 'cost-controller' leadership mentality. But the more you cut cost the more brittle the supply chain becomes, and the lesser its ability to flex and respond rapidly to sudden changes in demand. Fortunately, there is always likely to be a sizable segment of customer/market combinations that demand a consistent low-cost response.

The identified
dominant buying
behaviours in the
user/consumer base

The portfolio of
different service
strategies designed to
respond to identified
buying behaviours

The distinctly
different subcultures
required to underpin
the corresponding
value propositions

The different
leadership styles that
are required to shape
the corresponding sub
cultures

'User Segmentation'

'Value propositions'

'Internal Capabilities'

'Shape & create'

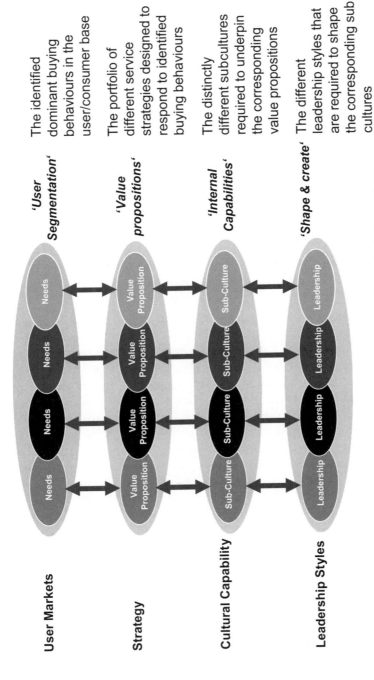

User Markets

Strategy

Cultural Capability

Leadership Styles

Supply-side supply chains are the mirror image of demand-side supply chains depicted here

Figure 8.1   Multiple supply chain alignment on the customer side

On the other hand, for those customers (it can be the same cost-driven customers albeit in a different situation) with values that are dominated by a requirement for speed, taking risk, a low emphasis on relationships and time-sensitivity, we need something very different in this case – an 'agile' response. I largely agree with Lee's definition[6] of 'agile' and the six rules of thumb to develop this property, although it is difficult to see how collaborative relationships can flourish in this customer segment as they come and go on an ad hoc basis. There is no loyalty here. However, there is a better chance of collaborating with suppliers (if you wish to do so) because in that particular situation, you are the buyer/customer!

Lee also provides examples[7] of major unpredictable and unplannable disruptions that have occurred – 9/11, SARS and natural disasters in general. Here, I think we are dealing with a special case of 'super-agility' which requires an additional category of market segment and a corresponding supply chain configuration. In my work in this area I and my co-workers have discovered what I describe as the fully flexible supply chain.[8] It has two variants – 'business event' and 'emergency response/humanitarian' supply chains. We have covered the humanitarian variant of fully flexible supply chains in great detail in Chapters 5, 6 and 7. For more details I refer the reader to Chapter 8 in my earlier book.[9]

2. *Adaptability (or is it flexibility?)* This is the term I am having the most difficulty with in Lee's Triple-A nomenclature. If there are structural shifts in a marketplace, which in turn are likely to drive the reshaping of the behavioural segment mix for a particular product/service category, then you simply engage a different supply chain configuration. For example, if a loyal customer is being served by the continuous replenishment supply chain, and that customer, for whatever reason, shifts across to, say, the low-cost/efficiency segment, you simply recognize that fact and 'engage' the lean supply chain lever. Or if a customer in the low-cost/efficiency segment experiences a major disruption (as in the case of Nokia and Ericsson quoted by Lee[10]), then the customer effectively moves to the innovative solutions type of behavioural segment and we engage the fully flexible supply chain configuration. Indeed, whether you call it 'adaptability' or 'flexibility', what you have to do in essence is shift gears from one type of supply chain configuration to another – fast. This is the 'quick-change supply chain in action, and it requires some smart organization design. Some leading enterprises are already in this mode.

This is a key discussion point because the word 'flexibility' gets bandied around a lot in the supply chain vernacular, and you have to ask yourself: what does it really mean in practice? In my view, what it does *not* mean is to bend and squeeze your current 'one-size-fits-all' supply chain configuration to fit every customer demand coming your way – that creates hundreds, perhaps thousands, of exceptions, which in turn drives costs up just when you are trying to get your cost-to-serve down!

What it does mean in an operational sense is to have your business 'hard-wired' with three, perhaps four, different supply chain configurations as depicted in Figure 8.1 and simply engage customers with the particular configuration most appropriate to their buying behaviour (or mindset) at that time. This approach doesn't change the original principle of no more that three or four supply chain configurations. Indeed, this is the very essence of 'dynamic alignment',[11] something we have been seeking to understand and explain in the marketing arena for a long time.

To be fair, Lee gets close when he remarks that '...smart companies tailor supply chains to the nature of markets and products'.[12] However, I disagree with his observation that '[they] usually end up with more than one supply chain, which can be expensive...'[13] Indeed, quite to the contrary, if we are able to eliminate overservicing in lean and agile-type supply chains, recognize underservicing in continuous replenishment supply chains and be paid the appropriate prices in each case, margins overall will improve significantly. We found as much at DHL Taiwan.[14]

The examples that Lee mentions, where companies develop different supply chain strategies around their different brands, is valid and quite consistent with my view that you use only the appropriate supply chain configuration in each market/customer situation.

In the end, it is all about keeping your eye on the marketplace and the customers within. Amazingly, and contrary to popular opinion, if you do that, things seem to move slowly and you rarely get caught out. Try watching grass grow – it's quite slow. But take your eye off the back lawn and go away for the weekend, and look at the grass when you return!

3. *Alignment* In my vernacular, 'Alignment' is the overarching organizing principle that needs to be applied to drive business success – that is, aligning your strategies, internal subcultures and leadership styles, with customers, suppliers and third-party providers in the marketplace. It is the only way to achieve sustained operational and (therefore) bottom-line performance.

    Under this broader definition of 'alignment' – indeed, 'dynamic alignment' – the related concepts of 'agility' and 'adaptability', as used by Lee, are simply constituent components, at a different (lower) level in the scheme of things. This differentiation is depicted in Figure 8.2. Indeed, taken together, the latter two properties provide the dynamism in 'dynamic' alignment, which explains a lot in the context of how supply chains must actually work in the real world.

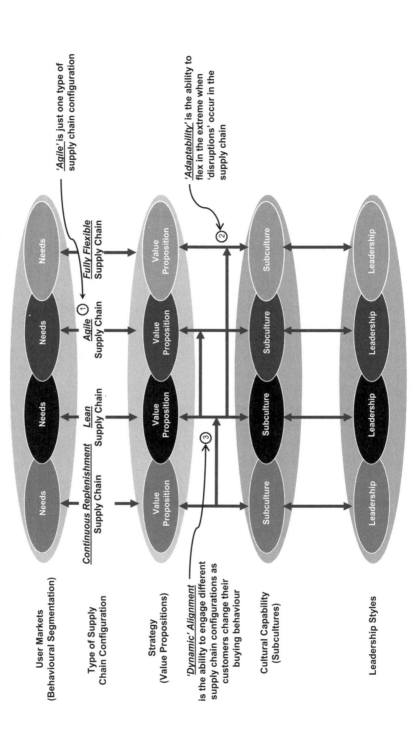

Figure 8.2   Revised definitions for 'agility', 'adaptability' and 'dynamic alignment'

My concept of 'dynamic alignment' therefore goes well beyond Lee's narrower interpretation which focuses mainly on aligning the 'interests' of all firms in their respective supply chains. I agree with that, but first we have to align the internal resources of the firm to have any chance of delivering high performance on a consistent and sustainable basis. And when it comes to aligning with customers downstream in the chain, we need different value propositions to address the range of buying behaviours evident in the target market. The same applies upstream when we are the buyers and seeking products and services from our source markets.

'The internal structure has to be a mirror image of the external structure – that is what "alignment" is ultimately all about!'

In truth, the missing link in Lee's article is a comprehensive explanation of how the internal culture of the firm plays such a pivotal role in executing these value propositions. That's really why so many of the firms he quotes in his article have been successful – cultural considerations are at the root of their success, but we only see the tangible results that emerge as the end result. Financial success is only a lagging indicator after all.

So let's step into where all these 'forces of darkness' live and operate. My research and experience indicates that there are at least 11 levers to pull in order to shape a particular subculture, all of which are well known in their own right – no mysteries there. However, the 'secret sauce' is in knowing which ones to pull, and in what sequence. And, of course, you need some point of reference to guide you in this process – namely, an understanding of the structure of the marketplace and the particular mix of dominant buying behaviours present. For best results the internal structure has to be a mirror image of the external structure – that is what 'alignment' is ultimately all about! The 11 levers are as follows: organization design; positioning of individual people within the structure; processes; IT systems; internal communication styles; KPIs and corresponding incentives; training and development; role modelling; recruitment; and the influence of leadership style.[15]

All of these components are well known in their own right, but the potentially different recipes are understood by few executives, and that is why we have seen very few successful business transformations over the last few decades. The problem is that reconfiguring the prevailing corporate culture in an organization into, say, three or possibly four subcultures in order to properly underpin newly configured supply chains takes time. To give you some idea, it took three years to achieve full alignment in an organization of 10,000 people. You can change the strategies on a Saturday afternoon, but it takes much longer to get the required subcultures in place and in a fit state to propel these strategies into your target market. Indeed, it is no coincidence that the best-performing enterprise supply chains in the last decade have come from firms which did not exist a generation ago. Hence, they were able to start with a clean sheet and design their supply chains from a zero-base, without legacy cultures to hinder progress. The old 'bricks and mortar' companies have mostly struggled for this very reason, and this reason alone. And they will continue to struggle unless new leadership cuts through the old conventions that are so deeply embedded.

Clearly, based on their respective records, companies like Zara (Spain), Li & Fung (Hong Kong), Adidas (Germany), JBS (Brazil), Dell (US), and 7-11 (Japan) have discovered how to mix the 'secret sauce' of culture. They know that, in the end, it is people and their leadership that matter most if the enterprise is to deliver ever-improving operational and financial performance.

ALIGNMENT INSIGHTS

- *'Agile' is just one of a number of different types of supply chain configuration.*

- *'Adaptability' is the ability to flex in the extreme when disruptions occur in enterprise supply chains.*

- *'Dynamic alignment' is the ability to engage different supply chain configurations as customers change their buying behaviours, for whatever reason. It is the overarching organizing construct.*

- *Above all, it is the deeper understanding of what is going on in the subterranean area of the enterprise, the engine room, that provides a predictive capability to guide management decision-making in an otherwise incoherent world, and leads directly to improved performance. There are no mysteries here except an ignorance of how culture influences the execution of strategy.*

NOTES

1   Adapted from 'The triple-A supply chain revisited', *Supply Chain Asia* (November/December), 2008, pp. 38–41.

2   Hau L. Lee, 'The triple-A supply chain', *Harvard Business Review* (October 2004), pp. 102–112.

3   Ibid., p. 112.

4   Ibid., p. 105.

5   Details of this emerging concept were first published in: J.L. Gattorna and D.W. Walters, *Managing the Supply Chain: A Strategic Perspective*, Macmillan Press, London, 1996; and J.L. Gattorna, *Strategic Supply Chain Alignment*, Gower Publishing, Aldershot, 1998.

6   Lee, 'The triple-A supply chain, *op. cit.*, p. 105.

7   Ibid., p. 106.

8   Primarily Kate Hughes who is doing her doctoral research at Macquarie Graduate School of Management, Sydney, Australia.

9   See J.L. Gattorna, *Living Supply Chains*, FT Prentice Hall, Harlow, 2006, Ch. 8.

10 Lee, 'The triple-A supply chain', *op. cit.*, p. 106.

11 I coined the term 'dynamic alignment' (previously 'strategic alignment') in 2005 and published early details of how it works in J.L. Gattorna. *Living Supply Chains, op. cit.*

12 Lee, 'The triple-A supply chain', *op. cit.*, p. 108.

13 Ibid.

14 See Chapter 16 for more details. DHL Taiwan was providing a largely fast express service to all customers. However, we discovered in fieldwork that this type of singular focus was overservicing some customers and disaffecting others who simply wanted a reliable relationship-driven service.

15 See J.L. Gattorna, *Living Supply Chains, op. cit.*, Ch. 3 for detailed descriptions of each of these cultural characteristics.

9 Designing Supply Chain Organizations for Peak Performance[1]

John Gattorna

I must be slow, because it has taken me over two decades of study, research and practice to come to the conclusion that the way we are organizing our supply chains is deeply flawed, and indeed we are setting ourselves up to fail from the outset by using conventional silo structures. It's akin to tackling a problem in the electronic age with the tools of a previous era, and no matter how you dress it up and fudge it, the results won't get better. So it's time to break the old models and try something new, just as some of our leading global companies have done and continue to do.

IN THE BEGINNING ...

Perhaps the best recent historical review I have seen recording the different types of organizational structures deployed in the logistics/supply chain arena is that of Soo Wook Kim.[2] He identified the following five types:

1. *non-SCM-oriented organization*, in which the main activities normally attributed to an SCM function are distributed across all the other functions;

2. *functional organization*, in which the supply chain function is just one of the functions, albeit on an equal footing;

3. *matrix channel organization*, in which the main SCM activities are distributed across all the other functions, and the SCM function plays a strictly coordinating role in a matrix-style format;

4. *process staff organization*, similar to the matrix channel organization, but with the SCM function receiving more prominence by reporting directly to the CEO/President;

5. *integrated line organization*, in which the SCM function encompasses the other main line functions and reports to the CEO/President.

It is clear from the five categories that the customer has not been at the centre of the minds of organizational theorists and practitioners as structures have evolved from distribution management in the 1960s, through logistics management in the 1980s, to supply chain management in the current era. If we search wider into the world of the organizational theorist we find Gareth Morgan's (2006)[3] work which provides a much richer and more eclectic perspective, using such metaphors as organizations as machines, organizations as (living) organisms, organizations as political systems and so on. His work, although not specifically directed at supply chains, provides useful insights into how we might reconceptualize supply chain structures to do the tasks required of them. It's a pity that designers of supply chain configurations have not invoked his work more widely. In any event, we are left with the impression from Morgan that the way organizations should shape their supply chain structures involves integrating more into the overall business design, and I agree with this proposition.

Perhaps the other major experiment in how to structure the way people work was started by Ricardo Semler at Semco in Brazil some 15 years ago and reported in both his 1993[4] and 2003[5] books. His suggested structure was unorthodox, indeed – akin to putting the inmates in charge of the asylum – but as noted author Charles Handy once commented, '... the way Ricardo Semler runs his company is impossible; except it works, and works splendidly for everyone'.[6] Semler believed in 'participative management' in which the workers, rather than management, would work out what should be done and do it for the company. He was bent on surfacing the creativity in his workers that tends to be lost in the conventional functional model. Interestingly, Semco is still thriving today, but few, if any, other corporations have followed his lead and adopted a similar structure.

BREAKING THE MOULD

'It is clear... that the customer has not been at the centre of the minds of organizational theorists and practitioners.'

It may not come as a surprise that the first enterprises to break with convention were in the fashion apparel business – because they had to, for survival. They hit the 'unpredictability ceiling' before most other industries. Two names come immediately to mind, and others are beginning to follow. A few words about each of these so-called 'pathfinders' follows below.

Zara

This Spanish-based company is taking the world by storm and has done wonders by showing how an enterprise can become more responsive to its customers than any of its competitors, by a country mile. And all this without any secret new technology or hitherto unknown processes. In the end, it's all about the way Zara's management mixes the recipe with otherwise known ingredients.

Zara came up with the idea of cross-functional teams to manage the design, production and delivery of the different apparel ranges to their target markets in women's fashion, men's fashion and children's wear. These teams worked closely with the store managers in the Zara retail chain and were co-located to facilitate rapid communications. The result: Zara is able to process a garment from sketch on paper to product in the store in 15 working days – none of its competitors can get anywhere near that. 'Postponement' techniques are invoked, coupled with lean supply chains on the in-bound side, but the end-result is an agile response to the changing fashion whims of their target consumers. A great success story, and one still in the making.

Vanity Fair

The VF Corporation is based in Greensboro, North Carolina, and is a leader in branded lifestyle apparel. This company also uses what it terms 'cross-coalition' teams to speed up their responsiveness to customers worldwide. In the process, the VF Corporation has effectively transformed itself from a manufacturing business (owning machines) to a sourcing business (owning brands) in less than a decade.[7]

Li & Fung

This Hong Kong-based company is perhaps the consummate example of using organization design to power growth. The Fung brothers coined the phrase 'network orchestrator' in their book, Competing in a Flat World.[8] They transformed the original trading business through rapid acquisitions and a new business model.

What Li & Fung has done is create 300 customer-oriented, multidisciplinary 'clusters' (or 'Little John Waynes' as it calls them). Each of these clusters of 50–60 personnel focus on one or more customers, and deliver revenue of $20–70 million.

On the customer side it has developed a genuinely customer-centric organization structure; and on the supply side these clusters focus on managing, and indeed owning, the relationships with nearly 10,000 factories worldwide. Li & Fung is therefore effectively the largest manufacturer in the world – and it doesn't own a single factory! With a very strong focus on customers, and an equally strong focus on supplier relationships, the company effectively orchestrates hundreds, perhaps thousands, of supply chains linking suppliers and customers to each other around the world.

More than anything else, the great success the company is now experiencing comes from the organization design which, by its very nature, focuses personnel '... on business challenges instead of functional (issues) that dominate in so many large organizations'.[9] Each of these clusters is interdisciplinary – full of self-starters who are highly incentivized through a remuneration package that is heavily weighted towards achieving results. Each cluster acts like the owner of their respective businesses, and is held together by a strong set of corporate values and financial disciplines. This is truly a success story quite unlike any other. But, even here, improvements and refinements are possible, and we will come to these a little later.

Adidas

In the run-up to the 2006 FIFA World Cup in Germany, the management at Adidas decided they had to design and implement a more responsive supply chain in order to capture the value of being one of the major sponsors of the four-yearly event. Traditionally, it had taken Adidas 120 days' lead-time to supply replica soccer shirts from a standing start. The management knew that this would not be good enough for the 2006 World Cup.

Jay Pollard, Lars Sorensen and their teams set about to break old business practices and produce a much faster, more responsive model.[10]

Here's how they did it:

- They set about instilling a change in mindset;

- They developed cross-functional fully integrated teams, with representatives from all disciplines.

- These newly formed teams were all co-located in the same building, called 'The World of Football'; this was done three years before the 2006 event.

- Sourcing offices around the world were similarly organized into clusters.

The new regime was road-tested at the 2004 European Cup, with incredible results. For example, 35,000 Greece replica shirts were produced in 20 days following Greece's unexpected win in the Cup final. This was an 80 per cent improvement over previous lead-times!

Adidas found that the new organization design allowed it to scale up and down faster, providing much greater flexibility than hitherto possible.

Overall, the lessons learned from this experiment were that, by throwing out the old 'silo' system and forming an end-to-end integrated supply chain with multidisciplinary clusters of personnel taking the product from design to shelf and into the consumers' hands, the operational and financial benefits were immense. Adidas now plans to replicate this method at future major sporting events.

Aera Energy LLC

Aera Energy LLC is a self-sufficient full-service oil and gas company based in California. The company was only formed in 1997, using assets jointly owned by Shell and Exxon Mobil.

The company was formed explicitly to extract oil from 'brownfields' – old fields that were being recharged – and to do so safely and at a low cost.

To achieve this objective Aera adopted a radically different approach to project management, and a similarly different attitude towards its suppliers.[11] In particular, the company adopted a variant of the cluster organization design discussed above, one they called the 'Daisy' organization structure as depicted in Figure 9.1.

The 'Daisy' organization structure focused and brought together all the processes in a particular project, from concept to implementation. Features of the 'Daisy' were:

- cross-functional teams

- all team members focused on particular process outcomes

- suppliers included as accountable team members.

The results have been nothing short of startling. The Belridge extraction project produced a 47 per cent reduction in drilling and completion costs, while achieving a similar reduction in health, safety, and environment (HSE) costs. Relentless execution led to these outstanding results, and the organization design was a prime reason for the success achieved in an otherwise difficult industrial operating environment.

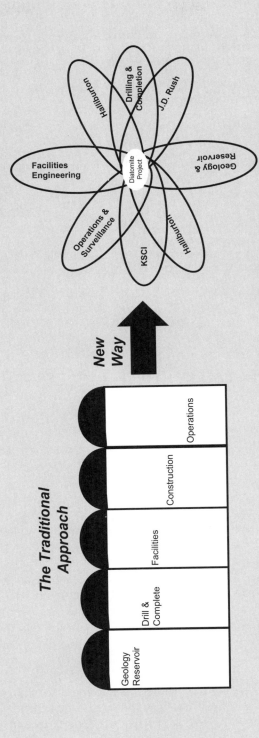

The Development Process Concept

The Traditional Approach

New Way

- Functional Teams
- Separate Plans, Separate (sometimes competing) Objectives
- Suppliers work in isolation from one another and are not a part of planning

- Process focuses on concept to implementation
- Cross-Functional Team
- Focused on Process Objectives
- Suppliers included as accountable team members – involved in planning

Figure 9.1   Adoption of the 'Daisy' organization structure at Aera

Source: 'Aera Energy: the next era in energy', http://www.aeraenergy.com.

> **Guidewire**
>
> This company is written up as a case study to demonstrate how a software company focusing on the global insurance industry managed to gain a dominant position through the development of a new project management process called 'Scrum'.[12]
>
> At the core of the 'Scrum' methodology is the so-called Sprint team. Each team is small, nimble and has no more than nine members.
>
> Every Scrum project starts with an understanding of the customer's vision – what outcome do they want?
>
> The customer and development team then defines the requirements to deliver this vision.
>
> The development team then works for 30 days (the 'sprint') to meet as many of the above stated requirements as possible. Meanwhile the customer continues to refine their vision to deliver the required business result.
>
> At the end of the first and every succeeding sprint, the customer and development teams review progress to check whether expected business value is being delivered.
>
> Finally, at some point the customer will stop the development process and the software product will be refined and released for wider use in the business. In this way, the customer is able to steer cost, date and business value on a continuous basis.

THE COMMON THREAD IN THESE SUCCESS STORIES?

All the above-described successful cases of fast responsive 'systems' had a common thread running through them – they all involved some type of 'team' design, composed of interdisciplinary personnel, all focused on a particular objective and incentivized by joint KPIs.

What has become clear is that (vertical) functional silos don't work because they are at least 90 degrees out of phase with the way in which customers buy (horizontally, across functions).

We became apathetic in the 1970s and 1980s, thinking we had the answers, and when organizations began to see that functional silos were not the panacea, we looked to weak matrix structures to compensate. However, while account managers working in matrix structures were well-meaning in their inscrutable focus on the customer, the rest of the organization did not share their enthusiasm.

Perhaps the only enterprises that did 'get it' were management consulting companies like Andersen Consulting (subsequently Accenture), which understood that you need both the vertical specialities to build capabilities and competences and the horizontal teams of mixed specialisms to go to market and solve individual client problems. From their successes we can conclude that you need *both* vertical silos of specialists *and* horizontal teams of mixed disciplines, depending on the exact nature of the customer's requirement. And this brings us full-circle back to the business of enterprise supply chains.

NEW SUPPLY CHAIN ORGANIZATION DESIGNS

What we need now are new supply chain organization designs for the new breed of supply chains as described in earlier chapters.

If it is true, as we propose, that there are a limited number of variants in customer buying behaviour patterns, and indeed that we mostly see the same three or four types irrespective of product/service category, then the way forward becomes clear. Now we can have the best of both worlds – strong functional specialisms where specific capabilities are developed and reside and customer-centric teams composed of representatives of all the appropriate functions necessary to fully 'align' with customer expectations.

So, for those relatively few customers whom we have identified as genuinely 'collaborative', we will engage the *continuous replenishment* supply chain, driven by 'clusters' of personnel seconded from the vertical functions. And here is the twist. Not only will all the functions be represented in these clusters (or teams), but we also have the opportunity to 'genetically' engineer the mindset of these clusters by taking into account the 'values' of each team member. It is not simply a matter of having all the technical skills covered; the right embedded bias in the team is just as important. This refinement goes beyond what Li & Fung is doing with its so-called 'Little John Waynes', but it is a necessary refinement to get maximum alignment with the customer's mindset, in this case driven by 'relationship' values. See Figure 9.2 for a schematic representation.

> '*The only enterprises that did "get it" ... understood that you need both the vertical specialities to build capabilities and competences and the horizontal teams of mixed specialisms to go to market.*'

Note the solid line drawn connecting the customer-centric 'relationships' clusters; they are accountable for meeting customer expectations, and the functions are there to support as required. The customer-centric clusters, however many there are, all report to a line executive, probably the COO or Global Customer Solutions Director. No more dotted lines for the customer-facing teams.

To service those customers in the *price-sensitive/efficiency* segment we need something very different. Here the emphasis is on refining the various processes involved to deliver the lowest possible cost-to-serve via the *lean* supply chain configuration. See Figure 9.3 for a schematic representation.

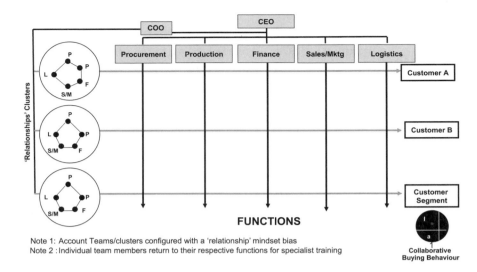

Figure 9.2   Continuous replenishment supply chain clusters

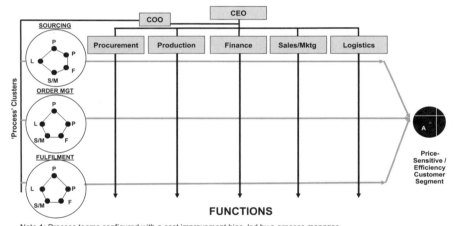

Figure 9.3   Lean supply chain clusters

As in the case of the continuous replenishment supply chain configuration, multidisciplinary clusters are formed. However, this time, each cluster focuses on a major process rather than a customer, and the various processes come together to deliver the lowest cost and most consistent service possible for that particular segment.

In order to satisfy those customers who demand a quick response in an otherwise unpredictable market place, we need something different again. In this situation, the multidisciplinary clusters are designed for speed, and the bias embedded in the *agile* supply chains serving these demanding customers is just that – speed. This approach is very much like Zara has done so successfully. See Figure 9.4 for a schematic representation.

It is possible that there will be subsets of the *demanding/speed* segment as depicted in Figure 9.4. For example, Zara has to service the demand for fashion in three different subsegments: women, men and children.

Finally, in cases of unexpected events or crises, the *fully flexible* supply chain configuration is required to deliver innovative solutions, super fast. See Figure 9.5 for a schematic representation.

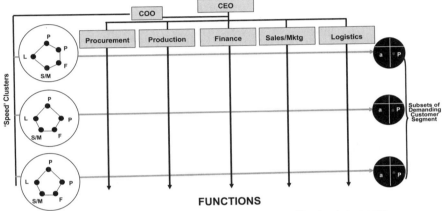

Note 1: Clusters are focused on different parts of the same segment but possibly different product categories
Note 2: Individual team members return to their respective functions for training and other specialist matters

Figure 9.4   Agile supply chain clusters

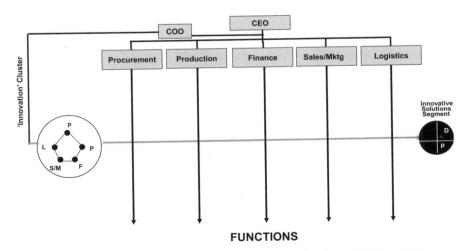

Note 1: This 'innovation' cluster may be composed of part time members who only convene in an emergency
Note 2: Individual team members return to their respective functions for training and other specialist matters

Figure 9.5   Fully flexible supply chain cluster

There may only be one cluster to service the *innovative solutions* segment and this could well be composed of part-time members or volunteers, who only come together in times of an emergency. The individuals in this cluster are likely to be highly trained multi-talented personnel, capable of quick thinking and quick action. There are plenty of examples of this type of structure in aid and military organizations all over the world.

BRINGING IT ALL TOGETHER

As discussed in earlier chapters, any given supply chain has an upstream supply-side component and a downstream demand-side component.

The key is to have in place organizational 'clusters' that power the different types of supply chain configurations based on customer demand patterns, and have mechanisms in place to link the various clusters in situations where supply chains are 'hybrid' in nature – that is, different on the supply side and the demand side, which is quite normal. This situation is depicted schematically in Figure 9.6 opposite.

> **ALIGNMENT INSIGHTS**
>
> - *Current organization designs for enterprise supply chains are fundamentally flawed because they assume a 'one-size-fits-all' world.*
>
> - *The only successful way to design supply chain organizations for the new world is to map the marketplace and the customer buying behaviours found there, and then try to reflect these with a corresponding structure on the inside of the organization.*
>
> - *In the end, the two structures (external and internal) need to coexist and support each other to properly service a disparate market.*
>
> - *The customer-centric clusters are multidisciplinary by nature – personnel are seconded into them from time to time to suit the particular customer type being served.*

NOTES

1 Adapted from 'Supply chain organization design – the secret sauce of peak performance' *Supply Chain Asia* (January/February 2009), pp. 15–20.
2 S.W. Kim, 'Organizational structures and the performance of supply chain management' *International Journal of Production Economics*, Vol. 106 (2007), pp. 323–345.
3 G. Morgan (2006), *Images of Organization*, Sage Publications, London.
4 R. Semler, *Maverick: The Success Story Behind the World's Most Unusual Workplace*, Warner Books, New York, 1993.

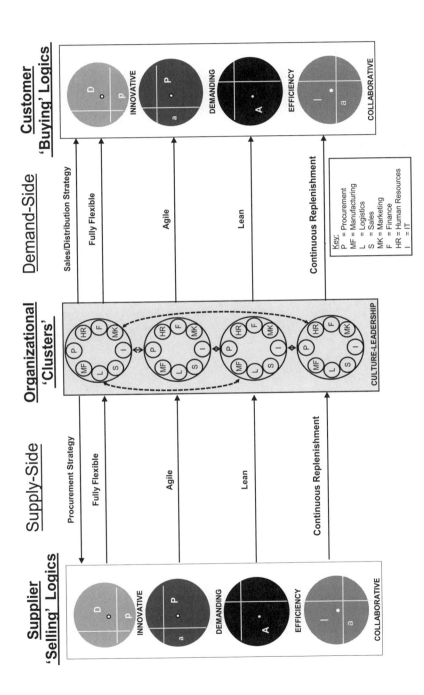

Figure 9.6   A new and dynamic business model for supply chains of the future

5   R. Semler, *The Seven-Day Weekend: Changing the Way Work Works*, Random House, London, 2003.

6   Commendation by Charles Handy, commenting on Ricardo Semler's first book, *Maverick, op. cit.*

7   One of the 'customers' for VF brands is Icon Clothing in Australia, a business unit of the Pacific Brands Group. This company, under visionary leadership, has done something similar – organizing and co-locating cross-functional teams around each individual brand. The result has been a significant improvement in operational and financial performance.

8   V.K. Fung, W.K. Fung and Y. Wind, *Competing in a Flat World*, Wharton School Publishing, Upper Saddle River, NJ, 2008.

9   Ibid., p. 86.

10 What they did is recorded in a seven-minute. DVD called: *The FIFA World Cup 2006 – The Ultimate Supply Chain Event.* Produced by Adidas and Deloitte, 2007.

11 See http://www.aeraenergy.com for more information.

12 *Guidewire (A): Sprinting to Success*: a case developed by IMD International, Lausanne, Switzerland, 2007, p. 12. Available at: http://www.effectuation.org/ftp/imd_p197878.pdf.

10 The Supply-side View and 'Reverse' Logistics

John Gattorna and Deborah Ellis

So far in this book we have tended to focus on the demand side because that is where the original signals that inform and guide us in the design of our enterprise supply chains come from. However, the 'supply-side' is just the mirror image of the 'demand side', as depicted in Figure 10.1. This means that we need to connect what we have learned about the markets we are serving to our source markets; otherwise everything gets out of synch.

The whole area of supply-side sourcing is coming back into focus once again as the world reels from the impact of the financial services melt-down on the real economy. Since the turn of the New Millennium, multinational corporations in particular have been pursuing global sourcing strategies in the relentless search for lower-cost sources of inputs to manufacturing. This in turn has had the effect of '... making supply chains longer and more fragmented, and this is exposing firms to greater costs and risks'.[1] The same research also found that most firms were still largely basing their procurement decisions on a minimum-price approach rather than a more sophisticated 'total cost of ownership'.[2] Finally, the same global trade appears to be significantly contributing to the emission of greenhouse gases because of the added transportation legs involved, and this flies in the face of efforts to reduce such emissions. Maybe we will see a change back to regional and local sourcing as a result of this new factor that is concerning the community at large. Indeed, from our own work we see a clear trend towards a subsegment within the overall 'collaborative' segment, that appears to be very empathetic towards the environment and will punish suppliers along the supply chain who do not take appropriate measures to minimize their carbon footprint.

SUPPLY-SIDE ALIGNMENT

Like demand-side alignment, supply-side alignment is multidimensional. It takes its lead from the market side and is depicted in Figure 10.2.

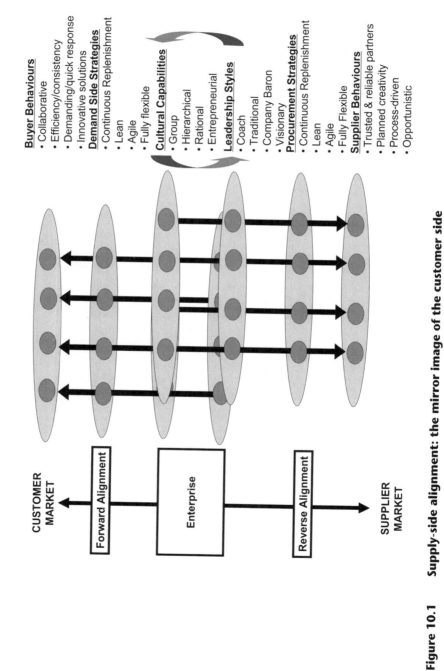

Buyer Behaviours
- Collaborative
- Efficiency/consistency
- Demanding/quick response
- Innovative solutions

Demand Side Strategies
- Continuous Replenishment
- Lean
- Agile
- Fully flexible

Cultural Capabilities
- Group
- Hierarchical
- Rational
- Entrepreneurial

Leadership Styles
- Coach
- Traditional
- Company Baron
- Visionary

Procurement Strategies
- Continuous Replenishment
- Lean
- Agile
- Fully Flexible

Supplier Behaviours
- Trusted & reliable partners
- Planned creativity
- Process-driven
- Opportunistic

CUSTOMER MARKET

Forward Alignment

Enterprise

Reverse Alignment

SUPPLIER MARKET

Figure 10.1   Supply-side alignment: the mirror image of the customer side

Source: Adapted from Figure 3.5.2 in J.L. Gattorna (ed.), *Gower Handbook of Supply Chain Management* (5th edn), Gower Publishing, Aldershot.

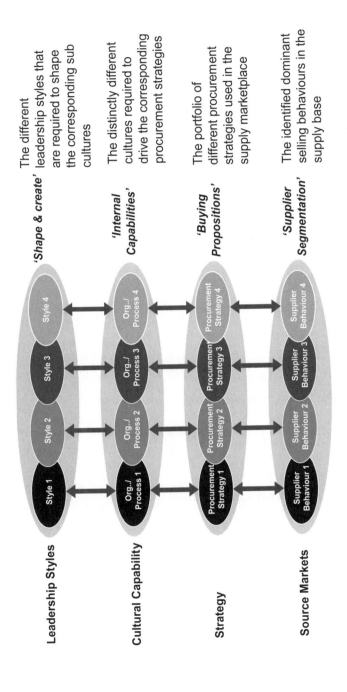

Leadership Styles — *'Shape & create'* — The different leadership styles that are required to shape the corresponding sub cultures

Cultural Capability — *'Internal Capabilities'* — The distinctly different cultures required to drive the corresponding procurement strategies

Strategy — *'Buying Propositions'* — The portfolio of different procurement strategies used in the supply marketplace

Source Markets — *'Supplier Segmentation'* — The identified dominant selling behaviours in the supply base

Figure 10.2   Reverse (procurement-side) multiple supply chain alignment

However, it seems that many of the activities practiced on the supply side (strategic sourcing, global sourcing, spend analyses and so on) have been taking place in a relative vacuum, with little direct reference to demand-side customer buying patterns. Even worse, assumptions are too often made inside the procurement side of the business about the assumed 'selling behaviour' of suppliers, and this leads directly to inappropriate procurement strategies. For example, Brazil's largest meat processor was endeavouring to gain a larger share of the domestic cattle herd for slaughter, and the conventional wisdom inside the firm was that all ranchers (suppliers) were sensitive to the price they are paid and would move to the buyer who offers a few more dollars per head. When a behavioural segmentation of sellers was undertaken, the results were quite unexpected. Over three-quarters of the ranchers were found to be inclined towards some element of relationship with the buyer and were open to a service package involving different combinations of technical assistance, training and development, credit and other non-price factors. As a result, the buying company was able to adjust its procurement strategies to reflect these underlying buying preferences and thereby better align with the supply market.

THE FOUR GENERIC SUPPLY-SIDE CHAINS

The four generic supply-side chains are just the mirror image of the demand-side; see Figure 10.3. The aligned procurement propositions are as indicated in the diagram.

HYBRID SUPPLY CHAINS

In the end, the most common situation in industry is that different combinations of demand-side and supply-side supply chain elements occur.

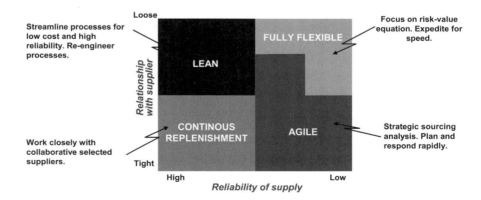

Figure 10.3   Four generic supply chains (procurement-side)

It is rare to see a pure lean or pure agile supply chain all the way through. This then brings into focus the question of organization structure that we have already covered in Chapter 9. Suffice to say that our recommendation is that enterprises embrace the multidisciplinary cluster design as discussed earlier, and depicted again in Figure 10.4.

'Almost all supply chains have a component of reverse movement, and both the level and the significance of reverse movement in supply chains is growing.'

As depicted, the individual clusters are designed around the characteristics in both the customer and supplier segments, in a pure sense. However, where there is a mix of different elements, say *lean* on the supply side and *agile* on the demand side, then the corresponding clusters will work in a coordinated way to get the desired alignment *at both ends*. This is the innovative new aspect in supply chain management that has the potential to lift performance by a quantum leap.

REVERSE LOGISTICS: BOTH DEMAND- AND SUPPLY-SIDE

Our concept of the supply chain is steeped in analogies associated with forward movement. We consider pipelines and flows and distribution and delivery – even the term 'supply' puts us in mind of activity leading to a final destination (inevitably, at some point, the customer). Increasingly, however, this concept misrepresents the real activity involved. Almost all supply chains have a component of reverse movement, and both the level and the significance of reverse movement in supply chains is growing.

Reverse logistics is a complex part of any operation, not least because it often involves the retailers or manufacturer's customers and suppliers – parties that are usually kept at arm's length. This demand-side/supply-side intersection also operates with logics and imperatives quite different to those of the rest of the operation.

Until recently, 'reverse logistics' referred to the return of product and packaging from either an intermediate or final customer to an upstream supplier to recover value or enable disposal. Wider definitions are now more appropriate to reflect the type of activity occurring and the range of opportunities being explored. An up-to-date definition might thus include the activities undertaken to avoid returns (such as in the terms of trade), the management of 'life-cycle' issues (such as the materials or the amount of packaging used) in the forward system so that less flows back, and the management of reuse and recycling to minimize environmental impact and/ or provide inputs to manufacturing.

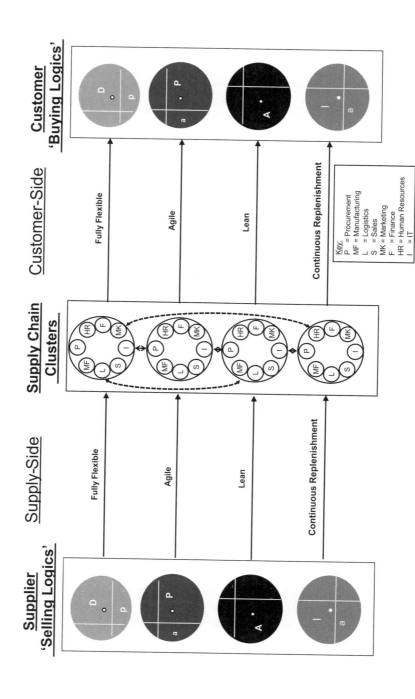

Figure 10.4 **New and dynamic business model for supply chains of the future**

Scale

The scale of reverse movements is significant. Even under the base definition of returns to recover value or enable disposal, the level is thought to be of the order of 15–20 per cent of the forward volume[3] and has been estimated to account for 4 per cent of total logistics cost in the US.[4] The level appears to be growing at a considerable rate. Federal Express, for example, has seen a 12 per cent increase in its returns business in the US in recent years.[5]

The growth in the level of reverse movements is deriving from shifts in product, consumer and market patterns and from increasing environmental pressures. The increased share of purchases undertaken via consumer direct channels (particularly the Internet) is thought to have been accompanied by high levels of returns related to sight-unseen purchasing. Shorter product life cycles, accompanied by increasing 'life-cycle responsibility', is driving higher levels of returns of electronics, phones and their associated peripherals such as printer cartridges and batteries. This has been reinforced by legislation in some places, examples being the EU Waste Electrical and Electronic Equipment Directive (WEEE), Japan's Household Appliance Recycling Law of 2001 and California's Electronic Waste Recycling Act of 2003.

Closed-loop systems (such as that associated with pallet pooling) are also expected to become more common as packaging becomes a key focus for reducing environmental impact.

State of Play

In many organizations the reverse logistics operation is at the stage of development of the logistics operation of 15–20 years ago. Activities and responsibility is fragmented, there is little data capture or analysis of cost or impact and there is little visibility across the organization. Possibly the most concerning issue, however, is the impact they can have on the forward operation. Return movements are typically irregular, which means they are time- and resource-intensive, and in mixed operations this need to respond intermittently usually draws that time and resources from the forward operation.

Objectives of a Reverse Operation

The objectives for a reverse operation vary by situation, but would typically include some or all of the following:

- Minimize the *net* financial impact:
    - minimize the cost of reverse movement; and/or
    - maximize revenue recouped; and/or
    - minimize inefficiencies caused by disturbance to other parts of the operation.

- Minimize reputation damage; protect brand; maintain customer loyalty.

- Meet legislative requirements.

- Minimize the environmental impact of the product across the life cycle.

Very often returns are actually managed only with a cost minimization objective, but more comprehensive consideration should also consider the wider impacts and opportunities.

THE IMPLICATIONS OF LIFE-CYCLE RESPONSIBILITY

As noted earlier, the growing recognition of the manufacturer's responsibility for a product through its life cycle of use is likely to drive a much higher level of reverse movements, but it should also drive change throughout the processes from design to disposal and even much broader considerations of the market need and how best to satisfy it over time.

At the design stage the focus is on the materials and packaging used and on increasing the options for recycling, reuse or refurbishment and on reducing the use of hazardous material.

Through the logistics process this responsibility will drive network designs that coordinate both forward and reverse movements with much more emphasis on the reverse process than in the past.

The life-cycle focus on how consumers and industrial customers use products and the basic need being fulfilled, together with the cost impact of end-of-life responsibility may, in some cases, suggest opportunities to replace product ownership with creative service offerings.

THE RETURNS PROCESS

The basic returns process involves screening, collection, sorting and disposition.[6] The effectiveness of each stage depends on clear guidelines. An absence of routing instructions at the very first stage of local screening, for example, results in products entering the reverse flow and accumulating cost only to ultimately end up in the same landfill site that they could have been directed to, possibly weeks earlier.

Figure 10.5 indicates the priorities at each stage to support an effective process. One of the major issues that constrain efficiency is the loss of product identity. Products are often returned without packaging or in a damaged condition, and thus their original item code is unknown. This precludes the

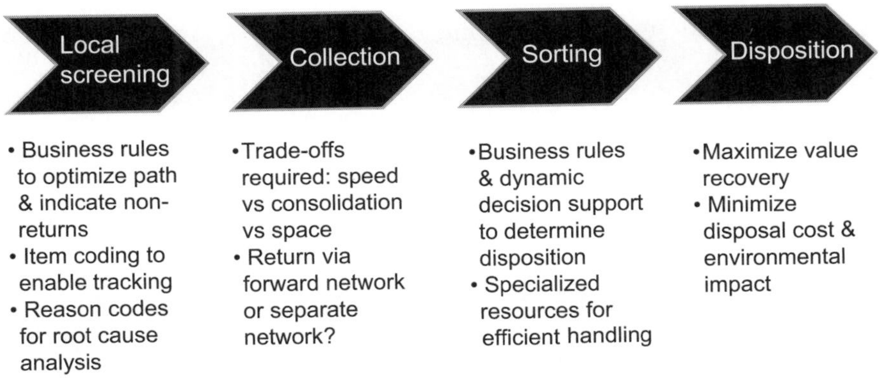

Local screening	Collection	Sorting	Disposition
• Business rules to optimize path & indicate non-returns • Item coding to enable tracking • Reason codes for root cause analysis	•Trade-offs required: speed vs consolidation vs space • Return via forward network or separate network?	•Business rules & dynamic decision support to determine disposition • Specialized resources for efficient handling	•Maximize value recovery • Minimize disposal cost & environmental impact

Figure 10.5   The returns process

item from tracking and from the usual analysis that supports sound supply chain decision-making. Coding systems need to be created that systematically capture some level of information about returned products to enable visibility, control and process development.

Innovative solutions are starting to develop for the last stage of the process, the disposition stage. Options for various conditions of finished goods include:

- Sell-as-is: resale through normal channels. via outlets or discount channels, via e-auction, via secondary markets (for example, the 'trailing edge' technology markets).

- Reuse: repair, refurbish, remanufacture or modify, recycle components.

- Dispose: scrap, donate, secure disposal.

TAKING A STRATEGIC VIEW

Reverse movements and returns need to be understood and managed strategically in the same way as the forward supply chain. The reverse flow transits a network of facilities (see Figure 10.6), has underlying patterns of activity (which, once appreciated, can be proactively managed) and is best handled with specialized capabilities. Clarity is required around the financial impact: the total reverse cost should be identifiable, and the per-unit cost should be monitored over time to enable changes to be identified and process improvements to be assessed.

Finally, a clear set of strategies around the major types of reverse movements are needed in order to optimize the financial and sustainability impact and to protect the core operation.

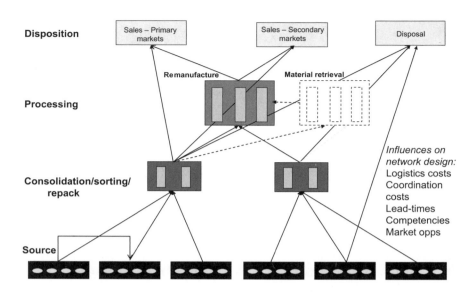

Figure 10.6   Defining and optimizing the reverse logistics network

The supply chain alignment 'logics' are an appropriate way of assessing and interpreting the type of operation and strategies that are most suitable for the different types of reverse movements. Figure 10.7 summarizes the implied reverse paths and the situations where each is likely to be suitable, and the four paths are discussed in a little more detail below.

The Agile Return Path – Where Time is the Key Driver

Where there is an opportunity for resale, *time* is usually the key driver in the returns process.

Studies undertaken on the Hewlett Packard Equipment Management and Remarketing (EMR) operation[7] found that laptops being refurbished for resale in secondary markets could take over four months through the various phases of staging and processing before being made available for sale. Obviously, the recovery value of computer equipment deteriorates rapidly and time lost is value lost in these markets. One source of delay in this process was the use of the same manufacturer for refurbishment as for original equipment production. Inevitably, new production was given a higher priority. A complicating factor in this market was also management's perception that they needed to limit sales of refurbished items to hold the price of new laptops up. Analysis as part of this study, however, found that the markets for each were different and there was little substance to this concern.

Time-sensitive returns should be treated as a value stream, not a waste stream. The priority is to manage lead-times, avoid bottlenecks and support the operation with a flexible organization structure geared around identifying and quickly capturing market opportunities.

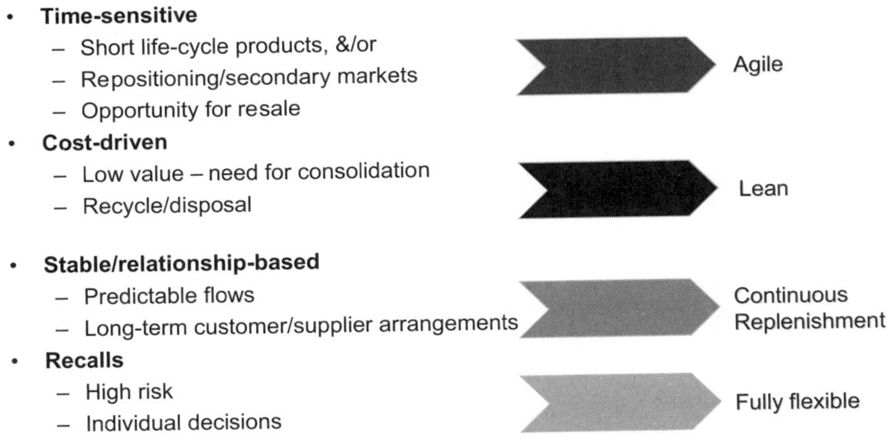

- **Time-sensitive**
  - Short life-cycle products, &/or
  - Repositioning/secondary markets
  - Opportunity for resale

Agile

- **Cost-driven**
  - Low value – need for consolidation
  - Recycle/disposal

Lean

- **Stable/relationship-based**
  - Predictable flows
  - Long-term customer/supplier arrangements

Continuous
Replenishment

- **Recalls**
  - High risk
  - Individual decisions

Fully flexible

Figure 10.7   Using 'logics' to interpret the appropriate reverse paths

The Lean Return Path – Where Cost is the Key Driver

Where items are expected to have no reclaimable value, or for regular and stable recycling of low-value inputs, the key driver is usually *cost*, and the emphasis is on routine patterns with minimal need for management intervention.

The household waste recycling process in which paper, glass, steel and aluminium are removed on a regular weekly/fortnightly basis and directed through a predictable separation process should be designed around the reliability and rigour of a lean path.

The Continuous Replenishment Return Path – Where Relationships are the Key Driver

Case Study: Bessemer

Bessemer is an Australian company that has made and distributed premium quality aluminum cookware for 40 years. They offer customers a 40 per cent discount on a new product with a trade-in of an existing product. Many of their customers are loyal devotees of their product, and this very attractive incentive keeps them repurchasing. As the items have a longer-than-normal life cycle, however, the repurchase period may be 8–10 years after the original sale.

On many dimensions this is a very savvy approach. Aluminum from returns constitute a third of Bessemer's total aluminum used in production. The cost per tonne at the time of writing (February 2009) of new aluminum was approximately US$1300. Recycled product also requires considerably less processing in the initial stages of production than new input material. The overall economics of the closed-loop recycled system are thus very attractive. The offer also enhances the 'premium' brand image by providing an additional benefit, and the recycling policy positions Bessemer as a responsible manager across the full life cycle of the product.

The return path is supported by the extensive national network used for forward movements, and the complexity is minimized because the returned item is introduced into the return path when it is exchanged for the new item. When each depot reaches an economic transfer quantity (usually a pallet), the items are dispatched, mostly with the vehicle delivering new stock. The quantities returned, after many years of this operation, are quite predictable

This is a classic example of leveraging a loyal customer base appropriately and developing a stable and cost-effective return operation around that relationship. The continuous replenishment return path will often be built on dependencies. In this case the manufacturing operation is highly dependent on the returns as inputs, and the marketing arm is dependent on the incentive to maintain and build an ongoing relationship with customers. Stable patterns also lend themselves to fine-tuning based around analytics, and in this case the variability of supply would be a key element in the analysis.

The Fully Flexible Return Path – Where It's All About Risk

Whereas the *fully flexible* supply chain features rarely in the forward supply chain, in the reverse supply chain it is a feature of every major manufacturers armoury – but hopefully only in their contingency plans. A fully flexible path requires fast, dynamic and creative responses to unforeseen situations. For most companies this means recall programmes, natural disasters or other similarly high-risk situations.

The recall programme is an important reverse logistics situation. It requires detailed contingency planning with specialized arrangements, as well as capacity commitments from logistics providers that can be turned on immediately they are needed. Despite all the planning, however, when the situation arises it will inevitably also require creative and fast decisions responding to the particulars of the event. Reputational risk is so high in these situations that cost cannot be a consideration.

NEW BUSINESS MODELS

The different requirements and opportunities associated with reverse movements are increasingly driving the separation of returns from mainstream operations into specialized streams of activity. The traditional business model is often not suitable to meet the requirements of this type of activity, and often the volumes are small or it is impractical to separate returns back to the original producer (as in the case of household recycling). In other situations a specialist body of knowledge develops around disposition – for example, recycling technology or placements into secondary markets. In response to these opportunities and constraints new businesses and new business models, focused on various aspects of reverse logistics, are emerging.

For example, in the electronics sector, companies have been formed that provide return and repair and/or warranty services for several competing businesses. Some of these start life servicing one dedicated client and then extend to non-competing and competing companies later as they chase efficiencies. Highpoint Australia, for instance, was originally formed to service its own returns (that is, Acer computers), extended the offer to non-competing companies (such as Palm and D-Link) and now also provide services for their competitors (such as LG and Benq).

The TIC Group in Australia is a third-party providing reverse logistics services to retailers. They clear stores of both product and packaging (for example, clothes hangers), sort off-site and arrange returns to vendors. The congestion and damage at store level caused by accumulating stock is reduced, and the complexity of sorting and chasing multiple vendors is alleviated.

Multis Product Sustainment Services provides product return streams and remarketing into secondary markets for HP, Sun and NEI in parts of Europe and the US. The company could possibly be described as a 'reverse distributor', with a body of market knowledge and access to customers that the original manufacturers cannot cost-effectively access.

ALIGNMENT INSIGHTS

- *The supply-side element of the overall supply chain is just the mirror image of the demand-side. This means that we need to apply what we have learned about the markets we are serving, to our source markets. For best results, both sides of the equation must be in synch.*

- *Reverse logistics has become a more complex topic than even a few years ago. For many organizations it is no longer a fringe activity and no longer just a cost-generating liability. For many it is a core element in their environmental response, and for others it is also a potential source of revenue.*

- *Effective return operations demand the same clear paths and processes as forward logistics; however, they will often have different drivers and are thus best managed through specialized streams of activity. True cost and value depletion need to be known, and clear disposition strategies are required for an effective operation.*

- *The potential for cost and revenue impacts, the transition to a paradigm of life-cycle responsibility and the growing awareness of risk in the supply chain all suggest that reverse logistics is likely to move up the supply chain agenda in the coming decade. As that occurs, it is unlikely that simply replicating the approaches used to develop the forward logistics operation will be appropriate, and innovation in processes and even new business models will be required.*

NOTES

1   M. Christopher et al. (2007) *Global Sourcing and Logistics*, Research Report, Cranfield School of Management, May 2007, p. 3.

2   Ibid.

3   C.D. Norek (2002), 'Returns management: making order out of chaos', *Supply Chain Management Review*, Vol. 6, No. 3, pp. 34–42.

4   O. Schatteman, 'Reverse logistics' in J.L. Gattorna (ed.) (2003), *Gower Handbook of Supply Chain Management* (5th edn). Gower Publishing, Aldershot, p. 267

5   S. Murray, 'Hidden beauty of the "uglies"', *Financial Times*, London, 17 May 2007, p. 16. Retrieved 1 March 2009 from AB/INFORM global database (Document ID: 1272705971).

6   Schatteman, 'Reverse logistics', *op. cit.*, p. 272.

7   V. Daniel, R. Guide Jr, L. Muyldermans and L.N. van Wassenhove, 'Hewlett-Packard company unlocks the value potential from time-sensitive returns', *Interfaces*, Vol. 35 (July/August 2005), pp. 281–293.

11 Sales and Operations Planning: The Critical Ingredient in Supply Chain Operations

Scott Githens

In this chapter we will take a brief journey into the principles and application of sales and operations planning (S&OP), the benefits that can be derived from S&OP and the application of S&OP principles to the four generic supply chains. For those supply chain types that operate within an environment of reasonable certainty – continuous replenishment and lean – the S&OP framework provides a powerful method of integrating and balancing decision-making across functions and organizations. For those supply chain types operating in a less certain environment – agile and fully flexible – the S&OP framework provides a powerful method of managing and allocating capacity to maximize customer service and financial and humanitarian outcomes.

Before applying S&OP thinking to each supply chain type, it is worth understanding what S&OP and its critical components are.

SUPPLY CHAIN PLANNING WITHOUT S&OP

Let's work through a hypothetical, yet all too common, scenario that illustrates how many organizations conduct supply chain and related planning:

1. The marketing department has a plan to increase sales volume over the next six months to bring sales back on budget. It will drive this demand through a television advertisement campaign.

2. The sales organization is not aware of this television campaign and its sales plans reflect steady sales, except in month 4 when they plan to offer a volume discount on sales above a certain volume to fill a gap in their forecast to budget.

3. The factory has a long history of developing its own forecast of what it needs to produce. Now is no different and its volume forecast, based on 'years of experience', does not include any of the volume increases that may be driven by the marketing and sales activity.

4. The third-party logistics provider (3PL), which supplies warehousing and line-haul freight services to the organization has its own volume plan.

5. The finance department of this organization has its own financial forecast. This is developed within the financial organization, thus not taking into account what sales or marketing plan to sell, or what the factory plans to produce.

'S&OP is a framework or process that allows an organization to develop a set of "do-able" or constrained, integrated plans.'

The outcome of this scenario is likely to include an increase in demand over the next six months, with a spike in month 4. The factory is not able to support this increase in demand without pre-build, which it did not do as it was not aware of the need until actual customer orders started to arrive. The result: delivery failures and lost customer orders. The shortage at the factory is not necessarily a bad thing from the 3PL's perspective, as it had neither the trucks nor warehouse space to cope with the month 4 volumes anyway. The CEO and board are frustrated as budget is not being met, and senior functional management are equally frustrated as their plans are not being achieved.

Surely there is a better way to run an organization? The answer is 'Yes, there is', and the solution is sales and operations planning (S&OP).

WHAT IS S&OP?

Essentially S&OP is a framework or process that allows an organization to develop a set of 'do-able' or constrained, integrated plans. These plans ensure that the organization's functions are all working towards the same goals and that the organization's capacity is optimized and best configured to meet the agreed strategic direction.[1]

Let's revisit the scenario introduced previously and see how this would play out in an organization using an S&OP approach.

1. The marketing department has a plan to increase sales volume over the next six months to bring sales back on budget by increasing consumer demand through a television advertisement campaign. It works with the sales organization to integrate this marketing plan into an overall sales plan that includes an increase in demand in month 4 due to a volume discount offer.

2. This sales plan is communicated to the factory via the S&OP process. The factory compares the sales plan to capacity and realizes that the spike in demand in month 4 will exceed production capacity. It also calculates that it has enough capacity to accommodate the month

4 spike if it produces and stores additional product in months 3 and 4.

3. The updated production plan is communicated to the 3PL via the S&OP process. The 3PL compares the production plan to capacity and realizes that the additional production in months 3 and 4 will exceed vehicle capacity. It calculates that it has enough vehicle capacity if the additional demand is spread over months 2, 3 and 4. This is run past the factory which confirms that it is capable of starting the stock build in month 2.

4. The sales plan with the spike in demand in month 4, together with the supporting production plan showing a stock build in months 2, 3 and 4, is communicated to the finance department. These plans are used to develop the financial forecast incorporating sales, working capital (inventory) and factory costs/utilization.

Result: additional demand in month 4 being supported from stock produced and distributed in months 2, 3 and 4, thus maintaining customer service as well as allowing delivery against budget and individual functional plans. The CEO and board are happy as the budget is being met, and senior functional management are happy as their plans are being achieved.

OVERVIEW & WALKTHROUGH OF S&OP

As discussed, S&OP is a framework or process that allows an organization to develop a set of 'do-able' or constrained and integrated plans. The easiest way to understand S&OP is to walk through a generic S&OP process. This process consists of four basic steps (see Figure 11.1).

Demand Planning[2]

The demand planning process develops an unconstrained view of demand (that is, what we could sell if we had no supply constraints). It involves the sales/marketing department developing a consensus point of view on unconstrained demand, taking into account known activities that are likely to change demand such as promotions, price changes, competitor activities and so on. The process culminates in a consensus forecast meeting where the unconstrained forecast is signed off as the agreed unconstrained forecast of demand.

Supply Planning

The supply planning process takes the unconstrained forecast from demand planning and applies this to available supply and capacity. This involves key supply functions (production planning, logistics/warehousing and so on) comparing the forecast to inventory and capacity. The aim of this comparison is to identify where and when demand and supply are not in balance.

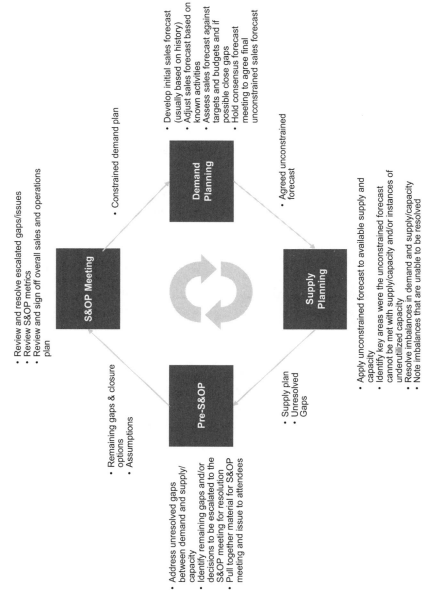

- Review and resolve escalated gaps/issues
- Review S&OP metrics
- Review and sign off overall sales and operations plan

- Constrained demand plan

- Develop initial sales forecast (usually based on history)
- Adjust sales forecast based on known activities
- Assess sales forecast against targets and budgets and if possible close gaps
- Hold consensus forecast meeting to agree final unconstrained sales forecast

- Agreed unconstrained forecast

S&OP Meeting

Demand Planning

Pre-S&OP

Supply Planning

- Remaining gaps & closure options
- Assumptions

- Supply plan
- Unresolved Gaps

- Address unresolved gaps between demand and supply/capacity
- Identify remaining gaps and/or decisions to be escalated to the S&OP meeting for resolution
- Pull together material for S&OP meeting and issue to attendees

- Apply unconstrained forecast to available supply and capacity
- Identify key areas were the unconstrained forecast cannot be met with supply/capacity and/or instances of underutilized capacity
- Resolve imbalances in demand and supply/capacity
- Note imbalances that are unable to be resolved

Figure 11.1   Illustrative generic S&OP cycle

The Pre-S&OP Session

The pre-S&OP session takes the outcomes of the demand planning and supply planning processes and identifies actions needed to balance demand and supply/capacity. In this session key representatives of sales and marketing (or similar) functions, together with key representatives of supply/capacity such as production planning and logistics, work together through the imbalances. In some cases, the actions required to balance demand and supply/capacity require sign-off from senior management, and these are referred to the S&OP meeting for this purpose. Thus, the outcome of the pre-S&OP session is a balanced demand and supply/capacity plan, together with any actions requiring sign-off from senior management to enable the balanced plan to be achieved.

The S&OP Meeting

The S&OP meeting is the culmination of the S&OP cycle. In this meeting the organization's leaders review the balanced plans developed in the pre-S&OP session, assess and resolve actions referred to the S&OP meeting and finally sign off the balanced plans. In addition, they review crucial metrics related to supply chain performance and drive improvement in this performance as appropriate. The outcome of the S&OP meeting is an integrated, constrained plan that the business will execute against.

CRITICAL SUCCESS FACTORS FOR S&OP

There are a number of critical success factors that should be understood when developing and executing S&OP, and these are discussed below.

One Plan/Multiple Translations

The output of the S&OP cycle is a common, constrained plan that the business will execute against. Although this is a common plan, it should be expressed in multiple units of measurement suitable for particular functional audiences and functional uses (see Figure 11.2).

Appropriate Aggregated View of the Business

The S&OP cycle is an aggregate planning cycle – that is, demand and supply/capacity is viewed and managed in aggregate units of measurement such as: product families, rather than detailed SKUs; customer groups, rather than individual customers; and overall production capacity, rather than individual work-centre capacity.

The actual level of aggregation is very much business situation-dependent; however, a key determinant is keeping the number of resulting groups in an S&OP cycle to a manageable number – usually less than ten and ideally around four or five (see Figure 11.3).[3]

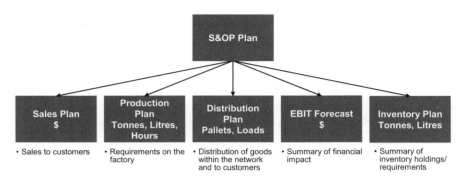

Figure 11.2   Illustrative S&OP output

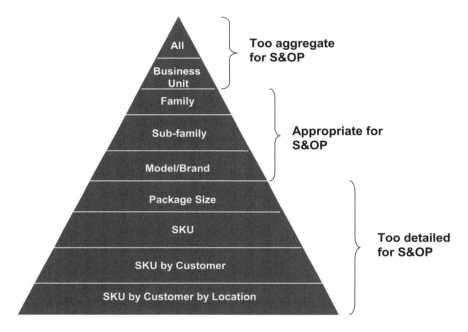

Figure 11.3   Illustrative product aggregation example

Realistic Capacity Constraining

One of the fundamental actions in the S&OP cycle is to assess the unconstrained sales forecast against supply and capacity. In the case of capacity it is important to use realistic capacities, with best practice being to use demonstrated capacity.[4] Using demonstrated capacities ensures that the resultant plan is limited by realistic constraints.

Time Fences

The reality of almost all fulfilment processes is that *it is much more expensive and disruptive to make changes at the last minute than to make changes to the plan ahead of time.* An effective S&OP cycle needs to have appropriate and agreed time fences that manage the process and degree of change allowed as we move closer to 'now'. There are effectively three 'zones' created by application of time fences (see Figure 11.4):

1. The *flexible* zone: This is the period of time far enough in advance that changes to plans have little cost or disruption impact, and changes here can be made relatively freely.[5]

2. The *firm* zone: This is the period of time far enough in advance that changes can still be made, although some execution activities may have been extensively planned or have actually commenced (an example being raw material procurement). For these latter type of activities, any changes need to be managed.

3. The *frozen* zone: This is the period close enough to 'now' that any change will cause significant cost and disruption. Changes in this zone should be very much the exception.

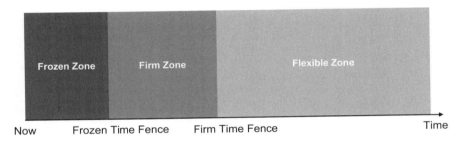

Figure 11.4   Time Fences

The actual settings of these zones are very dependent on the business's circumstances and cost profile. For example, a steelworks may quite validly operate to a three- to four-week frozen zone for steel-making, whereas a steel coil processing plant may only need a three-day frozen zone.

Effective and Simple Data Representation

For S&OP to be effective and 'user friendly', the plan and supporting data should be represented simply. The most effective approach is to use an S&OP 'plan on a page' format. Simple visual cues, such as colour coding for time fences and cell highlighting for imbalances, can be easily included using Microsoft Excel. Most organizations running an S&OP cycle use Microsoft Excel for their plan on a page, although leading organizations are beginning to use more sophisticated tools integrated into their Enterprise Resource Planning (ERP) systems (see Figure 11.5).[5]

Appropriate Resourcing and Involvement

For the S&OP cycle to be effective, active involvement of a number of key people across functions is required. In most cases, S&OP does not require significant additional people; rather, it modifies the activities of people

| | History | | | Frozen | Firm | | Free | | | | | |
	Jan	Feb	Mar	Apr	May	Jun	Jul	Aug	Sep	Oct	Nov	Dec
Demand												
Forecast	40	45	40	45	50	55	60	35	40	45	45	20
Orders	38	42	43									
Production												
Capacity	40	50	50	50	50	50	50	50	50	50	50	10
Plan	40	45	40	45	50	55	60	35	40	45	45	10
Actual	40	45	38									
Plan/Actual v Capacity	0	-5	-12	-5	0	5	10	-15	-10	-5	-5	0
Inventory												
Plan	50	50	50	50	50	50	50	50	50	50	50	40
Actual	52	55	50									

Now

Key Assumptions
1. Demand spike driven by expected investment buy ahead of price rise
1. Planned maintenance at Christmas reduces capacity

Figure 11.5   Simplified S&OP plan on a page

already in the organization. As a rule of thumb, the seniority of people involved in S&OP increases as one moves through the monthly cycle; however, involvement is primarily driven by knowledge of the subject-matter, functional expertise and decision-making authority.

There are usually one or two additional roles that are required to drive S&OP: the S&OP manager and (if required) the S&OP analyst. The S&OP manager is responsible for the execution of the S&OP cycle and is in effect the S&OP process owner. This role is often full-time during implementation and while the business is running S&OP in the early days. Later, it is possible for this role to be part-time. In some organizations, depending on the availability of data and/or the complexity of the process, an S&OP analyst may be required to support the S&OP manager.

A Well-Considered Decision Framework

The key aim of the S&OP cycle is to balance demand and supply. While there are a large number of possible options for achieving this, in most cases the circumstances of individual businesses will determine the actual 'decision levers' that can be used.

For example, BlueScope Steel, an Australian-based integrated steel producer and distributor produces steel slab in their Port Kembla Steelworks and rolls these slabs into products in two major rolling mills – one in Port Kembla and one in Western Port (approximately 1000 km south of Port Kembla). Their S&OP decision levers focus on determining which products to roll in Port Kembla versus Western Port to best match demand and available capacity, and, after making these balancing decisions, how much additional slab to make and release to the export market to maximize utilization of the steel-making assets.

When setting up the S&OP cycle it is important to identify the appropriate decision levers that apply to your organization, identify the appropriate point in the planning process when this decision can be taken and then identify who in the organization has the delegated authority to take this decision (see Figure 11.6). The combination of all these determines the key players in the S&OP cycle.

Effective Meeting Culture

For the S&OP meeting to be effective, a disciplined and tight meeting culture, as described below, is essential:

- Data submitted to the S&OP meeting is presented in a consistent and synthesized manner and is appropriate to support the decision-making and sign-off agenda of the meeting.

- Participants arrive at the meeting having reviewed the pre-reads and being prepared to participate in the meeting. They do not use the meeting to 'get up to speed' with the data and decisions required.

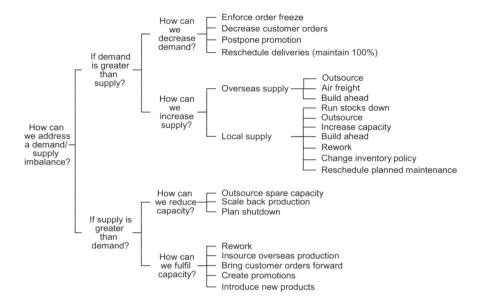

Figure 11.6   Illustrative S&OP decision framework

- Attendance at the meeting is vital. The meeting should be locked into diaries on an ongoing basis, and attendance should be delegated only as a last resort (see Figure 11.7). If attendance is delegated, then so is full decision-making authority.

- The S&OP meeting is not a discussion group. It is a decision-making forum that makes the hard decisions as escalated to it (see Figure 11.8).

Inappropriate meeting culture and behaviours will stop the S&OP meeting being effective, and this will usually be manifested in a significant increase in the meeting's duration and senior management ceasing to attend. At this point, the S&OP cycle has failed and needs to be reimplemented.

#	Item	Duration
1	Actions from Last Month's S&OP	5 min
2	Review of Metrics	10 min
3	Review New Plan	15 min
4	Review & Resolve Issues/Decisions	15 min
5	Sign off Plan Incorporating Decisions	10 min
6	Review Meeting & Continuous Improvement	5 min

Figure 11.7   Illustrative S&OP meeting agenda

Issue: Unable to Meet Forecasted Increase in Sales in Month 4

Issue Description

In order to meet budget, a volume discount in painted widgets during month 4 is being planned to drive additional sales volume. This discount is forecast to increase volume in this month by an additional 30% (an extra 2000 tonnes). This will exceed month 4 production capacity by 1500 tonnes

Supporting Facts

- Baseline forecast for month 4 is 5000 tonnes
- Promotional lift from volume discount is 2000 tonnes, total month 4 demand is 7000 tonnes
- Month 4 production capacity is 5500 tonnes
- Month 4 capacity shortfall is 1500 tonnes
- Month 2 and month 3 have 1500 tonnes excess capacity

Options for Resolution

1. Prebuild the additional 1500 tonnes in months 2 and 3 to ensure 7000 tonnes of painted widgets are available in month 4	**Risk/Impact** - Carrying cost of additional inventory $200k - Additional gross sales volume of $2m will meet budget
2. Run overtime in month 4 to increase production capacity to 7000 tonnes	**Risk/Impact** - $500k overtime costs incurred - Additional gross sales volume of $2m will meet budget
3. Cancel the volume discount to bring month 4 demand back to 5000 tonnes	**Risk/Impact** - Gross sales volume $2m below budget

Recommendation – Option 1 Prebuild

Option 1 recommended as it enables us to meet budget, and is less expensive than option 2 for the same budget impact

Figure 11.8   Example issue template

INDICATIONS OF VALUE FROM S&OP

A well-implemented S&OP cycle can drive significant value in an organization. However, it should be noted that, for the full value to be realized, the S&OP cycle needs to be supported by a basic level of integrated planning/manufacturing resource planning (MRPII) capability.

An indication ot the value that organizations capture from S&OP can be seen from the following examples and research:

- A leading Australasian industrial products manufacturer attributed the following benefits (confirmed in a post-implementation audit by an external party) to the implementation of S&OP and supporting MRPII processes:[6]
  - a 62 per cent reduction in finished goods inventory;
  - a 40 per cent reduction in work in progress and raw material inventory;
  - a 3 per cent increase in sales.
- Oliver Wight (a supply chain consultancy) assessed the benefits attributable to S&OP as a:[7]
  - a 21–30 per cent reduction in inventory;
  - a 13–20 per cent productivity improvement;
  - a 9–13 per cent purchase cost reduction;
  - an 18–25 per cent customer service improvement.
- The Revere Group (a business consultancy) assessed the benefits of S&OP as supporting:[8]
  - a 40 per cent reduction in inventory;
  - a 35 per cent increase in sales volume;
  - a 42 per cent increase in forecast accuracy.

THE APPLICATION OF S&OP TO DYNAMIC SUPPLY CHAIN TYPES

The S&OP cycle can be applied to all four of the generic supply chain types as identified by John Gattorna.[9] The application of S&OP principles does differ from type to type. S&OP is easier to implement with the continuous replenishment and lean types – that is, those servicing customer segments with medium to high predictability of demand, although it can add significant value to agile and fully flexible supply chains as well. It should also be noted that as more than one supply chain type can exist in an organization, more than one style of S&OP can also exist to support the different types (see Figure 11.9).

Supply Chain Type	Fit of S&OP	Focus of S&OP	Benefits/Positives of S&OP	Challenges of S&OP
Continuous Replenishment (CR)	A natural sweet spot for S&OP – good cultural & process fit across the organization and into key customers & suppliers	• Aggregate material in short/medium term • Capacity in longer term	• Collaborative nature of S&OP suits continuous replenishment cultures • Natural fit for the collaborative bias of CR customers	• Involvement of external parties can be challenging • Balancing the S&OP plan will mean you have to say no to some customers sometimes
Lean	An effective decision and alignment framework that helps integrate a somewhat siloed organisation	• Aggregate material in short/medium term • Capacity in longer term	• S&OP provides a good structured approach to frame optimization decisions • S&OP helps reduce functional barriers	• Analytical culture can drive S&OP into too much detail • Administration culture a challenge for S&OP-style meeting culture
Agile	An effective capacity management and decision framework to maximize the ability to respond (or not) to demand as it arises	• Capacity • Sensing & responding to rapidly changing circumstances in an optimal manner	• S&OP provides an effective communication medium • S&OP well placed to manage capacity rationing	• Need to keep S&OP at an aggregate capacity level • Convincing stakeholders that planning works at all
Business Event (*Fully Flexible*)	A useful analysis and decision-making framework that can be brought to bear during the event – with some tweaking normally required	• Material & capacity planning in the short to medium term (duration dictated by length of significant impact of event)	• Provides a proven framework (process & tools) that can be easily mobilized to make effective decisions	• Tempering senior management's reaction to circumvent S&OP with an ad hoc war room
Humanitarian (*Fully Flexible*)	An effective capacity management and decision framework for those events that are predictable at least in volume, if not on location	• Capacity • Sensing & responding to rapidly changing circumstances in an optimal manner	• S&OP provides an effective communication medium • S&OP well placed to manage capacity rationing	• Need to keep S&OP at an aggregate capacity level • Convincing stakeholders that planning works at all

Figure 11.9   **The application of S&OP to supply chain types**

Continuous Replenishment Supply Chains

Continuous replenishment readily suits an S&OP approach. The collaborative and consensus-based cultural bias of continuous replenishment supply chains is a natural fit with an effective S&OP framework. The focus of S&OP in these supply chains is at an aggregate material level in the short and medium term and shifts to more of a capacity focus in the longer term.

The collaborative and loyal nature of customers in continuous replenishment supply chains makes it a (relatively) easy task to include them in the framework. It is not uncommon for key trading partners to participate actively in the S&OP cycle, including attending the S&OP meeting. This participation by trading partners can include the customer sharing marketing and sales plans, as well as the more traditional purchasing plans during the S&OP cycle. Some organizations even go as far as having joint marketing and sales initiatives with their key customers using the demand planning portion of S&OP as the collaboration process.

Although the continuous replenishment supply chain is an S&OP 'sweet spot', challenges to an effective S&OP framework in this context can include the attendance of key trading partners in S&OP meetings. However, having these parties privy to the level of information involved in S&OP meeting can be challenging to many organizations, with the collaborative nature of the culture only partially alleviating the concerns of some people involved in the process. In addition, the collaborative nature can manifest itself in a risk of group-think during S&OP decision-making, so that care needs to be taken to ensure that all parties involved in the S&OP framework are maintaining the appropriate level of objectivity and fact-based decision-making.

Lean Supply Chains

Like continuous replenishment supply chains, lean supply chains readily suit an S&OP approach. Their focus on scale, synergy and efficiency is supported by an effective S&OP cycle that matches demand and supply/capacity and proactively manages the imbalances.

The more arm's-length nature of trading partners in lean supply chains usually manifests itself in limited involvement by external parties in S&OP. S&OP is focused almost totally within the individual organization, with some limited input, usually as information feeds only, from some service providers or selected major customers. The degree of cross-functional collaboration required to drive an effective S&OP provides significant value in lean supply chains as it tends to reduce the impact of the functional silos and administration culture of these organizations. At the same time, the structured and logical approach used by S&OP appeals to the logical and analytical bias of these organizational cultures.

Challenges of running an S&OP cycle in lean supply chains centre on the prevailing 'hierarchical' culture holding back a cross-functional S&OP team, although S&OP can also help break this issue down. In addition, the analytical nature of the lean culture can drive an 'analysis paralysis' that bogs down the S&OP. S&OP requires the right level of aggregate data to make an effective decision based on the risk/reward balance of the decision being made. The lean culture can struggle to take timely decisions in the S&OP framework with the level of data available. This manifests itself in decisions being deferred across multiple S&OP cycles and opportunities being missed.

S&OP is also applicable to those supply chains operating in an environment of low predictability of demand, although these agile and fully flexible types require certain modifications or focus in the generic S&OP cycle.

Agile Supply Chains

The S&OP approach provides a powerful framework for understanding capacity and available supply within an agile supply chain. The challenge with agile supply chains is the unpredictable nature of demand (and possibly supply) inherent in this type of chain. A key competency for these supply chains is to understand and manage the available and potential capacity and, as demand becomes more certain, to allocate this capacity in the most optimal way to meet financial and customer service objectives. Decisions can include deciding when to allocate or release available capacity versus when to continue to reserve capacity for other potentially more important customers, and, if capacity is close to full, when to defer or reject additional demand.

S&OP provides a robust and proven framework to allow this demand and capacity management to occur at the appropriate level of aggregation in the appropriate timeframe. S&OP in an agile supply chain is focused primarily on capacity management. When demand is known, it uses this information, but in most cases an agile S&OP is working with high-level forecasts of demand and assumptions (including probabilities) of the nature and timing of this demand. Key design considerations in an agile S&OP are identifying the key options available to consume capacity, the financial and customer service implications inherent in each of these options and then the timeframe required to exercise the option. For example, the export market for steel slab for most of this decade[10] has discounted the price paid for slab on the spot market, with better prices gained if the slab can be sold under a short-term contract. To obtain these contracts, the slab needs to be contracted two or more months in advance of being physically shipped. Thus a key decision in this S&OP centres on whether to release the slab two or more months in advance for a better export price or hold the capacity for even more favourable domestic orders? If these domestic

> **'A key competency for these supply chains is to understand and manage the available and potential capacity.'**

orders do not materialize, then the slab can be sold at short notice on the spot market at a discount.

A number of challenges are encountered when applying S&OP to an agile supply chain. These are centered on the need to operate at an aggregate level with significant assumptions around demand. These two combinations are not comfortable for people who are analytical by nature and/or like to work at a detailed level. The challenge for agile supply chains is to keep S&OP at this aggregate level and demonstrate that the 'unforecastable' nature of the chain does not invalidate the capacity-level optimization delivered by the S&OP cycle. Senior management who are involved in this S&OP need to be realistic about the level of accuracy achievable and make sure that they do not allow key stakeholders to disengage from the process on the perception that their agile supply chain is simply not able to be planned.

Fully Flexible Supply Chains

At first glance, S&OP does not appear to be appropriate in fully flexible supply chains. However, in some cases S&OP can add value, although if the S&OP framework is to be correctly applied, we need to address the two types of fully flexible supply chains separately.

'Emergency Response'/'Humanitarian' Supply Chain

The completely unpredictable events that make up some of this supply chain are not really suited to an S&OP approach – reactive project management being the more suitable approach.

However, there is a significant subset of events that, while not 100 per cent predictable in terms of timing or impact, can be predicted. For example, annual or semi-annual flooding episodes and the resulting humanitarian response can be planned for at a high level and S&OP provides a suitable framework to conduct this planning. In this case, the actual S&OP design is similar to that deployed for an agile supply chain: S&OP is focused primarily on capacity management. When the emergency event is known, S&OP uses this information, but in most cases an emergency response/humanitarian supply chain S&OP is working with high-level forecasts of demand and assumptions (including probabilities) of the nature and timing of the emergency event. Even more important in this S&OP are the assumptions and probabilities of the size of the emergency event and the degree to which the humanitarian supply chain is expected to be capable of meeting the event. These flag in advance the degree to which additional 'capacity' may need to be planned for from other sister organizations.

'Business Event' Supply Chain

Supply chains experiencing these styles of events should be able to leverage an S&OP approach to provide a pre-existing decision-making framework. The frameworks and processes used to gather demand and capacity and to assess and balance the two are well suited to assessing the impact of, and determining the actions required for, a major business event. It should be noted that the regular timing and rhythm of the monthly S&OP meetings may need to be broken to allow the analysis and decisions to be delivered in the required timeframe. It is also likely that some assumptions around demand or supply/capacity may need to be reviewed when operating S&OP in a business event mode. However, the basic logic and approach used in S&OP, together with the key roles involved in the process, provide a solid structure for determining how to respond to a business event.

Probably the key challenge in applying S&OP to a business event is to resist the urge for senior management to move into a 'war-room'-style response and circumvent the very capable existing S&OP process and the skilled planners. In most cases, the S&OP approach provides a better-quality response than a senior management war room. In addition, because of the need to use the S&OP framework 'on the run' during a business event it requires a well-developed and experienced S&OP capability to start with. You have to know the rules before you can break them.

> **ALIGNMENT INSIGHTS**
>
> - *S&OP provides a proven and powerful framework to ensure that individual functional plans and activities are integrated to maximize value to the organization, overall supply chain and ultimately the customer. As supply chains become increasingly complex, and resources more constrained, the importance of an effective framework to integrate planning and execution activities becomes more critical.*
>
> - *An S&OP framework adds significant value to each of the supply chain types. For those supply chain types that operate within an environment of reasonable certainty – continuous replenishment and lean, the S&OP framework provides a powerful method of integrating and balancing decision-making across functions and organizations. For those supply chain types operating in a less certain environment – agile and fully flexible, the S&OP framework provides a powerful method of managing and allocating capacity to maximize customer service, financial and humanitarian outcomes.*

NOTES

1   The American Production & Inventory Control Society defines S&OP as: 'A process to develop tactical plans that provide management the ability to strategically direct its businesses to achieve competitive advantage on a continuous basis by integrating customer focused marketing plans for new and existing products with the management of the supply chain. The process brings together all the plans for the business (sales, marketing,

development, manufacturing, sourcing and financial) into one integrated set of plans': *APICS Dictionary* (11th edn), 2005.

2   See S.F. Githens 'Forecasting and demand planning' in J.L. Gattorna, *The Gower Handbook of Supply Chain Management* (5th edn), Gower Publishing, Aldershot, 2003 for a more in-depth discussion of the topic of demand planning.

3   See T.F. Wallace *Sales & Operations Planning: The How-To Handbook*, T.F. Wallace & Co., Cincinnati, OH, 1999 for more discussion on selecting the appropriate level of planning aggregation.

4   The *APICS Dictionary*, *op. cit*, defines demonstrated capacity as 'Proven capacity calculated from actual performance data, usually expressed as the average number of items produced multiplied by the standard hours per item'.

5   For example, SAP AG has recently released an SAP Sales & Operations Planning solution as part of its Supply Chain Management Business Suite.

6   Conversation between the author and the supply chain manager of Industrial Products Company in 2007.

7   R. Ireland and C. Crum, *Linking CPFR & S&OP*, Whitepaper in the Oliver Wight Whitepaper Series, 2007. Available at: www.oliverwight.net/modules/fileshare/download.php?file=839.

8   M. Sosnowski, *The Right Way to Implement S&OP in Your Organization*, The Revere Group, 2005, http://www.reveregroup.com/articles/1381_060521.pdf.

9   See J.L. Gattorna, *Living Supply Chains*, FT Prentice Hall, Harlow, 2006.

10   Note that the significant and rapid increases in steel prices (plus raw materials and freight) seen in 2008 inversed this situation with most slab selling on the spot market for a higher price than contracted slab. This situation is an anomaly.

12 Supply Chain Integration Layer

Nigel Jones

Transforming an organization's supply chain from one which can be described as 'hard-wired', into one that operates in a multiple supply chain alignment configuration requires that a significant change take place within the organizational subcultures. John Gattorna[1] identifies 11 key elements that need to be addressed when undertaking such an exercise:

1. organization design;

2. positioning of personnel;

3. processes;

4. systems/information technology;

5. Key Performance Indicators (KPIs)

6. incentives;

7. job design;

8. internal communications;

9. training and development;

10. recruitment;

11. leadership style.

Although often bracketed and hidden as a subgroup under the heading systems/information technology, supply chain visibility is a key enabler to the successful delivery of strategic change initiatives in the wider supply chain domain. Of all the systems that will underpin the required subculture, supply chain visibility has the potential to materially shift the performance dial and should be seen as a prerequisite to a successful change programme.

Traditionally, supply chain visibility is often perceived as nothing more than 'logistics visibility', and, of course, the importance of timely, quality, reliable logistics visibility cannot be underestimated. However, to support an organization's desire and/or need to undertake the scale of change (both physical and cultural) to achieve 'multiple supply chain alignment', supply chain visibility needs to be considered in a far wider context.

'Supply chain visibility is repeatedly identified as one of the key building-blocks on the roadmap to a more efficient and competitive supply chain.'

This chapter sets out to explore the topic of supply chain visibility and reviews the use of Business Activity Monitoring (BAM) as one option with the potential to deliver this. Although it is a solution that has been available for over six years, the technology has only just recently been seen as a possible solution in the supply chain context. The following topics are reviewed:

- Exploring what supply chain visibility really is;

- Why it's required;

- Potential solutions;

- Business Activity Monitoring (BAM);

- The application of BAM to achieve supply chain visibility.

SUPPLY CHAIN VISIBILITY

What It Is

The subject of much discussion, supply chain visibility is repeatedly identified as one of the key building-blocks on the roadmap to a more efficient and competitive supply chain. Without a robust and reliable visibility tool across the wider supply chain there can be little confidence of lifting overall performance and capability. A study undertaken by the Aberdeen Group (2006)[2] found that, whereas in the early 1990s most companies focused on resolving internal data and process issues, recently the focus has increasingly shifted to the external supply chain, with improved visibility as the top priority. Interestingly, the same study showed relatively low levels of adoption of visibility capability across businesses, and quite low numbers of activities and events actually being tracked.

To understand why the issue of visibility is now apparently being prioritized so highly we need to know what is actually being defined as supply chain visibility and what its potential impact is on the business performance.

Surprisingly, it is not easy to find a generally accepted and robust definition of supply chain visibility, despite frequent reference being made to the term in the literature. Many parties, including software and logistics providers, claim to offer supply chain visibility as a capability. Often, however, what is being offered as supply chain visibility is no more than a logistics event management function over relatively small sections of a much larger network. One of the more comprehensive definitions put forward is as follows:

> *Supply chain visibility is the identity, location, and status of entities transiting the supply chain, captured in timely messages about events, along with the planned and actual dates/times for these events.*[3]

Even this definition, when looked at in detail, seems to depend on reference to an identifiable object, be it product or customer order. If we are to have what can be truly described as a supply chain visibility capability, then, by definition, it needs to also provide visibility of any processes being undertaken that ultimately support the movement of goods and services. This sentiment is supported by the Aberdeen Group, which reports that in 'best of class' 36 per cent of industry leaders have achieved data and *process* visibility across their supply chains.[4]

As concepts such as multiple supply chain management increasingly become a reality, supply chain visibility systems will need to adapt and meet the needs of this wider, more sophisticated definition. Later in this chapter we discuss how the solutions capability might support this wider interpretation of the supply chain, and how it will become a distinguishing feature and a particular strength of business activity monitoring.

Interestingly, the current focus of business seems to be heavily biased towards the physical activity within the supply chain: hence the corresponding narrow scope found in the majority of solutions is designed to meet immediate needs. However, turning to what business seems to be seeking to achieve through greater supply chain visibility in the future, it may be concluded that, as more companies adopt solutions, visibility will need to be deployed over supporting processes in order to retain a leading position.

Why is Visibility Required?

There are many reasons why organizations are, or should be, seeking greatly improved levels of supply chain visibility, and these can be aggregated under the following headings:

- to improve customer service delivery performance;
- to reduce costs;
- to monitor suppliers' performance;
- to support the additional reporting required to meet an ever tightening regulatory environment.

The specific areas of focus within each of these categories will vary, depending on an individual company's supply chain configuration, level of maturity and competitive environment. For example, a company with a widely spread international supply chain, consisting of hundreds of trade lanes could be expected to seek transport savings and proactive alert management over any shipping issues. The solution in this case could be expected to involve the tracking of many events stretching across the globe. In contrast, a company operating a shorter-range domestic business may require only a couple of milestones – for example, goods dispatched and goods delivered.

It is important that these needs are not considered only in a transactional context. Strategically, these capabilities will be required as basic enablers to meet increasingly stringent customer expectations as they themselves seek ever greater improvements.

POTENTIAL SOLUTIONS

There have traditionally been a number of different offerings available to businesses that deliver visibility over the supply chain. Potential solutions can generally be split into three broad categories, as described in Table 12.1.

Table 12.1   Major current visibility solution types

Classification	Descriptions
Commercial solutions	Purpose-developed solutions delivered by commercial technology vendor
Outsourced	A hosted solution potentially via third-party logistics provider or solutions provider
Self-developed	Developed in-house, varying levels of complexity and sophistication

Business Activity Monitoring (BAM)

The supply chain is not the only business function striving for greater accessibility to information; significant effort has been, and continues to be, applied to develop and deploy world-class data warehouses. New and emerging technologies are being used to manage and store information originating from many disparate systems across many different business functions. Since, by definition, supply chain management involves both upstream and downstream parties working together, joining their individual 'logistics networks' and associated systems, the need for efficiently managing information originating across disparate systems is especially important.

'A key feature of BAM is its ability to display data from disparate systems, in real time, by listening for changes.'

Business Activity Monitoring (BAM) broke on to the scene around 2002, stimulated by a growing interest in Business Process Management (BPM), which made it possible to understand more clearly the relationship between real-time IT operations and the corresponding business activities.[5] BAM is an emerging technology that monitors business events in real time and issues alerts that enable the business to react quickly to both problems and opportunities.

Fundamentally, BAM is about monitoring and measuring business activity across operational systems and business processes. A key feature of BAM is its ability to display data from disparate systems, in real time, by listening for changes and only picking up the data when a change has occurred.

First-generation BAM usage was mostly targeted at understanding business flow through IT systems, by counting processes, transactions and events, and displaying that information either through dashboards or historical reports. As experience with BAM has grown, its focus has moved from this relatively static role to a much more dynamic, high-value one in which business process interactions and trends are examined much more closely.

The high level of statistical and analytical intelligence now delivered with the best BAM solutions provides a much better and more accurate understanding of the business dynamics and therefore brings a tighter focus on addressing real business issues.

Second-level BAM strategies focus on business assurance and visibility, control services and complex pattern recognition. They blend the core strengths of BAM with these powerful analytical capabilities to provide an effective approach for targeting business problems in areas such as compliance, change management and quality improvement. The technology has now been applied in the supply chain environment and brings with it a high level of agility, offering a new solution and new functionalities in the area of supply chain visibility.

The Application of BAM

The following case study looks at the deployment of BAM to provide supply chain visibility across the global operations of Fonterra.[6]

Case Study: Fonterra

Fonterra is highly dependent on a variety of outsourced logistics providers to deliver its products in full and on time. Yet determining the status of an order at any given time has required a manual search through some 11 different systems – a tedious process, indeed. To compound that difficulty, most of time Fonterra didn't even know a problem existed until 'after the fact'. Issues management was highly reactive – once a cost had been incurred and/or customers were directly affected.

This lack of visibility resulted in high costs to the business! Estimates across the business showed significant opportunities for avoiding unnecessary costs while at the same time improving customer service. Lacking was the visibility and capability to proactively manage its logistics execution and suppliers. The avoidance of unplanned costs was, however, only one of a number of objectives to be addressed – others included:

- *Provide real-time visibility across the global network through a single source* Dependent on many disparate systems and individual suppliers, there was not one system that an individual within the company could ask the question 'Where is my order?' and be confident of getting an immediate response. In practice, the question could be answered, but someone would be expected to know the order's approximate progression (and hence system) through the extended supply chain.

- *Enable proactive event management* Traditionally, parties become aware of a failing within an extended supply chain only when a service failure is inevitable. As organizations place a greater emphasis on not only lifting service levels, but also ultimately supporting more sophisticated customer relationships, finding out after the fact is not acceptable. Fonterra, in particular, manages relatively long international supply chains, so being made aware of an issue as it develops can enable the implementation of resolution management that not only avoids any disruption, but also minimizes exception management costs.

- *Drive data accuracy and timeliness where it is deficient* Information and data sourced from a system is only as good as the raw data entered into it. Many solutions depend on intense ongoing manual data update, so a key need was for the solution to be able to manage and report on data activity associated with the supply chain as well as the physical activities taking place within it.

- *Provide data to drive continuous process improvement* Although many businesses consider the deployment of a visibility solution as a natural cost of doing business, the service improvements and avoided operational costs in themselves will in most cases be found to produce a healthy return on any required investment. Further and more significant financial value, however, is often found lying beyond what is deliverable through short-term operational improvements. A well-thought-out visibility solution will provide a wealth of data that can subsequently be used to identify and support major re-engineering activities. Given the importance of this information, Fonterra wanted to ensure that it not only retained ownership, but also had ongoing access to it from both a technical and capability perspective.

- *Provide a foundation for future strategic initiatives* Given the variety of supply chains that the business was likely define as necessary in the future, it was generally accepted that if Fonterra was to offer a multiple supply chain strategy, then it would need the capability to support and operate at levels of sophistication far exceeding those in place. If capabilities are to be developed that support an advanced, integrated, continuous replenishment supply chain, far greater levels of confidence with respect to the supply chain's performance are required. The visibility solution being decided upon had to both support and become an integral part of Fonterra's future supply chain solutions.

- *Retain ownership of supply chain data and associated intellectual property (IP)* Almost anything can be comfortably outsourced in today's operating environment. The concept of outsourcing the physical functions of the supply chain is by now an established practice. Frequently overlooked, however, is the intellectual value of supply information and the importance of retaining ownership of it. Such information often creates the point of difference between supply chains, and retention should be considered as a strategic imperative. Although Fonterra was, and still is, comfortable outsourcing significant components of its supply chain operations, a clear decision has now been made to retain exclusive ownership of any intellectual property with respect to the supply chain.

- *Provide the ability to link with a variety of regional and global 3PLs in different geographic areas* For organizations with global operations it is often the case that no single 3PL can provide an optimal solution. The capabilities and quality of local knowledge of most operators (even the biggest) will vary from region to region and from country to country. It is not only because of their differing capabilities or coverage that different 3PLs will be more or less suitable in different regions; often, small local operators may be able to pass on the benefits of a financial and/or tax structure that a large global operator cannot. Nevertheless, regardless of the reasons why, it is becoming increasingly unlikely that a single partner will be able to provide the 'best' total solution across the globe and, with it, their potential to provide a single window through which to observe the supply chain.

- *Provide a scalable solution that grows with the business at minimal cost.* Generally, outsourced visibility solutions are charged on the basis of throughput. Although these costs are unlikely to be strictly linear when compared to volume, it is usually found that, in outsourced/hosted solutions arrangements, costs will be calculated and charged on a volume basis – in other words, the more you put through, the more you pay. However, such an approach does not tend to suit all situations and can very quickly can become very expensive for organizations that are experiencing growth.

- *Operate with a low unit cost* The ability for valuable products, such as pharmaceuticals, to absorb high unit-cost activity tends to be greater than in the case of bulk commodities such as grain or dairy, which tend to be relatively low-value. This is particularly important in respect of customers serviced through what may be described as 'lean' supply chains. With a focus on efficiency and cost, a visibility solution and its role in avoiding unnecessary operational costs becomes pivotal to meeting such needs and expectations. Given this focus and awareness on cost and efficiency, such a solution cannot come at any price. Because of the proportion of business deemed to fit under this category Fonterra needed to find a solution that not only provided and supported increasingly sophisticated levels of capability when required, but could also do so at a low unit cost.

In addition to the various functional needs described in the objectives, Fonterra had also learnt that any visibility solution needs to involve much more than just data capture and information transfer if its true potential was to be realized. The solution deployed not only had to be a technology solution, but also had to recognize and accommodate the variety of business IP, knowledge, capabilities and operational bandwidth combinations that might be encountered across geographic regions and/ or within business units (see Figure 12.1).

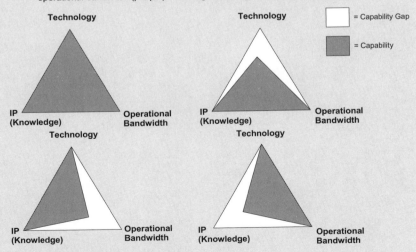

The solution had to cater for needs that could vary by region or across business unit – i.e. maturity of supporting technology, local supply chain expertise and the operational bandwidth (people) to manage resulting information and actions.

Figure 12.1   Needs triangles

Figure 12.2 Screen shot example of dashboard

Task Results

Subscribe Scheduled Delegations

| Accept | Release | Accept & Complete |

0 selected

Export Table...

	TASK ID	ALERT RULE NAME ▼	CREATED DATE	DELIVERY ▼	SALES ORDER	AIMS ZEST	CUSTOMER REQUIRED ETA	LOAD PORT ETD ▼	EXPIRATION DATE
☐	295817	Delivery shipment ETA outside of DIFOT	29/01/2009 09:05	81446787	10107739		2009-03-05	2009-02-21T00:00:00.000Z	5/02/2009 09:05
☐	294171	Delivery shipment ETA outside of DIFOT	27/01/2009 13:51	81444439	10109218		2009-04-07	2009-03-17T00:00:00.000Z	3/02/2009 13:51
☐	295195	Delivery shipment ETA outside of DIFOT	28/01/2009 17:15	81446358	10107726		2009-03-16	2009-02-11T00:00:00.000Z	4/02/2009 17:15
☐	295935	Delivery shipment ETA outside of DIFOT	29/01/2009 14:29	81447621	10109037		2009-01-16	2009-02-02T00:00:00.000Z	5/02/2009 14:29
☐	294954	Delivery shipment ETA outside of DIFOT	28/01/2009 09:20	81445302	10105541		2009-03-15	2009-02-09T00:00:00.000Z	4/02/2009 09:20
☐	294950	Delivery shipment ETA outside of DIFOT	28/01/2009 08:49	81445185	10107739		2009-03-05	2009-02-21T00:00:00.000Z	4/02/2009 08:49

Alert Name	Short Description	Type	Owner	Action	Timeout
Delivery shipment ETA outside of DIFOT	Assigned shipment ETA is not within 7 days of customer ETA at time of delivery creation	Monitor	CSE/ISS	Contact LOP if a review of the shipment is required. Contact customer with the arrival date at the CSE's discretion	7 days

Figure 12.3   Screen shot example of alert

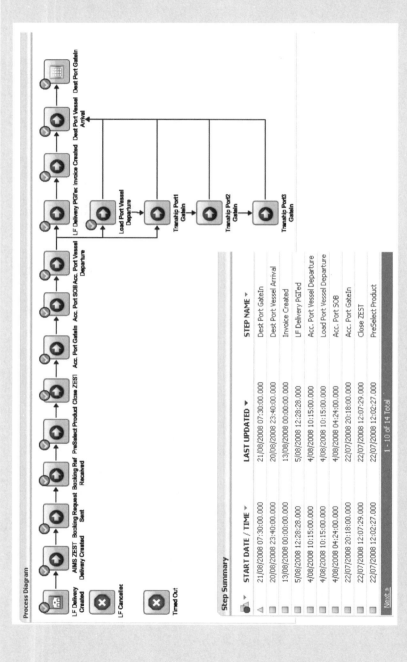

Figure 12.4   Screen shot example of tracking

Solution needs could vary across the business

Having explored a very wide range of potential solutions with varying degrees of success, especially with respect to matching the functional and data needs identified, attention turned to the potential to lever off the company's existing integration layer and deploy BAM.

Fonterra's integration layer (the system capability linking both its internal and external system interfaces) was, and continues to be, supplied by Webmethods, a product suite from Software AG. Although the company already deployed the Webmethods 'Trading Platform' functionality (with its comprehensive messaging capabilities), it had not previously deployed the BAM solution. When deployed, BAM delivered the dashboard shown in Figure 12.2 on page 184. Real time dashboards such as this provide management with easy to read visibility of business performance as it happens. The 'alert' capability depicted in Figure 12.3 (page 185) from BAM, are generated when business rules are broken, enabling prompt resolution. The comprehensive tracking capability depicted in Figure 12.4 opposite allows users to visualise and monitor the supply chain in real time. BAM also provides all necessary components for delivering the functionality to provide basic, robust supply chain visibility.

With the additional functionality available through the solution, such as automation, business process management workflow, sophisticated analytical capabilities and process modelling, Fonterra had easy access to a truly world-class supply chain visibility solution in the widest sense of the word. Having already met the comprehensive and extensive list of requirements previously defined, early experience suggests that as yet unutilized functionality within the solution will further enhance and lift capabilities beyond those of more traditional visibility solutions.

REALIZING THE POTENTIAL OF BAM

Transforming an organization's supply chain from a traditional 'hard-wired' environment to a multiple alignment business model as prescribed under dynamic alignment principles requires businesses to undergo significant change across the culture. A wide variety of system solutions is required to support such change, among them supply chain visibility which should be considered a key cornerstone for any such change.

Often confused with limited visibility over physical logistics activity, the definition of supply chain visibility required to support such a major change must be couched in the widest possible context and necessarily include both processes and physical movement.

Although there is a wide range of visibility solutions available, many support only the physical movement. A solution that has the potential to meet the increasingly challenging needs – although relatively untested in the supply chain environment – is Business Activity Monitoring (BAM), an emerging technology that monitors business events in real time and issues alerts that enable the business to react quickly to problems and opportunities. BAM is therefore ideally placed to support and provide supply chain visibility. For organizations with an integration layer already deployed to support their electronic connectivity with the world, the potential exists to deploy a BAM solution at relatively little cost and reconfiguration.

Although only recently piloted in this arena, early results suggest that not only does BAM technology have the potential to provide a cost-effective, comprehensive, fully scalable solution; it also has the potential to ensure that organizations can retain exclusive ownership of valuable intellectual property and data.

ALIGNMENT INSIGHTS

- *Changing an organization's subcultures in order to operate a multiple supply chain alignment strategy requires changes to both systems and processes; visibility is the key enabler to support both.*

- *Supply chain visibility is vital to:*

  - *provide the confidence that the efficiencies necessary to support a lean supply chain are being delivered; and*

  - *provide a platform that underpins the sophisticated capabilities necessary to deliver a robust continuous replenishment environment.*

- *Using emerging technologies such as Business Activity Monitoring (BAM) enables closer integration between process management, process control and visibility. The closer integration provided by such a solution can be a valuable tool for supporting the required culture change.*

NOTES

1   J.L. Gattorna, *Living Supply Chains*, FT Prentice and Hall, Harlow, 2006.

2   Aberdeen Group, *The Supply Chain Visibility Roadmap – Moving from Vision to True Business Value*, Aberdeen Group, Boston, MA, 2006.

3   F. Vernon, 'Supply chain visibility – lost in translation', *Supply Chain Management – An International Journal*, Vol. 13, No. 3 (2008), pp. 180–184.

4   Aberdeen Group, *Supply Chain Visibility Roadmap, op. cit.*

5   J. Crump, *Business Activity Monitoring(BAM): The New Face of BPM*, White Paper, Software AG, June 2006.

6   Fonterra Cooperative Group produces and sells more than 2.8 million tonnes of product in more than 140 markets globally.

13 Supply Chain Configurations and the Impact of Different Pricing Strategies

Chung Chee Kong

Supply chain management is a critical capability in most companies, as it is one of the most powerful dimensions of competitive advantage an organization can utilize in the marketplace. In order to derive value from the improved delivery of customer benefits through superior supply chain service, companies would be well served to consider how their pricing strategies should be realigned in light of the differential and/or improved supply chain offerings they are presenting to their customers.

While it is common sense that such alignment between supply chain service and pricing is a 'given' and should be managed well in most companies, unfortunately, the reality is quite the contrary.

The barriers to achieving good alignment are due to a multitude of reasons, including:

- lack of cross-functional skills and organization structure which facilitates development of coherent pricing, supply chain and customer strategies;

- inadequate IT infrastructure to support analysis and decision-making, which links the entire business operations from supply chain, to sales and marketing, manufacturing, finance/costing and so on (for example, cost–to-serve and 'pocket margin' information, customer segmentation);

- lack of a good understanding of customer needs and buying values/ behaviours;

- Organizational silos and KPIs which are more focused on 'optimizing' individual departmental performance rather than overall business performance.

This chapter will address the 'know-how' in terms of developing a coherent pricing approach which is aligned with the main supply chain configurations identified earlier in this book. A number of best-practice pricing management frameworks will be presented to illustrate how this can be applied in the context of supply chain alignment strategies.

COST IMPLICATIONS OF SUPPLY CHAIN CONFIGURATIONS

John Gattorna has already identified the four generic types of supply chain configurations (see Figure 13.1).

This supply chain configuration typology provides a framework to decide on the appropriate supply chain models, given the different supply chain characteristics (that is, predictability of demand) and depth of relationship with customers. Implicit in the framework are the implications of the customers' supply chain characteristics on the cost of operations, as well as the potential supply chain service offerings.

In general, when customer demand is predictable, safety stock requirements will be lower than would be the case with customers whose demand is less predictable. Demand predictability gives us an idea of the relative cost-to-serve for customers with different supply chain types. An indication of this is given in the statistical safety stock equation below:

Safety stock target = $K \times \sqrt{LT_{avg}} \times (\sigma_{Demand})^2 + (Demand_{avg} \times \sigma_{LT})^2$

where: K = safety factor (correlated to safety stock service level)
LT = lead-time
σ = standard deviation.

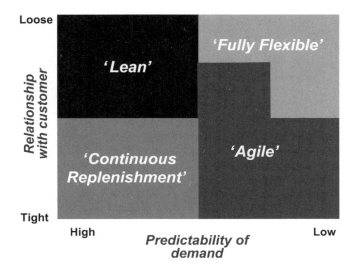

Figure 13.1   Four generic types of supply chain configuration

Source: John Gattorna, *Living Supply Chains*, FT Prentice Hall, Harlow, 2006.

However, beyond safety stock carrying cost, there are other supply chain costs which are incurred, the types and amount of which depend on the relevant supply chain configurations. Therefore, it is important to isolate and identify such cost-to-serve components in order to gain a better picture of cost-to-serve in different supply chain configurations.

For instance, for an *agile* customer, due to the need to provide a quick response, suppliers may have to provide:

- a costlier mode of transportation for speedy delivery;

- production schedule 'break-in' capability;

- greater allocation of manpower time and resource to allow speedy response;

- perhaps door-to-door delivery capability – for example, providing 'delivered' basis incoterm (for example, DDP), instead of CIF, CFR or FOB (all of which do not include end-to-end customer delivery).

In contrast, for a *continuous replenishment* customer, the cost-to-serve profile may be proportionately higher for the following components:

- account management activities;

- intercompany IT systems integration (for example, ERP to ERP);

- vendor-managed inventory (inventory carrying an associated cost).

On the other hand, the following costs may be relevant for servicing *lean* customers:

- order management (high transaction volume-handling, without the benefit of intercompany transaction integration automation);

- demand forecasting (manpower and IT).

Lastly, for *fully flexible* customers, it is not hard to imagine that there will be disproportionately higher expedited shipment/rush-order costs due to the occurrence of 'unplanned demand' and emergency requests.

It is therefore important to identify and quantify the various cost-to-serve elements for the different supply chain types, in order to understand the impact on customer profitability and subsequently how pricing strategies should be reconfigured. This then raises the following questions:

1. How do we identify the various cost-to-serve elements?

2. How do we measure, quantify and allocate the various costs?

3. How do we model customer profitability, given the cost-to-serve implications?

4. How will this affect the segment(s) in which the customer belongs?

5.   How will this eventually impact on pricing strategies, as well as on the service offerings, by customers/customer segments?

6.   Is there a better way of pricing our products/services, given an ability to deliver better customer value through improved supply chain performance?

We will address these questions in the following pages of this chapter. However, since it is not possible to provide one generic approach across all industries (as each industry has its own peculiar characteristics), we have chosen to illustrate the concepts and principles within the context of business-to-business enterprises. We hope it will be possible to translate these learning points and principles to other industries not specifically mentioned in this chapter.

'POCKET MARGIN' MODEL TO THE RESCUE

One useful tool or helping to map out the various supply chain cost-to-serve elements is the customer offerings chain map (Figure 13.2). This provides a structured framework to visualize and ascertain the range of 'offerings components' relevant for the different supply chain types.

Once the cost-to-serve elements are established, it is paramount that these are quantified, allocated[1] and tied to every sales transaction through an advanced profitability model such as the Pocket Margin Waterfall Model.

Such a model will allow us to gain a deeper insight into customer profitability, transaction level by transaction level, which, as a whole, offers us a better understanding of the returns for the different supply chain configurations provided to different customers. An example of a Pocket Margin Waterfall Model is shown in Figure 13.3. Note that it provides visibility to different

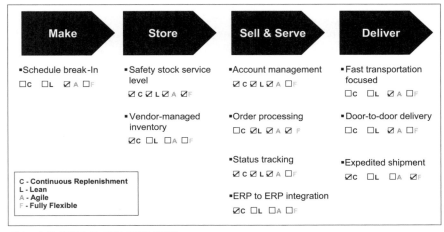

Only selected offerings components shown

Figure 13.2   Customer offerings chain map

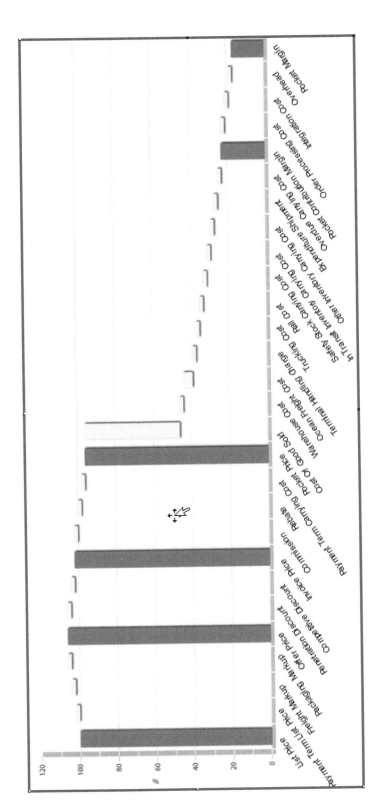

Figure 13.3   Sample Pocket Margin Model

costs and discount components that would result in price and margin erosion. Analysing the cost components element by element enables us not only to identify areas of margin erosion, but also to improve pricing policies and service offerings that are aligned with the objectives of the corresponding customer segments.

'Unless a business is relatively simple and has very few cost-to-serve components... a typical accounting-based profitability model is usually inadequate to provide a true reflection of customer profitability.'

With improved customer profitability insights (and, by extension, insights on the profitability of the dominant customer supply chain configuration models), companies can now use the information for development of a worth-based segmentation[2] which provides the foundation for aligning price and service offerings to customers.

SEGMENTATION: THE FOUNDATION FOR DIFFERENTIATED PRICE/SERVICE POLICIES

While most organizations will use some form of segmentation, more often than not, the chosen segmentation method (or segmentation criteria) lacks rigour and/or the data are not sufficiently accurate to be truly reflective of customer characteristics and contribution to business.

Based on our experience, it is common to find companies segmenting their customers into A, B, C segments, using relatively simple segmentation criteria such as revenue contribution, profitability contribution and so on. Such methods are known as worth-based segmentation.

Although this type of segmentation is useful to give an idea of the relative worth (or value) of the various customers to a business, in implementation it often falls short in terms of the rigour and level of accuracy of data used.

A classic example is profitability data. Unless a business is relatively simple and has very few cost-to-serve components (which is unlikely in a modern-day complex business environment), a typical accounting-based profitability model is usually inadequate to provide a true reflection of customer profitability. This is because such a model is unable to capture and fairly allocate costs based on actual consumption of resources by customers – for 'complicated' scenarios such as allocation of labour costs (for example, sales visits, customer service), expenses (for example, travel costs, customer entertainment) and carrying costs (for example, payment terms, inventory).

As a general rule, customer profitability data derived from the Pocket Margin Model is a better choice for segmentation purposes. In the case of one manufacturing company, a recast of customer profitability using

Pocket Margin principles revealed that the company's previous ranking of customers was not entirely reliable (see Figure 13.4). The implication of such mis-categorization of customer segments is that good customers may be unnecessarily 'penalized', whereas an undeserving customer may be unintentionally rewarded through differentiated customer treatment based on worth-based segments.

Another common shortfall we observed in the way worth-based segmentation (customer ranking) is developed is the lack of rigour in segmentation methodology, especially those adopting a simple ranking approach, using a single criterion. However, in most organizations, the worth of their customers to the business cannot be fully captured by a single criterion such as revenue or (pocket) profitability. There are other criteria which ought to be considered at the same time – for example, strategic importance, projected sales, depth of relationship – to provide a well-rounded view of customer worth.

An example of a multi-criteria segmentation methodology is given in Figure 13.5. It generates a worth-based index which can then be used to develop A, B, C worth-based segments. Obviously, using such a technique to develop customer segments provides an enhanced view of customer worth. These worth-based segments can subsequently be used to develop differentiated pricing policies (for example, discount entitlement by customer rank), volume allocation priorities (in the event of supply shortage) and service-level differentiations (further illustrated in the next section).

Besides worth-based segmentation there are other customer segmentation techniques that are employed by companies, depending on their level of

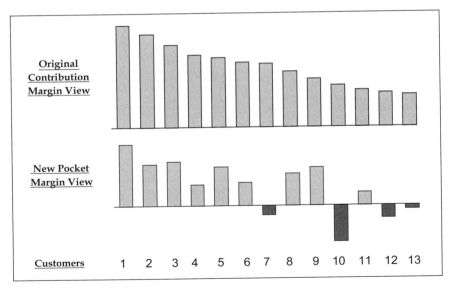

Figure 13.4   **Improved view of customer profitability**

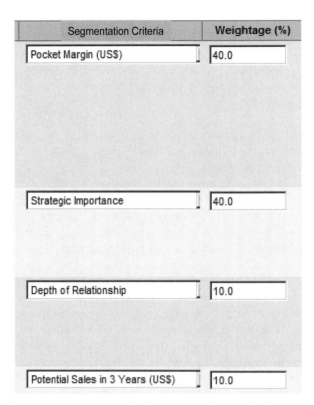

Segmentation Criteria	Weightage (%)
Pocket Margin (US$)	40.0
Strategic Importance	40.0
Depth of Relationship	10.0
Potential Sales in 3 Years (US$)	10.0

For each of the segmentation criterion, a scoring guideline is developed to define the relevant score given segmentation criterion value (for example, high strategic importance score = 10, medium strategic importance score = 5).

Figure 13.5   Worth-based segmentation methodology

sophistication and segmentation methodology maturity (see Figure 13.6). In fact, at any one time, companies many utilize more than one segmentation approach in order to gain customer insights from different perspectives.

To some extent, Gattorna's four generic supply chain configurations are a variant of behaviour-based segmentation. The customer 'behaviour' in this context is really the customer's demand pattern (that is, predictability of the demand), taking into account also the depth of the customer relationship.

One advantage of this segmentation approach is that, by understanding the different types of configuration (agile, continuous replenishment and so on), companies can now design service offerings that are better aligned with their customers' supply chain characteristics in order to create customer value while 'optimizing' the cost-to-serve side of the equation. An example of how we can operationalize this segmentation approach is shown in Figure 13.7 where a 'forecastability' index (that is, a coefficient of variation) is used to define 'demand predictability' while the 'depth of relationship with customer'

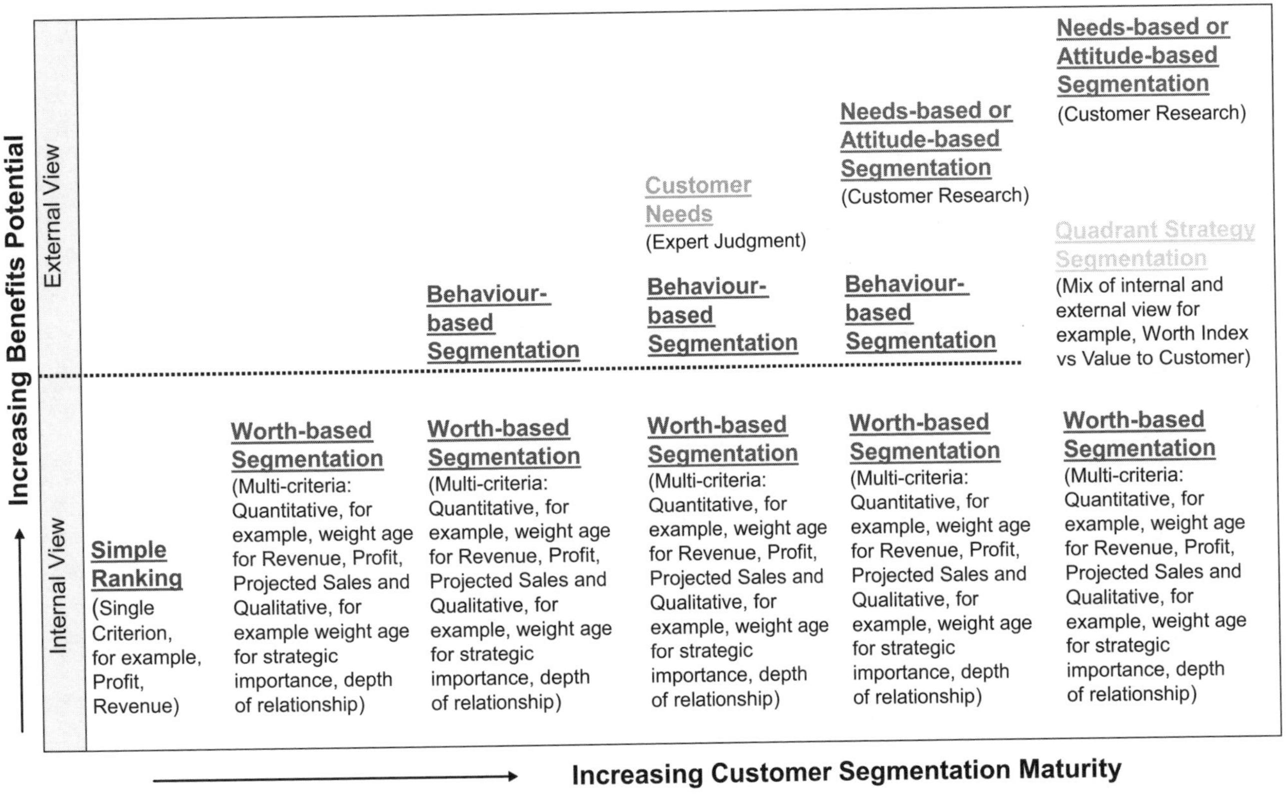

Figure 13.6 Customer segmentation maturity continuum

Increasing Customer Segmentation Maturity →

← *Increasing Benefits Potential*

External View | Internal View

External View			**Needs-based or Attitude-based Segmentation** (Customer Research)	**Needs-based or Attitude-based Segmentation** (Customer Research) / **Quadrant Strategy Segmentation** (Mix of internal and external view for example, Worth Index vs Value to Customer)
		Customer Needs (Expert Judgment)	**Behaviour-based Segmentation**	**Behaviour-based Segmentation**
Internal View	**Behaviour-based Segmentation**	**Behaviour-based Segmentation**	**Worth-based Segmentation** (Multi-criteria: Quantitative, for example, weight age for Revenue, Profit, Projected Sales and Qualitative, for example, weight age for strategic importance, depth of relationship)	**Worth-based Segmentation** (Multi-criteria: Quantitative, for example, weight age for Revenue, Profit, Projected Sales and Qualitative, for example, weight age for strategic importance, depth of relationship)
	Worth-based Segmentation (Multi-criteria: Quantitative, for example, weight age for Revenue, Profit, Projected Sales and Qualitative, for example, weight age for strategic importance, depth of relationship)	**Worth-based Segmentation** (Multi-criteria: Quantitative, for example, weight age for Revenue, Profit, Projected Sales and Qualitative, for example, weight age for strategic importance, depth of relationship)		
	Simple Ranking (Single Criterion, for example, Profit, Revenue)			

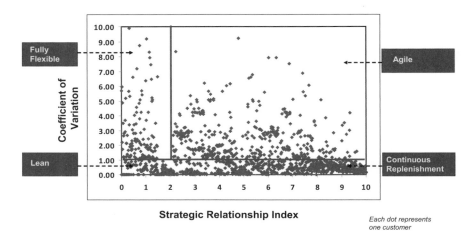

Strategic Relationship Index

Each dot represents one customer

Figure 13.7   Operationalizing supply chain type segments

is represented by a 'strategic relationship index'. The latter is a weighted index, taking into account both the depth of customer relationship and size of customer contribution (for example, revenue, pocket margin).

Customer segmentation can be described as the bedrock of pricing strategy. A well-formulated customer segment provides the springboard for price and profit improvement. Experience from companies such as Dupont reaffirms the significant value of having good segmentation. This has been well explained by Diane Gulyas, DuPont's chief marketing and sales officer, when she commented that '(Wall Street) analysts are blown away by the company's price increases and well executed customer segmentation' in response to an interview question on the rationale for the focus in that area.[3]

One 'best-practice' segmentation technique mentioned in the customer segmentation maturity continuum (Figure 13.6) is a 'needs-based segmentation' which groups customers according to their buyer values and drivers of buying decisions. Customer needs insights provide companies with additional information to help them tailor their offerings according to what the customers value.

PRICING POLICIES AND SERVICE OFFERINGS DESIGN: VALUE CREATION THROUGH 'ALIGNMENT'

Customer segmentation on a standalone basis does not generate business value unless we develop actionable plans to realign the way we price and serve our customers given these customer insights. The next step towards achieving the objective of this realignment is what we call 'offerings design'.

The main principle behind offerings design is to align our pricing policies and service offerings such that we do not overserve or underserve customers. Of course, our ability to realize this realignment will very much depend on the insights we gain about our customers and that in turn depends on how insightful and actionable our customer segmentation methodologies are.

Done properly, offerings design can positively influence all the key value drivers: revenue, cost and working capital.

Revenue enhancement is achieved through improving pricing policies either by enhancing the price points to increase transactional profit (for example, mark-up and surcharges) or employing strategic discounting to promote volume growth and/or customer loyalty.

Cost reduction can be achieved by allocating the organization's scarce resources (such as manpower, expense budget, inventory and so on) to where it has the most impact on the basis of insights about customers' worth to our business (and their buyer value, if customer needs insights are available).

Working capital improvement can be realized by differentiating service level (for example, inventory) based on segments the customer belongs to.

To illustrate this, take the example of a company which uses a combination of worth-based segmentation (A, B, C ranking) and supply chain characteristics segmentation (continuous replenishment, lean and agile).

In principle, customers with a higher ranking will receive better price/service levels. For example, within the 'lean' segment, 'A' rank customers will get a higher discount compared to 'B' rank, whereas 'C' rank customers will get no discount. By the same logic, 'A' rank customers will get a higher safety stock service level compared to 'B' rank customers, while for 'C' rank customers, we will not keep safety stock at all – that is, a safety stock service level of 50 per cent (see Figure 13.8).

Within the same customer rank, we can further differentiate price/service offers based on the supply chain characteristic segments the customers belong to. Taking 'A' segment as the comparison basis, we provide higher discount to 'lean' customers compared to 'continuous replenishment' customers, as 'lean' customers will generally value low price and usually have a lower cost-to-serve than 'continuous replenishment' customers (in other words, 'lean' customers are likely to have lower order management cost, lower IT infrastructure cost and lower safety stock requirements).

Similarly, within the 'A' segment, 'continuous replenishment' customers deserve a higher discount compared to 'agile' customers since they generally have a lower cost-to-serve. The obvious example is safety stock requirement. Even if we provide the same safety stock service level to the two segments, the

Supply Chain Characteristics Segments

Price/Service Offerings	CONTINUOUS REPLENISHMENT	LEAN	AGILE
A			
Discounts	3%	6%	2%
Min. Order Quantity Surcharge	None	None	None
Safety Stock Service Level	98%	95%	98%
Expedited Shipment	Yes	Yes	Yes
B			
Discounts	1%	2%	None
Min. Order Quantity Surcharge	Yes	Yes	Yes
Safety Stock Service Level	85%	80%	85%
Expedited Shipment	No	No	No
C			
Discounts		None	None
Min. Order Quantity Surcharge		Yes	Yes
Safety Stock Service Level		50%	50%
Expedited Shipment		No	Yes, but chargeable

Worth-based Segment

Figure 13.8   Offerings design in action

safety stock requirement for 'agile' customers will still be higher due to the lower predictability of demand (that is, a higher demand variability).

In the above example, the pricing strategy of price (discount) differentiation is designed such that only deserving customers (A versus B versus C) get a better price (to encourage loyalty). Furthermore, price differentiation also takes into account customers' cost-to-serve (agile versus lean versus continuous replenishment).

Obviously, the examples shown are simplified. In reality, price differentiation and alignment can be further achieved through various pricing policies which will help companies improve their price points. These may include applying cost recovery policies such as minimum order quantity surcharge, payment term mark-up and so on, thus creating value through price/revenue enhancement.

Of course, service offering differentiation (for example, safety stock service level, account management and so on) will provide further margin improvement through cost reduction (inventory carrying cost, support/ service cost and the like) by 'optimizing' allocation of internal resources.

In the above example, a matrix of worth-based and supply chain characteristics segmentation was used to guide offerings design. We saw how the different supply chain configurations affect the way we should define our pricing strategy/policies. Performing such price/service offering differentiation based on the customer's supply chain characteristics does provide us with a mechanism to create value for our customers while extracting value for ourselves.

If a company employs multiple segmentation approaches (say, including needs-based segmentation), the additional insights gained will further help fine-tune pricing policies and service offerings. Naturally, this becomes more complex due to multidimensional segmentation perspectives. In such situations, having a software solution[4] that handles an offerings design which employs multiple customer segmentation approaches will certainly lighten the analytical burden.

'VALUE PRICING': THE HOLY GRAIL OF PRICE OPTIMIZATION

We started this topic by commenting that superior supply chain capability can be a significant new dimension of competitive advantage (in addition to the traditional ones such as product design, quality, brand and so on). The question that comes to mind is: is it possible, and if yes, how can this competitive advantage be translated into an improved price position (that is, achieving a price premium) in the marketplace (assuming we deliver a comparatively better supply chain service relative to our competitors)?

Surely, price and service offerings alignment, to a certain extent, allow us to gain some improvement in the price level we offer to our customers. There is another pricing technique, however, which will take us to the next level in terms of 'price optimization' – namely, 'value pricing'.

As our objective is to introduce the concept of value pricing and how it is applied in the context of supply chain, we will not cover the technical details of how to calculate customer value. However, essentially, customer value can be defined in two forms: perceived value and quantified economic value. Not surprisingly, there are two value pricing techniques, each corresponding to the two forms of customer value. Value mapping is used for the former and customer economic value estimation is used for the latter.

The underlying logic for value pricing[5] is that, if we can quantify the value perceived or received by customers and if we have a comparative advantage over our key competitors, in the context of our analysis, supply chain delivery advantage, then we should be able to achieve a price premium in the market.

Figure 13.9 uses the value mapping technique to illustrate that, for the given (supply-driven) customer segment, the customers highly value the supplier's delivery reliability.

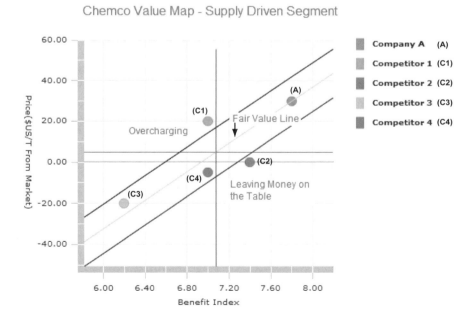

Figure 13.9   Value pricing

If a supplier is perceived to outperform its competitors in this aspect, it is perceived to provide higher customer value (in terms of the benefits index). The higher the benefit perceived by customers, the higher the price customers are willing to pay and this is still perceived to be fair as long as

'Quantifying such customer economic value provides the supplier with the ability to negotiate on the basis of value, rather than just purely on the basis of price.'

the price remains along the Fair Value Line. In the example in Figure 13.9, Supplier A's price is still perceived to be fair even though it is the highest. On the other hand, Supplier 2 is deemed to be underpricing as it generates more customer value than its pricing in the market (it is, in other words, value-advantaged). Supplier 2 has the option either to raise its price to attain a price premium or retain its current price position in order to gain market share.

In contrast, the customer economic value estimation technique quantifies the benefits the customer receives from us, relative to our customer's next best alternative (that is, our key competitor). If we provide more reliable delivery relative to our competitor, conceivably, we help our customer to reduce inventory-carrying cost, reduce warehouse rental or even cut down the production losses due to key raw material supply disruption (if our customer is another manufacturer who buys our product as a key raw material).

Quantifying such customer economic value provides the supplier with the ability to negotiate on the basis of value, rather than just purely on the basis of price. Most importantly, value pricing provides a way of translating a company's supply chain (or other) comparative advantage into tangible value creation.

Experience in the field has validated the usefulness of the value pricing technique in helping companies improve their price positioning. For example, as part of its pricing transformation initiative, one major chemical company (a leading producer with a significant presence in Asia Pacific), was able to identify a price premium through value pricing, for some of its products that are generally believed to be 'pure commodity'. In combination with a number of the best practices mentioned in this chapter, the project delivered benefits in excess of 1 per cent of revenue per year (which was more than US$10 million per year for a company with revenue of US$1 billion per year).

In conclusion, then, aligning pricing strategy and service offers to customer value (taking into account customers' supply chain characteristics) provides an opportunity for companies to create significant new value.

ALIGNMENT INSIGHTS

- *Customer segmentation provides the foundation for developing a company's pricing and service offer strategies.*

- *There are many ways of performing customer segmentation, each providing insights in terms of different aspects of customers' characteristics; their contribution to our business, their supply chain characteristics and impact on cost-to-serve, their buying behaviour, buyer value and needs and so on.*

- *Properly aligning price and service offers to customers' worth, needs and characteristics provides opportunities for companies to create new value for their business.*

- *Understanding customer value (perceived or quantified economic value) provides a way of achieving better price positioning (if we have a value advantage) and/or helping us focus on improving relevant capabilities which create value for our customers and eventually value for our own business.*

NOTES

1   Some components of the cost-to-serve elements within the Pocket Margin Waterfall are fairly straightforward to allocate, while others would require more sophisticated methods to derive the value and subsequently allocate the costs. For instance, order processing cost allocation would be facilitated by activity-based costing technique, whereas allocation of safety stock carrying cost by customer would first require a statistical safety stock model which allows calculation of safety stock requirements given the customers' demand variability.

2   Aka customer ranking.

3   Extract from Dupont's website 'Chief Marketing and Sales Officer talks about Marketing at DuPont. DuPont's Chief Marketing and Sales Offer, Diane Gulyas, spoke candidly with Judith Houchhauser, a full time MLDP participant, to share ideas on the direction of marketing at DuPont and the role of Marketing Leadership Development Program', http://www2. dupont.com/MLDP/en_US/david_bills_interview.html.

4   Typically, needs-based segments are derived from customer survey data. One powerful customer research method which provides the basic data to generate needs-based segments is conjoint analysis. It is beyond the scope of this chapter to dwell on conjoint analysis, but readers can refer to the various literatures which provide further details on why this is such a powerful technique for ascertaining buyer value. One such reference is B.K. Orme, *Getting Started with Conjoint Analysis: Strategies for Product Design and Pricing Research*, Research Publishers, Madison, WI, 2006.

5 Most of the modelling and analysis capabilities presented in this chapter (for example, pocket margin modelling, customer segmentation, offerings design, value pricing) are available in PriXLence™, Acceval's Pricing and Profit Management Software. PriXLence™ is an award-winning software which received the 'Best Customer ROI' Award from SAP, in recognition of its significant value creation impact.

14 Performance Measurement: Shaping Supply Chain Subcultures

Linda Nuthall

Performance measurement has the potential to fulfil a number of purposes in today's supply chain organizations. Indeed, if used smartly, performance measurement is one of the most powerful, efficient and effective tools available to management for strategic, tactical and operational decision support and, ultimately, for shaping the subcultures in an organization – and its supply chains.

In order for performance measurement to be fully utilized, it must first break away from the perception of being merely a cost management tool. Thankfully, this new perspective is becoming more widespread these days. Many executives are now acknowledging that successful performance measurement leads to improved alignment of operations with business strategies, a culture of accountability, and cooperation and collaboration between functions. It greatly improves understanding not only of internal operations, but also of suppliers, service providers and, most importantly, of customers, enabling more fact-based decisions about customer acquisition, retention, profit optimization and other revenue-enhancing tactics. Performance measurement 'done right' will also be a major facilitator and shaper of culture and subcultures within the organization.

This chapter explores the roles of performance measurement, including how it helps in shaping internal subcultures, a topic that has already been introduced in earlier chapters. To begin with, it gives an overview of some of the basic uses of performance measures which, when considered holistically, are what in fact make the cultural influence possible. It then explores how different types of measures can be used to foster different subcultures within organizations. The four generic supply chains described by John Gattorna in his book *Living Supply Chains*[1] are used to flesh out this concept.

WHY USE PERFORMANCE MEASURES?

'Successful performance measurement leads to improved alignment of operations with business strategies, a culture of accountability, and cooperation and collaboration between functions.'

Perhaps the most obvious use of performance measures is to simply report on what has happened within the organization, and between organizations, and to compare the results with previously defined targets. Knowledge of these 'performance gaps' helps to establish the need for change and provides the organizational tension necessary to drive change. Performance measures used to monitor the performance of various business units or divisions also provide information that contributes significantly to the rationale for resource allocation and investment decisions at the corporate level. A well-designed performance measurement system will systematically expose problems and their causes, therein providing management with a framework for informed decision-making. In the absence of such a framework, decisions would be made in a high-risk environment characterized by unsupported assumptions and biases.

Performance measures can also play a number of key communication roles (see Figure 14.1). They are perhaps the most effective way of communicating the strategic intent of the company from the boardroom, through all levels of management, to operations. Assuming that measures are always aligned with objectives, and that objectives at all levels of the organization are also aligned, the performance measurement system facilitates the education of all employees with respect to the organizational goals and the role that their area of responsibility plays in the achievement of these goals. Another important communication role of performance measures is performance feedback. Sharing performance measurement results throughout an organization, particularly higher-level measures, not only provides workers with a view of the 'broader picture', but can also invoke in them a sense of accomplishment, competence and control. Performance measurement also affords a mechanism for management to improve their understanding of operational processes, thereby increasing their ability to manage them. Being careful not to implement information overload, performance measures can communicate the relevant information from the 'shopfloor' to the appropriate levels of management in a way that exposes the nature of the various relationships between the variables. This enables informed end-to-end trade-off decisions rather than risking sub-optimization via lower levels of control.

Performance measurement is the primary tool at management's disposal for directing the behaviours within the organization. After all, when people know the criteria on which performance is being measured and perhaps rewarded or penalized, it follows that their behaviour will be such to enhance the outcome of these measures. This particular role of performance measurement is paramount with regard to an organization's chances of success given that evaluation and reward systems based on poorly chosen measures can be more

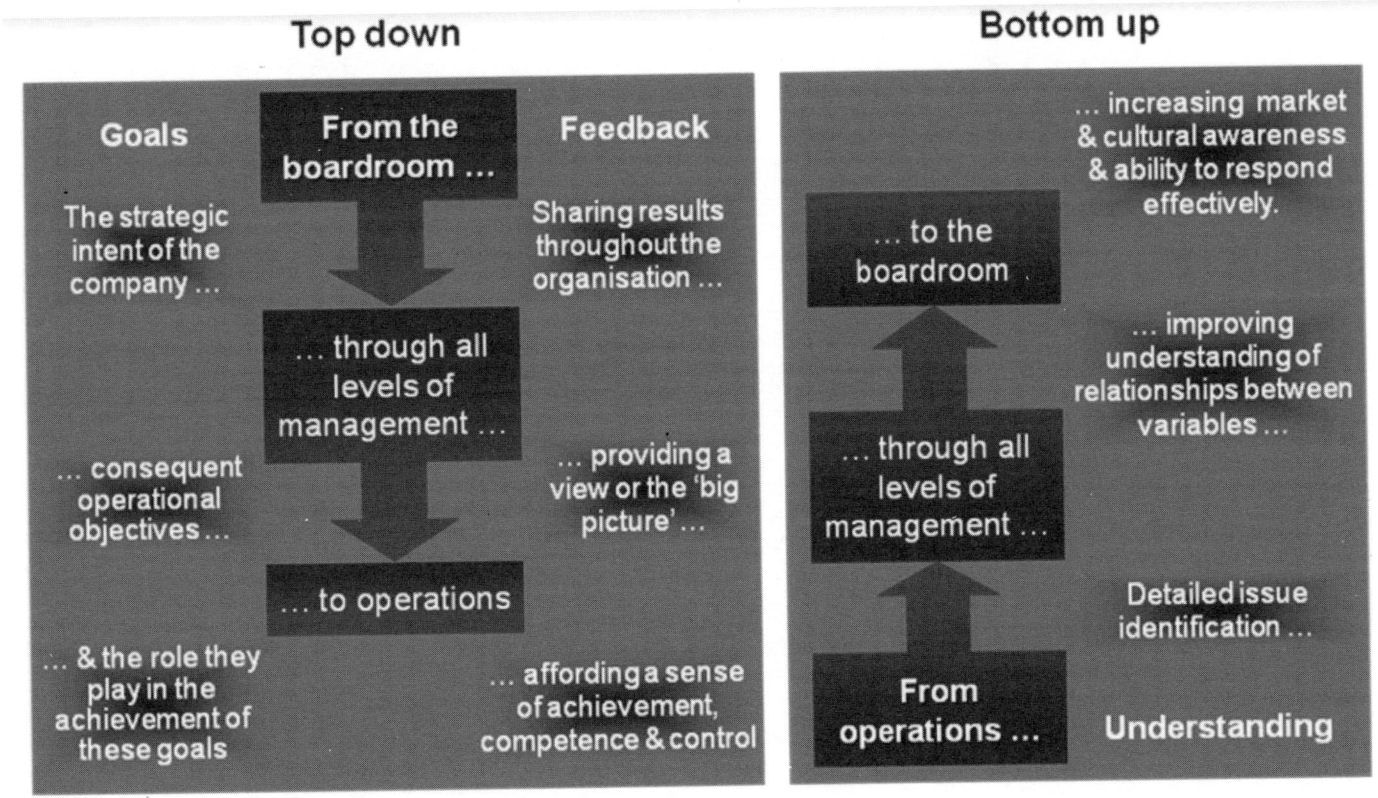

Figure 14.1   Communication roles of performance measures

destructive than effective. With no performance measurement system, or one that is misguided, individuals will be confused about what is expected of them, unclear about the quality of their work and unmotivated to change.

Having said that, it is important to add that high-performing organizations don't actually measure people, they measure processes and outcomes, and if designed smartly and with the appropriate input of key stakeholders, this does not translate into a lack of ownership and accountability. One will often encounter resistance to the introduction of new performance measures or, indeed, to reporting on existing measures. This reluctance is usually symptomatic of an unhealthy culture in which it is the people being measured rather than processes and outcomes, and blame and self-preservation dominate over creativity, curiosity, discovery and cooperation.

A truly effective performance measurement system will do more than steer behaviour in the right direction. It will help to create an environment in which the participants are encouraged to look for, recognize and pursue innovative improvement opportunities. Positive feedback, for example, ensures that people are aware that even little things count. This alone can provide the incentive to do more. Also, rather than simply monitoring, performance measures must show areas of improvement and areas of potential improvement. In this way, performance measures actually encourage innovation and problem-solving, and ultimately foster a culture of continuous improvement. Some of the most 'motivational' measures are indeed those that focus on potential performance, rather than actual. If consistent in their make-up and form, performance measurements enable organizations to make comparisons over time, between divisions or sites, with competitors, other industry players and so on. Indeed, even when operating procedures vary between organizations or operations, comparisons of results may highlight the potential benefits of alternative methods and approaches. Once this information is available, management has the opportunity to explore the implications of introducing such methods into other areas of operation. Benchmarking measures were developed to fulfil this role.

It is important to note that for benchmarking to be relevant and beneficial it should involve not only the measurement and comparison of operational output and results, but also the comparison of the processes that achieve these results. When properly understood and used as intended, benchmark performance measures can lead to inspired change.

GOOD PERFORMANCE MEASURES

While performance measurement systems have the potential to be the key to an organization's success, just as extreme are the tragic dysfunctional effects of employing the wrong measures. The provision of conflicting, or too many, performance measures is likely to result in a lack of conviction in decision-making, dissatisfaction among employees and consequent poor performance. While having suitable performance measures in place provides the foundation for informed decision-making, improper performance measures can lead to organizational paralysis by effectively disguising the critical issues and warning signs.

When determining the supply chain objectives of an organization, management must look to the overall corporate objectives for guidance. In other words, management must identify the role that the particular supply chain plays in moving the company, as a whole, towards the achievement of the corporate objectives. This process of goal 'alignment' must persist throughout all sub-organizations within the company and throughout each and every operational procedure to ensure that no part of the organization is working at cross-purposes. It follows, then, that in order to assess how the organization is performing in relation to its objectives, performance measures must be directly related to them.

> *'Measures must be clear, understandable and meaningful.'*

Leading organizations develop specific strategies to help them achieve their objectives. A strategy will consist of a set of actionable points that focus the efforts of all those involved. Measures should not only reveal the degree of achievement of the overall objectives, but also provide management with information on how well a strategy is being executed and on the appropriateness of the strategy itself. Measures properly aligned with the actionable points will convey the necessary information regarding the execution of the strategy, while the measures aligned with the objectives will provide feedback on the impact of the strategy on the system.

Supply chains come in many shapes, sizes and levels of complexity in terms of their configuration, operations and purpose. Good performance measures will sufficiently reflect these complexities so as to be realistic, but will also be simple enough to be understood. If performance measures are too simplistic, they undermine the process of consideration. Conversely, if they are too convoluted, they will simply not be used in any real way. To fulfil the purpose of motivating people, measures must be clear, understandable and meaningful. In other words, people must be able to see the relevance of the measures to their jobs and to the company's objectives.

Without breaking them down into their individual elements, many composite measures – such as DIFOTEF – lack tangible meaning, are difficult to understand and can mislead management decisions. A safer approach or rule of thumb is: if a process or outcome is deemed significant enough to measure, it should be measured directly.

Of course there are other characteristics of 'good' performance measures, many of which are discussed throughout the remainder of this chapter as the attention turns to the role performance measures play in shaping the subcultures of an organization. To explore this concept, we consider the four generic supply chains identified by Gattorna[2] – continuous replenishment, lean, agile and fully flexible. Each of these supply chain types is distinguished by its alignment to a customer segment with distinctly different 'dominant' buying behaviours. Consequently, the strategy employed to service each segment is different and, in turn, the performance measures employed to monitor, discover, direct and motivate must also be different or, at the very least, have different tolerances or emphases placed on them.

CONTINUOUS REPLENISHMENT SUPPLY CHAINS

The continuous replenishment supply chain is characterized by tight relationships with customers and high predictability of demand. These customers are all about long-term relationships. They 'expect' consistency, stability, personalized service and supply chain partners that work with them to resolve issues and improve performance. If their needs are met, these customers will be loyal to the end. They will communicate openly, share information and be willing, or rather expecting, to work collaboratively regarding demand and operations planning, and, indeed, all areas of the relationship. Furthermore, while a certain level of operational efficiency will result purely from the degree and timing of the information shared, price is not the primary focus of the customers in a continuous replenishment supply chain. Drivers of buying behaviour are more about guaranteed supply and consistent quality. It is worth noting also that these customers will not appreciate always dealing with different sales representatives. The desire for consistency goes way beyond product delivery.

Continuous replenishment supply chain customers could be described as the 'bread-and-butter' customer segment. For the most part, they have a low cost-to-serve – at least operationally – and the profit margins reflect this. They are predictable in terms of demand and, therefore, revenue and profitability are predictable as well. Too good to be true? It should be, but it could all just as easily turn sour. From time to time, issues will arise when a 'bread-and-butter' customer will require special attention. They will expect a jump to attention and an attitude that says 'Your challenges are our challenges. Let's sort this out together'. Be warned – don't disappoint! The cost of maintaining these relationships, even with the occasional 'over and above' treatment or loyalty reward, is nothing compared to what it would take to win them back after being, in their eyes, jilted.

So what does this mean for the performance measurement system? Once the customer segment's buying behaviour is understood, the organization's value proposition/mission statement, objectives and strategy for the segment can be designed. Given that the objectives provide the starting-point for developing the performance measurement system, let's give some thought to what one would typically expect to see in a strategic objective statement for a continuous replenishment supply chain – words and phrases like long-term, working together, collaboration, sharing, best quality, consistent service, etc. Consider the following questions:

- What are the ultimate measures of success?

- How do the customers themselves measure their suppliers?

- What are the warning signs if things are not going so well?

- How do the internal processes, through every level and function of the organization, contribute to success, and what are the measurable outcomes of these processes?

What are the Ultimate Measures of Success?

At the highest levels, one would expect to see measures such as: length of customer relationship; number of joint initiatives undertaken; number of face-to-face visits per customer; degree of information being shared in both directions; supplier's percentage of customer spend in each product/service category; and customer profitability. Together, these types of measures will reveal not only the degree of success and achievement of the strategic objectives, but also whether the customers being serviced by this supply chain really do belong in this segment.

How Do Customers Themselves Measure Their Suppliers?

Service reliability and quality are likely to be the predominant measures for these customers. Given that they give plenty of notice regarding their requirements, there is a basic, minimum requirement for consistency – lead-time consistency, product and/or service quality consistency, and even consistency of their points of contact with the supplier organization. The measures, therefore, will probably include: delivery on time, delivery in full and percentage of accepted quality.

In order to understand how customers view the performance of suppliers, and ideally pre-empt any performance glitches before they become 'serious' issues, suppliers must measure themselves in the same way – or at least incorporate these measures as part of their own performance measurement system.

Often, suppliers are left baffled by poor performance complaints from customers. The major cause of this 'disconnect' is that the parties are using different measures and/or that the measures used are being calculated in different ways. It is often just a question of language or formula. Composite measures are particularly prone to these problems.

What are the Warning Signs that Things are Not Going so Well?

As mentioned earlier, the costs associated with attempting to reclaim these customers, once their trust or faith in service has been damaged, are significant and quite possibly futile. A few well-designed measures to ensure that the relationship never reaches breaking point are therefore well advised and well worth the extra attention. In order to 'prevent rather than cure', an organization should not only measure such things as the number of customer complaints and response times to customer queries and complaints, but should also closely track the output of all the other high-level measures in order to quickly respond to unfavourable trends or blips. For example, the number of face-to-face visits for a particular customer suddenly decreasing or trending downwards may require management attention, or even intervention, in order to save a possibly neglected relationship. On the other hand, a sudden increase in the number of face-to-face visits may indicate communication or negotiation difficulties. If these departures from the 'norm' are not recognized and acted upon early, it may well be too late.

What are the Measurable Outcomes of Internal Processes?

Gattorna[3] describes the type of subculture required in the service of a continuous replenishment supply chain as a 'group' subculture. Measures that will best direct the behaviour and foster this type of culture will focus on the interaction or handover between processes and functional areas. The measures should help to educate workers as to how the output of their own processes impacts on those of other team members and ultimately, the customer. The high-level measures addressing consistency and quality will also cascade down throughout the organization. Adherence to plan, cycle-time variance and percentage of accepted quality are typical measures we would see in this environment.

> *'The costs associated with attempting to reclaim these customers, once their trust or faith in service has been damaged, are significant.'*

LEAN SUPPLY CHAINS

The lean supply chain is characterized by loose relationships with customers and high predictability of demand, based on history. These customers are all about price. They 'expect' efficiency and consistency and will always be 'shopping around' for the best deal. Loyalty is not a characteristic one would expect to find in this customer segment and customers will come and go and come again – almost on a transaction-by-transaction basis. Attempts to 'differentiate' value propositions with extra service and product features are virtually futile where these customers are concerned. Their buying behaviour is very 'commodity'-oriented. However, the upside of this segment is that demand is, for the most part, highly predictable, making efficiency possible

– that is, if forecasting and planning are done well. Unlike the continuous replenishment supply chain customers, lean supply chain customers are not big on sharing information and collaborating on operational decisions. Quite the contrary, they are likely to communicate from a distance and interactions may even be described as adversarial. The core focus of the supply organization in a lean supply chain is on excellent forecasting, planning and execution of standard, supported by basic processes.

The sorts of words and phrases one would typically expect to see in a strategic objective statement for a lean supply chain include lowest-cost, precise planning, and consistency.

What are the Measures of Success?

At the highest levels, one would expect to see measures such as: cost-to-serve; forecast accuracy; order-to-delivery cycle time; order-to-delivery cycle-time variation; productivity and asset utilization; number of active customers per month/quarter; and customer profitability. Together, these types of measures reveal a clear picture of how service in this segment is travelling. The organization is also likely to have measures for closely tracking and reporting on competitor pricing and activity. If a lean supply chain is 'wrongly' servicing specific customers, these types of high-level measures will alert management to this error and help them to rethink the customer's positioning accordingly.

How Do the Customers Themselves Measure Their Suppliers?

Service reliability and price are the predominant concerns of these customers. The measures, therefore, will probably include: cost of goods, delivery on time, delivery in full and percentage of accepted quality. No bells and whistles necessary.

What are the Warning Signs if Things are Not Going so Well?

From a competitive point of view, there is very little lag-time between cause and effect when things are not going well in a lean supply chain. With customers typically dealing with multiple suppliers in order to maintain consistency and low cost of supply, the impact of customer 'dissatisfaction' is almost immediate, particularly if the issue is one of price rather than of service delivery. If service delivery is the issue, these customers are likely to be amply vocal about it. The 'message', therefore, will arrive in concert directly and via the performance measurement system. Early warning of any service shortfall, indeed very early, before the event has taken place, provides the only opportunity for the supplier to 'soften the blow' with the customer and perhaps buy enough time and goodwill to weather the storm. Facilitating this level of sensitivity to operations requires measures that are sourced directly from the operations side of the business. Communication of these measures must be immediate (using exception reporting), and go directly to the person or persons within the organization with the authority and skill to take the appropriate action.

What are the Measurable Outcomes of Internal Processes?

Gattorna[4] describes the type of subculture required in the service of a lean supply chain as 'hierarchical'. Procedures, policies, standards and measures dominate this landscape. Measures that will direct the desired behaviour and foster this type of subculture will focus on adherence to plans and elimination of waste in materials, processes, time and information. Working in a 'Make-To-Forecast' (MTF) mode, a lean environment means trade-offs need to be made at a level high enough in the organization to ensure that no pockets of sub-optimization emerge. If they do, it could upset the delicate balance and put undue pressure on, or even erode, the already tight margins associated with serving this customer segment. Measures at the operational process level will therefore be very prescriptive, the most important of these being adherence to plan. Many operational measures will be populated in a lean supply chain. The two primary purposes of most of these measures are: 1) data discovery and input for the trade-off or optimization equation for the planning process; and 2) to provide feedback on, and motivation for, process improvement. The types of measures one would expect to see include: supply lead-time; production cycle time; lead-time and cycle-time variability; production change over times; productivity rates; utilization measures; and so on.

AGILE SUPPLY CHAINS

The agile supply chain is characterized by low demand predictability and, for the most part, a mixed relationships with customers. For a wide variety of reasons, ranging from organizational chaos and poor planning to genuinely unpredictable market forces, these customers demand very short order lead-times. Whatever the cause, the effect is that customers require rapid responses from their suppliers. In most cases, in order for a supply chain to be truly agile while maintaining some containment and control of cost, there will have to be 'buffer' or slack built into the system at various points along the chain. Production time, raw materials inventory, work-in-progress inventory, finished goods inventory, labour and so on. Strategies such as modular design, assemble-to-order and deferral are common in agile supply chains.

Many of these customers will have existing relationships with their supply organizations and may even have a continuous replenishment supply chain relationship for particular product or service categories, or for the 'base' volume of their business. As with all aspects of their business, these customers will want to collaborate with suppliers to determine the most efficient rapid response capability and processes possible. Others will be less collaborative in their approach, possibly for the simple reason that they operate in an environment where there is no time to develop relationships and urgent responses are necessary, whatever the cost. The common characteristics of the customers of the agile supply chain, regardless of the nature of the relationship, are the need for speed, priority service and, often, the need for fresh, innovative approaches, products and services.

What are the Measures of Success?

At the highest levels, one would expect to see measures such as: customer order-to-delivery time; new product concept-to-launch time; and measures that track and compare current performance with past performance and competitor performance. It is also very important to measure the true costs associated with servicing this customer segment in order to price products and services correctly and enable fact-based negotiation with any customer that may not be so accepting of the premium price tag that accompanies the premium service. This must incorporate not only the direct servicing costs, but also the costs associated with research and development, as well as the cost of carrying slack and buffer in the system to enable rapid response. Measures will therefore include things like: spend on research and development; maximum, minimum and average utilization of space, time and personnel; and damage, loss and obsolescence of inventory. Finally there will be measures that track the total cost to serve and customer profitability for the segment.

> '*The common characteristics of the customers of the agile supply chain... are the need for speed, priority service and, often, the need for fresh, innovative approaches, products and services.*'

How Do the Customers Themselves Measure Their Suppliers?

It will come as no surprise that the customers of an agile supply chain will be almost singularly obsessed with one measure – speed of response. This does not mean that quality should be sacrificed, but in a situation where all else is equal, the quickest wins this race. Even higher prices will take a back seat in this environment.

What are the Warning Signs if Things are Not Going so Well?

The key to pre-empting service issues in an agile supply chain is to constantly track the 'actual' against the 'planned' in terms of inventory balances and built-in reserves of resources. If these buffer elements are allowed to slip or lag, it will be prohibitively costly or even impossible to recover in time if an unexpected – albeit unpredictable – order comes through. If there are periods of low demand, this is an environment of monitoring and balancing, but when the order comes through, all systems are go.

What are the Measurable Outcomes of Internal Processes?

Gattorna[5] describes the type of subculture required in the service of an agile supply chain as 'rational'. This environment is 'aggressively customer focused' and, of course, fixated on speed. Measures that will direct the behaviour and foster this type of culture will focus on timing – of everything – as well as consistency of quality and adherence to plan. Flexibility is a core capability in a time-critical, unpredictable market rendering speed of customization and/or production changeover times as high priority. Innovation that focuses on improving response times should be highly regarded and rewarded in an agile supply chain environment, however, adherence to plan is also critical. This is because the 'balancing act' between cost and service must be done at the supply chain management level so as to safeguard against sub-optimization. The plan should focus on 'what', 'how much' and 'when', but not necessarily on the 'how'. In this way, operators are encouraged to be creative within their own area of expertise and responsibility without upsetting the overall balance. If this, indeed, does result in improved processes and responsiveness, the new standards can be communicated back to management for use in all subsequent planning tasks.

FULLY FLEXIBLE SUPPLY CHAINS

The fully flexible supply chain is characterized by low demand predictability and loose relationships with customers. In his book, *Living Supply Chains*, Gattorna[6] describes the two possible types of situations in which the fully flexible supply chain emerges. The first of these is the 'business event' – that is, an unexpected, or even unforeseeable, event that occurs within a business or to a customer of a business. The business will normally operate one or more of the other three supply chain types, or variations of these. The 'event' requires a response that is inspired, innovative and fast. It is fair to say that, if an effective solution is not found and delivered fast, it will be ruinous for the organization, or the customer, or both. These are, one would hope, 'one-off' events for which it is difficult, if not impossible, to plan, except to have access to resources that have the appropriate attitude, aptitude and knowledge to respond. In most cases, the fully flexible supply chain in a business context is a temporary state. Once the 'crisis' has passed, the pre-existing supply chain logics will return, perhaps slightly updated if there were lessons learnt from the event itself or the action taken. 'Business event' fully flexible supply chains are not price-sensitive. Quite the reverse: 'We need to fix this now, hang the cost' more or less sums up the attitude in this environment. The cost will, of course, have to be absorbed by the organization or individual for whom the action is being taken.

The second situation where fully flexible supply chains are commonly found is the 'emergency event' –that is, large-scale disasters, man-made or natural, where lives are at risk and all sorts of obstacles and challenges must be overcome. As with the 'business event', these situations require fast and creative solutions, often under the most difficult circumstances. In addition to dealing with the logistical challenges, 'emergency event' fully flexible supply chains also have financial accountabilities and limitations due to the fact that they are funded by governments, government agencies, aid organizations, charities, corporations and individuals. The responsibility of the respondents is therefore to both the customers (or victims) and those funding the campaign. But, wait, there's more. On top of all this, these supply chains are usually made up of groups and individuals from a wide range of skill and cultural backgrounds, who have probably never worked together before and who have a variety of 'objectives' and interpretations of how success will look in that particular setting. The element that ultimately holds these supply chains together is that they attract the right type of person, often volunteers. Whatever else they may bring to the table, they have the common desire to help and make it work.

Fully Flexible Supply Chain Measures

When a 'business event' catapults an organization into a fully flexible response, it will essentially hit the red button that launches those involved into an 'entrepreneurial' subculture. As mentioned earlier, this subculture must be pre-existing in some form, even if severely underutilized. Individualism is encouraged, risks are taken and mistakes are essentially forgiven. Whereas performance measurement will focus on speed, incentives and rewards will be based on elements – namely creativity and innovation – that are less easily measured due to their subjective nature,. The costs associated with the action taken will be borne by the organization or individual at the source of the demand. This means that, even though costs are not perceived as a constraint to the response, they must nonetheless be captured and reported on.

In the fully flexible 'emergency event' supply chain, strategies and measures will focus, first, on saving lives and, second, on safeguarding against further threats. With very little planning time and possibly very little specific knowledge of the obstacles ahead, operations in this environment are likely to be directed on a task-by-task basis and measures will probably consist of such questions as 'Is it done yet?' and 'Did it work?'. Tracking, monitoring and managing funds is also critical in these supply chains and difficult trade-off decisions must often be taken in the absence of complete information and under very intense time pressures. Clearly, the better the measures and communication channels, the better the decisions and the results.

CLOSING COMMENTS

Just a couple of final thoughts on organizations housing multiple supply chain types. It is completely feasible that a single organization will service multiple customer segments that exhibit different buying behaviours. Some organizations may have sufficient resources to enable completely dedicated and independent supply chains. Fantastic – supply chains that never have to cross over or compromise, at least not operationally. Most organizations, however, will need to operationally service more than one customer segment from the same resource base, at least in part. In these environments, planning should still be carried out for each segment independently, in order to ascertain its optimal arrangement. Once this is done, aggregate planning and optimization can take place, as well as informed decision-making on resource and cost allocation. The best performance measurement approach to adopt in the sections or processes that are shared by multiple supply chain types is therefore adherence to plan. To avoid reverting to a 'one size fits all' world, the trick is to determine at which operational junctions the different supply chains must branch out in order to facilitate different responses, underpinned by the appropriate subcultures, to best align with the customers they serve.

ALIGNMENT INSIGHTS

- *When determining the objectives and measures for a particular type of supply chain, management must look to the overall corporate objectives for direction. Goal 'alignment' must persist throughout all sub-organizations within the supply chain, and each and every operational procedure, to ensure that no part is working at cross-purposes with others. In order to assess how the supply chain is performing in relation to its objectives, performance measures must be directly related to them.*

- *A supply chain strategy will consist of a set of actionable points that focus the efforts of all those involved. Measures that properly align with these actionable points will convey to management the necessary information regarding the 'execution success' of the strategy.*

- *If the execution of the strategy is successful, measures that align with the strategic objectives will provide feedback on the appropriateness of the strategy itself.*

NOTES

1   J.L. Gattorna, *Living Supply Chains*, FT Prentice Hall, Harlow, 2006, Figure 2.4, p. 46.
2   Ibid.
3   Ibid., Ch. 3, Figure 3.3, p. 74.
4   Ibid.
5   Ibid.
6   Ibid., Ch. 8, pp. 179–197.

15 Using Network Optimization Modelling Techniques to Resolve Supply Chain Complexity and Achieve Aligned Operations

Deborah Ellis

INTRODUCTION

As the geographic reach of supply chains widen and tools become available to enable extended visibility and control over larger operations, and as we abandon the 'one-size-fits all' convention, the number of variables and trade-offs that must be considered in supply chain planning and design increase dramatically. Most supply chain networks, for even mid-sized businesses, are now too complex for managers to make critical changes relying only on their experience and a set of spreadsheets. But many do!

Complex problems require sophisticated resolution tools,[1] and, for strategic and tactical decisions in the supply chain, this now equates to decision support tools. The design of the network, including such questions as where to manufacture and how to appropriately service each market, are usually the most significant in any supply chain. This chapter discusses the most common decision support tool used to support strategic and tactical supply chain network design decisions – the network optimization model. We briefly review how such models operate and place them in the context of the other tools that support supply chain decisions. Case studies are then used to explore the directions network models are now taking, in particular: their role in supporting global sourcing and distribution networks; the recent breakthroughs in the integration of inventory into contemporary models; and the use of network models to factor carbon emissions into strategic and tactical supply chain planning.

Finally, this chapter outlines possibly the most significant opportunity that network optimization presents, which is its role as a tool to achieve 'aligned' operations. By recognizing the demand patterns and buying priorities of different groups of customers and embedding this information in the model, the options for the supporting network, service structure, and the resultant cost-to-serve can be derived. This becomes a powerful tool to design the one or several supply chains that make up an aligned operation, and to be able to assess the impact *before* making major changes *on the ground*. It is also an important development in terms of reducing both the strategic and operational complexity of the supply chains under management.

NETWORK MODELLING IN CONTEXT: DECISION SUPPORT TOOLS USED IN THE SUPPLY CHAIN

'A selection of scenarios are fed into a simulation model to look in more detail at how they might perform over time, particularly in relation to specific events or disruptions to normal operations. This can be a powerful way of testing the 'resilience' of the network.'

Although strategic and tactical decision support systems (DSS) have been used in the supply chain for a considerable time, they have now moved from the leading edge to being a part of the everyday armoury of the supply chain designer/manager. There is a developed industry supporting modelling, the software is largely off-the-shelf rather than custom-written, and models are being used in mid-sized businesses as well as large corporations. These developments have led to some confusion, however, about the role of network models compared to other decision support tools used in the supply chain. The boundaries are blurring a little, but in general the most established decision support tools, and their role in planning, can be broadly categorized as shown in Table 15.1.

These tools are not alternative approaches but complementary, each supporting a different, but related, set of decisions. They are beginning to be used in this fashion where there are multifaceted issues to be addressed. Network design options are developed using a network optimization model, for instance, and then a selection of scenarios are fed into a simulation model to look in more detail at how they might perform over time, particularly in relation to specific events or disruptions to normal operations. This can be a powerful way of testing the 'resilience' of the network after potential disturbances, and the results can be fed back into the network model to either build protection into the structure on an ongoing basis or to develop plans via a series of 'contingency' scenarios.

Similarly inventory optimization can be run iteratively, using outputs from a network model in order to identify the inventory positions that can be supported by the various networks, and, conversely, inventory-derived scenarios can be tested with the network model. These might include, for example, various combinations of centralized and regional distribution centres supporting different parts of the range.

Inventory has always been a limitation in network models. The inventory dynamic is particular to the stock-keeping unit (SKU), and the same aggregations that work for manufacturing and logistics do not work for inventory: hence the use of iterative approaches rather than full integration

Table 15.1   **Supply Chain Decision Support Tools**

Network Optimization Models	
Used to design the optimal facility and process 'footprint' and/or select the appropriate 'paths' through the supply chain to meet a given level of demand, or to most effectively utilize a scarce resource.	**Strengths:**
	• A *macro-view* – the clarity created by aggregation. Enables managers to 'see' the patterns and major trends and to make decisions in complex environments.
Models are usually built, and results viewed, at an aggregate level.	• The size of the problems that can be addressed. One model, for example, can trade off raw material supply options against DC locations and end-customer delivery options.
They evaluate trade-offs with an objective to minimize total cost, or maximise overall profitability within given constraints, for example, service levels.	• The network model is essentially a static model, looking at average 'buckets' of volume rather than changes over time.

Simulation	
Simulation tools enable the behaviour of a part of the supply chain to be observed over time.	**Strengths:**
	• A *micro-view* – granularity enables managers to understand the key relationships and processes within the supply chain.
Rules are created which describe how the system should work, and the impacts on other parts of the operation are tracked as inputs are varied.	• Can capture variability, randomness and 'events'.
Agent-based simulation (ABS) models, a subset of simulation models, are gaining more attention in supply chain situations because of their ability to capture more complex relationships and individual decision-making processes.	• Simulation models cannot choose between a large set of options. Most useful when comparing the performance of a small number of predesigned alternatives.

Inventory optimization	
Mathematical algorithms developed in the 1990's for multi-echelon inventory chains have now been commercialized.	**Strengths:**
	• Supports decision-making on inventory at both the granular and the very high level, for example, safety stocks are developed by SKU by location, but the impact of availability policy can be tested at the aggregate level.
These systems take account of the uncertainties around demand and supply and the various lead-times, and the interconnectedness of each level of the network. They optimize the inventory by SKU at any point to meet service-level objectives.	**Limitations:**
	• Can only optimize inventory within a given network. Does not indicate the 'ideal' network for inventory cost or total cost.

into the network model. Significant advances are being made in this regard, however, and a case study later in the chapter describes a format for integrating inventory into network modelling.

Although the focus here is on strategic and tactical decision support, the underlying capability that drives these tools is now also being seen in operational areas of the supply chain. Optimization has typically been associated (in the supply chain) with longer-term, strategic and occasionally tactical decision-making. The time and system resources required precluded operational applications. Now, however, the exponential growth in computing power has enabled optimization techniques to be used to support planning and scheduling at the operational level, as illustrated by DHL's Asia-Pacific roll-out from 2008 of an optimization-based planning and scheduling system across its operations.[2]

THE NETWORK OPTIMIZATION MODEL: HOW IT WORKS

A network model is a representation of part of the supply chain. Just as with the models of the economy, reality can never be exactly replicated. In most cases, however, a well-constructed supply chain model can be validated against financial reports to a high level of accuracy which gives confidence in its predictive powers (usually a much higher level of confidence than the economic models can ever achieve).

A network model can be conceptualized as a number of levels (echelons) of activity – that is, from suppliers, to manufacturing and on to one, two or more distribution levels and finally through to customers/markets. At the manufacturing and distribution levels, actual facilities are represented and within these facilities a set of processes are defined. Suppliers, facilities and processes all have costs and capacities, as do the 'links' between each. Product, in the form of raw material, work-in-process and finished goods, flow through the network, the volume and direction being pulled by the 'demand' for finished goods in specific markets. As volume 'flows' through a node (facility or process), or along a link, cost is incurred (see Figure 15.1). This cost can either be a unit cost and/or a share of the fixed cost of the facility or process.

The model essentially starts out as a very large file set, with volume files and cost and capacity files related to suppliers, facilities, processes and links. These are ultimately combined by the software into a complex 'algorithm' which depicts the network. This algorithm is then 'solved' to satisfy an objective function, either to minimize the cost of operating the network or, by also capturing revenue, to maximize profitability, subject to specific constraints.

The model is a strategic view of the supply chain. In order to produce results which make sense at the strategic level, *aggregations* of the key

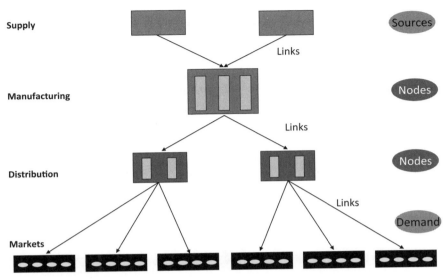

Demand 'pulls' product through a network of nodes and links, accumulating cost at each stage...

Supply — Sources

Links

Manufacturing — Nodes

Links

Distribution — Nodes

Links

Demand

Markets

Figure 15.1   Network optimization model structure

elements are usually required. Thus, products, suppliers and customers are typically aggregated into meaningful groups. The decisions surrounding these aggregations are arguably the most significant decisions in the whole modelling process. The groups need to reflect the aspects of products, customers and suppliers that drive different costs through the part of the network being examined.

For *product groups*, the key drivers are typically handling and manufacturing characteristics. Logistics aspects such as cube, weight and pick format are often relevant. Manufacturing dimensions are naturally industry- and scenario-specific, but are typically related to the different lines and processes utilized and the key activity cost drivers, such as fill time in a bottling operation.

For *customers and supplier grouping*, location is, of course, a key driver as it determines transport time and cost. Location, though, is rarely sufficient to capture different service requirements and thus the cost of servicing different types of customers. Customer groupings which in some way reflect these requirements are also usually required in order to develop meaningful outcomes.

It is in this aspect of designing a supply chain model around customers (and even suppliers) that dynamic alignment provides a framework that can significantly enhance the model results, as illustrated in the discussion and case study later in this chapter.

Although the initial model runs are 'constrained' to replicate activity in the validation period, the model is either built (or later extended) to enable a set of feasible alternatives to be tested. Thus additional nodes, processes and links are built into the model (see Figure 15.2).

Although the various packages differ a little in how they capture activity and cost inside a facility, the underlying logic invariably relates back to an activity-based costing approach (see Figure 15.3). It is at this point that the method of aggregation is critical. A product group needs to reflect a consistent process and use of resources in the plant or distribution centre. An 'ugly' product, such as a refrigerator that requires two-person handling and specialized equipment at various stages as it transits the distribution centre would be mismatched with smaller appliances that are handled on a standard pallet and picked by one person.

THE MODELLING PROCESS

The process of building a model of a supply chain starts with establishing a clear direction. This requires understanding of the key issues (and opportunities) facing the business and identifying a set of scenarios to be tested related to these issues. Although a model can be a broad representation of the business generally, the types of scenarios determine the level of detail that needs to be captured in particular parts of the operation and in the aggregations. If there are no critical issues and thus scenarios relating to distributors, for example, then they may be treated as a customer. In another situation, where choices between distributors and direct distribution are to be tested, much more detail about both distributors and their customers should be included in the model.

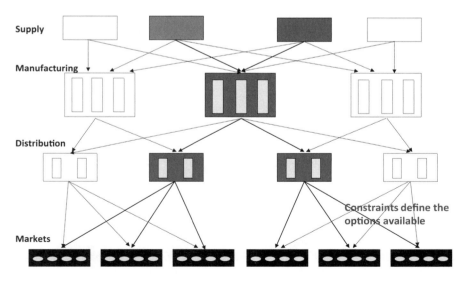

Alternative paths are made available which the model tests against the current...

Supply

Manufacturing

Distribution

Constraints define the options available

Markets

Figure 15.2   Network optimization model: testing options

Distribution and manufacturing facility cost and capacity is defined at facility, process and product group level...

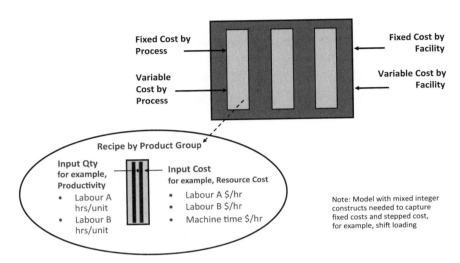

Figure 15.3   Representing facility costs and capacities

The use of models to date has often involved one-off solutions or strategic direction-setting projects managed by consultants. As the tools have become more user-friendly and as supply chain issues have moved up the strategic agenda, we are starting to see many more organizations making ongoing use of models to support annual planning cycles and specific tactical planning requirements.

A model that is to be used in-house, as an ongoing strategic or tactical decision support tool, is usually broader, covering not only the immediate business issues, but also areas of potential future opportunity or concern.

Whether the model is for a one-off strategic review, or will be used in-house for both strategic and tactical support, the initial process is similar. The project plan moves from considerations of broad strategy to detailed data collection and modelling and back to broad strategy. Specifically the key stages in a modelling project are:

1. Developing an initial list of *scenarios* to be tested. The list will invariably be extended and changed as the initial results start flowing from the model, but this 'first cut' indicates the general direction of concerns and focus.

2. *Designing and building the model.* Modelling software provides a 'shell', but the characteristics of the particular operation, and the priorities driven by the likely scenarios, must be interpreted and engineered into the model. The model is constructed on a recent historical data period

– for example, the last financial year. Volume data is extracted from the transactional files for this period and is aggregated by the appropriate product, supplier and customer groupings. Costs and capacities for the same period are defined and built into the model. Key cost drivers must be identified and the relationships between cost and volume needs to be defined – this is similar to an activity-based costing exercise. Models can be either single-period or multi-period where there are seasonality issues or tactical planning decisions to be made.

3.   *Validation*. Once the volume and costs are defined, the model can be constrained to run for the data period. This would involve 'forcing' volume down the appropriate paths that were actually used in this period with the aim of replicating the operating cost for the period. A number of refinements are usually required to fine-tune the cost relationships until management is confident that the model is capable of capturing the key dynamics of the business and until it generates costs for major activities that are close to those experienced in the data period.

4.   *Optimization*. This is usually the most exciting and thought-provoking stage of a modelling project. The constraints that forced the validation model to perform as the business did in the data period are relaxed and the model is given the freedom to optimize – or find a 'better' (lower-cost/more profitable) method to source, produce or deliver its volume. Although most solutions during this period are impractical for various reasons, the trends provide very strong indicators of the opportunities for quantum change. There are often 'anti-intuitive' results which can open up whole new ways of viewing the operation. Invariably, the results in this stage suggest new scenarios to be tested in the next stage.

5.   *Scenario testing*. The list of scenarios is reviewed and updated. The model may also be calibrated to take account of significant changes since the original data period. New versions of the model are then used to run each of the scenarios. There may be several versions of a particular scenario to refine it or to test the sensitivity to changes in key assumptions.

6.   *A costed strategy*. After the various results have been absorbed, a final scenario or set of scenarios (often reflecting a staged implementation), which combine the preferred options into a realistic strategy, is run. This becomes the base for planning and capital allocation for the operation over a given timeframe.

WHEN IS A NETWORK OPTIMIZATION MODEL APPLICABLE?

As discussed, network optimization models provide insight at the strategic and tactical level. Until now, much of the focus has been on support for strategic decisions. Types of strategic issues that can be addressed include:

- Sourcing decisions: alternative supply models; levels of value added from suppliers; direct delivery versus consolidation.

- Manufacturing decisions: number and location of plants; offshore versus onshore manufacture; what to manufacture where; timing of capital expenditure.

- Distribution network decisions: how many DCs; location and role of DCs; cross-dock versus warehousing; reverse logistics support network.

- Channel decisions: distributors versus direct; number of distributors; structure to support e-commerce channels.

- Market decisions: optimum market allocation of limited supply; structure needed to support service levels by segment; structure needed to support sales forecasts/new markets/expansion plans (and cost to support growth); optimum outlet number and location to support sales.

- Merger and acquisition: extent of synergy; opportunities for consolidation; reconfiguring merged networks.

- Contingency planning: alternatives for major supply and demand variations; facility/line interruption responses; levels of redundant capacity to cover interruption scenarios.

At the tactical level the decisions span the medium-term aspects of the areas indicated above and the types of applications would relate to:

- how to most effectively utilize available resources (limited supply, manufacturing plants and lines, distribution centres) to meet anticipated demand;

- planning and providing information for those involved in assigning resources over the short to medium term, including: plant and line capacity; transport capacity planning; and storage and handling capacity;

- tactical contingency planning: optimizing responses to real or anticipated interruptions.

MODEL PROVIDERS

Most organizations now use off-the-shelf software as the 'shell' for their network model and use experienced consultants to assist them to build the initial model. Network optimization software is available as 'best-of-breed' or within modules associated with some of the established ERP systems. These models still vary considerably in capability and orientation, with some designed for distribution-only networks and others able to model a full production and distribution network. The other key differences relate to the solver, the mathematical optimizing engine which determines the accuracy of the results and the level of detail that can be incorporated – for example, the model's ability to capture non-linear relationships such as fixed costs.

Some of the established models and their suppliers are listed in Table 15.2. In recent years there has been considerable consolidation and the suppliers have changed, but each of these models has been on the market for some time.

Table 15.2   Selected network optimization model providers

Supplier	Model
Optiant	PowerChain Network Design (formerly SLIM)
i2	Supply Chain Strategist
ILOG (LogicTools)	Logicnet Plus
Llamasoft	Supply Chain Guru
Barloworld	CAST
Insight	SAILS
Axxom Software AG	Orion-PI
Oracle	JD Edwards One Strategic Network Optimization

APPLICATIONS AND NEW DIRECTIONS: GLOBAL SUPPLY CHAINS

Many of the applications of network models are now global supply chains, where sourcing, distribution or both are carried on across borders and with extended lead-times. A classic example of this type of model is that used by Fonterra in New Zealand.

Case Study: Fonterra

Fonterra is one of the top six dairy companies in the world, and the world's largest exporter of dairy products. Its annual turnover is approximately $US11 billion ($NZD13.9 billion to 31May 2008). It is a cooperative and is owned by 11,000 New Zealand dairy farmers, who are also its major suppliers. Fonterra exports from New Zealand to over 140 countries. Much of its product is processed into dry powder for export. It also has large operations outside New Zealand, including 11 plants in Australia, and joint-venture and co-pack operations in other countries.

Fonterra uses a Network optimization model to configure and refine its distribution network within New Zealand and to Europe, the United States, Asia and Africa. The level of detail in the overseas destinations varies, with Europe and the United States depicted to customer level but with Asia and Africa modelled only to 'Fonterra DC' level. (A standalone, 'within-Asia' model is being developed to address more detailed options without overcomplicating the primary model).

The global operations model is currently structured as:

- 120 product groups, with *ambient* and *refrigerated* as the first screen

- 40 plants

- 80 stores (DCs) and

- 150 customer groups (although some of these are single large customers).

The 'customer' is defined as the point at which title is transferred. Most export business is under CIF terms, so the 'customer' is located at the receiving port.

The pallet is used as the standard unit of measure. Fortunately, the business has a high proportion of products which comply with the simple rule of thumb, 1 pallet =1 square mete r= 1 tonne, which makes the single unit of measure both practical and intuitive.

The model is a cost minimization model, designed to optimize distribution. Inbound supply and production are not included. The distribution channels modelled include plant direct to Fonterra DC, plant to distributor, plant direct to customer, in addition to the DC to distributor and DC to customer options.

The location and level of utilization of distribution centres is a key issue that the model is used to address. The network consists of some distribution centres that operate on a variable cost basis and others that are predominantly fixed-cost, and the models optimizes use across both types. It is also used to locate and define the dimensions of new facilities: for example, the decision to build a new $NZ80 million refrigerated warehouse at Waikato resulted from modelling 20 alternative location and configuration options.

Despite being distribution-focused, one of the core issues that this model addresses is driven by issues further up the supply chain. Fonterra has a highly seasonal supply dynamic. Milk is produced during the spring and summer seasons, and 42 per cent of the volume needs to be processed within three months. Then there are three winter months during which there is almost no supply or processing. This creates a complex distribution problem as inventory 'peaks' and then depletes across the year. The model is constructed as a multi-period model to enable the seasonal variations to be taken into account.

Fonterra has a team of five people working on various aspects of network modelling. Their agenda for the future includes: use of the model to assess several merger and acquisition options under consideration; plans to extend the model into the supply chains of some of their key customers to enable an end-to-end optimization of the combined operations; and development of an 'Asian' model to look more closely at scenarios related to co-packing and blending operations across Asia.

Fonterra takes a project approach to using the model, treating the sets of scenarios that address particular issues as a 'project'. Like many model users, the team finds that the biggest challenge is assembling data and vetting the quality across such a large network. In a recent project, 80 per cent of modelling time was associated with data collection.

INTEGRATION OF INVENTORY INTO NETWORK OPTIMIZATION MODELLING

As noted earlier, one of the problematic aspects of network modelling has been the inability to fully integrate inventory into the optimization equation. The difficulty arises because network models are mathematical programming models and inventory planning has relied on probabilistic models. Network models are also built at an aggregate level and the natural groupings of products that suit the capture of cost through the network usually do not have a consistent inventory dynamic.

Various approaches have been taken, and it now appears that progress is being made in more fully accommodating inventory trade-offs.

Case Study: North American Homewares Chain

A model built for a North American homewares chain[3] by two of the leaders in the network optimization field (Shapiro and Wagner) moved beyond the iterative approaches used in the past. Methods were developed that enabled inventory-holding cost to be incorporated into an optimization model of the supply chain. This allowed the model to minimize the total supply chain cost and to more fully trade off both operating cost and inventory-holding cost options.

In 2005 the chain had 50 stores served by direct shipments from suppliers (55 per cent) and shipments through two cross-dock facilities (45 per cent). They stocked approximately 30,000 SKUs with a turnover of $US750 million and had an aggressive expansion plan that aimed to double the number of stores in five years. The network optimization modelling project was undertaken to 'define an optimal and realistic network expansion plan and operating guidelines'[4] for the immediate term and for the five-year time horizon. The current network was modelled ,as well as options for additional channels via either new cross-dock facilities or distribution centres.

The approach used to incorporate inventory was to construct inventory simulation models outside the network model on a sample of SKUs with different inventory dynamics, using the historic relationship between inventory and throughput at current facilities. These models were used to define a set of relationships between throughput and inventory that could be used more generally.

Product groups were then developed that aggregated products by logistics criteria and also criteria related to their inventory performance (such as fast or slow sales, lead-time and stocking capability). When the model was built, in addition to the usual distribution centre and cross-dock processes (such as pallet unloading and break bulk) an additional process of inventory holding was incorporated at all potential stockholding facilities. The information from the simulation models was then used to create throughput/inventory holding cost relationships at each facility for each product group. Holding cost related to the yearly investment cost per unit and the cost of capital.

At distribution centres this relationship had a fixed component and two variable components (see Figure 15.4). The two levels of variable cost reflect the economies of scale in inventory, driven by factors including the need for proportionally less safety stock where inventory is located at fewer facilities (usually estimated via the square root rule). In smaller facilities, in this case at retail stores, the volumes are lower and inventory was found to have a more direct relationship to throughput.

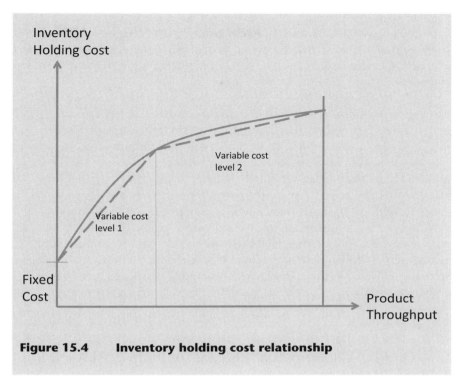

Figure 15.4 **Inventory holding cost relationship**

The model was solved with a cost minimization objective and produced a very significant potential savings of 20 per cent of annual operating cost. The savings were driven by shifting parts of the direct-to-store volume into cross-dock facilities and by the reduction in inventory holding cost achieved by shifting inventory for some (mainly high-value) items back up the network into distribution centres. This improved inventory turns from 3.7 to 4.1 (with potentially greater increases via opportunities identified by the inventory simulation models to modify the underlying inventory control methods and policies). The model was also able to provide the initial phased strategy for the introduction of cross-dock and distribution centre facilities to support the five-year expansion plan.

'One of the problematic aspects of network modelling has been the inability to fully integrate inventory into the optimization equation.'

THE GREEN SUPPLY CHAIN

An emerging, and potentially very important, application of network optimization models is in supporting the integration of carbon emission factors into network design decisions.

It is apparent that many countries will soon have a mechanism for pricing greenhouse gas emissions beyond a 'cap' limit. This will impact on the cost of manufacturing and distributing, and change the optimal network to support sales. In Europe such a mechanism already exists, and Australia is expected to have an emissions trading scheme by 2010. As well as pressure from regulators, there is also considerable demand building from shareholders and customers for businesses to be environmentally responsible and to show evidence of action to minimize their impact.

Some model vendors have adapted their models to explicitly capture emission levels from activities through the chain. The level of emissions can be used as a constraint and the model solved for minimum cost within specified levels of emissions. A cost per tonne of emissions can also be attached to generating activities (reflecting emission pricing) either for all activity or for activity/emissions beyond specified levels (reflecting a 'cap' level). The model is then solved to minimize cost (or maximize profitability) including emissions. Combinations of constraints and cost can also be 'tested'. The parameters of the carbon emission problem are very sympathetic to the underlying logic of mathematical optimization models, so that even some of the software which has not specifically incorporated emissions terminology can be used to build models which test network design options that include carbon emissions.

USING NETWORK MODELS TO ACHIEVE ALIGNED OPERATIONS

Dynamic alignment, as introduced elsewhere in this book, seeks to use different supply chains to respond most appropriately to the major demand patterns in the market. Conceptually there are striking parallels between the way dynamic alignment 'views' an organization's supply chains and the way network models depict the supply chain.

Dynamic alignment recognizes demand as the key driver for all supply chain activity. Network models ultimately 'pull' volume through their virtual supply chains to satisfy demand. Dynamic alignment recognizes that, while it is critical to focus on the difference between customers, it is impossible to cost-effectively provide customized service to every customer, so that a small number of significantly different options are optimal. Similarly, strategic network models typically operate at an aggregated level, where the most significant differences between customers and products are the basis for groupings. This aggregation is critical to revealing the underlying strategic imperatives.

The following case study illustrates the clarity that combining the conceptual framework of dynamic alignment with the mathematical framework of the network model can bring to a complex distribution problem.

Case study: Building Industry Supplier

A building industry supplier had a broad customer base which ranged from distributors and large commercial building contracts to large and small end-user installers. Although these customers were buying the same or very similar products, the service expectations, buying patterns and underlying needs were very different.

When an optimization model[5] was developed for this business, a critical aspect was to capture these key buying differences in the customer grouping and to factor in the format of the order and the 'service package' that was purchased. The customer groups developed were based on the way the customer brought (project or not-project) and the level of direct support needed from the supplier. On one end of the spectrum were distributors (including all formats of resellers) who ordered regularly for stock and whose priority was reliable, consistent service. Commercial Project and Residential Project were segments of customers identified as having long-term relationships with the supplier but ordering for one-off project situations with specific requirements. Their priority was responsiveness and flexibility. At the other end of the spectrum, Commercial and Residential Support customers were generally (but not always) smaller end-users who required delivery to site but also often needed easy access for last-minute requirements. These customers valued technical support and day-to-day relationships with their supplier who they saw as the 'hub' of their trade network.

The 'service/product' packages these customers purchased were defined for modelling as: Bulk (larger, stock orders picked up or delivered); Crane-ups (deliveries, with narrow delivery windows to meet crane schedules); House Lots (larger mixed orders picked up or delivered); Standard Orders (smaller mixed orders picked up or delivered); and Immediate Orders (pick- ups with no advance notice). Many of these 'service/product' packages were purchased by more than one type of customer.

Product groups were determined by the product's weight, handling and manufacturing characteristics (as manufacturing was also considered in the model). The network that was developed running models based on management scenarios and using these parameters is illustrated in Figure 15.5. It features three major paths

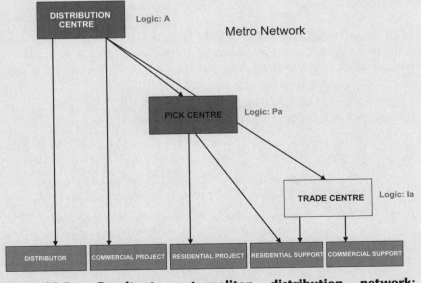

Figure 15.5　　**Resultant metropolitan distribution network: building supplies company**

to the customer. The Bulk path is designed for high-volume, regular activity and includes supply to facilities in the other two paths. (This is the lean supply chain of dynamic alignment). The Pick path is more responsive, capable of shorter lead-times and geared for a less predictable workload (equivalent to the agile supply chain). There would be one or two of these facilities to support a metropolitan area. The Trade Centre path (closest to the continuous replenishment supply chain) is a multi-facility network located close to the end-user's home or site location, providing not only small-volume and top-up products, but also technical support and the relationship aspect of the tradesperson's service needs.

The strength of combining the decision support capability of the optimization model with the concept of alignment is the ability to minimize cost within the context of a focused and appropriate service network. By bringing together the physical aspects of the business and its products and juxtaposing on this the buying behaviour of customers, the natural 'pathways' through the complexity of a supply chain begin to emerge.

FUTURE POSSIBILITIES

Network optimization models are a key tool for the design and ongoing development of any reasonably complex supply chain. They provide both a structured framework through which to rationalize and view the operation and the mathematical support to develop more optimal solutions than are usually achievable via experience and a set of spreadsheets.

The future for network models includes their integration with other decision support tools, such as simulation and inventory optimization and their role as a decision support tool for incorporating carbon emission factors into network design.

Finally, the discussion around the ability to use a network model to translate the architecture of dynamic alignment into the construction of a logistics service network points to their untapped potential to turn innovative strategy into a tangible and achievable action agenda.

ALIGNMENT INSIGHTS

- *Large, complex supply chains can only be successfully managed if the core patterns and key drivers of cost and effectiveness can be identified.*

- *Dynamic alignment brings a conceptual framework to identify and understand the key underlying pattern – the pattern of demand.*

- *Network modelling provides a tool for the business to test and determine the service/cost equations which most effectively responds to the different types of demand.*

- *Network modelling has moved from the leading edge to become an essential tool in the armoury of the supply chain decision-maker.*

NOTES

1   W.R. Ashby, *An Introduction to Cybernetics*, Chapman & Hall, London, 1956.

2   Quintiq press release, Netherlands, 3 June 2008, http://www.quintiq.com/news/archive-news/2008/dhl-asia.aspx.

3   J.F. Shapiro and S.N. Wagner in association with F.G. Arriaga and S. Marenco, 'Strategic inventory optimisation', unpublished paper, February 2008.

4   Ibid., p. 17.

5   Carpenter Ellis Pty Ltd, 2006. See also J.L. Gattorna, *Living Supply Chains*, FT Prentice Hall, Harlow, 2006, pp. 151–154.

16 DHL Taiwan: Aligning the Express Business with Customers

Stuart Whiting

In 2006 DHL Express embarked on an aggressive strategy to reach substantial revenue and profit targets. Upon realizing the scale of growth required, the management board recognized that substantial changes to the existing network, infrastructure, business model, operating processes and employee skill sets would be needed to achieve these objectives.

Recognizing the role that its customers played in its success, the company undertook a number of research surveys with the aim of precisely identifying where DHL Express needed to focus attention in order to avoid commoditization of its services, and thereby identify where DHL could differentiate itself in the eyes of customers.

In analysing this data DHL Express Taiwan recognized an opportunity to quickly differentiate itself in the marketplace by better aligning to customers' buying behaviours, particularly their demand for increased responsiveness.

However, to achieve this, the company realized, would necessitate not only a change in strategies, but also a change in the culture and leadership style within the organization; otherwise there was bound to be slippage in the implementation. In the past, DHL's approach would have been to optimize internal operations outwards to the customer. This new approach required it to design different products and services to optimize DHL's network and infrastructure, based on identified customer needs and behaviours. The customer therefore became the reference point for all action.

Martin Christopher comments: '... this new perspective sees the consumer not at the end of the supply chain but at its start. In effect this is the philosophical difference between supply chain management... and demand change management.'[1] Baker agrees when he says that '... managing demand chains is ... fundamentally different to managing supply chains. It requires turning the supply chain on its head and taking the end user as the organization's point of departure and not its final destination.'[2] Whether you call them supply chains or demand chains, the point is clear – start with the customer and reverse engineer backwards from the outside, in.

As a member of a global network comprising 220 countries and territories, DHL Taiwan saw the need to adopt a model that would complement and enhance other change programmes and initiatives already underway in the country and across the Asia Pacific region, thus further ensuring that it contributed to the delivery of the management board's medium- to long-term aspirations.

John Gattorna's *Living Supply Chains*[3] provided the concept of 'dynamic alignment', a model that proposed the application of a *dynamic*, yet systematic, response to customers' buying behaviours, which in turn resulted in an increased share of customers' wallets, provided a way of maintaining momentum in existing markets and, most importantly of all, building sustainable customer relationships as a foundation for future quality revenue growth. However, adopting such a model essentially meant that DHL would have to transition from a 'one-size-fits-all' supply chain mindset,to tailored approaches based on identified customer behaviours. This was the missing link which promised to deliver a quantum improvement in performance. And so it did.

> *'We quickly ascertained that there were up to 15 different buying behaviours present in the marketplace. Transitioning from the "one-size-fits-all" to 15 different responses would be almost impossible.'*

HOW DHL TAIWAN APPLIED THE CONCEPTS OF 'DYNAMIC ALIGNMENT'

Living Supply Chains became our roadmap, and we quickly embarked upon customer surveys amongst our top 260 customers, by sales channel, in order to identify the buying behaviours prevalent in our marketplace – and the required responses. These interviews were conducted over a period of two months and undertaken by our most seasoned and mature commercial representatives to avoid diverting existing resources from their day-to-day customer relationships and selling responsibilities.

While the surveys and customer interviews were being undertaken we also took the opportunity to customize Gattorna's dynamic alignment model to our own express transportation business – mainly to help us identify not only the necessary steps, but also the consequences and actions that would be required at each stage. Our approach is represented in Figure 16.1.

Upon digesting the results of these interviews, we quickly ascertained that there were up to 15 different buying behaviours present in the marketplace. Transitioning from the 'one-size-fits-all' to 15 different responses would be almost impossible. Consequently, the management team consolidated the 15 into four dominant types, (note that the P-A-D-I terminology, 'Ia', 'A', 'AP' and 'Dp' used below is taken directly from the coding methodology for segmenting customers along behavioural lines as first introduced by John Gattorna),[4] as shown in Figure 16.2.

λ 260 of DHL Taiwan's customers surveyed for preferences

λ 15 Preferences identified and segmented into 4 dominant 'types'

λ Against preferences product definition aligned and applied

λ Against products, services and value adding offerings defined

λ Customer account management & X functional support defined

λ Business Processes revised & enhanced to provide alignment

λ Business review process to monitor and improve initiatives

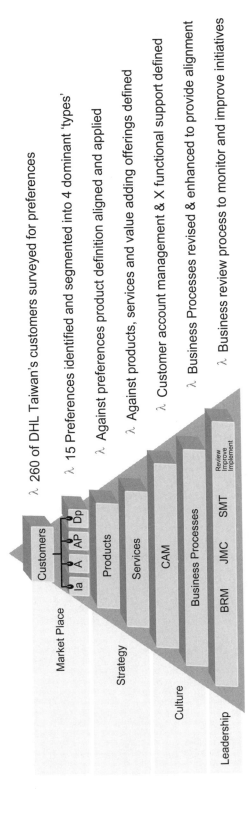

Figure 16.1   DHL Taiwan's dynamic alignment model

Source: DHL Taiwan.

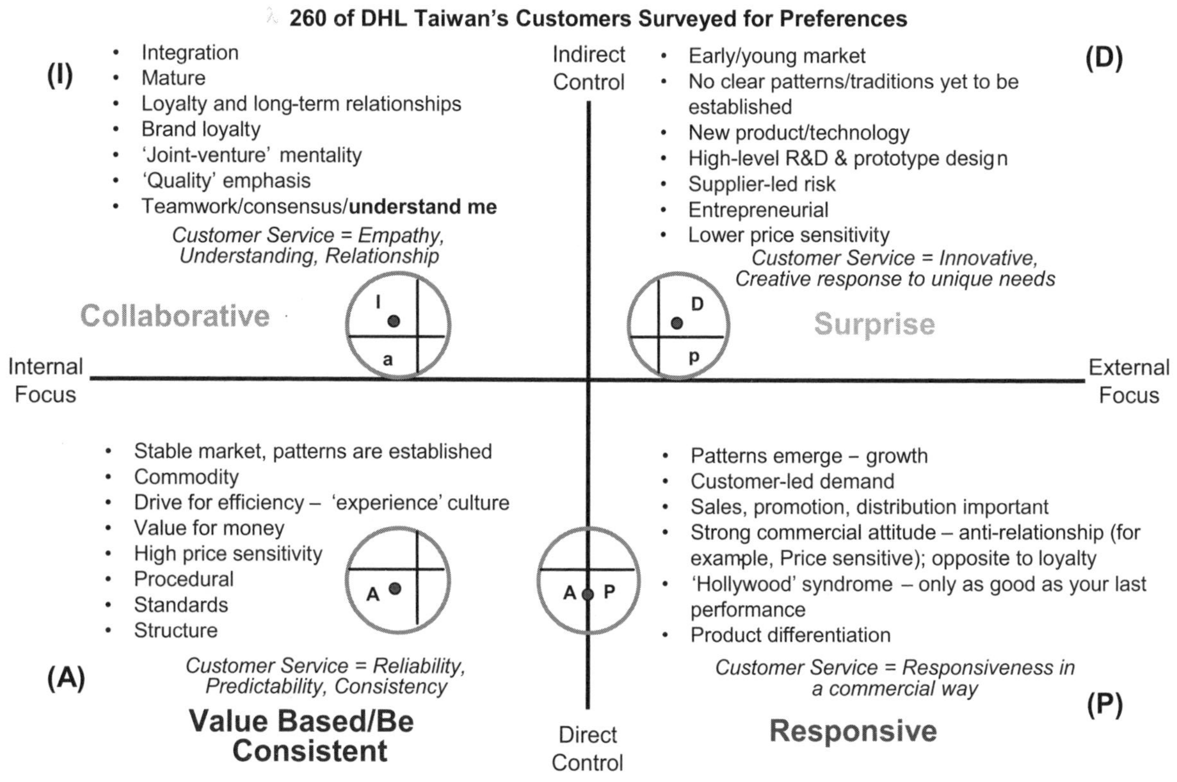

λ **260 of DHL Taiwan's Customers Surveyed for Preferences**

(I)

- Integration
- Mature
- Loyalty and long-term relationships
- Brand loyalty
- 'Joint-venture' mentality
- 'Quality' emphasis
- Teamwork/consensus/**understand me**

Customer Service = Empathy, Understanding, Relationship

Indirect Control

(D)

- Early/young market
- No clear patterns/traditions yet to be established
- New product/technology
- High-level R&D & prototype design
- Supplier-led risk
- Entrepreneurial
- Lower price sensitivity
  Customer Service = Innovative, Creative response to unique needs

Surprise

- Stable market, patterns are established
- Commodity
- Drive for efficiency – 'experience' culture
- Value for money
- High price sensitivity
- Procedural
- Standards
- Structure

Customer Service = Reliability, Predictability, Consistency

- Patterns emerge – growth
- Customer-led demand
- Sales, promotion, distribution important
- Strong commercial attitude – anti-relationship (for example, Price sensitive); opposite to loyalty
- 'Hollywood' syndrome – only as good as your last performance
- Product differentiation

Customer Service = Responsiveness in a commercial way

Responsive

Direct Control

External Focus

(P)

Collaborative

Value Based/Be Consistent

(A)

Internal Focus

Figure 16.2 **DHL Taiwan's four dominant market buying behaviours**

Source: DHL Taiwan.

Responses covering products, services, value-added services, customer account management, business processes, measurement and review were developed and consequently validated with multiple customers for each of the dominant behaviours in follow up meetings.

Surprisingly, we found that, in order to align with customer, product and service needs, we had to do little to our basic 'core' service offering. Rather, we needed to systematize the value-added/advantage solutions we offered around our 'core' products and services. We quickly embarked on bringing these services and products, previously offered under the old heritage 'Red and White' DHL Express, up to the new 'Yellow and Red' DHL as represented in Figure 16.3.

A total of 22 'bottlenecks' were identified within the existing business processes, and over the ensuing six months process re-engineering was undertaken by cross-functional teams to correct this situation. As details emerged and familiarity with the output intensified, the most significant realization by the senior management team was the need to segment our customer service and care in line with the four dominant buying behaviours, 'Ia', 'A', 'AP' and 'Dp' previously identified. Consequently, the team worked to create a segmented customer service/care approach aimed at improving customer responsiveness and alignment that served dominant 'I', 'A', 'P' and 'D' behaviours with the flexibility to incorporate secondary behaviours according to customer need, i.e. the 'a' within 'Ia' and 'p' within 'Dp'. In the case of 'AP' customers the service offering would be a blend of both 'A' and 'P'. The additional challenge was to manage this change and end state segmented customer service/care approach at no additional cost. The four segmented customer service/care approaches are detailed below:

- *Type 'A' Value-based/Consistent customers:* required customer service agents (CSA – the traditional DHL Express customer service model), offering a transactional 'lean' service at the lowest cost-to-serve.

- *Type 'P' Responsive/On-demand customers:* required customer service executives (CSE's), who manage responsive solutions/programmes with customers at a premium above Value-based customers.

- *Type 'I' Collaborative/Understand Me customers:* required key account desk (KAD) personnel, providing a service for customers who desire a more collaborative relationship with DHL Express and are willing to pay a premium above *Value-Based* customers, but not as much as Responsive/On-demand customers.

- *Type 'D' Surprise customers:* required a special services desk (SSD) solution to manage 'critical/event' transactions where service and a creative solution are an absolute priority over price, and consequently this service is at a premium above all others.

These four core segmented customer service/care approaches are depicted in Figure 16.4.

Figure 16.3   DHL Taiwan's value and advantage solution service offering

Source: DHL Taiwan.

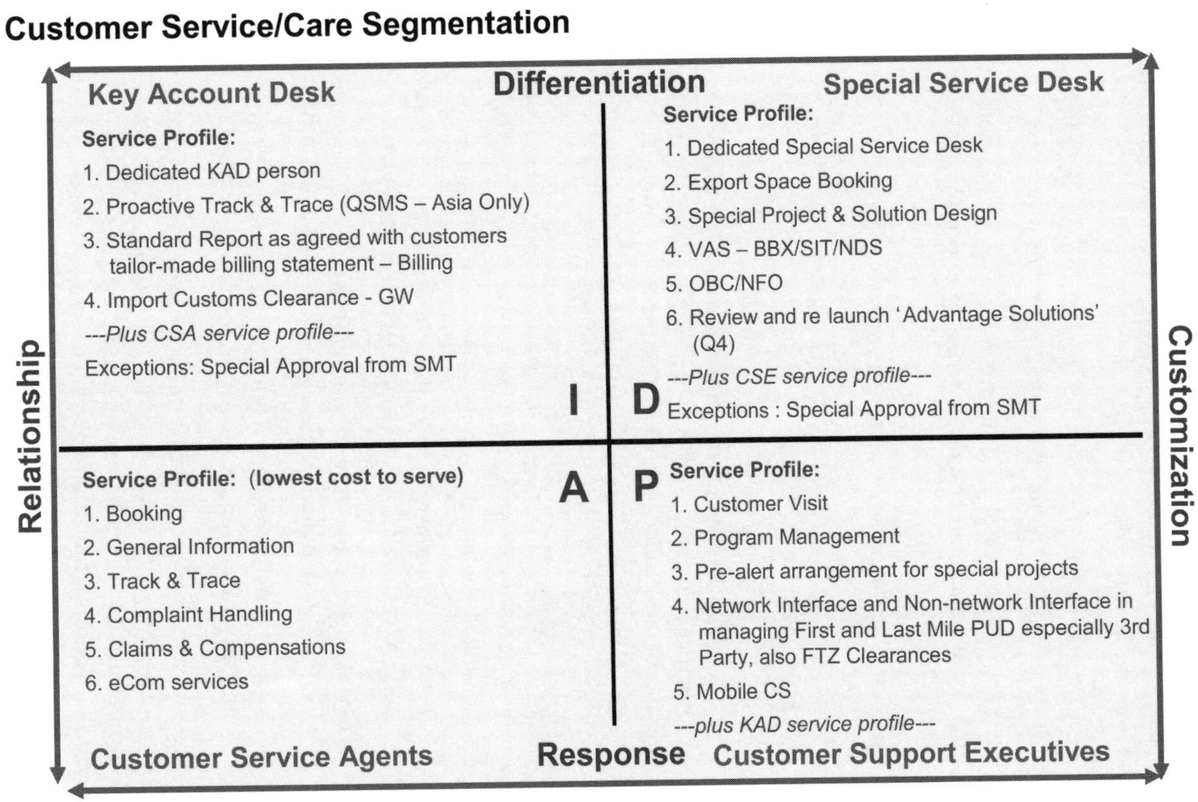

Customer Service/Care Segmentation

Figure 16.4   DHL Taiwan's segmented customer service/care approach

Source: DHL Taiwan.

CONSEQUENCES OF APPLYING 'DYNAMIC ALIGNMENT'

- Customer service/care is now segmented into four different responses.

- Customer service and cost-of-sales have been clearly identified by dominant buying behaviour types.

- Customer tariffs (rates) are now aligned to customer buying behaviours, incorporating trading and potential volumes/transactions.

- DHL Taiwan is now able to differentiate itself at the point-of-sale, in account management and, in terms of responsiveness, versus its competitors.

- Customers now receive proactive performance reports.

NET IMPACT

1. Customer retention improved – this is one of a number of key (sales) performance indicators (KPIs) where we measure the trading and volume of trade each customer has with DHL, by product, trade lane and geography. Any loss of business over a period of time would then classify the customer as 'lost' or 'down-trader'.

   a. Type 'A' retention improved by 8.74 per cent; in one year, starting August 2007, DHL Taiwan only lost 3.5 per cent of trading customers.

   b. Type 'P', including 'P' retention improved by 15.65 per cent; and since August 2007 no customers have been lost.

   c. Type 'I', including 'Ia' retention improved by 12.9 per cent; and likewise no customers have been lost since August 2007.

   d. Type 'D', including 'Dp' retention improved by 7.44 per cent; similarly, no customers have been lost in this segment.

   These results have confirmed that improved collaboration and responsiveness has significantly improved retention, most importantly in our profitable customer segments 'P' and 'I' which represent an important share of total country revenue.

2. Customer service cost as a percentage of revenue has improved by 13.8 per cent.

3. Customer up-trading – another key sales KPI which measures a customer's average revenue per day over a defined period of time and then measures quarterly performance against this average to ascertain current and year-on-year revenue per day – also improved significantly:

a.   Type 'P', including 'AP' customers +27 per cent.

b.   Type 'I', including 'Ia' customers x 1.2 market growth.

c.   Others +8.9 per cent.

4.   DHL now conducts an annual customer satisfaction survey across all customer channels – in the meantime, we have undertaken a 'mini' survey of our key account desk (KAD) 'I' and customer support executives' (CSE) 'P' customer base to ensure that progress is being made. The results are as follows:

a.   Type 'I', including 'Ia' customers +15 per cent.

b.   Type 'P', including 'AP' customers +12 per cent.

5.   DHL Express Taiwan achieved first place amongst DHL Express Asia countries in the 'Mystery Shopper Survey', an independent survey measuring professionalism and ability to manage an array of customer enquiries.

'The greatest challenge in implementing dynamic alignment principles in an organization of any size is culture; employees and management need to accept change and be party to this change process.'

6.   By coding customers by their dominant buying behaviours using the P-A-D-I regime, DHL Taiwan employees across all functions are now able to immediately align their thinking, response and behaviour to achieve the best outcome for the customer and the company.

ALIGNMENT INSIGHTS

- *The greatest challenge in implementing dynamic alignment principles in an organization of any size is culture; employees and management need to accept change and be party to this change process in order to be successful. In addition, constant communication across all channels, utilizing multiple mediums, is necessary to ensure full understanding. Communication, regardless of medium, needs to be as simple as possible, tailored to each audience and constantly reinforced in order to gain the necessary comprehension and support. Consequently, an open 360° forum also needs to be established, allowing for full discussion across all functions and positions. It is the senior management team's responsibility to ensure that feedback, participation and questioning is encouraged and allowed at all times.*

- *Of equal importance is the need for the organization to be realistic in setting targets and goals in undertaking this type of transformation. In total, it took 14 months of analysis, re-engineering, beta testing and customer involvement to achieve an operating model that could be fully deployed across an organization of 1,100 people. Once deployed, continual evaluation is required in order to evolve and adapt to the impact such changes had on the organization – and, where possible, proactive action and communication is best. However, the leadership needs to react in a timely way as the programme develops and problems/resource issues arise. It is critical to ensure that the organization's culture is sufficiently dynamic to recognize, escalate and quickly resolve problems as and when these are identified.*

- *When victories are won or failures occur, it is important to openly share why success was attained and what was learned from failure. It is important to show progress, success and setbacks at all times and the senior management team has to demonstrate passion, empathy and a sense that anything is possible, provided that all employees work together as a team.*

- *In managing the organization's subcultures, it is also critical that the leadership be fully on-board and behind the initiative. When the going gets tough, it is too easy to find fault and revert to old behaviours. The critical part now is ensuring that this change becomes part of the organization's DNA, ever-evolving and ever-adapting to the changing marketplace. As such dynamic alignment is not a 'change programme' or 'productivity/efficiency-driven initiative'; it is a 'way of life' and a new business model that needs to become a part of every employee's day-to-day life. Herein lies the challenge!*

NOTES

1   M. Christopher, *Logistics and Supply Chain Management*, FT Prentice Hall, Harlow, 2005.

2   S. Baker, *New Consumer Marketing*, John Wiley & Sons, Chichester, 2003.

3   J.L. Gattorna, *Living Supply Chains*, FT Prentice Hall, Harlow, 2006.

4   Ibid., pp. 14–29.

17 Aligning Fonterra's Global Supply Chain Network

Nigel Jones

The analysis and categorization of customers by their dominant buying behaviour (Figure 17.1) enables organizations to focus resources and efforts effectively, thus ensuring that value within the supply chain is maximized where it is practical and possible to do so. Some key characteristics used by Gattorna[1] to describe customers categorized as 'collaborative' through 'dynamic' alignment suggest that this group, in particular, should be treated as a priority for undertaking shared initiatives, such as:

> *'Categorizing customers by their buying behaviour is, however, only the start, and a further significant investment in time and effort is required before value can be unlocked.'*

- Build trusting relationships.

- Encourage teamwork/partnerships.

- Foster information-sharing.

- Seek joint development work.

Shared initiatives are viewed as particularly important because they can unlock value across the extended supply chain, which often exceeds that possible through companies working on their supply chains in isolation.

Categorizing customers by their buying behaviour is, however, only the start, and a further significant investment in time and effort is required before value can be unlocked across the extended supply chain. This chapter is based on work undertaken by the New Zealand-based Fonterra Cooperative Group, the world's largest dairy exporter, and the lessons learned from our continuing experimentation on the ground. The work is based on a number of initiatives that the company has undertaken, involving some of its international customers and the supply of bulk dairy ingredients, sourced from New Zealand, and delivered to multiple customer destinations around the world. The value created through this work has varied on a case-by-case basis (depending on the complexity and geographic stretch); however, the percentage efficiencies delivered have sometimes been measured well into double-digits.

Across a broad range of product categories, there are a finite number of dominant *customer buying behaviours*

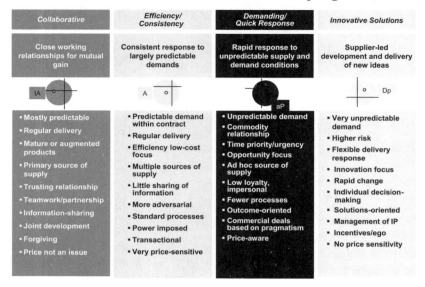

Collaborative	Efficiency/ Consistency	Demanding/ Quick Response	Innovative Solutions
Close working relationships for mutual gain	Consistent response to largely predictable demands	Rapid response to unpredictable supply and demand conditions	Supplier-led development and delivery of new ideas
• Mostly predictable • Regular delivery • Mature or augmented products • Primary source of supply • Trusting relationship • Teamwork/partnership • Information-sharing • Joint development • Forgiving • Price not an issue	• Predictable demand within contract • Regular delivery • Efficiency low-cost focus • Multiple sources of supply • Little sharing of information • More adversarial • Standard processes • Power imposed • Transactional • Very price-sensitive	• Unpredictable demand • Commodity relationship • Time priority/urgency • Opportunity focus • Ad hoc source of supply • Low loyalty, impersonal • Fewer processes • Outcome-oriented • Commercial deals based on pragmatism • Price-aware	• Very unpredictable demand • Higher risk • Flexible delivery response • Innovation focus • Rapid change • Individual decision-making • Solutions-oriented • Management of IP • Incentives/ego • No price sensitivity

Figure 17.1   Dynamic Alignment segments

Source: Adapted from fieldwork at Fonterra, 2001. Refer to Figure 2.2 in Gattorna (2006), p. 14.

The study picks up after the initial analysis and segmentation of customers, as prescribed by dynamic alignment principles, has been undertaken. However, we do not explore the processes used to undertake the shared initiatives, but focus instead on the critical key features that require consideration prior to the process getting fully underway. The steps followed include:

1. sponsorship;

2. provisional value assessment and preparing to share value;

3. setting rules and expectations on both sides;

4. establishing a baseline.

SPONSORSHIP

Although, by definition, a 'trusting relationship' can be expected to underlie a 'collaborative' environment and there are likely to be examples of information-sharing and shared projects, the real value is found and unlocked by taking these pre-existing traits to new levels. Growing the relationship sufficiently to unlock new, bigger opportunities requires formal ownership by senior management in both companies. A structure is needed around relationships that focus on delivering outcomes and removing potential internal roadblocks.

The structure that was found to work most effectively across extended supply chains involves the creation of a formal steering team supporting the sponsor and the development of a single-page objective statement to ensure alignment between parties (see Figure 17.2).

It is important that the steering team is a live/engaged team, to ensure that monthly meetings are conducted effectively (conference call is more than adequate, if necessary). The purpose of these forums is to ensure continued alignment with respect to a variety of items including:

- allocation of internal resources;
- updating of wider company strategies that may impact on existing initiatives or create new opportunities;
- reviewing/adjusting priorities;
- arbitrating over any conflicts or operational issues.

The importance of ownership and structure should not be undervalued, although before committing serious management time, it is necessary to have at least a reasonable level of confidence that an adequate return on investment can be delivered. It was found that the absence of any return on investment had the potential to quickly erode goodwill and ongoing commitment in all camps.

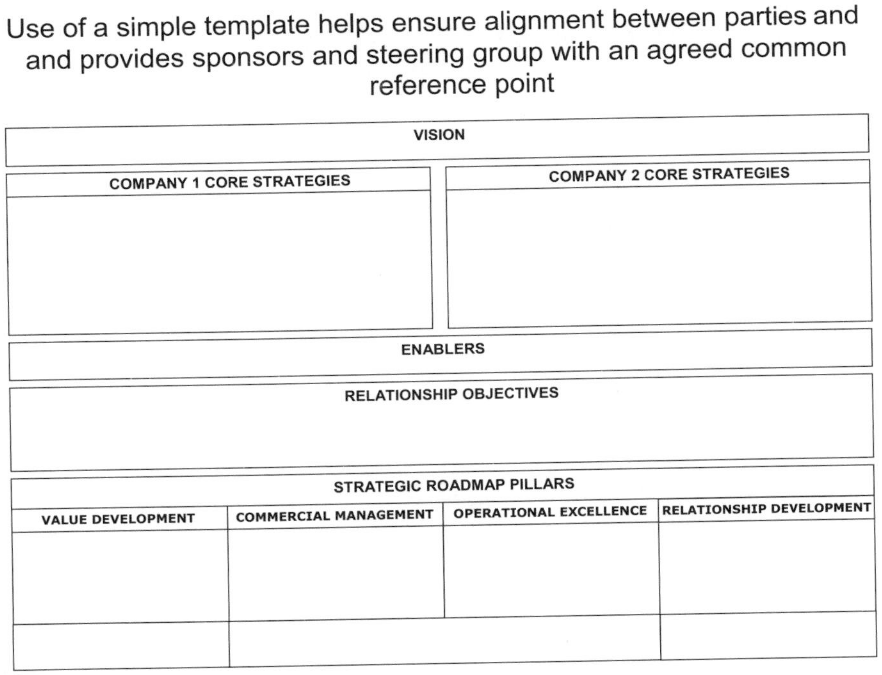

Use of a simple template helps ensure alignment between parties and and provides sponsors and steering group with an agreed common reference point

VISION

COMPANY 1 CORE STRATEGIES	COMPANY 2 CORE STRATEGIES

ENABLERS

RELATIONSHIP OBJECTIVES

STRATEGIC ROADMAP PILLARS			
VALUE DEVELOPMENT	COMMERCIAL MANAGEMENT	OPERATIONAL EXCELLENCE	RELATIONSHIP DEVELOPMENT

Figure 17.2   Objective matrix

ASSESSING VALUE POTENTIAL

The purpose of assessing value potential is purely to gain a level of comfort of what, if any, locked-in value may exist across the extended supply chains: is there a prize worth embarking upon?

It soon became clear that such exercises were not about unlocking the actual value itself, but, rather, increasing confidence that the potential existed in the first place. The process undertaken was a high-level review of key supply chain characteristics and features. Depending on the picture that developed from this review, the understanding gained would either create the necessary confidence or not.

When undertaking such exercises, they need to be specific to the supply chain environment under review, but at the same time sufficiently generic to ensure that the outcome can be translated across a variety of customer experiences. To achieve this goal, a series of questions were developed under a range of headings, including:

- dollar transaction amounts involved;

- volume of product;

- forecasting;

- order management;

- inventory management;

- physical logistics (warehousing and transport);

- manufacturing.

The actual questions varied in detail; some were quite specific concerning the order interface, while others were more general concerning the physical handing of product. Once each question had been considered, a rating and relative weighting was allocated and recorded on a spreadsheet. Once the rating exercise had been completed, each was then plotted.

The matrix produced plotted volume (that is, financial materiality) on one axis and the relative supply chain complexity on the other. This enabled, at a glance, the relative scale of perceived value across the extended supply chain to be appreciated, at the same time providing an initial insight into where the value lay – for example, either removing significant and costly complexity over small volumes (lower right quadrant in Figure 17.3), or refining a relatively simple supply chain which involved significant scale (upper left quadrant in Figure 17.3).

Although originally undertaken in order to explore the relative materiality across the full scope of supply chains involving a particular customer, the

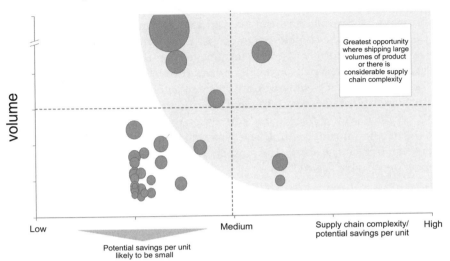

The potential to deliver value from joint initiatives is greatest where large volumes and supply chain complexity are present

Greatest opportunity where shipping large volumes of product or there is considerable supply chain complexity

volume

Low

Potential savings per unit likely to be small

Medium

Supply chain complexity/ potential savings per unit

High

Figure 17.3   Value location

exercise was then extended and used to compare opportunities across the full range of customers previously defined as 'collaborative'.

The importance of being objective, realistic and pragmatic when assessing the potential for value can not be stressed enough. If, at the end of the process, it is questionable that sufficient value actually exists to warrant further exploration, this judgement should be accepted. Such a conclusion does not mean that the relationship has been inappropriately defined as 'collaborative', it simply means that at that time, and given the existing transactions, there is not enough certainty to justify extensive focused engagement.

It was suggested earlier in this chapter that one of the key benefits of undertaking shared initiatives across an extended supply chain was to unlock value, which often exceeds that possible from working in isolation. If such an exercise is to be successful, it is critical to ensure that sufficient attention is focused upfront to foster and protect the goodwill found in collaborative relationships. Two major steps in defining this process were:

- setting rules and expectations;
- establishing a baseline.

SETTING RULES AND EXPECTATIONS

Having established the existence of the potential for sufficient value to warrant progressing more formal engagement, it was important to establish clear rules for sharing any value that would be derived from subsequent exercises. In practice, it was only very occasionally found that value would be naturally split evenly between the parties, so determining how value should be formally split warranted serious consideration. In addressing this challenge it was found that the commercial managers responsible for the wider relationship were ideally placed to take the lead on this matter. The approach actually taken may vary. However, it is good practice to ensure that this issue is locked down prior to initiating any exercise One approach that proved particularly valuable in that it brought objectivity to the task was the use of a simple decision tree (see Figure 17.4). By answering the questions shown on the decision tree in Figure 17.4 with a simple yes or no until the end of a particular branch is reached, the most appropriate approach to ensure a fair allocation of value is arrived at.

ESTABLISHING A BASELINE

Before the value being generated can be measured it is first necessary to understand the starting-point – that is, the baseline. The baseline represents the 'as is' supply chain in terms of processes, flows and cost.

It was found that the most successful approach for defining and agreeing on this important definition of the supply chain was to hold a highly focused face-to-face workshop, drawing upon the expertise and knowledge of a small group of representatives from the companies involved.

Identifying a collaborative partner and opportunity is only the start; upfront, the sharing of value has to be clearly understood

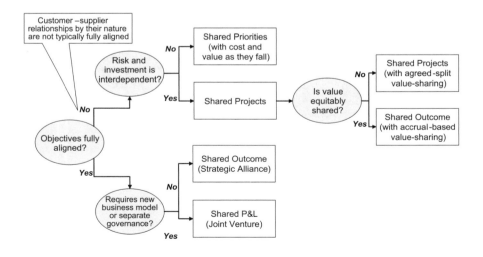

Figure 17.4   Value split

The key purpose of this workshop is to create a visualization of the supply chain (process, flow and cost) that will guide and focus work during subsequent phases. During this initial engagement workshop the aim is not necessarily to get a 100 per cent perfect representation, but to come away with a good enough understanding to enable the identification of likely areas for further investigation and confidence in terms of the current baseline costs and how they are distributed.

'The most successful approach for defining and agreeing on this important definition of the supply chain was to hold a highly focused face-to-face workshop.'

Tools used to complete the mapping exercise are listed below. The approach found to work most successfully was one based on a simple value-stream mapping exercise. This can be conducted using a variety of tried and tested techniques including the likes of:

- Pareto analysis;

- process mapping;

- histograms.

To facilitate an efficient and effective workshop, parties should be prepared in advance; attendees should ensure that they bring to the workshop a comprehensive understanding of their supply chain, its processes and its key cost drivers and their quantum.

The output of the exercise is a fully documented and quantified current state. As initiatives are undertaken to improve upon this starting position, the documents produced in the initial workshop become the key reference point against which future progress is reported, benefits distributed and the value being delivered through the collaborative relationship is proven or otherwise.

ALIGNMENT INSIGHTS

- *After completing a behavioural segmentation of customers by their buying behaviours, particular attention should be paid to the group defined as 'collaborative'.*

- *Although, by definition, a 'trusting relationship', with information-sharing and shared projects, might be expected to underlie a 'collaborative' operating environment, the real value is found and unlocked by taking these pre-existing traits to new (higher) levels. For the relationship to grow sufficiently in order for new, bigger opportunities to be unlocked, formal ownership by senior management in both companies is a prerequisite.*

> • *If, at the end of a value-assessment exercise, it is found that insufficient value exists to warrant further exploration, no further action should be taken at that time. Such a conclusion does not mean that the relationship has been inappropriately defined as 'collaborative'; it simply means that at that time, and given the existing transactions, there is not enough certainty to justify a more extensive, focused engagement.*

NOTE

1   J.L. Gattorna, *Living Supply Chains*, FT Prentice Hall, Harlow, 2006.

18 Supply Chain Alignment – Brazilian Style

Carlos Frederico Bremer, Rodrigo Cambiaghi Azevedo,
Carlos Aravechia and Lucas Cley da Horta

MANAGING SUPPLY CHAINS: LESSONS FROM SOCCER

Business management and soccer have a lot in common – try analysing both in terms of their evolution. During the World Cup Finals of 1958 in Sweden and 1962 in Chile, the Brazilian national team, popularly called *seleção*, established true supremacy over all the other competitors, thanks to the individual abilities and creativity of its players. Their skills were of such a high calibre that the team's tactical organization and strategies completely evaded detection. This supremacy persisted until 1970 when Brazil beat Italy in the final game at the Azteca Stadium in Mexico City with a squad that had, among other players, Rivelino, Jairzinho, Tostão and, of course, Pelé.

However, after the 1970 World Cup, Brazil went into the worst slump in its soccer history. Why such a sudden change? Was Brazil no longer able to produce good players? Unlikely. Take, for example, Zico, Socrates and Falcão, to mention just a few. The fact is that it took more than 20 years for Brazil to recognize that soccer, as a competitive game, had evolved. Leaving aside all feelings of nostalgia, tactical organization and physical performance, along with ability and creativity, became fundamental ingredients for successful teams. Brazilian players had to learn that fantastic dribbles were still very important, but within a tactical context. Even the most skilled strikers were taught that they have a responsibility to support defenders and midfielders when the team is on the defence – introducing the notion of teamwork. This is still an ongoing learning process in Brazil, but recent results have shown that the *seleção* is regaining its previous respectable position in the world of soccer.

Business managers can learn much from this example. When, in the early 1990s, authors such as Tom Davenport and Michael Hammer[1] started addressing the concepts of business process and business process management inside organizations, what they had in mind at that time was that the individually optimized performance of each department inside an organization did not necessarily define the best setting for the company's performance as a whole. In other words, the fact that a company was composed of, for instance, a brilliant sales team, the most expert production workers and a group of geniuses in R&D did not necessarily guarantee the company's market and financial success and longevity. For clarity's sake, these concepts never implied that companies should be run by unskilled hands and minds. Individual and departmental skills still remain crucial in meeting any kind of business challenge, but, as in soccer, strategies, tactics and coordination also came to be considered determinants of market competitiveness.

However, even though a business process concept was introduced almost 20 years ago (and has been accompanied by debates around it ever since), our experience working with hundreds of companies worldwide reveals that companies are still struggling to adapt to this business requirement. Transformation agendas towards business process models include, among others, issues related to companies' political structures, evaluation and remuneration systems, and, of course, people skills. Information technology has been used as one of the main transformation vectors towards process-oriented business models. More recently, service-oriented architectures (SOA) have been highlighted as a new means of propulsion to overcome this challenge.

We have spent years researching, testing and analysing how supply chains could be better coordinated through business process management and, as a consequence, after several attempts and improvements, we came out with a first version of our SCM process-oriented framework. This framework, composed of five core management processes, as depicted in Figure 18.1, has allowed companies to coordinate their supply chains from strategic to operational levels, through all traditional departments, from customers to suppliers. The efficacy of this framework has been verified by the significant financial and operational results obtained by companies that have opted to follow its guidelines.

'Individual and departmental skills still remain crucial in meeting any kind of business challenge, but, as in soccer, strategies, tactics and coordination also came to be considered determinants of market competitiveness.'

Before discussing how this framework can be utilized to achieve dynamic alignment for supply chains, it is important to understand clearly the scope of each process and their relationships. The five interrelated processes presented in Figure 18.1 can be introduced as follows:

- *Strategic planning and management.* This is the business process responsible for the formulation of the corporate strategy for a time horizon normally spanning from five to ten years. In addition to

Figure 18.1   Original SCM Business Process Framework

formulating the company's strategy map, the process is in charge of deploying it into strategic projects for the organization as well as in mapping its Critical Success Factors (CSFs) and Key Performance Indicators (KPIs). Results of the process also include tactical planning directives such as the company's business plan and budget, which are used as inputs to the S&OP process.

- *Sales and Operations Planning (S&OP).* This is a tactical planning process responsible for deploying the strategic plan into a set of integrated plans. It continuously pursues the alignment between the decisions taken at the strategic and operational levels and thus it plays a major role in the coordination of any supply chain. The main outputs of this process relate to sales, production, purchasing and product inventory plans, as well as to the financial evaluation of company performance for the planning period following, which usually spans from six to 18 months.

- *Fulfilment management.* This process is in charge of transforming plans into reality and therefore it encompasses activities including the deployment of the tactical plans within each specific area of the organization, as well as planning functions mainly related to Distributed Requirement Planning (DRP), Master Production Schedule (MPS) and Materials Requirement Planning (MRP). The fulfilment management process is also in charge of receiving customer orders and replying with an order delivery date through functionalities such as Available-To-Promise (ATP). In this way, the process sets the customer expected service level which must be accomplished by the order management process. A core activity of the fulfilment management process is a cross-departmental meeting that exposes eventual variabilities in the execution processes (for example, customer order cancellation, production delays and unavailability of vessels) as well as new market opportunities, and decides, on the basis of financial and service-level impacts, how the supply chain should react to them.

- *Order management.* The main goal of the order management process is to guarantee that the company is able to serve all customers as planned by the fulfilment management process. Activities related to order scheduling and order releases (for purchasing, manufacturing and delivery) are part of the order management process. One of the most important activities in this process is a meeting to discuss the alignment between the fulfilment plan previously defined and any deviations in the execution processes. Identified misalignments have to be properly addressed, and the impact at customer service levels must be carefully analysed.

- *Material flow management.* Located at the lowest level of the framework, the material flow management process is in charge of managing, and consequently improving, the material flow throughout all facilities of an organization (suppliers, plants, warehouses and so on). Methodologies such as Lean/Six Sigma are applied in this process in order to pursue perfection throughout the company's value streams.

FRAMEWORK EVOLUTION AND THE ACHIEVEMENT OF DYNAMIC ALIGNMENT

When we began implementing this framework in several organizations almost ten years ago, we were able to achieve significant business results for all the companies we worked with, mainly because of the better company-wide alignment achieved within and among the processes. The framework showed itself to be an essential tool in attaining the operational excellence pursued by organizations. However, throughout all those years, one particular issue kept challenging us: *how could these processes be tailored inside an organization in order to explore the different market (customers and suppliers) behaviours that exist?*

The 'one-size-fits-all' strategy was definitely a hindrance to realizing higher levels of business performance but, at the same time, traditional market analyses and segmentation methods were unable to advance our efforts in finding the answer to this question. We knew at this time that we had to look beyond conventional wisdom. Thus, when John Gattorna[2] presented the *dynamic* alignment framework and its underlying P-A-D-I logic, we definitely felt that we had found the missing link needed to grapple with our long-term problem. The identification and management of different customer and supplier segments based on their buying/selling behaviours made it possible for us to amplify the optimization of key decisions throughout all core management processes. It was also clear that, while our traditional core processes framework should be used to pursue operational excellence, two additional processes ought to be highlighted in the framework in order to assure forward and reverse alignments within any supply chain. These two processes are: the demand and supply management processes. The framework evolution is depicted in Figure 18.2, and the demand and supply management processes are discussed in sequence.

The demand management process allows the identification of customer behaviours in the marketplace, as well as determining specific supply chain strategies for each market segment. It continuously monitors the customer market in order to collect customer behaviour signals, analyses them and, finally, distributes them to all other related core processes. Among its main responsibilities are: the segmentation of the customer base; the definition and management of the service basket offered to each customer; the definition and management of order prioritization rules; the determination and administration of commercial and logistics service level agreements; product pricing, demand sensing and demand shaping tasks; and sales quota management.

On the other hand, the supply management process permits the incorporation of suppliers' behaviours into all other processes supporting the designation and management of specific procurement strategies as proposed by Gattorna. In addition to clustering suppliers according to their selling behaviours and determining segment-specific procurement strategies, the supply management process is in charge of selecting, developing and evaluating suppliers, developing and managing service-level agreements, designing tenders and contracts, addressing outsourcing decisions, and analysing and mitigating supply and regulatory risks.

In the following section we present two cases in which these processes were implemented, paying special attention to how the dynamic alignment concept was applied in different business contexts.

'The demand management process allows the identification of customer behaviours in the marketplace, as well as determining specific supply chain strategies for each market segment.'

TWO CASE STUDIES

The following two case studies illustrate how the dynamic alignment concept was applied, together with our core SCM business process framework. The cases illustrated here share important similarities and complementarities. Regarding similarities, both companies are considered global leaders in their performance segments, with markets and facilities located on different continents, and they are rated as large enterprises with annual revenues in excess of US$1.2 billion in

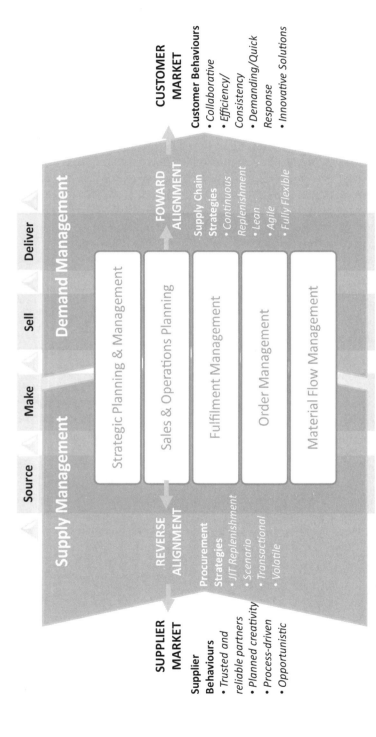

Figure 18.2   SCM Business Processes Framework with dynamic alignment

the first case and over US$20 billion in the second. As regards complementarities, two main aspects are highlighted: initially, whereas the first company was restructuring its supply chain management practices in a market containment strategy (market share and profitability retention), the second led the reform according to a much more expansionist strategy (increase of market share and global presence). An additional important complementarity is related to the market alignment targeted; whereas the first concentrates on achieving dynamic alignment with its customer market, the latter prioritizes its supplier markets. The names of the companies are kept confidential throughout the narrative.

Case Study 1: Achieving Dynamic Alignment in the Hermetic Compressors Business

Our first case study illustrates the re-engineering of the SCM practices in a company manufacturing hermetic compressors.[3] This business is characterized as very complex due mainly to the presence of a few powerful Original Equipment Manufacturers (OEMs) as customers, high demand variabilities and a large product portfolio manufactured on capital-intensive production lines.

In 2003 the world's leading manufacturer of hermetic compressors rose to the challenge of improving its supply chain management practices in order to guarantee a better service level to a complex growing market, as well as more attractive returns to its shareholders. The OTD (Order-To-Delivery) project was launched as a global initiative for all business units located in several countries in the Americas, Europe and Asia.

The initial focus of the OTD project relied on the definition and implementation of a global S&OP process, with the goal of coordinating tactical plans from several different areas, with a 12-month rolling horizon. The process was structured by geographical regions (S&OP Americas, S&OP Europe and S&OP Asia) with a global consolidation occurring monthly in its headquarters under the supervision of the company's executive committee.

A second phase of the OTD project focused on short-term planning and execution, aiming to guarantee the feasibility of the plans generated at the S&OP process aligned with eventual short-term variabilities. These goals were reached through the implementation of the fulfilment and order management processes which reduced the manufacturing planning cycle time from monthly to weekly. These changes enabled the adoption of frozen time fences and a more accurate ATP logic.

The operational results of those initial transformation phases were astonishing. Counting from the first day of the project back in 2003, the current customer order lead-time dropped from 33 to 17 days, the service level, in terms of orders delivered by the promised date, improved from 55 per cent to 88 per cent, the On-Time and In-Full (OTIF) indicator leaped from 30 per cent to 60 per cent, and global inventory level was reduced by over US$60 million.

Although these results were impressive, the company realized that there was still room for further improvements. Although the implemented processes definitely established a better level of management practice, when the primary configuration of these processes was viewed, it was felt that, while on average the company was now able to better service its customers, most of the time it was overservicing some and underservicing others. The logic within the processes did not take customer behaviour into consideration. This situation compelled the company to embark on an experimental project to search for a demand management process arrangement which could take into account the different buying behaviours of its customers.

To accomplish this, the project started developing a strategy alignment map to rank, according to each market-facing area and the performance attributes that were driving the company strategy (supply chain reliability, flexibility, responsiveness, costs and assets management). This analysis was followed by a market requirements map in order to understand how customers were evaluating company service as well as to provide a detailed customer demand variability analysis for the long and short term and also to analyze the existing contracts and agreements established with their customers.

A customer segmentation was performed based on the P-A-D-I logic resulting in four main customer segments: 28 per cent Partner customers (Ia and I); 37 per cent Volatile customers (D, Dp, iD, DI); 20 per cent Fair Deal customers (iA, Ap); and 15 per cent Hype customers (dP, aP).

The design of the demand management process thus ended up encompassing eight sub-processes: customer segmentation and prioritization, service menu definition, supply chain network design, KPIs definition and control, sales negotiation targets definition, commercial and logistics conditions negotiation, commercial and logistics agreement management, and quota management. These sub-processes allowed the S&OP to be reconfigured and fulfilment and order management processes to take into account the four different customer segments identified. For instance, the S&OP was able to establish different inventory policies for each customer segment and the fulfilment and order management processes started to take into consideration different customer service menus (for example, warranty lengths, consignment models), as well as different supply chain attributes such as reliability, flexibility and responsiveness. The project ended up addressing the need for a new organization structure in order to support the proposed demand management process.

Case Study 2: Dynamic Alignment in the Bovine Meat Industry

The second case study explores the quest for dynamic alignment in the bovine meat industry. In recent years this industry has been hit by massive challenges. Increasing global consumption and price fluctuations, as well as economic and sanitary aspects imposed by some important markets, have forced companies to seek business alternatives in order to guarantee the availability of their products and improve market share. As a response to such market factors, traditional exporters began to internationalize their operations by acquiring companies in consumer markets such as Europe and the US. With these acquisitions, companies were able to reduce local economic and sanitary restrictions.

In addition, specifically in Brazil, this industry has also been confronted with some particular circumstances such as: cattle shortages; increasing prices; market participation being dispersed among several competitors; lack of standardization of cattle quality due to the presence of many different breeds and cattle-rearing practices in the country; and steers representing approximately 80 per cent of the final meat costs. All these conditions make cattle supply a fundamental part of a profitable business model for any bovine meat processor.

As a result, in September 2007 the global leader in bovine slaughtering felt the need to assess its value chain in order to discover possible improvements that might lead to superior operational and market results. The assessment was structured around seven business dimensions: company vision, strategy, business processes, performance indicators, technology, people and organization. The assessment of these dimensions led to the proposal of a roadmap of initiatives, aligned to the vision of the main executives of the company, about the future market environment. Figure 18.3 illustrates the seven business dimensions analyzed in the assessment and the generation of the initiatives roadmap.

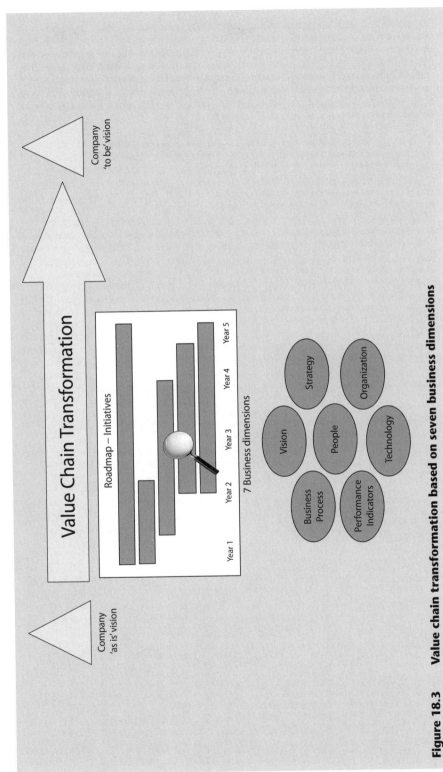

Figure 18.3   Value chain transformation based on seven business dimensions

The proposed roadmap was built around the company's core SCM business processes framework (Figure 18.2). In so doing, it contemplated initiatives such as implementation of the sales and operations planning process, fulfilment management and order management processes, besides the definition of new inventory policy, the implementation of additional functionalities for the actual information systems, the review of the current organizational structure, the application of basic training in supplying chain management concepts to more than 100 employees engaged in planning processes and so on.

With the goal of rethinking company positioning in the value chain, as well as aligning the executives around the future vision and strategies of performance, an initiative to review the company's strategic planning and management process was also undertaken. As a result, the company's goals up to the year 2012 were assessed and redefined along with the guidelines to reach them. Among these objectives, the need to continuously guarantee the cattle supply at the lowest possible cost and at a high-quality standard by means of a greater integration with its suppliers was also emphasized. The company decided to assume the leadership in this integration challenge, which should overcome some historical issues. In Brazil, the relationship between cattle farmers and slaughterhouses during recent decades has been marked by poor relationships and consequent disputes. The poor standardization of slaughtering procedures had brought about a historical misalignment between cattle farmers and slaughterhouses. Moreover, the imbalance between demand and supply reinforced the cattle farmer as the stronger party in this relationship – in other words, it is not slaughterhouses who decide to buy cattle, but ranchers who decide to sell to them. To integrate the supply side of the bovine meat industry means to question that relationship pattern, seeking to identify different supplier behaviours and consequently define different procurement strategies as well as assessing their impact on the core SCM business processes. With this intent, a pilot project was launched with the objective of increasing the cattle-purchasing volume in one of the most important cattle-producing regions in Brazil. The main idea behind the project was to identify the dominant supplier behaviours of the cattle producers using the reverse alignment concept. The project was structured into five main phases:

Collection of information, A closed-question questionnaire was developed and applied by telephone interviews with cattle suppliers located in the pilot region. By the end, more than 300 interviews had been performed.

Segmentation of the cattle farmers, The response to the questionnaire permitted the segmentation of all the cattle farmers into four main selling behaviours according to the P-A-D-I logic: Ia, Di, P, and Ai. It was decided to stereotype these behaviours using popular industry jargon in order to represent some characteristics of the relationship between cattle farmers and slaughterhouses. In this way, the concept could be more easily applied throughout the organization. In this case, Ia-behaviours were denominated 'chatting' if sensitive to personal contact and appreciative of friendship; Di-behaviours were called 'e-ranchers' due to the ability and interest of such suppliers in using new technologies; P-behaviours were labelled 'suspicious' because of the belief that the relationships are mostly unfair; and Ai-behaviours were named 'traditionalists' because of cultural habits and the desire to extract the maximum from the cattle. The participation of each segment in the sample, as well as their main characteristics, is described below.

Chatting (Ia) corresponds to 37 per cent of the sample. They:

- are open to partnerships
- are sensitive to personal contact
- want to be heard and understood

- appreciate friendship;
- are sensitive, but they see a fair price for their cattle as part of a reliable relationship.

E-ranchers (Di) correspond to 9 per cent of the sample. They:

- intend to invest in the property
- see value in innovation
- have little knowledge of sale options (for example, future contracts)
- are frequent computer and Internet users
- are the least sensitive of all groups with regard to the price of cattle.

Suspicious (P) corresponds to 19 per cent of the sample. They:

- do not believe in partnerships
- do not believe in long-term relationships – loyalty is not a business rule
- expect an agile response from slaughterhouses if problems arise (for example, quality inspection)
- are sensitive to payment methods
- are opportunists when it comes to the price of cattle – they always sell to those who pay more.

Traditionalists (Ai) correspond to 35 per cent of the sample. They:

- want to extract the maximum from their cattle and farm resources
- would like payment for hide and small parts
- look for differentiated price
- are possible partners
- are very sensitive with regard to the price of cattle – the price is fundamental for negotiation.

Services definition and development. From the analysis of identified dominant behaviours, a group of specific services with the needs and expectations for each profile were defined and developed. Also, the distribution channels were structured according to which services were offered to the cattle farmers.

Training. All involved in the purchasing process, as well as those responsible for the new services, were trained in the concepts, processes and proposed new segmentation.

Value capture. A set of key performance indicators was used to monitor the results, as well as to identify improvement in the services offered to the cattle farmers. Slaughtering share was defined as the main driver for the project. The target is to achieve 18 per cent of slaughtering share in the producing region, considering that the baseline was 3 per cent at the launch of the project.

Thus far, the entire analysis and segmentation based on selling behaviours provided the company's executives with a great opportunity to rethink the relationships with their cattle suppliers. Before the project, the executives' belief was that about 80 per cent of all cattle farmers would fit into the Suspicious

(P) profile. However, only 19 per cent were confirmed to be so. The greatest percentage (37 per cent) fitted the Chatting (Ia) profile. The mental model behind the purchasing approach based on the 'one size fits all' concept was left aside, allowing the company to identify and manage its many supply chains. The subsequent step in this project was the roll-out of the segmentation processes for all remaining cattle-producing regions.

ALIGNMENT INSIGHTS

- *Business process management is a fundamental concept when managing supply chains.*

- *The framework depicted in Figure 18.1, which encompasses the management processes (1) strategic planning and management, (2) sales and operations planning, (3) fulfilment management, (4) order management and (5) material flow management, is an essential tool in attaining the operational excellence pursued by organizations.*

- *Demand and supply management are the business processes in charge of assuring forward and reverse alignments respectively within any supply chain.*

NOTES

1   T.H. Davenport, *Process Innovation, Reeingineering Work through Information Technology*, Harvard Business School Press, Boston, MA, 1993; M. Hammer and J. Champy, *Reengineering the Corporation: A Manifesto for Business Revolution*, HarperBusiness, New York, 1994.

2   J.L. Gattorna, *Living Supply Chains*, FT Prentice Hall, London, 2006.

3   Hermetic compressors are compressors used, for example, in home appliances such as refrigerators and freezers.

19 Supply Chain Alignment – European Style

Janet Godsell

Europe is the second smallest continent in the world and is a collection of 56 countries. Russia is the largest, covering a vast 17,000 km^2 and with a population of 145 million. In contrast, the smallest is the Vatican, a land-locked sovereign state of less than 0.5 km^2 and a population of only 800. This politically and geographically diverse continent is a challenging environment in which to practise the principles of dynamic alignment.[1] If it can work in Europe, it can work anywhere. Over the last eight years I have been involved in a variety of research[2] and consultancy activities exploring the concept of supply chain alignment. This study has involved over 70 Europe-based companies, many of which are the European subsidiaries of global multinational enterprises. This chapter seeks to provide insights into the realities of applying dynamic alignment in Europe. It begins by describing some of the 'hard truths' of the current state of supply chain alignment in Europe, where reality is often a long way from theory. It then offers some concrete advice for those wishing to pursue an 'alignment' agenda. The chapter concludes with a consolidating case study and a summary of the key insights for alignment.

SUPPLY CHAIN MANAGEMENT IN EUROPE: A FEW HARD TRUTHS

The core of dynamic alignment is developing a supply chain strategy that is aligned to the needs of the marketplace. Implicit in this definition is an assumption that Europeans have a common understanding of what Supply Chain (SC) and Supply Chain Management (SCM) actually mean. In reality it is rare for two individuals within the same company to define these terms the same way, let alone two people from different organizations. A recent study by Burgess[3] supported this view and concluded that these terms lack 'consensual definition' which indicates the lack of maturity in this field. Further indicators of the immaturity of supply chain strategy in Europe include the following:

- There is a limited presence of supply chain directors in the top management teams of European companies. Those who do exist rarely have the responsibility for the full scope of the supply chain, manufacturing being the most notable exception. They are more commonly 'rebranded' logistics or purchasing directors.

- The vast majority of organizations still have a 'one-size-fits-all' approach to developing supply chain strategy, and it is not customer-driven.

- The most common form of customer segmentation is account value – a method that has no direct link to supply chain strategy, either in terms of design or execution.

- It is difficult to find examples of supply chain alignment. Alignment is still in its infancy and is best described by 'pockets' of good practice.

This does not mean that those wishing to pursue dynamic alignment should be disheartened. Indeed, the converse is true. As with all the best things in life, it is not achieved without effort. Supply chain redesign is a considerable undertaking for any organization and tests its project and change management skills to the limit. However the upside is that any improvement to an organization's alignment vis-à-vis the competition will deliver significant competitive advantage.

'In reality it is rare for two individuals within the same company to define these terms the same way, let alone two people from different organizations.'

European companies with superior levels of alignment were found to have three things in common:

1. They had one of two contrasting organizational structures. They were either vertically integrated or virtual organizations. These organizational designs force clarity in terms of the supply chain design, and more specifically provide clear accountability of who 'manages the supply chain'. In vertically integrated organizations this was typically the supply chain director. In a virtual context, this was usually a fourth-party logistics provider (4PL).

2. The supply chain had been specifically designed to meet the needs of the business context in which it operated. For vertically integrated organizations this was achieved through a supply chain redesign. Given the relative youth of the virtual supply chains studied, they had been designed from the outset to leverage the opportunities of the new economy.

3. Business and customer focus were at the heart of their organizational cultures. This was reflected in their performance measurement systems which revealed a balance of functional and cross-functional measures. The cross-functional measures focused on business-wide financial performance and customer service. Employees within these organizations took an active interest in these measures and might even monitor them on a daily basis.

So, for those still encouraged to pursue an agenda of dynamic alignment there follows some practical insights from Europe to get you started.

FIVE TYPES OF ALIGNMENT

The dynamic alignment model is elegant in its simplicity. Unfortunately, as with many models, the application is not so straightforward and requires expansion of the underpinning framework. Given the broad scope of dynamic alignment and its relative immaturity within Europe, it was found that companies found it useful to break the concept down into a number of more manageable chunks. These served not only to aid understanding of the concept, but also to help the organization embarking on the journey to understand where pockets of good practice might exist within its supply chain. The result was the identification of five types of alignment (strategic, customer, internal, supplier and end-to-end) as illustrated in Figure 19.1.

1. *Strategic alignment* is the alignment between the core elements of business strategy – product, marketing and supply chain. The strategies are mutually reinforcing and there are fora in place to proactively manage trade-offs between the functions to optimize the benefit to the business.

2. *Customer alignment* is the alignment between the supply chain and its primary customers. It is achieved by identifying the relevant bases of segmentation for the customer base that defines the resultant customer value profiles, and provides a link to supply chain strategy.

3. *Internal alignment* is the alignment between the core supply chain processes (Plan, Source, Make, Deliver)[4] and the customer value profiles to deliver the defined differentiated supply chain strategy.

4. *Supplier alignment* is the alignment between the internal differentiated supply chains and the supplier base. It looks beyond traditional approaches to supplier management to identify ways in which the internal supply chains can be extended to suppliers.

5. *End-to-end alignment* is a sum of the previous four parts, with the intention that the sum is greater than the constituents. It seeks to ensure the overall alignment of the supply chain and avoid conflict or sub-optimization between the different elements.

These are the core building blocks of dynamic alignment and will be discussed in more detail, with practical examples. throughout the rest of this chapter.

SUPPLY CHAIN STRATEGY IS CRAFTED, NOT COPIED

Supply chains are highly complex living systems that span the boundaries of many different organizations. No two supply chains are the same and

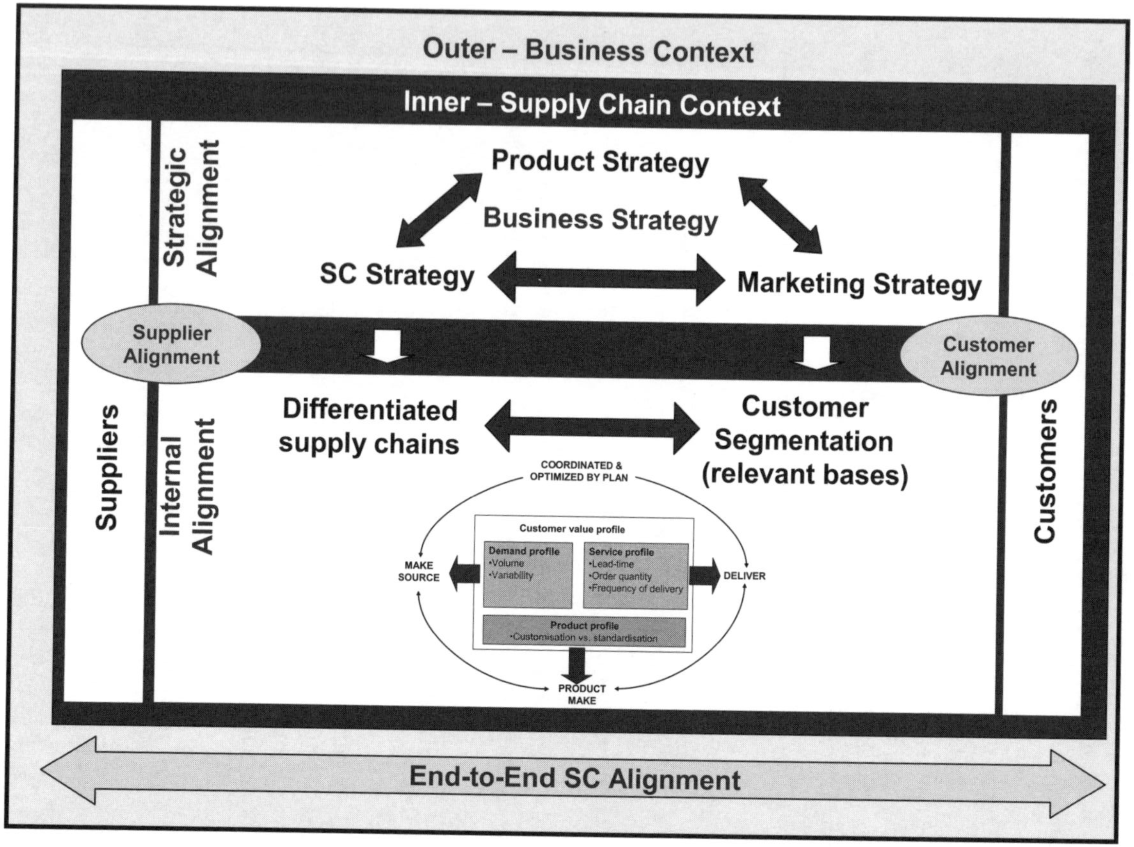

Figure 19.1   The five types of alignment

'best practices' cannot be directly copied or transferred from other supply chains. Organizations need to define their own set of 'best' or 'tailored' supply chain practices that support the delivery of their business strategy. For example, the retailer Tesco has an 'everyday low price' (EDLP) business strategy. The proposition to the consumer is 'lowest cost' which it can only deliver by having a supply chain strategy that is focused on achieving lowest operating cost. The focus for the supply chain, both internally and externally, is on minimizing cost and passing those savings onto the consumer. Tailored practices include vendor collaboration with co-managed inventory programmes and flow logistics and distribution (including cross-docking, direct store delivery, and differentiated flows). There is congruence between the supply chain strategy and the overall business strategy.

This key learning point from Europe is supported by the latest finding from the Massachusetts Institute of Technology (MIT) Supply Chain 2020 project.[5] Supply chain strategy is context-specific. It has to be developed to support the business strategy of a specific organization and cannot be copied. This is the key to strategic alignment.

START WITH THE CUSTOMER, BUT WHICH ONE?

A good business strategy has a clearly identified set of customers to which it responds, and these, it could be argued, are the customers for the supply chain. Unfortunately, the real world is more complex, particularly where a supply chain has many different customers. Fröhlich and Westbrook[6] introduced the term 'arc of integration' to describe the aspects of a supply chain that an organization chooses to actively manage. Experience has shown that this is commonly referred to as the supply chain and is positioned as part of the extended supply chain as illustrated in Figure 19.2.

Figure 19.2 illustrates the extended supply chain for an international tobacco company. Its span is from the end-consumer who smokes the product, back to the farmers who grow the tobacco crop. The extended supply chain is from 'smoke to seed' and includes many different types of customer. The consumer purchases the tobacco products from retailers, who in turn are served by distributors, who are provided with the product by the country-specific commercial organization. Operations, or the internal supply, is organized around the principles of the Supply Chain Operations Reference (SCOR)[7] model. It includes the main planning (plan), purchasing (source), manufacturing (make) and logistics (deliver) activities to deliver the physical product (cigarettes) at the right time, in the right quantity, to the right end-market commercial organization.

The end-customer of the extended supply chain is the consumer, but for the supply chain it is the end-market commercial organization. This is the decoupling point[8] for the supply chain and is the point at which the

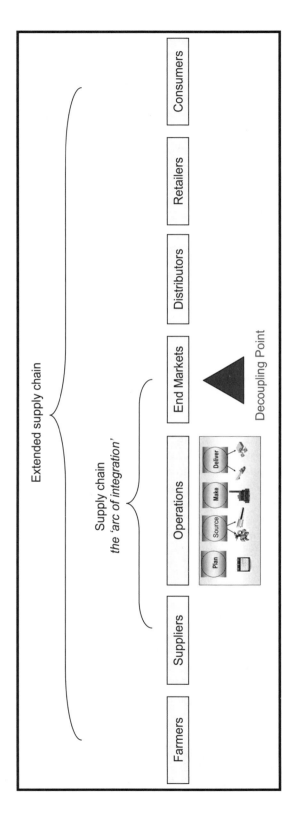

Figure 19.2   The supply chain as part of an extended supply chain

strategic inventory of finished goods is held. Whilst the tobacco company would ultimately like to extend its 'arc of integration' and get closer to the end-consumer, its immediate challenge is to align its supply chain to its vast number of end-market customers. Such clarity of scope is a fundamental prerequisite for effective supply chain alignment. Realism and pragmatism are also crucial to success. The virtues of responding directly to consumer demand are advocated by many. However, the immediate challenge and necessity can be very different, depending on the context in which the company operates.

Once the relevant set of customers for the supply chain has been identified, the next step is to segment the customers. Dynamic alignment argues for the use of behavioural segmentation. Experience from Europe would support this view but only when:

- the supply chain's 'arc of integration' stretches to the end-consumer or retail outlets that service the end-consumer;

- Customer Relationship Management (CRM) data within the company contains the appropriate information to enable behavioural segmentation to be effectively applied across all customers.

A prescriptive approach to segmentation is not advised. As suggested by Porter,[9] all bases need to be considered and the most relevant ones identified. Pragmatic decisions then need to be made regarding the forms of segmentation that are most beneficial to the organization in the short and long term. Where behavioural segmentation is not feasible, research from Europe suggests that there are three elements that interact to determine the customer value profile – namely, demand, customer service and product profiles. The key attributes of these profiles are described in Table 19.1.

INTERNAL ALIGNMENT: THE CRUCIAL MISSING LINK

Gattorna and Walters[10] allude to the concept of internal alignment when they suggest that supply chain strategy needs to be supported by the correct culture and leadership capabilities to enable effective implementation. European experience suggests that there are a number of elements to internal alignment.

Supply chain strategy is driven by understanding the customer value profiles for the customers directly served by the supply chain. Of the three customer value elements, demand profile was identified as the primary driver of supply chain strategy, with the customer and service elements being of secondary importance. Experience from Europe suggests that demand profiling should be carried out for each individual SKU. Where possible, demand for promotional SKUs should be isolated and plotted as different SKUs. The analysis is primarily based on plotting the volume for each SKU versus its variability (coefficient of variation). All SKUs are plotted and then high,

Table 19.1   **The three elements of a customer value profile and their key attributes**

Element of customer value profile	Key attributes
Demand*	Quantitative, quasi-objective analysis
	Determined at an individual stock-keeping unit (SKU) level
	Where possible, demand for promotional SKUs should be isolated and plotted as different SKUs
	Analysis primarily based on volume versus variability (coefficient of variation)
	All SKUs should be plotted and then high, medium and low quadrants identified on both axes based on a scale relevant to the demand
	Secondary filters can be applied to test the feasibility of SKUs in more marginal quadrants – for example, do individual low-volume, high-variety SKUs contribute sufficient margin to justify their production?
Customer service	Qualitative, quasi-subjective analysis
	Should be determined for each individual customer at the relevant point in the supply chain
	Exact dimensions (for example, lead-time, frequency of delivery, quality) to be determined through pilot testing
	Interview-based, but should have the ability to capture the data for all customers and be updated regularly
Product	Quantitative analysis
	Explores the degree of standardization versus customization or individual SKUs.

* Thomas Diefenbach led the development of this approach to demand profiling as part of his Cranfield MSc Logistics and SCM thesis (2008) and follow-up project with an FMCG company. Critical input was also provided by Chris Clemmow, Andy Birtwistle, Professor Denis Towill and Dr Janet Godsell.

medium, and low quadrants are identified on both axes, based on a scale relevant to the demand. Secondary filters can be applied to test the feasibility of SKUs in more marginal quadrants – for example, do individual low-volume, high-variety SKUs contribute sufficient margin to justify their production? This enables an understanding of the demand pattern for a product (base, semi-wave, surge and cavitation)[11] which has a major impact on the type of supply chain strategy developed, as illustrated in Table 19.2.

European companies did not have an appetite for managing more than three supply chains. Practically, they perceived little difference in the continuous replenishment and lean supply chain types and adopted the lean type to deal with both base and semi-wave demand types. As illustrated in Figure 19.3, different elements of the customer value bundle drive different elements of the supply chain strategy, although they all interact to determine the optimum strategy.

Table 19.2   Demand type and matching supply chain types*

Demand type	Type of supply chain
Base	Lean
Semi-wave	Regular or very predictable pattern of demand Relatively high-volume and low-variability demand at an SKU level
Surge	Agile Unpredictable pattern of demand Relatively low-volume and high-variability demand at an SKU level Includes promotions and certain types of new product introduction (for example, limited edition packs)
Cavitation	Fully flexible (innovation) Extremely unpredictable pattern of demand Includes the introduction of radical new innovations/reaction to unforeseen change in external environment (for example, fire in competitor's factory)

* After J.L. Gattorna, *Living Supply Chains*, FT Prentice Hall, Harlow, 2006.

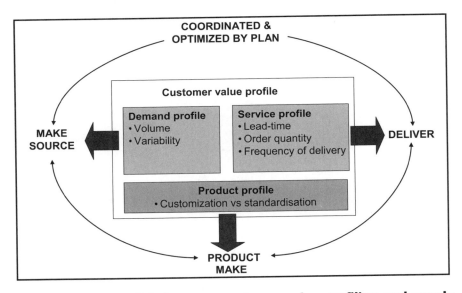

Figure 19.3   The link between customer value profiling and supply chain strategy

Demand profiling had a direct impact on the manufacturing (make) strategy, which in turn drove the purchasing (buy) strategy. The customer service profile had a direct link to the logistics strategy (move) and the product profile to the product and manufacturing (make) strategies. The implications of the different supply chain strategies on individual supply chain processes could then be considered and the 'tailored practices' articulated. An example for a global consumer packaged goods (CPG) company with a presence in Europe is illustrated in Table 19.3.

Table 19.3 **Examples of tailored practices developed to support different supply chain strategies for a global CPG company with a presence in Europe**

SC type	Tailored Practices		
	Lean	**Agile**	**Fully Flexible**
Product	Premium/Value for Money Standardised	Premium	Premium Innovation
Demand signal	Statistical forecast Automatic trigger for demand		End market confirms demand Assumptions are clear Normalized through global S&OP
Plan	Fixed order cycle/planning wheels (maker to stock (MTS), little human intervention)	Fixed order quantity/block planning (MTS, some human intervention for logistics optimization)	Global demand aggregation & supply planning
Source	Multiple suppliers Full trucks Electronic kanban	Fixed kit to order One 1st tier supplier (similar to automotive)	Many specialist suppliers Co-development
Make	Multiple factories in region MTS – Production wheels Modern, high-volume, high-speed machines Standardized – minimal specifications Lights out – minimal human intervention	One factory or 'factory in factory' in each trade bloc MTS – Fixed batch size Scheduling tool – smart planning Low capital/high labour	Make to forecast (MTF)/make to order (MTO) Stranger factory principles May be outsourced
Deliver	Fixed schedules & routes (hub & spoke) Full containers – production volume flex to accommodate	Batched infrequent full trucks May ship to hubs for consolidation	Ship to hubs for consolidation
Inventory policy	Low stock cover (weeks) Managed between limits	Higher stock cover (weeks) Managed between limits	Higher stock cover (weeks)
Management	Regional		Global

Ironically, given the pivotal importance of internal alignment, it was found to be the type of alignment that was most frequently overlooked – the crucial missing link.

EXTENDING ALIGNMENT TO THE SUPPLY BASE

Campbell and Du Preez[12] call this 'reverse' alignment, but it is more widely recognized within Europe as supplier alignment. Ironically, for many organizations it is easier to align with their suppliers than it is to align internally. Supplier alignment moves beyond the more widely recognized practices of category, supplier and contract management to consider the opportunities for extending the internal supply chain strategies (for example, lean, agile and fully flexible) into the supply base. For instance, as illustrated in Table 19.3, in a lean supply chain with a relatively stable demand for high-volume products, a multiple sourcing strategy using automatic replenishment on electronic kanban could be employed. In contrast, the agile supply chain requires a designated first-tier supplier to consolidate kits for a fixed order quantity. Some of the components may be the same, but the method of supply and price paid are different. A well-defined and relatively stable internal supply chain strategy is crucial if supplier alignment is to be successful. Changes in internal strategy (for example, changes from insourcing to outsourcing) can have a disruptive effect on the supply base and undermine the basis of the relationship.

Leading practice in Europe has seen organizations beginning to measure the degree of supplier alignment. This involved a two-prong assessment to identify alignment gaps, a supplier alignment questionnaire and process gap analysis. The output of the assessment was used to identify joint alignment improvement projects. Assessing supplier alignment was a time-consuming and involved process, and its application was limited to strategic suppliers. It is an interesting concept and one that could be extended to all five types of alignment.

THE ROLE OF S&OP IN MAINTAINING ALIGNMENT

As we have seen in earlier chapters of this book, Sales and Operations Planning (S&OP) is perhaps the most powerful planning process within an organization for maintaining alignment. Wallace & Stahl[13] define S&OP as:

> ... a set of decision-making processes to balance demand and supply, to integrate financial planning and operational planning, and to link high level strategic plans with day-to-day operations.

In essence S&OP seeks to address all aforementioned types of alignment. Its process and tools enables alignment gaps to be identified, solutions proposed and escalated to the appropriate level for a decision to be made. It enables the business at all levels to manage by fact and make decisions that maximize absolute profit in the short and long term. Leading practice from Europe suggests two more developed applications of the process:

- as a tool for tracking the degree of alignment in the business, and proactively responding to emerging alignment gaps; and

- as a tool for product/SKU life-cycle management (PLCM) and product 'health check'.

If the supplier alignment assessment tool could be extended to all five types of alignment, the S&OP process could be modified to include an alignment review. Alignment issues could be tracked and actions put in place to close the gaps. This idea is still very much at the concept stage but is nonetheless being actively pursued in a handful of companies.

'S&OP enables alignment gaps to be identified, solutions proposed and escalated to the appropriate level for a decision to be made.'

Using S&OP as a tool for PLCM is a slightly more developed concept but is still in its infancy. As illustrated in Figure 19.4. Kirill Popadyuk (2004)[14] explored this concept and developed a framework based on the Boston Consulting Matrix. It explored the differences in 'tailored practices' (inventory policy, supply chain priorities and cost) depending on the stage

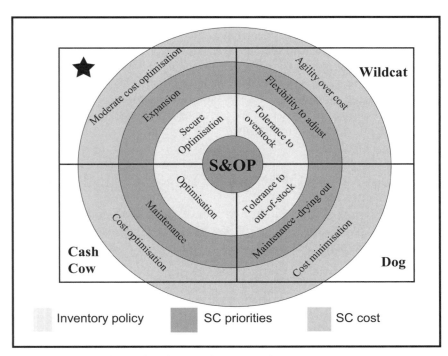

Figure 19.4   The role of S&OP in managing PLCM

Source: After Popadyuk (2004).

a product was in its life cycle. For instance, at launch when the future of a product was uncertain (wildcat), overstocking was tolerated, the supply chain required the flexibility to respond to variations in demand and hence agility was more important than absolute cost. In contrast, when a product was mature (cash cow) the whole strategy was focused on optimization. S&OP was used to review the stage a product was in its life cycle and ensure that it was being routed down the most appropriate supply chain pathway. Once again, demand profiling is the crucial link. It is an activity that needs to be regularly repeated (suggestion is quarterly) to ensure internal alignment.

Putting It All Together: PharmaCo Case Study

PharmaCo is a leading European retailer of health and beauty products. It employs over 50,000 people across a network of 1,500 stores ranging from small community pharmacies to city centre department stores. At the heart of every PharmaCo store is a pharmacy. It is the pharmacy supply chain that was the focus for this case study. PharmaCo had the benefit of a vertically integrated value chain. The value chain provides prescription medicines to individual consumers and nursing/care homes. There are two principal buying behaviours, so patients require medicine for two reasons:

1. a repeat prescription for a chronic condition that requires ongoing treatment (base/semi-wave demand)

2. acute prescriptions for an unforeseen illness (surge demand).

Of all the prescriptions fulfilled by PharmaCo 8 per cent were repeats and created a stable pattern of demand. The mix between repeat and acute prescriptions varied from store to store, but there was a strong correlation between store types (city centre, high street, travel, out of town and so on). For instance, out-of-town stores have a transient customer base and therefore a low percentage of repeat prescriptions. Consequently, they need to stock a much wider range of products than a high street store which serves a defined community and can even tailor its inventory to the prescribing preferences of the local doctors. The service-level agreement between PharmaCo and the government was very strict, and PharmaCo had a duty of care to provide over 20,000 standard products to their consumers within 24 hours. Customer service was paramount, but was balanced against supply chain cost.

In 2002 PharmaCo conducted a full redesign of its pharmacy supply chain. The objective was to maintain this challenging level of customer service while minimizing supply chain costs. The solution was an innovative hybrid solution tailored around the base/semi-wave: surge demand split (that is, demand profiling). PharmaCo built a new state-of-the-art dispensing warehouse for the top 2,000 standard product lines (by volume), which were managed internally. It leveraged the daily store delivery system developed for its store operations, piggy-backing on the existing warehouse and distribution infrastructure. This provided next-day delivery to all stores before opening. For the new dispensing warehouse to be commercially viable, it had to set a new standard within PharmaCo for warehouse efficiency. All members of management and operating staff were recruited new to role and underwent significant team-building training to help shape the appropriate culture for the new operation. The warehouse manager had excellent leadership skills. They ensured that everyone involved in the operation were focused on achieving a customer service level in excess of 99.5 per cent, while seeking to continuously improve internal efficiency. The remaining 18,000 standard lines were outsourced to a specialist pharmaceutical distributor. The distributor had an extensive network that provided twice-daily deliveries to pharmacies and hospitals across the country. PharmaCo was able to leverage its scale and scope for the long product tail and its speed of response as a contingency source for the core 2,000 lines – particularly if same-day delivery was required.

Essentially, PharmaCo managed the lean supply chain 'in-house' and outsourced their 'agile' requirements. Whilst the lean/agile split was primarily determined by volume, the relative positioning of the split also took into account the overall commercial impact. Originally, PharmaCo had managed the top 3,000 lines internally, but on review the company found that whilst that may have been a cheaper option for those particular product lines, the total supply chain cost was less if it increased the outsourced volume. This highlights the importance of optimizing the total overall supply chain cost rather than the cost through individual chains.

There was a third strand to the PharmaCo supply chain: 'special' products which, as the term suggests, need to be specially prepared to meet the requirements of individual patients. These orders are dealt with by a dedicated team at PharmaCo and although they account for only 1 per cent of the items that the team purchases, they required 40 per cent of the supply team resource! This is testament to the effectiveness of the lean supply chain, in which 99 per cent of the supply by volume was managed using only 60 per cent of the resource.

Supplier alignment was an interesting challenge in the pharmaceutical industry case study. There were essentially three categories:

1. *Branded* – products under patent protection which are sold to strict margin agreements for which there is little/no room for negotiation.

2. *Generic* – products which are no longer under patent, for which there is relatively fierce competition. Given the size of the PharmaCo, business generic manufacturers are keen to supply and tendering is very competitive.

3. *Parallel imports* – commercial opportunities do exist to leverage the benefits of products imported from other European countries. This is a very opportunistic business and there is little continuity of supply.

The lean supply chain has fairly predictable demand, and this was aligned to the supply of product from branded and generic suppliers. The supply organization was keen to leverage the commercial opportunities afforded by parallel imports, but this had to be balanced with the disruption to the supply chain. It was lumpy supply from an opportunistic source that was replacing the stable demand placed on an existing supplier. It is in situations like this, where S&OP is used to assess and find the solution, that provides the best return to the business in the short and long term. As summarized in Table 19.4, the PharmaCo case study is a good example of dynamic supply chain alignment in Europe because it demonstrates all five types of alignment.

Table 19.4   Summary of the attainment of all five types of alignment in the PharmaCo supply chain

Type of alignment	Key practices
Strategic	Understanding that customer service could not be compromised, but had to be delivered with maximum commercial benefit to PharmaCo.
	A clearly defined segmented supply chain strategy (lean, agile and special) that was focused on delivering customer service at minimum cost.

Table 19.4　　*Concluded*

Type of alignment	Key practices
Customer	Consumer intimacy enabled PharmaCo to use buying behaviour as a method for segmenting consumers. This was a result of their vertically integrated value chain. Understanding the link between store segmentation and buying behaviour, which enabled pharmacy inventory profiles to be developed. Sensitivity to the local context. The pharmacist had the ultimate responsibility for determining the inventory profile.
Internal	State-of-the-art warehouse facility, purpose-built to meet stable high-volume demand (a lean facility). Management and operations staff selected and trained to develop a culture that supports a high level of customer service while striving to continuously improve efficiency. Leveraging the scale and scope of the existing store delivery infrastructure. Separate supply chain for non-standard customized products (specials).
Supplier	Category and supplier management techniques employed. Understanding of the long-term business impact of trade-offs between commercial opportunities (e.g. parallel imports) and impact on the supply chain. Leveraging the capabilities of an outsourced distributor for the long product tail (leverage scale and scope) and contingency supply for top 2,000 products (leverage speed and agility).
End-to-end	Given the high degree of strategic, customer and internal alignment the end-to-end alignment was generally good. Parallel imports had to be managed carefully to ensure that they did not disrupt supplier alignment.

ALIGNMENT INSIGHTS

Europe has proven to be an engaged and testing environment for dynamic alignment. Some practical lessons from Europe to help organizations in their quest towards alignment include the following:

- *There are four different types of alignment (strategic, customer, internal and supplier) which interact to determine an organization's dynamic alignment.*

- *Extended supply chains have many different customers. The key is to understand which 'customer' the supply chain directly serves and use an understanding of this 'customer' (customer value profile) to drive the supply chain strategy.*

- *In a business-to-business environment, demand profiling is usually the starting-point for developing supply chain strategy.*

> • *Supply chain strategy should be extended into the supply base – this is the heart of supplier alignment.*
>
> • *S&OP is an important set of business processes and tools for maintaining all five types of alignment.*

NOTES

1   The study of alignment commenced in 2001 and used the strategic alignment model. See J.L. Gattorna and D.W. Walters, *Managing the Supply Chain: A Strategic Perspective*, Palgrave, Basingstoke, 1996, p. 26. This has subsequently been developed into the concept of dynamic alignment in J.L. Gattorna, *Living Supply Chains*, FT Prentice Hall, Harlow, 2006, p. 16.

2   The research was primarily conducted as part of two research projects led by the Supply Chain Research Centre (SCRC) at Cranfield University. Both projects were supported by the Engineering and Physical Sciences Research Centre (EPSRC), grant numbers GR/N34406 L\2\21 and IMRC40. Further details are available at the SCRC website: http://www.som.cranfield.ac.uk/som/research/centres/lscm/research.

3   K. Burgess, P.J. Singh and R. Koroglu, 'Supply chain management: a structured literature review and implications for future research', *International Journal of Operations and Production Management*, Vol. 26, No. 7, (2006), p. 703.

4   These are the core forward-facing supply chain processes as defined in the Supply Chain Operations Reference (SCOR) model developed by the Supply Chain Council. For further details on the SCOR model see http://www.supply-chain.org.

5   This research project seeks to explore the essence of supply chain excellence. For further details on the research visit see http:// www.sc2020.net.

6   M.T. Fröhlich and R. Westbrook, 'Arcs of integration: an international study of supply chain strategies', *Journal of Operations Management*, Vol. 14, No. 10 (2001), p. 17.

7   See Note 4.

8   The point in the supply chain which provides a buffer between differing input and output rates.

9   M.E. Porter, *Competitive Advantage: Creating and Sustaining Superior Performance*, Free Press, New York, 1985, p. 233. A very comprehensive approach for identifying the most relevant bases of segmentation.

10   See Note 1.

11   Gattorna, *Living Supply Chains*, *op. cit.*, p. 46.

12   B. Campbell and A. Du Preez, 'Securing immediate benefits for e-sourcing' in J.L. Gattorna (ed.), *The Gower Handbook of Supply Chain Management* (5th edn), Gower, Aldershot, 2003, p. 346.

13   Tom Wallace and Bob Stahl are two of the leading commentators on S&OP. For more information refer to their website: http://www.tfwallace.com/pages/content/sop_101.html.

14   K.N. Popadyuk, 'Product life cycle and its influence on supply chains', *Marketing in Russia and Abroad*, No. 2 (2005), pp. 25–35. This was the output from a break-out session on a customer-driven supply chain workshop with a Russian manufacturer of consumer packaged goods. It was based on the output from Kirill's doctoral studies.

20 Corporate Social Responsibility in Enterprise Supply Chains

Mark Reynolds and Leeora Black

For the last 20 years we have all, as consumers, enjoyed the plummeting price of manufactured goods. The repeating cycle of newer–better–cheaper has encouraged us to buy bigger, brighter flat-screen televisions, smaller, cleverer mobile gadgets and larger, leather-lined luxury cars, at prices nobody would have thought possible in the 1980s. At the same time, retailers have sourced our day-to-day food and clothing items from all over the world and made them cheap as well. On the face of it, globalization has been a remarkable consumer success.

But how is all this stuff getting to us? How are the farms, forests and mines that provide the raw materials being operated? We know that most of the factories transforming materials into finished products operate in countries like China, but what do we know about their cost-cutting practices, their pollution discharges and how they treat their people? What about all the global transport legs that bring the goods to us? And in our own backyard, what happens to the old stuff we discard from our businesses and homes?

As legal concepts like 'chain of responsibility' become the norm, these are important questions for supply chain professionals and corporate management to reflect on. Corporate Social Responsibility (CSR) and sustainability thinking provide the models to tackle these questions and others of similar importance to the future of our supply chains.

THE ORIGINS OF CSR

Modern ideas about corporate social responsibility emerged during the twentieth century, especially in industrialized nations after the Second World War. However, beliefs about the nature of business's responsibilities to society are as old as the corporate form itself – about 400 years old.

Although groups of people have combined skills and resources to conduct business since pre-biblical days, the advent of the 'chartered company' around

400 years ago is when the real story of CSR began. In those days, a king might charter a ship to develop new trade routes or explore new lands. The British East India Company was an example of this early corporate form. The purposes of such businesses were to act on behalf of a society to advance a society's interests, represented through the king. It was only much later that the idea of business for personal profit developed.

'Given that each business has a unique configuration of products, services, people, assets, markets and customers, the specific social responsibilities of business will vary.'

Herein is the core philosophical question that drives debate about CSR – what is, or should be, the relationship between business and society? Some (a shrinking minority) think that the only responsibility of business, apart from obeying the law, is to return profits to its shareholders.[1] Others believe that business has wide-ranging responsibilities to act ethically and responsibly, and to play its part in the development of society and the protection of the environment.

The idea that business has any responsibility at all to its suppliers and other stakeholders, beyond paying the bills, is clearly consistent with the view that business has broader responsibility – in other words, that business has 'corporate social responsibilities'. Defining the exact nature of those responsibilities can, however, be a challenge.

Given that each business has a unique configuration of products, services, people, assets, markets and customers, the specific social responsibilities of business will vary. National and cultural differences also play a big role. For example, business in the USA has traditionally played quite a large role in philanthropy. With the US government taking a smaller role in social welfare than, for example, in countries like Australia, CSR developed as an idea that business should make philanthropic contributions towards solving social problems.[2] In Western Europe and the UK, where government plays a larger role in social welfare, ideas about the social responsibility of business are more likely to focus on corporate governance and sustainability. Australian business is influenced by both US and European interpretations of CSR. Corporations such as mining companies operating predominantly in developing countries and remote regions find themselves under great pressure to act as leaders in social, community, education, health and workforce development.

With the increasing globalization of business and the rise of the multinational enterprise in the twentieth century, we are seeing more convergence at the international level on concepts of corporate social responsibility. This is nowhere more clearly spelled out than in the work of the International Organization for Standardization (ISO), which is developing a voluntary standard on corporate social responsibility called ISO 26000 for release in 2010.

The ISO Working Group on Social Responsibility has issued a definition that includes the key elements of an agreed international definition of CSR:

Social responsibility is the responsibility of an organization for the impacts of its decisions and activities on society and the environment, through transparent and ethical behavior that:

- *is consistent with sustainable development and the welfare of society*
- *takes into account the expectations of stakeholders*
- *is in compliance with applicable law and consistent with international norms of behavior; and*
- *is integrated throughout the organization.*[3]

The core CSR issues the ISO CSR standard is expected to cover are:

- organizational governance;

- environment;

- human rights;

- labour practices;

- fair operating practices;

- consumer issues;

- community involvement/society development.

These seven issues encapsulate all the areas of CSR activity. Consideration of CSR in the supply chain is included within the theme of 'fair operating practices'.

THE GROWING IMPORTANCE OF CSR

If CSR is not really a new idea, then why does it seem to be rising in prominence right now? The answer may be because society is changing, and so too are the attitudes, values and expectations of people about business.

There is a lot of evidence for how societal values are changing. The World Values Survey,[4] run from Michigan's Institute for Social Research, is the largest investigation ever conducted of attitudes, values and beliefs around the world, covering societies where the per capita annual income is as low as $300 a year to societies like Australia's that is generally wealthy by world standards.

Over the last 30 years the World Values Survey has run five large waves of surveys in 65 countries representing 80 per cent of the world's population. The main finding from these surveys is that, as the gross national product of countries rises, people's values change from traditional and survival values to self-expression values. It makes sense. When people are primarily concerned about the basics of human survival – putting a roof over their head, finding work and eating enough – they tend to value the satisfaction of basic material needs. But as societies become wealthier, people start to value more highly things like individual expression, personal freedom, citizen involvement in government decisions, humanistic values and preserving the environment. These values are called 'post-materialist values'.

The World Values Survey has found in country after country that as wealth rises, so too does the proportion of people holding post-materialist values. Prolonged periods of prosperity, such as has been enjoyed in Australia over the last 50 years, tend to encourage the spread of post-materialist values.

'As the gross national product of countries rises, people's values change from traditional and survival values to self-expression values.'

Although economic growth is still valued, an increasing share of the public is willing to give environmental protection and other values priority over economic growth when these goals conflict.

We can see evidence of rising post-materialist values since the 1960s. First there was the civil rights movement where increasing numbers of Americans began to value more highly equal rights and diversity. Consumer rights and women's rights came next, in the 1970s. In the 1980s we began to focus more on environmental issues. In the 1990s we broadened our understanding of the environment and started to talk about sustainability. The 2000s may come to be known for the rise of corporate responsibility and accountability values.

An increasing proportion of people born since the end of the Second World War have been infused with these post-materialist values. It is natural and self-evident to most of us that we should care about the environment, human rights, equal opportunity, fairness, and individual rights and self-expression.

It is natural to us to want to manage the organizations we work for in accordance with those values.

When you think about it, corporate social responsibility is really an approach to managing organizations based on post-materialist values. A CSR approach to managing the supply chain is therefore one based on managing a supply chain to ensure protection of the environment and human rights in a manner which is fair and ensures good business outcomes for all the businesses and consumers who are a part of the supply chain.

CSR AND SUSTAINABILITY

A question often asked is 'How do CSR and sustainability relate?' The answer is that they have closely aligned interests in the environment sector and a great deal of common ground generally.

Differences in philosophy and intent mean that the focus of a sustainability programme is usually narrower than CSR. Sustainability programmes can be expected to deliver stronger environmental results with less attention to the social and corporate governance dimensions of a CSR programme.

At the philosophical level, we have seen that CSR brings a positive, humanist and values-based approach to supporting the business, social and natural environments in which a company operates. Many businesses these days can point to good things they have done for their communities, for their business partners and for the natural environment as a result of taking their corporate social responsibilities seriously. These are praiseworthy achievements.

Sustainability philosophies generally drive an even more rigorous and wide-ranging approach to doing good for the natural environment by taking a long view into the future and challenging us to act today in ways that leave future generations no worse off across every measure of resource usage and waste output.[5] Views on how to do this range from the 'hard' sustainability of Herman Daly's 'steady state economics' which seriously questions the basis of economic growth[6] to the 'soft' sustainability of harm minimization which asks us to treat the environment in 'more sustainable' ways.[7]

Major mining, manufacturing and energy businesses have to grapple hardest with the philosophical chasm between just 'doing better' and really 'doing good'. A few remarkable companies have become poster children for the sustainability movement by seeking to climb Mount Sustainability all the way to objectively measured levels of 'good', such as zero emissions and 100 per cent recycling of products.

Companies like Interface Carpets[8] which have publicly committed to such goals are driven by strong sustainability philosophies articulated by leaders such as Interface's Ray Anderson who describes himself as a 'recovering plunderer' driven by environmental vision. The term 'recovering plunderer' refers to his life-changing experience in 1994 when he was asked to present his environmental views to his employees. He says, 'I had no environmental vision. In my whole life, I had never given a thought to what my company was doing to the earth.' Then he encountered Paul Hawken's book, *The Ecology of Commerce.*[9] In Ray Anderson's words, 'Within 50 pages, I am a convicted plunderer of the earth. It is a spear to the chest.'[10]

Ray Anderson has gone on to make Interface Carpets a world leader in recycling and closing the loop on material flows to eliminate waste.

Visionary leadership like Ray Anderson's is advancing steadily among industries which have a high environmental impact. We can expect to hear more about extraordinary sustainability journeys like that of Interface Carpets. Fortunately, not all businesses need to change so much. For many businesses, the philosophical leap is smaller, the actions easier to introduce and the differences between CSR and sustainability less significant.

At the practical level, we observe that effective CSR programmes usually aim to take a balanced view across many worthy corporate initiatives including governance, ethics, health, safety, community and the environment. The Westpac Bank case study below is an excellent example. In contrast with CSR-driven programmes, practical sustainability programmes are usually more focused on measurable environmental targets such as energy efficiency, zero emissions or zero waste, as exemplified by the Herman Miller case study which follows.

CASE STUDIES: ACHIEVEMENTS IN CSR AND SUSTAINABILITY

Case Study: Westpac Banking Corporation

Do banks have supply chains? Yes, says CSR leader Westpac Banking Corporation which launched its Sustainable Supply Chain Management (SSCM) programme in 2003. SSCM refers to the supplier-facing component of Westpac's strong commitment to CSR across all its corporate activities.[11] Westpac has the impressive record of being the world's most highly rated bank on the Dow Jones Sustainability Index almost every year since 2002. The SSCM section of Westpac's website sets the scene for suppliers with the words:

> Westpac recognises that our social, ethical and environmental impacts reside as much in our supply chain as in our own activities. In our supply chain we seek to ensure that:
>
> Our suppliers are aware of the specific environmental, social and ethical issues, risks and opportunities relevant to their operations and products
>
> Our suppliers operate to internationally recognised standards of practice
>
> Our higher spend and risk suppliers have management systems in place to address associated issues, risks and opportunities
>
> These systems are delivering effective performance management and improvement.[12]

Westpac follows through on these commitments by working closely with suppliers to help them lift their CSR standards year by year to ensure that Westpac's supplier base continually develops towards better alignment with Westpac's own CSR aspirations. Over the last five years more than 500 of Westpac's suppliers have completed a comprehensive SSCM questionnaire. The responses provide Westpac with a unique supplier CSR capability database revealing rich information on the maturity, strengths and weaknesses of their supply chain partners.

Case Study: Herman Miller

As a world-leading manufacturer of high-end furniture for office, health care and home, US-based corporation Herman Miller manages a complex supply chain. Herman Miller's annual CSR report' titled A Better World, addresses all the expected dimensions of CSR, with special emphasis on sustainability and the environment.[13] Like Westpac in the case study above, Herman Miller has a long history of serious corporate commitment to sustainability. And, to a far greater degree than corporations in the services sector, manufacturers like Herman Miller face a multiplicity of environmental issues within their own four walls as well as up and down their supply chains. Energy use in factories, hazardous chemicals and production waste generation are just a few of the issues facing a manufacturer whose products combine metals, wood, fabrics and plastics in highly engineered configurations.

Manufacturers like Herman Miller also have the power to drive product design in directions that strongly impact on sustainability, for better or worse. The pivotal role of product design in determining whole-of-life sustainability performance of their furniture has made 'cradle-to-cradle design' one of Herman Miller's key initiatives. Their Design for Environment (DfE) protocol calls for each new product design to be thoroughly evaluated for materials chemistry, safety of inputs, disassembly and recyclability. Doing this requires the extensive involvement of supply chain partners, including raw material suppliers, component suppliers, transport providers and end-of-life recycling and reclamation services. Herman Miller's intent is reflected in the tough goals set out in their Perfect Vision programme:

In 2004, we established a new environmental mandate with our Perfect Vision program. This initiative set a target date of 2020 to meet the following sustainability goals:

- *100 percent reduction of VOC (volatile organic compound) emissions to air*
- *100 percent reduction of process water use*
- *100 percent reduction of hazardous waste*
- *100 percent reduction of solid waste to the landfill*
- *100 percent renewable electrical energy use*
- *100 percent of sales from our Design for Environment (DfE)-approved products*
- *100 percent of owned and/or leased company buildings meet or exceed USGBC's LEED Silver certification.*[14]

Herman Miller demonstrates the technical rigour needed to back up a thoughtful CSR philosophy for a manufacturer and ensure that all members of its extended supply chain work together to deliver on the sustainable vision.

THE IMPORTANCE OF SUPPLY CHAIN ALIGNMENT

Those with professional training in cross-disciplinary fields such as agricultural science, ecology or Water conservation will automatically recognize that true sustainability always requires systems thinking because a 'sustainable' product cannot exist in isolation. End-to-end supply chains can only be configured to achieve sustainable outcomes if each part of the supply chain is arranged to do so from a systems perspective. And as the Herman Miller case study demonstrates, that means involving suppliers and customers

293

and other parties such as energy providers and waste recyclers. Clearly, supply chain thinking becomes more and more essential as our expectations of sustainability harden.

Alignment between multiple supply chain parties is a legendary challenge. The in-house aspects of CSR – such as internal governance – can be addressed without alignment but, as soon as supply chain partners are involved in CSR or sustainability programmes, the critical first step will be aligning interests, goals, behaviours and strategies. Progress on a more complex system outcome like true supply chain sustainability will be practically impossible to achieve without extensive work on alignment among supply chain partners.

> *'Those with professional training in cross-disciplinary fields such as agricultural science, ecology or Water conservation will automatically recognize that true sustainability always requires systems thinking because a "sustainable" product cannot exist in isolation.'*

THE ALIGNMENT MODEL AND SUSTAINABILITY

We have already examined the important role of post-materialist values in directing more attention towards CSR and sustainability. Values-driven change is particularly motivating for two of the four types of corporate subculture described by the alignment model. A 'group' subculture is strongly values-oriented and an 'entrepreneurial' subculture responds well to visionary leadership. Energized by inspiring leadership, both of these corporate subcultures will tend to embrace CSR and sustainability as the 'right things to do'. The Interface Carpets and Herman Miller cases discussed above are both characterized by powerful personal leadership from the top of the organization.

The other two types of corporate subcultures identified by the alignment model are the 'hierarchical' and the 'rational'. These subcultures are more strongly driven by numbers and facts. Increasingly, we are seeing scientists, engineers and accountants taking a lead on sustainability because their analyses show them that quantified performance measures and benefits will be driven in the right direction by sustainability thinking. Given the right encouragement, these analytically-oriented subcultures will prove to themselves that initiatives to save energy and waste will also save money and often provide surprising side-benefits in areas such as intellectual challenge and staff motivation.

This sounds like good news – all four corporate subcultures can find reasons to get excited about CSR and sustainability in ways that drive positive change in supply chains. The evidence of this excitement is all around us as more and more companies sign up to reducing the footprint of their supply chains.

Another motivator for sustainable thinking has always been there in the background and has recently become more prominent – namely, risk mitigation. Supply chain businesses with specific exposure to high-profile risks like coastal shipwreck have usually taken care to manage and mitigate their physical risks. Another class of risks is resource shortages. These risks gained profile back in the 1970s when the Club of Rome leapt into prominence by predicting 'limits to growth'[15] based on shortages of essential industrial raw materials. Such concerns seemed to fade through the 1980s and 1990s as cheap energy and technical innovation kept the industrial world powering along.

From 2003 the price of oil began to move upwards at double-digit annual percentage growth rates. By 2007 it was clear that energy was becoming neither cheap nor low-risk. Other commodities like steel and coal also headed steeply upwards in price, and a new set of supply chain input risks put themselves on the table.

All supply chain businesses now have compelling reasons to examine and understand every aspect of their exposure to resource inputs, energy usage, freight transport, carbon emissions, pollutants, waste discharges and product disposal implications from beginning to end of the life cycle of their products. CSR and sustainability now take centre stage.

FUTURE DIRECTIONS FOR SUSTAINABILITY AND CSR IN SUPPLY CHAINS

We have learned a lot since the 1970s. The latest edition of *Limits to Growth – The 30-year Update*, points to accelerating environmental degradation, energy consumption and waste disposal challenges as presenting more immediate and inescapable limits than supplies of many input materials.[16] It is becoming obvious that the best efforts of those already committed to cleaning up our planet are being overwhelmed by the pace of growth elsewhere. Individual businesses can point to great achievements in sustainability, but globally we have managed far too little dematerialization over the last 30 years to be confident of stabilizing humanity and the world on a sustainable course.

What has to change is well understood. 'Dematerialization' sums up a shift to a new form of prosperity based on less 'stuff'. This is a highly confronting prospect for supply chains dedicated to volume growth as the tangible sign of success. The change will probably have to come about by broadening the legislated interests of corporations from their shareholders to all their stakeholders – in other words, by making CSR in its broadest sense a mandated requirement.[17] How could such a thing happen? Only by means of remarkable changes forced by currently unimaginable and unwelcome events.

So as we run up against increasingly hardened limits to growth we must expect the coming pace of change to leave us breathless and the mean time between surprises to become frighteningly short. Our best protection will be to stay ahead of waves of forced change by engaging early with every one of our supply chain partners to work in the best interests of all our stakeholders, who can help lead the way towards a truly sustainable world.

ALIGNMENT INSIGHTS

- *Aligned strategies, subcultures and leadership are essential to turn around 'the way things are done round here' and make corporate social responsibility and sustainability as natural as breathing for corporate management and staff.*

- *Sustainability thinking can be introduced in various ways. Different corporate subcultures, aligned with different customer needs, will respond best to aligned communication approaches. CSR and sustainability values, leadership, technology or incentives should be selected for emphasis in communication, according to the needs of each culture.*

- *Large-scale sustainable outcomes can only achieved with the help of finely tuned and aligned supply chains that connect together all the activities through the life cycle of products. Alignment between all supply chain partners is the key to eliminating waste, dramatically improving resource efficiency and making the world a better place for all.*

NOTES

1   The apostle of this view is influential US economist Milton Friedman who is famous for saying (amongst other things): 'So the question is, do corporate executives, provided they stay within the law, have responsibilities in their business activities other than to make as much money for their stockholders as possible? And my answer to that is, no they do not.' See J. McClaughry, 'Milton Friedman responds: a Business and Society Review interview', *Business and Society Review*, Vol. 1 (Spring 1972), pp. 5–16.

2   For a discussion about the development of CSR in the USA see A.B. Carroll, 'Corporate social responsibility: evolution of a definitional construct', *Business & Society*, Vol. 38, No. 3 (1999), pp. 268–295.

3   From ISO 2600, http://www2.dupont.com/MLDP/en_US/david_bills_interview.html.

4   See http://www.worldvaluessurvey.org.

5   *Our Common Future*, Report of the World Commission on Environment and Development (commonly known as the Brundtland Commission), Oxford University Press, Oxford, 1987, provides the famous definition of sustainability: 'Sustainable development is development that meets the needs of the present without compromising the ability of future generations to meet their own needs.'

6   Herman E. Daly, *A Steady State Economy*, UK Sustainable Development Commission, 2008, http://www.sd-commission.org.uk/publications.php?id=775.

7   John M. Hartwick, Intergenerational 'Equity and the investment of rents from exhaustible resources, *American Economic Review*, Vol. 67 (December 1977), pp. 972–974.

8   See http://www.interfacesustainability.com/whatis.html.

9   P. Hawken, *The Ecology of Commerce*, Harper Business, New York, 1994.

10   Ray Anderson, quoted in E. King, 'How boss saw green light – and lifted profits' *New Zealand Herald*, 2 September 2008, http://www.nzherald.co.nz/clothing-textiles-industry/news/article.cfm?c_id=151&objectid=10530079.

11   See http://www.westpac.com.au/internet/publish.nsf/Content/WI+Corporate+Responsibility.

12   http://www.westpac.com.au/internet/publish.nsf/Content/WICR+Suppliers.

13   See Hermann Miller, *Hermann Miller's Better World Report*, 2008, http://www.hermanmiller.com/hm/content/environment/shared_assets/files/2008_A_Better_World_Report.pdf..

14   Ibid., p. 54.

15   D.H. Meadows, D.L. Meadows, J. Randers and W.V. Behrens III, *Limits to Growth*, Universe Books, New York, 1972.

16   D.H. Meadows, J. Randers. and D. Meadows, *Limits to Growth: The 30-Year Update*, Chelsea Green Publishing Company, White River Junction, VT, 2004.

17   For a thorough treatment of this argument see G. Speth, *The Bridge at the Edge of the World*, Yale University Press, New Haven, CT, 2008.

21 Building Sustainable Supply Chains for the Future

Michael Bernon

In recent years there has been an increase in all aspects relating to 'green issues'. As a consequence, organizations are under incessant pressure to manage their supply chains in a more socially and environmentally responsible manner. A number of issues have emerged that have led to this, including the debate surrounding global warming, pollution, land degradation, deforestation and water usage, to name just a few. However, social factors such as child labour, the right of association and a fair wage have also become prominent. Supply chains have a significant impact on these factors: hence, managing them in a sustainable way has become a key management concern.

This increased awareness is influencing a range of stakeholders in a number of ways, and organizations need to respond to meet these new demands. Pressure comes from a variety of sources. Consumer buying decisions, for example, are increasingly being influenced by information consumers receive from the media. No company is exempt. Even Wal-Mart, the world's largest company, found that customers were being deterred from shopping in its stores following a series of negative campaigns and legal battles highlighting its poor record on labour rights.

Sustainability is emerging as an issue for investors, too. They recognize that companies that have unsustainable practices pose a threat to their investment. Therefore, many are beginning to supplement their traditional investment criteria with additional forms of data. Information on sustainability performance is now becoming readily available and published by a number of indices. Two examples are the Dow Jones Sustainability Index and the FTSI4 Good Index, which provide asset managers with a ranking system for those companies that are listed on their stock exchanges.

Legislative bodies, such as the European Union (EU) and national governments, are increasingly looking at business to take responsibility for the environmental impacts of their activities. In Europe, for example, under the concept of the 'producer pays' principle, the recent EU directive for the Waste of Electrical and Electronic Equipment (WEEE) now places an obligation on manufacturers to collect and recycle products at the 'end of life'.

However, the response by many organizations to sustainability has been simply one of managing the image of the organization – a situation commonly referred to as 'green wash'. For others, it takes a superficial form

'Building sustainable supply chains requires new thinking which involves embracing a holistic, integrated and dynamic way of doing business.'

typically addressing a single issue, such as carbon footprinting. However, this is a limited view of sustainability and not only does not fully address the complexities of the subject, but also fails to take advantage of the many benefits associated with implementing a sustainable supply chain strategy.

This is an understandable situation as embedding sustainability requires a high degree of commitment and a deep understanding of the issues. Even with this, the science to support decision-making is often subjective, complex or underdeveloped. Without care, this can lead to poor decisions being taken. Indeed, a number of recent apparent advances, initially hailed as breakthroughs, have turned out to have detrimental side-effects. An example of this is the debate over biofuels. Once seen as an answer to a cleaner fuel for vehicles, biofuel is now derided as having a negative effect on land use and has also been linked to the current increase in world food prices.

In addition, over the past decade supply chains have been changing dramatically. Many have become geographically dispersed and truly global in nature, often consisting of complex networks. In addition, the trend towards outsourcing, especially to low-cost economies, means that operations previously done in-house are now performed by third-party organizations and hence not directly under a company's control.

Therefore, building sustainable supply chains requires new thinking which involves embracing a holistic, integrated and dynamic way of doing business. Companies that fail to take this approach will, at a minimum, leave themselves vulnerable to business risk. Those companies that embrace sustainability can achieve significant reduction in operating costs, while for others it will lead to competitive advantage through innovative new product networks.

DEFINING SUSTAINABILITY

Sustainable development has been defined in a number of ways, but probably the most recognized reference can be taken from the Bruntland Commission[1] which defined it as *'development that meets the needs of the present without compromising the ability of future generations to meet their own needs'*.

In practice, this is expressed as the 'triple bottom line'[2] or 'people, planet and profit' and promotes the view that companies have a responsibility to look beyond profit maximization and take responsibility for their environmental and social performance. The 'people' element refers to the fair treatment of individuals that the organization either directly employs or interfaces with across its supply chains. 'Planet' considers the impacts an organization's activities have on the environment. This is often referred to as the ecological footprint[3] and requires a 'cradle-to-cradle' approach. Finally, 'profit' is the economic benefit obtained by society through commercial activity.

The three pillars of the triple bottom line should not be seen as a trade-off, but rather as complementary to each other. Often, sustainability is viewed negatively by business in the fear that managing the environment and societal issues will be costly. However, as will be shown, there are clear economic benefits from taking a sustainable approach.

BUILDING A FRAMEWORK FOR SUSTAINABLE SUPPLY CHAIN MANAGEMENT

To understand sustainability in a supply chain context it is useful to define its scope or the 'system boundary'. The Supply Chain Council's Supply Chain Operations Reference (SCOR) model[4] describes the five principal supply chain management processes as being source, make, deliver, return and plan. For traditional supply management, each of these processes has a well-established meaning. However, when viewed through the lens of sustainability, they take on additional meaning. An exhaustive review of these issues is beyond the scope of this chapter, but a number of the more prominent social and environmental considerations are introduced below.

Source

Labour standards and child labour
Sourcing is probably the one area where people are most familiar with the issues. This is due to the numerous news reports covering a succession of brand-name companies which have been exposed as using non-sustainable labour practices in the sourcing of their products. Famously, during the 1990s, Nike was exposed for the use of child labour and having poor labour standards in the factories with which they contracted to produce their goods.

However, even with the high media exposure over the past decade, the pressure to source goods at low cost means that the practice has not been fully eradicated. Organizations today continue to have products produced in factories where basic labour rights are still being denied. In August 2007 Top Shop, a clothes retailer, was accused of using 'slave labour', while later that year fashion group Gap had to withdraw a range of children's clothing after it was alleged to have sourced them from a factory in India using child labour.

And in 2008 Primark terminated three long-standing contracts with suppliers in India for using child labour after the BBC exposed their practices on UK television.

Food miles   Sourcing also includes the environmental considerations of where we source products from. The term 'food miles' has come to describe the vast distances some of our greengrocery products are now travelling to get to supermarket shelves. Because of consumers' desire to eat seasonal produce all year round, vegetables are now grown in countries where growing conditions are more favourable all year round – an example being green beans from Kenya. However, because of the short shelf life of most fruit and vegetables and the distances involved, many of these products are air-freighted to their destination. In one study, it was found that a basket of 26 organic vegetables had travelled 226,000 kilometres to get to retailer's shelves.[5] As a consequence, the associated emissions are significant.

Make

The production processes involved in the making of goods have a significant impact on the environment. These environmental factors include energy use, greenhouse gas emissions and pollution to land and air. One sector alone, the cement industry, is responsible for emitting an estimated 5–9 per cent of the world's CO_2 emissions.

It is also the part of the supply chain where raw materials are consumed. Hence, good environmental stewardship of manufacturing facilities can have a positive impact.

Deliver

Transport   'Deliver' includes the transport and warehousing operations across the supply chain network. The key to success here lies in the efficiency and effectiveness of the transport planning and systems in place. One of the major issues for transport is associated with the emissions from freight movements. In the UK, freight emissions account for approximately 6 per cent of total CO_2 emissions.[6] It is projected that this figure is likely to increase. In addition, in recent years the movement of goods has shifted away from the less polluting transport modes of sea and train to road and air.

'In one study, it was found that a basket of 26 organic vegetables had travelled 226,000 kilometres to get to retailer's shelves.'

At an operational level, a number of studies have shown that these impacts can be reduced by simply doing things better. For example, in the UK, the Department for Transport offers advice to haulage companies on driver training, maintenance of vehicle fleets, alternative fuels and so on that reduces not only the emissions of vehicles, but also operating costs. Poor vehicle utilization in most sectors also means that there are significant opportunities here. Finally, continued improvements in vehicle engine efficiency and body design will reduce emissions.

Return

Retail returns
Although not widely appreciated, managing product returns has become a major issue for many retailers in recent years due to a number of factors. Changing channels to market (including the growth of Internet sales and home delivery), 'no quibble' money-back guarantees and increasing market volatility coupled with shortening product shelf life are some of the reasons for this. Current research shows that retailers can expect return levels of between 2.5 per cent and 20 per cent by volume, with some catalogue companies experiencing up to 30 per cent returns.

Although some returns can be put back into stock and sold as new, most travel back through reverse logistics networks, as discussed in Chapter 10, to eventually be sold off at a reduced price in secondary markets or recycled, asset-stripped or put into landfill. This represents a significant failure of supply chain management and an unsustainable waste of the natural resources and energy used to produce the products in the first place.

Product recalls
Product recalls are another example of returns. During 2007 Mattel hit the headlines with the news that it was recalling millions of toys, primarily because of lead-paint contamination. The company announced a US$30 million charge to its second-quarter earnings after its first recall announcement.

Plan

A significant number of supply chain planning criteria can impact on an organization's sustainability. The better the supply chain is planned and managed, the less waste it will drive. So, as an example, let us consider just one aspect of waste caused by 'product obsolescence'. This can be defined as the point at which a product has no future anticipated consumer demand and will be disposed of. Planning criteria that can have an effect on the level of obsolete stock include short product life cycles, promotional activity (such as BOGOFs, special packs and price promotions), product variety and parameters for setting inventory levels.

Another critical planning activity that can lead to obsolescence is forecasting. Forecasts convert signals about future market demand into a time-phased plan for the supply of products. Organizations need to balance the need for customer-service with the level of inventories they hold. Poor forecasting overestimates the need for inventory, which can directly lead to obsolescence.

THE EXTENDED SUPPLY CHAIN VIEW: CRADLE-TO-CRADLE

The SCOR model is a useful place to start in defining the scope of supply chain activity, but, for the purposes of managing sustainability, it does not go far enough in describing the full 'product life cycle'. This means that we also need to consider three further elements, namely: design, consumer use and dispositioning.

- *Design*. The design phase is where ideas for new products are specified. This is critical as many of the aspects relating to the sustainability of products will be defined at this stage through the selection of materials, where it will be made, the production processes used, transportation methods and so on. One area that has received attention in recent years is the design and use of packaging in the transport of products across the supply chain. A number of initiatives can be cited here, including material substitution to renewable sources, light weighting, returnable transit packaging and recycling, to name but a few.

- *Consumer use*. Apart from providing after-sales service, most organizations naturally forget about their products once they have been sold. However, a sustainable company will consider the impact its products have during their usage. For example, the 'standby facility' on most electrical devices, such as TVs, is designed to help people turn their equipment on and off quickly. However, it is estimated that in the UK around two power stations' worth of electricity each year is being wasted by leaving equipment on standby.[7]

- *Final disposition*. Once a product has finished its useful life it will normally be discarded by its user. Final dispositioning refers to the various ways in which products can be disposed of – for example, landfill, recycling, second use and so on. Within the sustainability agenda, organizations have a responsibility to disposition their products effectively with the least impact on the environment.

The system boundary for a sustainable supply chain can now be described as having eight phases as illustrated in Figure 21.1. To build a sustainable supply chain, companies need to evaluate each of these phases in terms of the impact on the triple bottom line. Equally, an understanding of the interactions between these phases is also paramount.

SUSTAINABLE SUPPLY CHAIN MANAGEMENT STRATEGIES

To implement a sustainability strategy, supply chain managers need to consider a hierarchy of four distinct approaches – namely, risk mitigation, cost minimization, value advantage and sustainable supply chain transformation.

Figure 21.1   The eight phases of supply chain sustainability

Risk Mitigation

Risk mitigation involves assessing supply chain operations in terms of identifying the risks associated with non-sustainable practices. These risks range from direct financial penalties from breaking environmental and social regulations to negative media exposure that can have an enduring impact on a company's image.

One recent case is Mattel, the world's number one toymaker which had to recall 18 million of its toys due to a series of non-sustainable practices across its supply chain. These included their contract manufacturers in China painting toys with lead paint. Not only did this have a severe direct financial impact through the cost of the recall – estimates range as high as US$30 million – but the company's image as a trusted toy maker was also damaged.

In 2007 the fashion retailer Gap had to withdraw a range of its children's clothing destined for the USA and Europe after an undercover investigation by the UK's *Observer* newspaper exposed the use of child labour in one of its contract manufacturers in India.[8] The *Observer* reported the case of a 12-year-old boy who said that children were beaten if they were seen not to be working hard enough. Gap had previously made commitments on the non-use of child labour and apologized, but by this time the reports had been shown on TV news channels in a number of countries.

Cost Minimization

Cost minimization views sustainability as a method of reducing cost in the supply chain while also having a positive sustainable impact. Many examples have shown that there is a direct relationship between reducing environmental burdens and reduced costs through gains in efficiency. For example, transport efficiencies through better vehicle utilization reduce vehicle miles which in turn reduce CO_2 emissions. In another example, a number of Tesco refrigerated trailers are now painted white instead of the corporate blue. White reflects sunlight and blue absorbs it, and the company has found that the temperature inside a white trailer can be as much as 22°C lower.[9] This means refrigerating the trailers requires less energy, which saves cost while also reducing emissions.

In another example, due to public concerns about food miles, one study evaluated the methods of importing wine from Australia to the UK. The report, undertaken by WRAP,[10] concluded that changing the way in which the wine was transported from bottles to bulk containers could reduce carbon emissions by as much as 40 per cent and also cut shipping costs. In addition, light weighting of the glass bottles (a method of reducing the material content of packaging without affecting the properties) could also significantly reduce the emissions while also reducing the cost of purchasing glass.

Value Advantage

Value advantage can be achieved by providing customers with products and services based on a sustainable platform. Everywhere you look today, companies are keen to show how they are reducing their impact on the environment or how they can even help you to do your bit. Innocent, a producer of smoothie fruit drinks claims to be the world's first company to use 100 per cent recycled PET plastic bottles. Proctor & Gamble are asking you to 'Turn to 30' (in other words, do your washing at 30°) when using its Ariel soap powder in your washing machine as this can save up to 41 per cent energy consumption. Costa Coffee, the UK's largest coffee shop, is planning to use only sustainably grown beans sourced from a Rainforest Alliance Certified™ plantation.

Retailers are also keen to show their green credentials. In 2007 Tesco announced a commitment to carbon-label all of the 70,000 product lines it stocks. Consumers who shop at Tesco stores will soon be able to decide which products to buy on the grounds of their carbon intensity. However, it should be noted that by the middle of 2008 the company only had 20 product lines with a carbon label!

Sustainable Supply Chain Transformation

Sustainable supply chain transformation describes an instance of radical change to the way in which a network currently operates, based on the principles of sustainability. A 'sustainable collaborative network' is one such model. Here, companies join together in a synergistic arrangement and share their logistics infrastructure to reduce the impact of running separate networks. A recent announcement by the IGD in the UK describes one such initiative in which 47 retailers and manufacturers have come together to evaluate how they can reduce transport road miles through collaboration. An initial estimate suggests that they expect take some 800 lorries off the UK road network.[11]

CALCULATING YOUR CARBON FOOTPRINT

One of the major environmental concerns is global warming. There is much debate over the science, but it is generally accepted that the increased levels of carbon emissions is leading to climate change. Supply chain activity represents a significant impact on emissions – predominantly carbon dioxide (CO_2). Therefore, companies need to measure their 'carbon footprint' to assess the quantity of emissions produced as products pass through their supply chain.

'Walkers now believes that it should disclose the carbon intensity of their products and is one of the first companies to carbon-label a number of their products.'

At the product level, a carbon footprint is a measure of the total amount of greenhouse gas emissions that are attributable to an item as it passes along the supply chain. Although CO_2 is the standard measure, there are six greenhouse gases, each of which has a different global warming potential. For example, methane has a factor of 21 times that of CO_2. Therefore, the measure for carbon footprints is normally expressed as tonnes CO_2 equivalent (CO_2e).

When commissioning a carbon footprint study it is essential to capture all the relevant emissions within the whole system boundary relating to a particular product. Typically, the following categories need to be considered:

- emissions produced directly from an organization's activities;

- emissions from the use of electricity;

- emissions produced across the extended supply chain;

- emissions produced during consumer use;

- emissions produced at 'end of life'.

Carbon Labelling

The Carbon Trust has undertaken a significant number of carbon footprint studies including one with Walkers Snack Foods Ltd. A number of initiatives have been undertaken as a consequence. One of the major changes concerned the sourcing of its potatoes. Through carbon footprinting, the company recognized that it could significantly reduce its food miles by sourcing its potatoes locally in the UK and now claims to use only British-grown potatoes in the production of its range of crisps.

Following this, Walkers now believes that it should disclose the carbon intensity of their products and is one of the first companies to carbon-label a number of their products. More recently, major retailers such as Wal-Mart and Tesco (mentioned earlier) have also committed to measure the carbon intensity of their products.

A number of issues exist with carbon footprinting, however, and any direct comparison between products needs to be done with care. The main issue is one of methodology. Although there has been a convergence of standards, currently there is no single protocol, and hence measurement is being done in different ways.

Case Study: Marks & Spencer

One company that is on the sustainability path is Mark & Spencer (M&S). In January 2007 CEO Stuart Rose announced 'Plan A', a five-year programme[12] which includes 100 environmental and social initiatives. Plan A will encompass the whole M&S supply chain and has far-reaching implications for the way M&S do business in that it covers the challenges of climate change, waste, sustainable raw materials, fair partnership and health.

M&S have announced five key commitments:

1. To make its operations in the UK and the Republic of Ireland carbon-neutral by minimizing energy use and maximizing the use of renewables.

2. To stop sending waste to landfill from its stores, offices and warehouses, reduce the use of packaging and carrier bags and find ways to recycle and reuse the materials it uses.

3. To ensure that its key raw materials come from the most sustainable source possible, in order to protect the environment and the world's natural resources.

4. To improve the lives of hundreds of thousands of people in its supply chain and in their local communities.

5. To help thousands of customers and employees choose a healthier lifestyle.

To drive these initiatives forward, Marks & Spencer recognize that it cannot do this in isolation and has engaged a range of stakeholders from customers, employees and suppliers to provide ideas, information and resources. Partnerships have also been developed with a variety of organizations, including Oxfam, WWF, Breakthrough Breast Cancer, Save the Children, The Carbon Trust, Waste Resources Action Plan and Groundwork to provide specific knowledge and skills.

GOING FORWARD

It is clear that, for many organizations, sustainability is emerging as a significant business issue. The subject is complex, and companies need to take an integrated approach by aligning their supply chain strategy with their strategy for sustainability. This will become essential as companies realize that the desire for sustainability is in effect creating a subsegment of the 'collaborative' (Ia) behavioural segment mentioned in earlier chapters. That is why companies such as Marks & Spencer which rely so heavily on brand loyalty are making such an effort – their consumers want the comfort that they are buying products that are meeting all possible environmental and social standards. Those that are successful in achieving these standards will see reduced operating costs and create competitive advantage by offering new value propositions to their customers. As stakeholders increasingly demand higher standards, those companies that fail to take action will leave themselves vulnerable to significant business erosion.

ALIGNMENT INSIGHTS

- *Companies which do not take an integrated and aligned approach to sustainability leave themselves open to business risk.*

- *Building sustainable supply chains requires a product life-cycle perspective, encompassing all supply chain processes.*

- *Companies which embrace sustainability exhibit low-cost operations and can achieve competitive advantage over their rivals through innovative products and services.*

NOTES

1   The Report of the Brundtland Commission, *Our Common Future*, Oxford University Press, Oxford, 1987.

2   J. Elkington, 'Towards the sustainable corporation: win–win–win business strategies for sustainable development', *California Management Review*, Vol. 36, No. 2 (1994), pp. 90–100.

3   W.E. Rees, 'Ecological footprints and appropriated carrying capacity: what urban economics leaves out', *Environment and Urbanization*, Vol. 4, No. 2, (1992), pp. 121–130.

4   Supply Chain Council, http://www.supply-chain.org (accessed 20 September 2008).

5   A. Jones, 'Eating oil – food supply in a changing climate', Sustain/Elm Farm Research Centre Report, December 2001, http://www.sustainweb.org/pdf/eatoil_sumary.PDF

6   A. McKinnon, 'CO$_2$ emissions from freight transport in the UK'. Report prepared for the Climate Change Working Group of the Commission for Integrated Transport, Logistics Centre, Heriot-Watt University, http://www.cfit.gov.uk/docs/2007/climatechange/pdf/2007climatechange-freight.pdf (accessed 20 September 2008).

7   M. Kinver, 'TV "sleep" button stands accused', BBC News Online, 22 January 2006, http://news.bbc.co.uk/1/hi/sci/tech/4620350.stm (accessed 22 January 2006).

8   D. McDougall, 'Child sweatshop shame threatens Gap's ethical image', *The Observer*, 28 October 2007, http://www.guardian.co.uk/business/2007/oct/28/ethicalbusiness.india (accessed 20 September 2008).

9   Tesco's Greener Living, 'How we are helping', http://www.tesco.com/greenerliving/getting_around/how_we_are_helping/default.page (accessed 20 September 2008).

10   'Bottling wine in a changing climate', case study, WRAP, http://www.wrap.org.uk/downloads/15149-07_BottlingWine_CS_lr.8d312f6c.3807.pdf (accessed 20 September 2008).

11   J. Sibun, 'Food and drink giants share trucks to reduce costs and carbon emissions', *Daily Telegraph*, 19 June 2008, http://www.telegraph.co.uk/finance/newsbysector/retailandconsumer/2791863/Food-and-drink-giants-share-trucks-to-reduce-costs-and-carbon-emissions.html (accessed 20 June 2008).

12   See Marks & Spencer, 'Plan A'. *Annual Report and Financial Statements 2008*, http://annualreport.marksandspencer.com/business_review/plan.html.

22 Managing Disruptions in Contemporary Supply Chains

Kevin B. Hendriks and Vinod R. Singhal

Senior executives are becoming aware that their company's reputation, earnings consistency and ability to deliver better shareholder returns are increasingly dependent on how well they manage supply chain risks. National and local media are filled with news reports on the increase in supply chain disruptions and the fact that many companies are unable to cope with these disruptions. Some recent examples include the disruptions due to Hurricane Katrina, Mattel's recall of 21 million toys due to safety issues; Boeing's unexpected delay in introducing its much anticipated 787 Dreamliner because of difficulties in coordinating global suppliers and the recalls of contaminated meat, pet foods and pharmaceuticals products. As supply chains have become more efficient, have they also become more vulnerable to disruptions? Lean, globally dispersed networks of suppliers, producers, distributors and customers must live with the possible consequences of disruptions.

It seems that many companies are not adequately prepared for assessing and addressing supply chain disruptions. For example, a recent survey by Marsh Inc. reported that not a single respondent out of 110 risk managers surveyed indicated that their current supply chain risk management practices are highly effective.[1] A study by FM Global found that insufficient time, inadequate personnel and insufficient budget were the biggest obstacles in dealing with supply chain risks.[2] A recent survey by Accenture of 151 supply chain executives in US companies found that 73 per cent of the executives said that their companies had experienced supply chain disruptions in the past five years.[3] A study by FM Global of more than 600 financial executives worldwide found that supply chain risks pose the most significant threat to profitability.

This chapter addresses three issues that are critical in managing supply chain disruptions. First, it provides a brief summary of some of the results from our research on the long-term financial consequences of supply chain disruptions. One of the reasons why many companies are not adequately prepared for assessing and addressing supply chain disruptions is that they do not have a good understanding of the magnitude and persistence of the negative consequences of disruptions on financial performance. Whilst anecdotes make for splashy headlines, they do not provide the objective evidence that many senior executives are looking for so that they can better understand the financial consequences of supply chain disruptions in order to make decisions about the initiatives and investments they should undertake to manage disruptions. Second, it offers insights into the factors that can increase the chances of disruptions to guide managers as they assess this risk. Third, the chapter highlights some of the best strategies and practices in managing disruptions using case studies from Wal-Mart, Mattel and Boeing.

THE LONG-TERM FINANCIAL EFFECTS OF SUPPLY CHAIN DISRUPTIONS

We have tracked and analyzed the financial performance of nearly 800 instances of supply chain disruptions that were announced in the *Wall Street Journal* and/or the Dow Jones News Service during 1989–2004. These announcements were about publicly traded companies that experienced production or shipping delays. Although disruptions can be caused by uncontrollable factors such as geopolitical instability, natural disasters or terrorism, most of the disruptions that we have come across seemed to be caused by controllable factors such as forecasting accuracy, performance of suppliers, complexity of supply chains, alignment among supply chain partners and the ability to manage and control the internal and external supply chain network. The performance effects of supply chain disruptions are estimated over a three-year time period starting one year before the disruption announcement date and ending two years afterwards. To control for industry and economy effects that can influence performance changes, the performance of the firms experiencing disruption is measured against benchmarks of firms that are in the same industry with similar size and performance characteristics. We use the following metrics in our analyses:

- shareholder returns as measured by stock returns that include changes in stock prices as well as any dividends declared;

- operating income (sales minus cost of goods sold minus selling and general administration);

- return on sales (operating income divided by sales);

- return on assets (operating income divided by total assets).

SHAREHOLDER VALUE EFFECTS

Figure 22.1 depicts the shareholder value effects of supply chain disruptions. The evidence indicates that supply chain disruptions are viewed very negatively by investors and shareholders. The announcement of a disruption is associated with a 7.18 per cent drop in shareholder value. When one examines the relative stock price performance during the time periods before and after the disruption announcement, the shareholder value effects are much worse than those observed on announcement.

Figure 22.1 shows the following:

- During the year before the disruption announcement, stocks of disruption-experiencing firms underperformed their benchmarks by nearly 14 per cent.

- Even after the announcement of disruptions, firms continue to experience worsening stock price performance. In the year after the disruption announcement firms, on average, lose another 10.45 per cent relative to their benchmarks.

- Although the negative trend continues in the second year after disruption, the magnitude of underperformance of 1.77 per cent is not as high as that during the year before and the first year after the disruption announcement.

- Over the three-year period the average level of underperformance on shareholder returns is 40 per cent. One way to judge the economic significance of this level of underperformance is the fact that, on average, stocks have gained 12 per cent annually in the last two decades. Even if a firm experiences one major supply chain disruption every ten years, the annual return would be close to 8–9 per cent, which is a significant difference when one takes into account the effect compounding over a long time period.

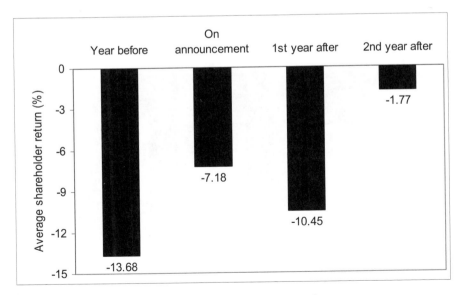

Figure 22.1 **Average shareholder returns from one year pre-disruption announcement to two years post-disruption announcement**

- More importantly, during this time period firms do not recover from the negative stock price performance that they experienced in the prior two years, indicating that the loss associated with disruptions is not a short-term effect.

PROFITABILITY EFFECTS

The magnitude of stock price underperformance associated with supply chain disruptions and the lack of any recovery may surprise many and could raise the issue whether the significant stock price underperformance is supported by a corresponding reduction in profitability or is simply a matter of stock market overreaction. This issue is explored by documenting the long-term effects of disruptions on operating income. Figure 22.2 presents the average effect of disruptions on profitability. Supply chain disruptions have a devastating effect on profitability. On average, firms that experience disruptions experience a 107 per cent decrease in operating income, a 114 per cent decrease in return on sales and a 92 per cent decrease in return on assets.

We also find that the shareholder value and operating performance effects are negative irrespective of which link in the supply chain is responsible for the disruption. These results show the heavy price one link in the supply chain pays for the poor performance by other links in the supply chains. Such losses should provide an incentive for the various links to align their supply chains to minimize disruptions. It also underscores the importance of effective

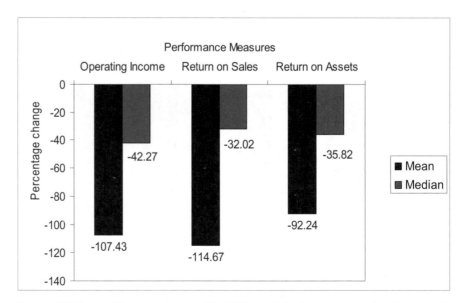

Figure 22.2   Changes in profitability-related measures due to supply chain disruptions during the year before the disruption announcement

supplier relationship and customer relationship management to increase supply chain efficiency, reliability and responsiveness.

To summarize, our analysis clearly indicates two things:

> *'Supply chain disruptions have a devastating effect on profitability. On average, firms that experience disruptions experience a 107 per cent decrease in operating income.'*

- Supply chain disruptions have a negative across-the-board effect on stock price, profitability and share price volatility. It does not matter who or what causes the disruption, why it happens, what industry a firm belongs to, or when the disruption occurs – disruptions devastate corporate performance.

- Supply chain disruptions have a debilitating affect on performance as firms do make a rapid recovery. They continue to operate at a lower performance level for at least two years afterwards.

These findings have major implications for senior executives:

- Senior executives must become aware of the primary sources of disruptions in their supply chains and what can be done to mitigate the risks of their occurrence. They should then take proactive actions to mitigate the possibility of disruptions. Disruptions, even if infrequent, have the potential to destroy value that might have been painstakingly created over years.

- Although the focus on making supply chains more efficient and lean makes economic sense, senior executives must recognize that lean and efficient supply chains face a higher risk of disruptions. There is a direct relationship between efficiency and risk. Firms can no longer afford to focus solely on cost reduction. Major supply chain investments and initiatives must also consider how these investments and initiatives affect the risks of disruptions. Furthermore, such investments and initiatives must often be undertaken not because they reduce costs, but because they increase the reliability and responsiveness of supply chains. Such investments and initiatives should be viewed as insurance against avoiding shareholder value destruction should disruptions occur.

DRIVERS OF SUPPLY CHAIN DISRUPTIONS

The analysis of the effect of supply chain disruptions on financial performance is valuable because it provides firms with a perspective on the economic effect of poor supply chain performance. The evidence clearly indicates that ignoring the possibility of supply chain disruptions can have devastating economic consequences. As one reflects on this evidence, a natural question is: what are the primary drivers of supply chain disruptions? The chances of experiencing disruptions are higher now and in the future than in the past because of some recent trends and practices in managing supply chains. In light of this recent heightened awareness of the risk of supply chain disruptions, many experts have offered insights into the factors that can increase the chances of their occurrence. Some of these major factors are discussed below with the intention that they can serve as guideline for managers as they assess the chances of disruptions in their own supply chains.

- **Competitive environment**. There is no doubt that most industries are facing a vastly different competitive environment today than a decade or so ago. Today's markets are characterized by intense competition, very volatile demand, increased demand for customization, increased product variety and short product life cycles. These trends are expected to intensity in the future. These conditions make it very challenging to match demand with supply. In particular, firms are facing increasing difficulty in forecasting demand and adjusting to unexpected changes in product life cycles and changing customer preferences.

- **Increased complexity**. The complexity of supply chains has increased due to global sourcing, managing large number of supply chain partners, the need to coordinate across many tiers of supply chains, and dealing with long lead-times. This increased complexity makes it harder to match demand and supply, thereby increasing the risk of disruptions. The risk is further compounded when various supply chain partners focus on local optimization, when there is lack of collaboration among supply chain partners, and when there is lack of flexibility in the supply chain.

- **Outsourcing and partnerships**. Increased reliance on outsourcing and partnering has heightened interdependencies among different nodes of the global supply networks and increased the chances that a disruption or problem in one link of the supply chain can quickly ripple through the rest of the chain, bringing the whole supply chain to a rapid halt. While many experts have talked about the virtues of outsourcing and partnerships, for these to truly work well it is important that supply chain partners collaborate, share information and plans, and have visibility in each other's operations. Such changes require major investments in connected information systems, changes in performance metrics, commitment to share gains and building trust among supply chain partners, all of which are not easy to achieve.

- **Single sourcing**, Single-sourcing strategies have reduced the purchase price and the administrative costs of managing the supplier base, but may have also increased the vulnerability of supply chains if the single-source supplier is unable to deliver on time.

- **Limited buffers**. Focus on reducing inventory and excess capacity and squeezing slack in supply chains has more tightly coupled the various links, leaving little room for errors. Just-in-time delivery and zero-inventory are commonly cited goals, but without careful consideration of the fact that these strategies can make the supply chain brittle.

> *'Overconcentration reduces the flexibility of the supply chain to react to changes in the environment and leads to a fragile supply chain that is susceptible to disruptions.'*

- **Focus on efficiency**. Supply chains have focused too much on improving efficiency (reducing costs). Firms are responding to the cost squeeze at the expense of increasing the risk of disruptions. Most firms do not seem to consider the inverse relationship between efficiency and risk. Strategies for improving efficiency can increase the risk of disruptions.

- **Overconcentration of operations**. In their drive to take advantage of economies of scale, volume discounts and lower transaction costs, firms have overconcentrated their operations at a particular location, or with their suppliers or customers. Overconcentration reduces the flexibility of the supply chain to react to changes in the environment and leads to a fragile supply chain that is susceptible to disruptions.

- **Poor planning and execution**. Poor planning and execution capabilities result in more incidents of demand–supply mismatches. Plans are often too aggregate, lack details and are based on inaccurate inventory and capacity information. Lack of good information systems hinders the organization's ability to be aware of what is happening. Lack of forward-looking metrics affects the ability of firms to anticipate future problems and be proactive in dealing with these problems. Firms also have limited visibility into what is happening in upstream and downstream supply chain partners. Most firms have limited abilities and capabilities to identify and manage supply chain exceptions. This is further compounded by the lack of synchronization and feedback between supply chain planning and supply chain execution.

DEALING WITH DISRUPTIONS

The importance of managing supply chain risks raises the natural issue of what are some of the best strategies and practices in supply chain risk management. We highlight some of these using case studies from Wal-Mart, Mattel and Boeing.

Case Study: How Wal-Mart Responded to Disruptions Caused by Hurricane Katrina

Hurricane Katrina, a low-frequency event with a 1 in 200 annual odds, caused unimaginable devastation and disruptions in communities in Louisiana and Mississippi. Although the federal, state and local governments failed miserably to respond to the devastation caused by Katrina, Wal-Mart was one of the few success stories showing how organizations should respond to such disruptions. The key to Wal-Mart's success was a clear strategy for dealing with disruptions, detailed planning and careful execution of the plan.

Wal-Mart started tracking and monitoring Katrina six days before the storm hit New Orleans. Using data from the National Weather Service and private meteorologists, Wal-Mart managers closely followed the storm's likely path and began shipping critical items to the distribution centres near the stores in the area where Katrina was likely to hit. These items were based on studies of customer buying patterns in hurricane-prone areas and the items that store managers usually need in order to ensure that their stores are operational. The trucking and transportation division was alerted to the need to load and ship critical items like back-up generators and dry ice to stores at short notice. Back-up communication plans with store managers and other key personnel were established, and their roles and responsibilities in dealing with the disruption were reviewed and clarified. Plans were adjusted and modified on a real-time basis as Katrina changed its path. This detailed planning paid off as Wal-Mart turned out to be the only lifeline for many victims of Katrina. Wal-Mart provided relief days before the Federal Emergency Management Agency FEMA could reach the affected areas, and was able to reopen it stores in record time, which provided further help and relief to its customers.

Wal-Mart's success in dealing with Katrina highlights the importance of developing capabilities to deal with supply chain risks. Developing these capabilities requires leadership, commitment of resources, and detailed and tedious planning. Building robust capabilities for dealing with supply chain risks involves the following steps:

1. *Analyze what could potentially go wrong.* This may require brainstorming, thinking about the unthinkable, observing disruptions that your company and other companies have experienced, and involving experts in creating scenarios of what could go wrong.

2. *Identify and analyze possible alternatives to deal with different types of risks.* This may require benchmarking of best practices with other companies, scenario analysis and idea generation. Various alternatives should be considered to mitigate the high-risk factors. Such alternatives include developing contingency plans to deal with the risk should it surface, options for spreading and transferring risks through insurance, forward contracts and flexible contracts, as well as making changes in the way the supply chain is designed and operated so that these risks are mitigated in the future.

3. *Develop plans to deal with disruptions.* This involves outlining what needs to be done to deal with disruptions, when it will be done, how it will be done and who will do it. The plan needs to assign responsibility and authority to employees to carry put the plans. Without such plans, employees are left clueless about what to do, which actually creates more chaos and magnifies the negative consequences of disruptions.

4. *Monitor the situation.* Companies should develop a system to monitor risks. Leading indicators need to be tracked, control limits need to be set to determine out-of-control conditions, two-way communication with the supplier and customers must be done on a continuous basis, and visibility systems must be in place.

5. *Execute the plan.* When disruptions occur, the appropriate plans should be activated and the effectiveness of these plans in mitigating the negative impact should be continuously monitored and adjustments made on real-time basis.

6. *Improve the risk management process.* Firms must continuously strive to improve their risk management processes. As and when risk is dealt with, efforts must be made to document the outcomes of the risk mitigation plans and highlight what worked and what did not work. These lessons should be shared across the organizations and used to improve the risk management process. Benchmarking a firm's process against other firms that have well-functioning risk management process can identify best practices and help make a firm's process more robust and effective.

Case Study: Mattel's Product Recall of Lead-tainted Toys

Mattel Inc.'s recall of nearly 1 million lead-tainted toys highlights the challenge companies face when they source globally in search of low costs. The toy industry has moved so much manufacturing to China to cut costs that nowadays 80 per cent of the toys that come to USA are made in China. The relentless pressure that Chinese manufacturers face to cut costs creates incentives for them to cut corners. Lead paint is not only cheap and readily available, but its use can speed up the production process, all of which leads to lower costs. In addition, because it had a trusted 15-year relationship with the Chinese manufacturer, Mattel allowed it to do its own testing, but the manufacturer did not perform the tests. Furthermore, the regulatory agencies did not have the resources to police the large volume of toy imports from China.

There are four key lessons for managing supply chain risks to be learnt from Mattel's recall. First, relentless focus on cost reduction can often have unintended consequences. Companies should consider backing off somewhat on cost reductions to avoid creating incentives for suppliers to cut corners on quality and safety. Second, even if you are not responsible for the disruption, you still pay. Interestingly, lead-tainted toys accounted for about 5 per cent of the total toys recalled by Mattel. Yet the damage that the recall caused to the overall reputation of Mattel's brand and image greatly exceeds the direct cost of recalling 5 per cent of the toys. Third, while much has been said about building long-term relationships with suppliers and trusting suppliers, companies must still be very watchful and monitor the processes at their key suppliers, particularly those that affect safety and health issues. Finally, as supply chains become more global, companies must make sure that they have traceability capabilities in their supply chains. This is critical because it is difficult to solve the problem if you cannot isolate the source. This issue has become urgent because of contamination problems in food products, pet foods, and pharmaceuticals. The most recent case is the recall of the blood-thinning drug heparin. Nearly 80 deaths in the USA are attributed to contamination in heparin. The lack of traceability in the heparin supply chain has made it very difficult to trace the source of the problem in order to address the contamination issue.

Incidents such as the product recall by Mattel have clearly caused customers to become sceptical about products that are being sourced from China. This is a critical issue that affects all big retailers who depend on overseas suppliers. To get better control of their supply chain and restore customer confidence, large and influential retailers such as Wal-Mart, Target, Toys 'R' Us, and Sears are requiring their suppliers to meet a new set of child-product safety requirements that goes far beyond existing government regulations. They are also encouraging suppliers to mark children's products with traceability information, including the factory where the goods were made, so that corrective actions can be taken should the products have quality and health issues.

Case Study: Boeing's Dreamliner Delays

The Boeing 787 Dreamliner has been very popular, with orders for 892 planes from 60 airlines and delivery slots sold out beyond 2014. Unfortunately, Boeing cannot meet the promised delivery dates for these planes. Recently, Boeing announced the third delay in the production of the plane, pushing first deliveries at least 15 months later than initially promised. The delay in the Dreamliner is an example of how outsourcing and globalization can create significant supply chain risks which, if not managed well, can derail a company's best-laid plans.

To reduce the cost of developing the plane on its own, Boeing outsourced the design and build of major sections of the aircraft to suppliers. The supply chain is quite global with nearly 15 major suppliers across nine countries. For example, the forward fuselage II and the wing are manufactured in Japan, the centre fuselage and the horizontal stabilizer in Italy, the wing tips in Korea, the trailing edge in Australia, the landing gear in the UK, the cargo access doors in Sweden, and the passenger-entry doors in France. Each of these first-tier suppliers uses its own set of suppliers, and so on, resulting in a highly complex and distributed supply chain. The sub-assemblies are transported by ship, air, road and rail to facilities around Seattle for final assembly.

The supplier problems range from language barriers to glitches when some suppliers further outsourced the work. Boeing overestimated the ability of suppliers to do the tasks that Boeing could do easily on account of years of experience. The company also lacked deep insight into what was actually going on in the suppliers' factories. Suppliers faced major issues in ramping up capacity. Coordinating across the various suppliers across the globe turned out to be more challenging than Boeing had anticipated. To deal with the delays, Boeing has bought out the interest that one of its supplier had in a joint venture and has hinted that similar moves are under consideration as it attempts to take control of key parts of its supply chain. Boeing managers are now taking a more aggressive role in getting insight into suppliers' operations, including stationing Boeing employees in every major supplier's factory. Boeing is also trying to build real-time visibility of their suppliers' operation, as well as developing a better understanding of how the plane comes together. Boeing's CEO is actively engaged in monitoring the plane's progress.

The lesson here is that companies should be careful when they make outsourcing decisions and must balance the benefits of expected cost savings against the increased costs of managing supply chain risks. The Boeing strategy underscores the limits and hazards of outsourcing.

ALIGNMENT INSIGHTS

- *Given the significant negative consequences of disruptions, it is critical that managers not only think of alignment in the form of generic types of supply chains such as lean, agile, flexible ,and continuous replenishment, but also think in terms of aligning these generic types of supply chain with the risk of disruptions. Even within a generic type of supply chain, managers have different design and operating choices that can have widely different implications on the risk of disruptions. The design and operating decisions must be aligned with the risk preferences of owners, customers and various supply chain partners.*

- *The alignment between supply chain design and operating choices and risk is dynamic. For example, Mattel outsourced its manufacturing to*

> *become more lean and efficient and, in the process, increased the risk of disruption. The product recall and its economic consequences may motivate Mattel to make adjustments in its supply chain, and these adjustments may require compromising on efficiency to reduce the risk of disruptions.*
>
> - *For supply chains to be truly aligned, supply chain partners need to have visibility and transparency into each other's operations and must have traceability capabilities. This will allow supply chain partners to have a clear picture of what is happening in the supply chains so that they can be proactive in avoiding disruptions and dealing effectively with disruptions, should they experience any.*

NOTES

1   *Stemming the Rising Tide of Supply Chain Risks: How Risk Managers' Roles and Responsibilities Are Changing, Research Report*, Marsh, a unit of Marsh & McLennan Companies (MMC). Available at: http://www.marshriskconsulting.com/st/PDEv_C_371_SC_228136_NR_306_PI_994639.htm.

2   *Managing Business Risk in 2006 and Beyond*, Research Report, FM Global and Harris Interactive.

3   'Supply chain disruptions result in lengthy recovery times, affect customer service and profitability, Accenture study finds', press release by Accenture Ltd, October 2006.

4   K.B. Hendricks and V.R. Singhal, 'The effect of supply chain glitches on shareholder value', *Journal of Operations Management*, Vol. 21 (2003), pp. 501–522; K.B. Hendricks and V.R. Singhal, 'An empirical analysis of the effect of supply chain disruptions on long-run stock price performance and risk of the firm', *Production and Operations Management*, Vol. 14 (2005), pp. 35–5; K.B. .Hendricks and V.R. Singhal, 'Association between supply chain glitches and operating performance', *Management Science*, Vol. 51 (2005), pp. 695–711.

23 The Coming of Age of Third-Party Logistics Providers

Jeremy Clarke and John Gattorna

A SHORT AND CHEQUERED HISTORY

The first third-party logistics providers (3PLs) arrived on the scene in the 1970s, mainly as the result of diversification by either transportation or public warehousing companies. It is significant that the very operational mindset of those early 3PLs has, in many cases, carried on through to today and herein lies part of the problem.

For a long time, principals/shippers with products to be moved and stored have harboured a suspicion that 3PL contractors presented them with a service risk, because they were unlikely to understand the business, and indeed care for the business as much as they themselves did.

On the other hand, 3PLs did offer the prospect of scale, with the corresponding cost reduction, just as freight forwarders had been doing for some time, themselves an agency variant of the 3PL business model. Unfortunately, many of the early contracts entered into with 3PLs were for the wrong reasons – for example, to overcome industrial relations problems – and so expectations were seldom met.

In the last decade, the better-performing 3PLs have made significant strides to overcome the 'credibility' gap with their shipper clients, but doubts still linger, and for good reason. Indeed, the problem is not just on the 3PL side. Shippers, while expecting the benefits of scale in the form of cost reductions and 'continuous improvement', have generally not done their bit to free up the contractual complexity that has dogged shipper–3PL relationships, and so create an atmosphere where innovation, creativity and trust could thrive and prosper.

In the meantime, globalization has meant that principals are looking for ever-wider coverage of their business, and in turn this has driven much of the rationalization that has gone on at the top end of the 3PL provider market around the globe. Companies such as Deutsche Post Worldwide

Network (DPWN) have stitched together a complete portfolio of services through acquisitions and are therefore in a strong position to meet the ever-increasing demands of their global and multinational customers. However, the process of acquiring multiple companies with different cultures and overlapping service offerings is going to take time to digest and settle down. In the meantime, shippers have to be patient and forgiving if they want these third-party services to exist at all in the years to come.

'Unfortunately, many of the early contracts entered into with 3PLs were for the wrong reasons – for example, to overcome industrial relations problems – and so expectations were seldom met.'

THE EVOLUTION OF LOGISTICS SERVICES

Historically, transport, warehousing, shipping, containerization and other core logistics services have represented one of the least dynamic components of global trading activity. They have been more a commodity function than a key contributor to trading success. But the world changed during the last decade or so. Markets became, and are still, increasingly competitive. As a result, we have seen a wholesale transformation in the production activities our various supply chains support. Product life cycles have shortened, and manufacturing points and markets have diverged to opposite ends of the globe, relocating away from the brand to the back-door of low-cost manufacturers. Products must fight harder for market share. Meanwhile, the supply chains that deliver products must achieve more, for less. None of this is new. But by understanding the evolution in supply chains that has supported these changes, we should be better able to predict and understand the structural requirements of the future.

With globalized manufacturing, product transhipment miles have increased dramatically, forcing organizations to scrutinize their logistics arrangements and their role in successful product positioning. For like-for-like commodity products, the supply chain has the potential to become the key differentiator and source of marketing advantage. Even where products have distinguishing or unique features (brand, design, after-sales service, consistency of supply, quality control and so on), the efficiency and cost-effectiveness of product movements remain key components of competitive advantage. In either case, to be successful, organizations need to put the right structures in place to manage their supply chain arrangements.

MODELS OF SERVICE DELIVERY

Standard Terms

Against such commercial pressures, it's not surprising that we've been in the midst of a gradual but complete transformation in the global supply chain and the structures by which logistics service providers and their shipper customers manage their relationships. If we looked back to the original providers, we would see that their contribution to product positioning in markets was limited. Service standards were low or standardized; integration between one provider and another (domestic through to international) was limited or non-existent; and the relationship between provider and shipper was separate and distinct (and encouraged to be so because the rationale for outsourcing was premised on the distinct and higher skill sets and experience of the parties). The post-1970s era saw massive growth in outsourced provider services across all the core functions, with logistics providers' apparent expertise in the services they offered driving the growth in outsourcing to third parties.

In line with the separate and distinct nature of the service, the original providers restricted responsibility and liability to a minimum. Providers would only accept responsibility and liability for the specific section of the logistics chain for which they were contractually and directly responsible: warehouse operators, for example, only accepted liability for products in their warehouse. If a provider was required to arrange downstream or upstream services, a complex chain of contractual agency relationships often evolved (of which the UK British International Freight Association (BIFA) terms are an example), by which the responsible provider arranged services for shipper customers (for example, a warehouse operator arranging onward road carriage to an end-customer), and act as the customer's agent, rather than the responsible – and liable – principal. This led to freight forwarders, essentially responsible for coordinating upstream services, arranging for services to be provided by third parties in their capacity as agents for the shippers, with no, or minimal, liability or responsibility for these procured services. Such an approach defined the starting-point for basic outsourced logistics services and led to the evolution of standard industry commercial terms in order to provide a contractual base for such arrangements. In the UK this included the standard terms and conditions of organizations like the Road Haulage Association, the UK Warehousing Association, BIFA, the Freight Transport Association and others.

Such simplistic structures had, and continue to have, their place. However, they are more appropriate for short-term, ad hoc or 'spot' service agreements involving standardized transport and warehousing services with relatively small volumes. Standard terms, which in large part protect providers, did not provide an appropriate structure for what was then the fastest growing segment of the logistics market, namely the dedicated long-term outsourced service solution. With standard terms, the risk/reward profile was often skewed against the shipper in favour of the provider, and there were very few, if any, built-in critical service levels and key performance measures. Moreover, when such terms are separately used in different locations around the world, they lead to a plethora of regionally different and potentially conflicting legal terms which, from the shipper's perspective, were neutral at best and provider-friendly at worst. As the volume and value of logistics services increased, such complexity would have become impossible to manage, although they were much aided by standard international conventions like CMR, the Montreal Convention and the Hague-Visby Rules. As shippers searched for providers with international reach as a means of responding to the increased pressures facing globalized supply chains, the use of bespoke and individually negotiated service contracts increased. As a consequence, standard terms have become less popular as a medium for large-scale supply chain arrangements.

Dedicated Logistics Service-level Agreements (SLAs)

While industry created a rudimentary structure for the relatively unsophisticated supply chain arrangements of the 1970s, they were never a platform for the dedicated arrangements that shippers increasingly demanded. The nature of the new dedicated logistics service agreement was defined by dual-party, multi-jurisdiction, increasingly complex services with detailed service levels and key performance measures, and 'as principal' liability for the providers – the opposite elements, in fact, to standard agency terms.

As international trade has increased, so has the complexity and scale of the supply chains which support the products flowing through to market. Rather than allowing the costs of logistics to grow proportionately, much effort has been expended in improving efficiency and reducing unit supply chain costs – reducing dwell times, lowering inventory, reducing damage/returns, improving planning regimes and, more recently, lowering carbon footprints – in each case across the supply chain. The early advent of enterprise resource planning (ERP) and other IT tools to connect providers with shippers and end-customers provided the communication tools necessary to properly integrate services across national and regional boundaries. Providers are gradually becoming better connected and are slowly moving towards aligned supply chain service provision in which they perform an integrated function between their shipper's internal organization and its wider external supply chain. This has enabled much more demanding targets to be met in the drive to control exponentially rising logistics costs and to improve efficiency.

For such efficiencies to be realized, providers needed commitments from shippers in order to amortize the much greater investments required to set up dedicated infrastructures. In turn, with such commitments and extended responsibility, the previously marked distinctions between one provider and another – for example, freight forwarders and carriers – have become blurred. This is the case for both SME 3PLs and, more obviously, the global providers like DHL. For example, it has become established practice for freight forwarder providers to enter into long-term contracts with shipper customers under which the freight forwarder provider will also provide ongoing services on a regular basis on agreed terms. Provider carriers, similarly, have entered into long-term contracts under which they perform the roles of carrier and provide freight-forwarding-type services.

Whilst shippers have become more reliant on their 'partner' provider's contracted services, in return for the commitments required to create the infrastructure, shippers have made providers accept increased levels of responsibility and liability for the extending supply chain. This was consistent with shippers' preference for a 'one-stop-shop' interface with global providers and, in turn, with the evolution of fourth-party logistics (4PL) service models, with larger cross-border providers taking responsibility for managing and coordinating the performance of more localized providers in different regional and national locations. See Case Study 1 below.

Case Study 1: A 4PL Solution – Corus and TDG

In January 2006 Corus, one of the world's largest steel producers, approached TDG to assist them with the task of improving its business's road transport services and increasing overall efficiency. The main issue facing Corus was the fragmented nature of its supply chain. Management of Corus's logistics operations was divided between three separate divisions, almost 20 different business units and over 70 sites, and Corus was using a number of different haulier companies. Greater coordination was much needed. Although the individual hauliers were working efficiently and effectively, overall Corus's transport distribution network was not.

In the spirit of 4PL, TDG provided coordination and information services for the Corus supply chain by introducing a central control centre at Scunthorpe called the 'Corus platform' to coordinate activities and essentially act as an interface between Corus and the haulier companies (see Figure 23.1).

The introduction of TDG to Corus's business and the move from 3PL to 4PL has to date proved an enormous success for Corus with significant environmental and financial benefits (both parties anticipate that TDG's estimate of a 7–8 per cent cost saving will be realized).

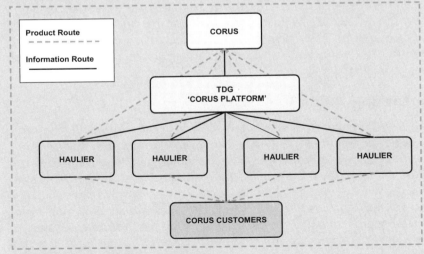

Figure 23.1   The Corus platform

Such dedicated solutions have become increasingly complex, with contractual structures seeking to accurately compare pre- and post-solution costs (so-called baseline costing), providing 'gainshare' reward mechanisms, with providers receiving a percentage of costs savings or even a financial upside for achieving improved efficiency. At the centre of such arrangements were the dedicated service levels and key performance measures by which the services were to be performed and objectively measured. Linked to such metrics were further reward and penalty measures in the form of target bonuses and liquidated damages to penalize service failures. The provisions allocating risk and liability balanced the interests of both parties, with a greater sharing of responsibility and liability.

So the move away from short-term spot contracts (with no volume or term commitments) to longer-term dedicated and exclusive outsourced service contracts for each leg of the supply chain was inevitable.

Value-added Services

A key advantage of the move to specialized supply chain solutions was the insight gained by providers of their shippers' businesses. As outsourced service providers, the providers were always uniquely placed to add ancillary activities to their service offerings. The increased market competition endured by shippers, the need to realize economies of scale and innovation, and the changing legislative and environmental backdrop enabled providers to offer increasingly innovative services to their customers.

Many of these services fall outside the scope of conventional logistics services and would traditionally have fallen to the customer itself. So, for instance, freight forwarders arranging the long-term carriage of manufactured goods from the Far East to Europe came to offer quality-control checks immediately upon receipt of the goods at the Far East Regional Distribution Centre (RDC). In such cases, the shipper might expect to make considerable savings as a result of the reduction in returns, the faster and earlier turnaround time for faulty product and the avoidance of wasted transportation costs incurred by shipment to the UK. Yet, despite such initiatives, many shippers continue to be frustrated with their service providers, in relation to both the standard of supply chain service and costs.

Partnership Models

Although many benefits were realized by way of the fast-growing market for dedicated solutions, the clearly defined and limited roles that were at the centre of outsourced service contracts underlined the separate and arm's length nature of the relationships. Since the late 1990s these relationships have become increasingly complex. Such complexity is driven by the forces we have already referred to: from the globalization of manufacturing increasing product miles and the need to control and reduce costs, through to the growth in market competition with the reducing product life cycles that follow.

Curiously, many conventional outsourced service contracts were dressed up as partnership arrangements (in the conventional, rather than legal, sense at least) between shipper and provider. Often such arrangements bore little resemblance to the spirit of partnership, being only a spin on conventional arm's-length, third-party contracts.

However, joint ventures, in the proper sense of the term, can be an effective medium for logistics companies conducting supply chain business. Long-term joint venture companies can be set up, partly owned by shipper and partly owned by the provider. The roles of each party can be both specifically and loosely defined according to expertise and need. The returns for both parties are in the form of profit share, rather than, in the case of conventional providers, a contracted fee. Both parties commit to promote the joint venture and have a mutual interest in its success. On the one hand, providers perform the services. On the other hand, shippers commit volumes. And both generally commit to procure additional third-party volumes to leverage the investment.

Such scenarios are far removed from the classic situation in which third-party providers would receive a blanket fee for lack-lustre services performed at high cost. Safeguards must be built in to control costs and guarantee services, but, once these are in place, the shared risk and reward structure is likely to motivate an improvement in the relevant part of the supply chain

'Arm's-length commercial contract structures... are being replaced, in part at least, by less formal arrangements that facilitate and encourage providers to interface with shipper customers and to cooperate more fully with their upstream and downstream counterpart providers.'

and, in turn, provide an advantage for both parties over their respective competitors. The downside of such structures is that they can become burned by their own legal formality, inflexibility and inward focus. Such criticisms can often be overcome at the critical early stage by means of a 'contractual' joint venture rather than the formation of a separate company structure. In place of the separate legal structure, a single contract separately provides for all management, director and shareholder issues and apportions responsibility for asset contributions and operational responsibilities. Crucially, detailed ring-fencing and accounting provisions (defined by contract rather than by formal shareholdings) define cost responsibilities and the sharing of liabilities and profits. Such relatively simple contractual structures are an ideal foundation for testing new supply chain solutions, but they are not properly understood and are therefore rarely used. Interestingly, they reflect the more liberalized approach to collaboration and risk-sharing increasingly seen in collaborative framework agreements (see below).

More recently we've seen providers going back to the drawing board. In order to meet their shippers' requirements, providers are having to remodel conventional outsourced service structures. Arm's-length commercial contract structures, with the stand-off position they encourage, are being replaced, in part at least, by less formal arrangements that facilitate and encourage providers to interface with shipper customers and to cooperate more fully with their upstream and downstream counterpart providers. Where a provider has 4PL global reach, it is more likely to be required to take full responsibility (legally, as principal) for the services provided by other providers and not to hide behind contractual limitations of liability. This has arisen because shippers want their providers to take a greater role in their organizations' success through better integration and understanding and, in turn, to leverage more and wider-ranging improvements. Consequently, 4PL providers are increasingly becoming a component of their shipper customers, and must acknowledge and share risk accordingly if they are to be credible and grow. See Case Study 2 below.

Case Study 2: Shared Risk Partnership Agreement – DHL and MFI

In December 2007 DHL Excel Supply entered into a five-year deal with the high-street furniture retailer MFI to manage the business's distribution centre (DC) and its home delivery operation. Critical to this arrangement was the level of investment to be made by DHL to the new joint venture.

Under the terms of the contract DHL agreed to invest more than £10 million of capital to improve information technology at the new facility dedicated to MFI and to develop additional space at the warehouse. The £10 million investment made by DHL was in addition to the £13.2 million warehouse fit-out costs which had already been completed by DHL.

The deal, which represents one of the biggest 'shared-risk' partnerships that DHL has entered into with a customer, indicates the lengths to which 3PLs will now go to win new business and gain a competitive advantage by making the transition from contracting on the principles of low risk and low margins, to increased risk but also potentially higher rewards.

The subject of 'shared-risk' partnership has latterly been thrown into sharp relief by the global economic downturn. The opportunities afforded by such models appear, on the surface, to have been blown away as a result of examples failing, like the partnership DHL has entered into with MFI, the UK furniture retailer which went into administration in November 2008 with little prospect of trading out to a full recovery. Examples like MFI and Woolworths don't foretell the end of such trading partnerships.

The key to success lies in corporate history: now, as ever before, long-term success requires organizational 'fit' and good management. But prior to embarking on such relationships, careful due diligence and objective risk assessments are required. In the case of MFI, its business model had long been questionable. Arguably, even pre-2008 MFI wasn't viable – its model was premised on the availability of easy credit and strong economic growth. With hindsight it is clear that little or no tolerance was built-in to cover a serious economic downturn or a change in bank lending policies. The eleventh-hour management buy-out in September 2008 of only half the stores followed previously difficult trading even in a benign economy. Given the valuations achieved by companies in the boom years, it's salutary that Merchant Equity Partners, the pre-management buy-out owners, bought MFI for £1 in 2006.

So in 2007 DHL was not entering into partnership with a historically solid company. Quite the contrary: DHL's 2007 risk assessment of the MFI business model may have assumed the overall trading environment would continue along positive lines, subject only to good, median and poor performance outcomes within that environment and, on that basis, the numbers must have worked. It is doubtful that the risk model was also run on the basis of the conditions prevailing in the last quarter of 2008 and the first quarter of 2009. If it had, then it's unlikely that the deal would have been done, given the investment involved.

Because the 'shared risk' model is, by nature, more risky, service providers will have to adjust their pre-contract risk assessments to take into account the potentially more volatile trading environments that will prevail over the next three years. Caution suggests that the risks will be better taken with organizations having either a history of successful trading spanning good times and bad or new business models which have a low cost base and a good prospect of beating the downturn. Such companies will be the only ones in a position to outsource good new logistics business and, more than ever, they will want and expect their 3PL service partners to support them through the hard times in return for an upside when trading strengthens. Rather than declining, the shared risk model is likely to flourish, so choose your partners carefully.

Collaborative Framework Agreements (CFAs)

The deep knowledge and understanding which providers have of their shipper customers, and which originated with the outsourced service contracts, has come to form a new foundation for much deeper levels of collaboration between previously arm's-length and contractually divided trading relationships. This collaborative and newly evolving commercial relationship has impacted on the nature of the structures required to support such innovative solutions and precipitated the evolution of Collaborative Framework Agreements (CFAs) into the contractual mix. See Case Study 3 below.

Case Study 3: Turning the Supply Chain Green – Collaboration

At the forefront of supply chain collaboration in the UK is the Institute of Grocery Distribution (IGD). Through its Efficient Consumer Response Programme (ECR UK) the institute aims to provide tools to companies to enable them to strike up collaborative distribution practices to bring about increased vehicle utilization and reduce road miles travelled in order to reduce the environmental impact of food and grocery distribution throughout the UK.

To date, 37 leading food and consumer goods companies have joined the programme. One example of the type of initiative being undertaken is that being carried out by manufacturers Nestlé and United Biscuits. Nestlé was running over 15 truck loads from its factories in the North to its distribution centre in the Midlands. Not all of the 15 truckloads could be tied to a return journey so around two or three were running empty on the return leg. Through ECR UK, Nestlé was able to identify that United Biscuits were running empty trucks from a nearby factory in the North to the Midlands. As a result, Nestlé and United Biscuits entered into a collaborative arrangement in order to avoid the empty truck movements.

To date, the IDG has reported that the project has surpassed its target of saving 48 million miles by an additional 5 million road miles – equivalent to removing 900 lorries from Britain's roads or conserving 26 million litres of diesel fuel per year.

CFAs focus specifically on creating a platform for multiple (but also dual) providers and shippers to collaborate more fully and to realize the elusive 'last mile' in terms of any added contributions that could be made to both the shipper's supply chain (or that of its industry) and, in turn, its wider business. As such, these structures are less focused on the operational day-to-day business of the supply chain (as per the conventional outsourced service agreement and its detailed service levels), but rather on what might be achieved by way of cost savings and efficiencies with innovation and blue-sky thinking – new value-added activities, innovative processes, new IT applications and even greater collaboration between, for instance, competitors. Anything, in fact, that directly or indirectly touches on the supply chain and has the potential to improve the shipper's current operations and, in turn, its business. Although the road from spot industry terms to dedicated outsourced contract to CFA has been long, the potential benefits to be realized from each step are, and have been, significant. For shippers and providers with real vision and a determination to succeed, there is no turning back on this process.

This evolution to CFAs marks an end to the traditional, clearly defined provider role existing under simple outsourced service contracts. Those roles will almost certainly continue to exist, but the returns, along with risk and liability, will be limited. In the new supply chain paradigm, the greater opportunities for providers will flow from collaboration and the willingness to take on an even greater multifunctional role within shippers' organizations. This involves providers collaborating across supply chain stakeholders in order to then stretch their reach into the shipper, realizing opportunities and improvements in new service areas and support. The real returns will not be attached to commodity logistics (such as transport, warehouse, scheduling and handling) where the risk should be relatively low, but instead directed to innovative value-adding areas and wider organizational innovations. Almost certainly, shippers will increasingly assess providers' willingness to perform standardized services at highly competitive (and low-margin) rates as the 'entry card' for winning the higher-margin collaborative and value-adding services where the long-term rewards lie. In stark contrast to the standard industry term model of the 1970s, the CFA model is very long-term and involves much more investment and risk, but it carries exponentially higher rewards. As a result, the successful providers will increasingly become an integral part of their shippers' organizations. In all likelihood, such relationships will be supported by mixed conventional contracts and CFA models under which providers evolve from an outsourced supplier to an integrated component of the shipper.

CFAs usually sit side by side with, and incorporate, shared risk models of trading. All the significant opportunities for growth from new logistics business will incorporate such concepts. So in real terms, the standalone conventional outsourced contract for services with limited and defined risk will decline. Such work will still need to be done, but either it will be contracted separately and carry low margins commensurate

> *'Shippers will increasingly assess providers' willingness to perform standardized services at highly competitive (and low-margin) rates as the "entry card" for winning the higher-margin collaborative and value-adding services.'*

with the risk or the low risk commodity service requirements will be bolted on to the broader CFA contract as a 'loss leader' to the much more profitable shared risk service elements. As such, those service providers only willing to take on low- and defined-risk contracts will decline and eventually become extinct.

THE RISE AND RISE OF NEW BUSINESS MODELS

The 3PL was a new business model in the 1970s, but by the mid-1990s it was clear that principals/shippers were generally unhappy with the service they were getting for the costs involved. Many of the early aspirations and expectations had disappeared, and shippers were looking for the next innovation in business models.

This came in 1994 when Accenture (formerly Andersen Consulting) came up with their Fourth Party Logistics model or, as it became known, 4PL. From the shippers' perspective, this new model showed a lot of promise, and indeed has been applied successfully in many industrial situations worldwide over the last 14 years. What this model did was offer a single point of contact for shippers, and, most importantly, it overcame the strategic weaknesses of earlier 3PLs. The 4PL concept was, in effect, a non-asset owning management company that acted as a type of air traffic control tower, and it had some very special capabilities embedded in its structure.·

It was owned in large part by one or more of the major shippers doing business; this is an important principle that many subsequent players did not fully comprehend – namely, that the enterprises which own the business retain a majority interest in the new service company.

It was an organization designed for a specific purpose and, as such, key capabilities were specified and quickly introduced into the structure simply by inviting those parties that had these capabilities *in situ* to join in return for a small equity. So the organization was, in effect, a best-of-breed enterprise, held together by equity holdings of various sizes.

As such, the 4PL did not have the contractual complexity encountered by the former 3PLs, and which inevitably had led to an adversarial operating environment – that condition was eliminated in the stroke of a pen.

Innovation and strategic thinking was encouraged in this new enterprise and played an equal role with operations. In the latter case, a 3PL would often be invited in as a minority party to manage the operations, even though it might also be fulfilling a 3PL role, along with other 3PLs selected to carry out a range of physical tasks.

Unfortunately, many 3PLs were threatened by the 4PL development and set out to transform themselves into a 4PL variant of their own design. This led to a lot of confusion in the marketplace among shippers, and the founding principles of the original 4PL concept became blurred or were lost. As a result, so-called 4PL providers came into the market and failed to deliver. A variation of this is the lead logistics provider (LLP) where one 3PL undertakes to manage other 3PLs in a particular contract for a shipper. This arrangement has also met with limited success, especially where 3PLs of similar standing are in this master–servant-style relationship. It may work in China where a more sophisticated 3PL might manage an array of smaller, unsophisticated providers that service outlying areas at low cost, but it doesn't translate well where providers of equal sophistication are involved.

WHERE TO FROM HERE? THE BEST-OF-BOTH-WORLDS STRATEGY

In reality, we need single-mode providers, multiple-mode providers such as 3PLs, and we also need an overarching management entity to provide all the pieces of the jigsaw puzzle. They all have complementary roles to play. Taken together, they can be moulded into a 4PL or, in the more modern vernacular, a joint services company (JSC) that coordinates the efforts of the two lower levels and brings knowledge, technology and innovation into play. The three levels can, and must, work in unison for the benefit of the shipper and the health of the various operators involved in the model. The important principle is that all parties must make money on a sustained basis ,and share the rewards for reducing operating costs over time. 3PLs should continue their vital role of fulfilling the physical tasks involved and may also have a role in the JSC, in this way getting two bites of the cherry. There is no limit to the possible permutations and combinations of 4PLs/

JSCs going forward because the concept transcends industry borders and buyer–seller boundaries. But success only comes if you stick to the proven principles. No short-cuts allowed. See Case Study 4 below.

Case Study 4: Taking These Concepts on the Road to the Middle East

One such experiment is currently taking place in Oman, where Petroleum Development of Oman (PDO), an oil exploration and development company, is moving through a phased approach towards a fully-fledged joint services company designed to service all its logistical needs. The task that the JSC has to fulfil is to service all the logistics needs of PDO's well engineering group which is engaged in exploring and developing oil in PDO oilfields. This involves managing everything from coordinating the procurement and delivery of oilfield equipment and consumables to remote oilfield locations, to the management of the specialized 3PLs that move 300-tonne rigs between drilling locations. The information technology is provided by a local Omani company, Bahwan Cybertek, and the management of the three specialized Omani 3PLs (Truckoman, Ofsat and TOCO) is undertaken by Bahwan DHL, a joint venture between the Bahwan Cybertek Group and DHL Exel. PDO's own Logistics Group also provides much of the knowledge and operational experience to the JSC.

This is the first time an organization structure of this type has been used anywhere in the world in the oil exploration and development industry, and early results indicate a quantum improvement in performance is on the way, not only in the form of cost savings but also in the additional revenue generated from the oil pumped as a result of quicker and more efficient rig moves. In addition, the faster movement of rigs has meant a reduction in the total number of rigs required for drilling operations.

This model, once proven and perfected, will be very transportable to other industries and applications inside Oman, and will significantly impact on the country's economy. It will also be transportable to other oil-producing countries in the Middle East and elsewhere in the world. Innovations can sometimes come from unexpected places in unexpected forms. Watch this space.

ALIGNMENT INSIGHTS

- *Supply chains continually move forward. Consequently, the innovations of yesterday become the standards of today. Shippers and providers, individually and together, must continually seek out potential opportunities for re-engineering and realigning their organizational processes (R&D, marketing, manufacturing, sales and so on) with their extended supply chains in order to simultaneously maximize the potential of the whole entity.*

- *Organizations that are supply chain sector leaders will create tailored structures to support their operations. One size does not fit all. The structures will vary with the subject and objective: from dual-party conventional outsourcing agreements dealing with standard operations to multiparty collaborative framework agreements incubating blue-sky innovations.*

- *The easy wins for the two items above are done and dusted. The increasingly demanding economic climate of today requires a more collaborative, concerted and constant effort to realize the deeply hidden opportunities over the next decade. Only providers and shippers prepared to embrace greater notional risk and make the required long-term investment will succeed in this new world.*

24 Tax-aligned Supply Chains

Brett Campbell and Alyson Rodi

B old supply chain initiatives are a proven way of reducing operational costs and increasing profits. But many initiatives fall short of their potential to maximize shareholder value. Why? Because companies often invest in deep operational improvements, but ignore broader issues of structural tax planning. They make critical supply chain decisions without understanding their full tax implications. They focus on pre-tax gains instead of after-tax returns.

Organizations should consider viewing their supply chains from a tax-planning perspective. By looking for opportunities to reduce taxes on their functions, assets and risks, the overall effective global tax rate can be reduced and earnings per share improved. The opportunities are especially robust in the key supply chain activities of procurement, logistics, product life-cycle management and supply chain technology.

By including tax considerations, companies are able to make more realistic decisions about where to make, source, locate, move and store product – it is not as simple as just looking at the unit price of an activity, a unit of work, or a material purchased. Users who trade across large or multiple boundaries should be including tax information to make better supply chain management decisions.

In fact, a tax-oriented view can reinforce – and even add to – the business case by substantiating key decisions and creating cost savings that improve the return on investment scenario. In looking at the tax implications of supply chain decisions, an executive or a company may uncover a competitive advantage that would otherwise have been missed – for example, in resourcing or relocating part of the supply chain to a different part of the globe. Therefore, taking the tax information into account can lead to changing the supply chain structure, the sourcing rules and the supplier base. All these factors directly impact on the company's competitive capability in the market.

Much of this tax information, or at least the tax information required for any supply chain initiative, is not necessarily intuitive. Ask a supply chain person what the net impact of tax on his/her supply chain is and, after a clouded look comes over his/her eyes, you typically receive a non-intuitive response because the users do not necessarily understand all the details or implications of tax across trading partner boundaries. This is why it is important to include tax considerations at all stages of a supply chain initiative, so that the tax perspective can be clearly articulated and its benefits can be accurately quantified.

WHAT A IS TAX-ALIGNED SUPPLY CHAIN (TASC)?

'When the two initiatives are integrated, the results can be powerful. Organizations can enjoy the expanded benefits of enhanced supply chain efficiency while taking advantage of tax savings opportunities.'

TASC is a strategy for improving financial performance and competitiveness. This is achieved through the global optimization of the 'order-through-delivery' process across all the needs and costs of an organization, including tax and treasury.

TASC can increase shareholder value by reducing operating expenses and working capital requirements, lowering effective tax rates, improving cash flow and asset utilization, and developing new intangible assets and improved profits. Business benefits are maximized by adopting an integrated approach to supply chain and tax improvements.

Standalone supply chain initiatives focus only on pre-tax cost reduction. They often overlook the fact that, for each dollar of operating savings generated, it is possible that only a limited portion of the benefit will fall to the bottom line after taxes. Similarly, when tax planning is performed independently of supply chain planning, it can fail to take into account how planned supply chain initiatives will reduce operating costs, increase profits and, in some cases, create additional tax compliance burdens and complexity. Figure 24.1, based on a theoretical example developed by Deloitte Touche Tohmatsu, contrasts the benefits achievable in supply chains with and without tax planning.

When undertaken in isolation, tax planning and supply chain initiatives often fall short of realizing the maximum after-tax return from supply chain improvements. Conversely, when the two initiatives are integrated, the results can be powerful. Organizations can enjoy the expanded benefits of enhanced supply chain efficiency while taking advantage of tax savings opportunities

IS A TAX-ALIGNED APPROACH RIGHT FOR YOU?

Most organizations could benefit from reviewing the tax implications of their supply chain strategy. TASC may be a major opportunity if your organization:

1. has significant supply chain operations in several countries;

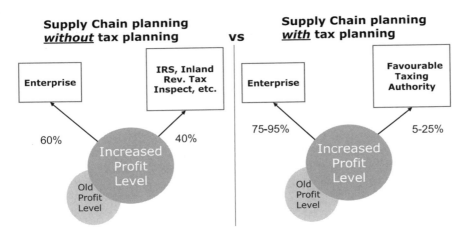

Figure 24.1   Benefits of supply chains with and without tax planning

Source: Deloitte Development LLC.

2.   is undergoing significant changes (for example, merger and acquisitions, restructuring);

3.   is pursuing aggressive cost-reduction goals, including standardizing business processes;

4.   is planning new manufacturing, distribution or R&D facilities;

5.   is adopting a new supply chain infrastructure.

TASC opportunities exist in these circumstances because the supply chain strategies and tactics that organizations employ frequently entail major changes to how and where they operate. By altering the geographic mix of where various functions are performed, assets owned and where risk is borne, organizations can significantly alter their global tax profile.[1]

It is appropriate to consider TASC in all stages of an organization's life cycle from start-ups to mature corporate groups operating on a country-by-country basis.

A SUPPLY CHAIN-EFFICIENT CENTRALIZED BUSINESS MODEL

The essence of TASC lies in global or regional centralization of functions, activities and risks with a view to eliminating duplication, improving efficiency and reducing total costs. In the most common forms of TASC, a central entrepreneur or principal, typically based in a location where it is subject to a low effective tax rate, is responsible for undertaking key functions and coordinating and directing the activities of a network of related affiliates (and sometimes third parties) that support the business/operations of the principal.

The principal assumes a major part of the total supply chain risk. Physical activities (for example, manufacturing, distribution, sales) are undertaken in the locations that are most suitable from a commercial perspective and are allocated an appropriate return with the residue accruing to the principal.

A supply chain-efficient business model is illustrated in Figure 24.2.[2] The model incorporates a number of components. It may be appropriate for an organization to consider some or all of these components in its TASC strategy.

Manufacturing Strategies

TASC strategies related to manufacturing typically focus on the segregation of key assets (for example, product design, brand intellectual property) or risks (inventory, manufacturing capacity) between the manufacturer and the principal. As such, the manufacturing entity would be characterized as a consignment, toll or contract manufacturer, rather than a fully integrated manufacturer. In these arrangements, the principal has a high level of control over the manufacturing process, including setting product specifications and standards and also determining the quality and quantity of production output.

In the case of toll or consignment manufacturing (as per Figure 24.2), the principal generally remains the owner of the raw materials which are manufactured on its behalf. The manufacturer performs a service for the principal and is paid an appropriate fee. An alternative strategy is to use contract manufacturing which involves the manufacturer purchasing the raw materials and then selling the finished goods to the principal. It should be noted that the tax implications may differ depending on whether toll or contract manufacturing is used (see the discussion of an integrated tax approach below).

Sales Strategies

The sales strategy for the finished goods may involve the use of a buy/sell or limited-risk distributor (SalesCo in Figure 24.2). Under this arrangement, SalesCo would purchase goods from the principal for resale to customers in its designated area. However, the parties would agree that most of the risks inherent with ownership of the goods would actually be retained by the principal. The parties would typically agree that SalesCo bears minimal risk regarding the finished goods being sold. For example, SalesCo would typically not bear risks associated with inventory obsolescence, bad debts, warranty/product liability or currency exchange.

The minimal risk that SalesCo bears with respect to the sale of the finished goods will be reflected in its lower profit margin. The residual profit would be allocated to the principal as compensation for the additional risks that it has agreed to bear with regards to the finished goods.

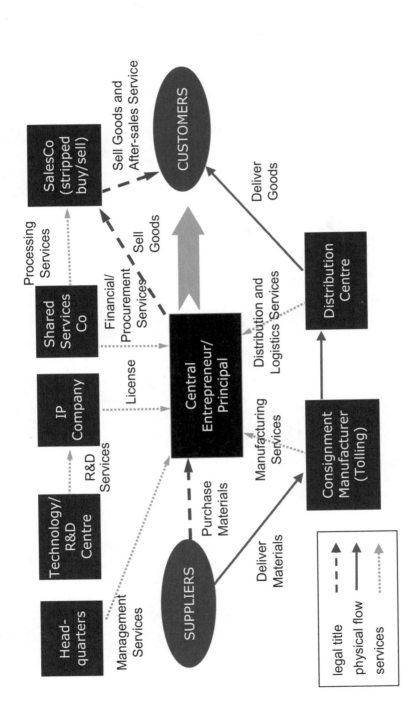

Figure 24.2   Example of a supply chain organization structure for a TASC

Source: Deloitte Development LLC.

Commissionaire arrangements are a variation of the limited risk SalesCo model described above and are often used in Europe. Under a commissionaire arrangement, assets such as inventory and receivables are owned by the principal rather than the distributor. The distributor effectively acts as an agent for an undisclosed principal and the customer may not even be aware that they are actually contracting with the principal. Again, under this arrangement, the principal is entitled to be compensated for the risks of ownership which it bears.

Shared Services (Including Procurement)

It is possible for companies to centralize procurement or other shared services within their corporate groups. For example, a procurement centre could perform various functions in support of the principal or the manufacturing and sales/distribution entities. Its functions could include identifying materials and services, negotiating with vendors to achieve better pricing and performing quality assurance on vendors' supplies to the organization. A procurement (or shared services) company would ideally be located in a low-taxed jurisdiction.

Intellectual Property (IP) Management

The management of IP within a TASC strategy generally involves an intangible holding company (IP Company in Figure 24.2) to hold, develop and maintain valuable IP of the global organization. The development of IP may be facilitated by the use of technology/R&D centres which would work, under the direction of the IP company, to research new technology/ideas on behalf of the IP company. The technology/R&D centres would be paid a fee for this service, and the IP company would own the IP developed. The IP company may also license the IP developed to the principal for use within the business or for exploitation by third parties.

The IP company would be located in a suitable jurisdiction (that is, in terms of IP protection and taxation issues). Whilst the IP company would generally be located in a low-tax jurisdiction, there may also be advantages in locating it in a relatively high-tax jurisdiction (such as Australia) with R&D tax concessions. Such R&D tax concessions can provide a tax shield in the early years of development or in the event of failure to develop new IP.

It may also be possible for the principal to perform the functions of the IP company in addition to its other functions. The principal could license the developed IP to other parts of the organization or to third parties.

AN INTEGRATED TAX APPROACH

The selection of a preferred location for the principal (and other support entities – for example, IP Company and Shared Services Co in Figure 24.2) needs to take into account commercial and tax considerations. From a commercial perspective, the location must be appropriate for the business (for example, logistics, infrastructure, staff mobility). From a tax perspective, an appropriate location should offer a tax-efficient regime with a low effective tax rate and a comprehensive network of double tax treaties.

In Europe, popular locations for principal companies include Switzerland, Ireland, the Netherlands and Belgium. These locations are attractive because of low corporate income tax rates or the ability to obtain favourable rulings which have the effect of lowering the normal corporate income tax rate.

In the Asia-Pacific region, Singapore is a typical location for setting up a regional principal because of its low corporate tax rate, ability to negotiate favourable tax rulings and because no dividend-withholding tax is imposed on dividend payments from Singapore. Hong Kong is also a popular location for a regional principal (notwithstanding that Hong Kong only has a limited double tax treaty network) because of its low corporate income tax rate.

In selecting an appropriate location, it is important to consider all taxes, including corporate income tax and indirect taxes (VAT/GST and customs duty). The tax issues that frequently arise in connection with the implementation of a TASC strategy include the following:

- *Transfer pricing.* What margin should be left in the manufacturing company or SalesCo? This will depend on the function which these companies perform, the risk that they are assuming and the assets which they hold. The objective is to locate the key profit drivers (risk, assets) with the principal who receives an entrepreneurial return (subject to a lower rate of tax in the principal's home jurisdiction). The other entities would perform routine functions and derive a cost-plus return.

- *Permanent Establishment (PE).* Do any of the principal's activities in countries where the manufacturer or SalesCo is located give rise to a PE (that is, a taxable presence) in those countries? A PE can arise in some jurisdictions by virtue of toll manufacturing activities. The activities of sales agents can also give rise to a PE issue. If a PE exists, profits attributable to that PE will generally be subject to tax in the foreign location where the manufacturer or SalesCo is located.

- *Parent Company-controlled Foreign Company (CFC) rules.* Where applicable, the application of these rules can result in the parent company being subject to taxation in respect of undistributed profits of foreign, related parties in certain circumstances.

- *Indirect taxes (value added tax/goods and services tax, customs duty.* Depending on the structure, there could be multiple VAT/GST registrations, and indirect taxes can have a cash flow impact on the new structure. From a customs duty perspective, the value for duty needs to be determined and administrative requirements adhered to. These taxes may also impact on the choice of location for the principal.

- *Conversion costs.* There may be a tax cost associated with converting existing aspects of the supply chain into the new structure (for example, cost of migrating existing IP offshore to a new IP company).

The impact of these and other tax issues needs to be factored into the choice of the appropriate TASC strategy for an organization and in the selection of a location for the principal.

GENERATING VALUE

Leading manufacturers are looking beyond the operational and cost-reduction benefits of supply chain initiatives to broader opportunities for value creation. By integrating tax planning with their supply chain initiatives, they are elevating the entire process to a new level and generating additional tens of millions – if not hundreds of millions – of dollars in savings.

The result is improved efficiency – both operational and tax-related – that can reduce compliance risks and lead to measurable gains in cash flow and profitability. Best of all, at least some of the financial benefit of these initiatives can be realized in the short term, thereby helping to fund the overall supply chain re-engineering efforts. Combined with the ongoing benefits that can be achieved, this near-term payback can help seal the business case for undertaking the supply chain initiative in the first place.[3]

ALIGNMENT INSIGHTS

- *Organizations with international divisions should look for the opportunities to maximize their operational efficiency and at the same time take advantage of tax-saving opportunities. This may shift the focus from shorter-term pre-tax gains to longer-term after-tax returns.*

- *Procurement, network optimization, product life-cycle management and information technology systems are some of the functions that can be optimized in a tax-efficient manner.*

- *Taking a tax-oriented view can reinforce, and even enhance, the business case for supply chain initiatives by substantiating key decisions and creating cost savings that improve the return on investment equation.*

Note on Professional Advice

This chapter is intended as a general guide only, and the application of its contents to specific situations will depend on the particular circumstances involved. Accordingly, readers should seek appropriate professional advice regarding any particular problems that they encounter, and this chapter should not be relied on as a substitute for this advice. While all reasonable efforts have been made to ensure that the information contained in this chapter is accurate, Deloitte Touche Tohmatsu and its member firms accept no responsibility for any errors or omissions it may contain, whether caused by negligence or otherwise, or for any losses, however caused, sustained by any person that relies on it.

NOTES

1   Based on an original article written by Deloitte's Dan Irving, Gary Kilponen, Raffi Markarian and Mark Klitgaard published in *Supply Chain Management Review* (April 2005), p. 58.
2   Deloitte Touche Tohmatsu has developed a number of organizational models which can be applied to tax-aligned supply chains. This example shows a supply chain-efficient centralized business model with the principal at the centre.
3   Irving et al., *op. cit.*

25 The Emergence of National Logistics Cities

Pieter Nagel, Michael Proffitt, Keith Toh and
Roger Oakden

The concept of a Logistics City and achieving this status is becoming recognized as a means of attaining sustained economic growth, as evidenced by a number of examples around the world. This chapter examines some aspects of Logistics Cities, with a view to proposing how this may also be achieved in Melbourne, Australia. For this purpose, a hierarchical planning framework is proposed by the Institute for Logistics and Supply Chain Management (ILSCM) at Victoria University. This planning framework is seen as necessary for achieving dynamic alignment in the development of infrastructure to be used by the relevant stakeholders.

THE LOGISTICS CITY PHENOMENON

A number of cities around the world aim to improve their international standing, competitiveness and attractiveness through the development of Dense Trade Clusters. The ultimate progression of a logistics-intensive economy within a region of a country is the multifaceted development of goods movement activities into a Logistics City. The purpose of this is to achieve economic, social and environmental sustainability for the surrounding region. Logistics Cities achieve significant economic growth, possessing an ability to attract investments and projects from leading global, regional and local logistics services, thus securing further strength in their capability to interact with global supply chains. Within a Logistics City reside industrial parks that include dedicated infrastructure, strategically located within a Free Trade Zone (FTZ). This leverages the excellent connectivity and superior handling efficiency of a local airport or seaport to enable quick turnaround of consignments, value-added logistics services and regional distribution activities. For example, the Logistics City in Dubai is a designated 'Free Trade Zone Pathway' connecting the Free Zone of Dubai Logistics City and the adjacent Free Zone of the Jebel Ali seaport within a single customs bond area.

Inland ports, intermodal hubs and freight villages are developments of these logistics-intensive clusters within Logistics Cities, depending on the complexity of activities undertaken.[1] Common characteristics of these clusters are the quality of road, rail and IT/communications infrastructure, depth and strength of goods distribution, skill sets of the workforce and sustainability (urban, economic and environmental). There is also a Central Business District (CBD) close by

'A Logistics City... leverages the excellent connectivity and superior handling efficiency of a local airport or seaport to enable quick turnaround of consignments, value-added logistics services and regional distribution activities.'

that provides a range of financial and business services, health care, education and tourism to support the Logistics City (see Figure 25.1).

One of the major enablers of such Logistics Cities is world-class infrastructure, including Information and Communications Technology (ICT). Globalization and the internationalization of supply chains has placed significant emphasis on Electronic Data Interchange (EDI) of trade documents such as trade declarations through systems like CargoWise EDI, TradeGate, TradeXchange and TradeNet,[2] enabling seamless trade transactions with a critical involvement of customs services.

It is a contemporary truism that competition between regions and countries has increased as a result of globalization and technology development. A region's ability to take advantage of globalization in the context of the connectivity of one economy to another economy plays an important role. National or regional governments support investment and may align laws and regulations to free up global trade and transportation in support of industry and commerce. The global connectivity of a metropolitan area and its ability to retain and further develop its 'competitive advantage', and that of its industries, requires a significant review of the way in which the country interfaces with the rest of the world. Also required is a strategy that addresses a well-structured and relevant solution to the longer-term sustainability of a region's economy in the global trading arena. The concept of the Logistics City may be seen as a major part of this strategy.

The ILSCM focused its research on the concept of a Logistics City, which it defines as the final progression of a Dense Trade Cluster.[3] Dense Trade Clusters are described as nodal points which can be positioned away from traditional land, air and coastal borders to enable international trade. The facilitation of trade is accomplished by strategic investment in logistics-related infrastructure, such as multimodal transport facilities, and by promoting value-added services.[4]

The concept of a Logistics City broadly represents a geographical metropolitan area with a dominant logistical function, providing appropriate infrastructure and physical facilities (for example, roads, rail tracks, terminals, IT infrastructure and so on) and substantial existing logistical services (such as warehousing, distribution, freight forwarding). However, related business

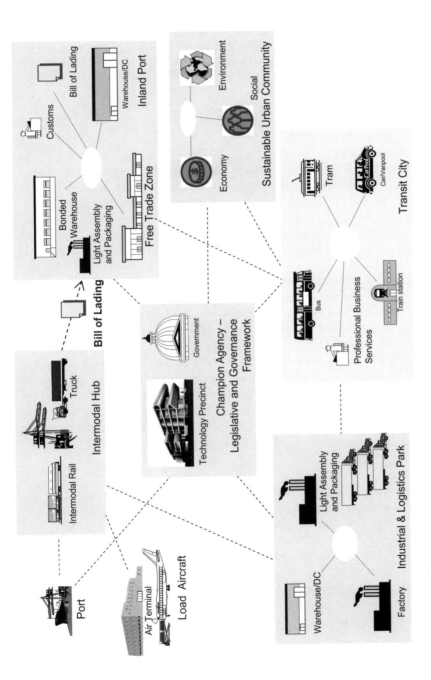

Figure 25.1   Schematic of a conceptual view of the Logistics City

value-added services (legal, finance, light assembly and the like) and social infrastructure (like education, health and recreation) are also necessary elements for the Logistics City as an integrated concept.

In addition to the above-mentioned initial investigation, three so-called Logistics Cities currently being planned and developed, or in an expansion phase, are found in the literature. These are:

- Dubai;[5]

- Lingang, adjacent to Shanghai, China;[6]

- Zaragoza, in Spain.[7]

These Logistics Cities differ in size and are focused on different elements, infrastructures and services provided. For example the Logistics City in Dubai is seen as the logistics area of the comprehensive structure of Dubai World Central. In contrast, the Logistics City of Lingang includes all other elements of Dubai World Central and is referred as a Logistics City. On the other hand, Zaragoza, located inland, appears small in comparison to Dubai and Lingang.

Although these examples differ in size, they bear commonality in terms of core infrastructure and services. These Logistics Cities include, or are adjacent to, ports that include seaports, airports and inland ports. All of them provide sufficient transport and communications infrastructure and logistics facilities, as well as the related logistics services, although these differ in terms of size and services provided. Value-added business services such as light assembly, banking and hospitality are integrated in Logistics Cities; hence the value-added services as an enabler, mentioned by ILSCM,[8] can be seen as a necessity for the development of Logistics Cities. In addition, the free trade zones and research/education facilities seem to be an important part of the Logistics City concept. All the identified Logistics Cities are part of their region's economic development plan.

There are many different perspectives concerning the constituents of a Logistics City, and therefore the designations may be ambiguous. There is no academically rigorous conceptual model that can be used to clearly identify its distinct physical characteristics, mode of operation, valued-added business services and social components. In their study of intermodal freight literature, Bontekoning et al.[9] state that, typical for a research field in the pre-paradigmatic phase, there is a lack of a consensus definition and a common conceptual model. A comprehensive review of the emergence of Logistics Cities may be found in Sengpiehl et al.[10]

However, the Logistics City concept may be applied very freely. The concept has emerged out of the industry domain and has been the subject of significant commercial and government interests over the world because of its potential regional economic contribution. We view metropolitan areas, such as Hamburg (harbour city), Singapore (logistics cluster) and Rotterdam (port city), with their long seaport and trade history, as well as their massive transport infrastructures, logistics service activities and value-added business services, as Logistics City concepts, even though they are not named as such. Van der Lugt and de Langen[11] support this conclusion by describing the changing role of seaports as locations for logistics-intensive activities. Meidute's[12] comment that logistics centres are generators of business and regional economic growth strengthens this view.

MELBOURNE AS A POSSIBLE LOGISTICS CITY

ILSCM[13] has found that the integrated development of a Logistics City has significant potential to increase the competitiveness of a region and strengthens the regional and economic development of regional Melbourne. Whilst it is important to learn from international examples, it is clear that a Logistics City model for Melbourne must take into account its uniqueness

as an origin–destination city (as opposed to a transit-type city) and that it will have to be unique to these particular circumstances. The model must provide a framework that enables comparison and understanding of the differences between different Logistics Cities. Perhaps more importantly, where there may be perceived differences or 'grey areas', the model should facilitate acceptance and understanding rather than be dogmatic in implementation.

'Transit Cities are regional cities and suburbs that provide easy access to a range of transport, housing, shops, services and job opportunities. They are designed around concepts of providing a safe and vibrant community that sets a new standard in urban design.'

It is clear that the Logistics City model is not solely based around the movement of freight. Apart from the case studies of existing Logistics Cities carried out by ILSCM, which have identified common elements such as infrastructure and services, other areas provide readily accessible concepts and criteria from which the design elements can be drawn. These provide knowledge and experience in terms of city and urban planning. The various areas of work that impinge on the design criteria for the Logistics City model may best be depicted in Figure 25.2.

Certainly, the logistics elements for the model are well known in terms of the physical infrastructure required as well as the catalogue of services provided by the logistics sector. Figure 25.2 features an important point: this is the first attempt to integrate city planning (urban planning) with the freight network, although there are well-documented design models for Transit Cities and Activity Centres in Victoria, Australia. The impact of freight movements on urban and environmental aspects are less well known in terms of an integrated design concept.

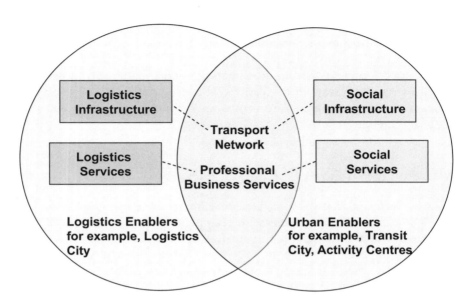

Figure 25.2   Overview of the relevant areas for the Logistics City model

The Transit Cities initiative is a major Victorian government programme to revitalize the metropolitan and regional centres of Melbourne, making them economically stronger and better places to live and work. Transit Cities are regional cities and suburbs that provide easy access to a range of transport, housing, shops, services and job opportunities. They are designed around concepts of providing a safe and vibrant community that sets a new standard in urban design. By encouraging development around public transport, Transit Cities will be able to deliver these outcomes to residents. Transit Cities are based on the principles of transit-oriented development, a form of urban development that clusters a greater mixture of land uses around a high-quality transport service. The transport node is encouraged to be a combination of train, light rail or bus, and the terminus is designed to be the focus for the development.

Similarly, the Logistics City may be described as a planned development around a 'nucleus' freight terminal. In this instance the freight terminal provides the functionality for freight transition and exists with the functionality of a freight hub. This progression from freight terminal to Logistics City is shown in Table 25.1.

Each progression stage is enabled by some defining functionality (that is, functional enabler). This functional enabler is the key to the classification of the freight facility (that is, freight terminal, freight hub and so on) and also provides the criteria for determining what is considered to be compatible and non-compatible use at each level. At the level of the Logistics City, the benefits are derived from the agglomeration of population, namely the availability and diversity of labour and market

Table 25.1   Classification of Logistics City components based on functional enablers

Conceptual: Progression (Type)	Functional: Enablers	Transactional: Execution or Operational Elements
	Urban agglomeration economies	Business Intelligence, Business HQ Functions, urban sustainability
	Industrial agglomeration and location economies	Business Integration, Business Operations
Freight Hub	Freight Consolidation/ Deconsolidation	Logistics Services
Freight Terminal	Freight Transition	Terminal Operations, Customs, Intermodal Operations

size. This must be made available via common infrastructures (for example, utilities or public transit) as well as access to urban amenity. In order for local economies to develop there must be infrastructure for education that provides logistics education.

Unless a Logistics City has a value proposition for its market (or beneficiaries) it will not happen. The value proposition should be developed in terms of the Logistics City model. Some of the benefits are identified in Table 25.2.

A GENERAL MODEL OF THE LOGISTICS CITY

To enable a common understanding of the Logistics City concept, a data model, as shown in Figure 25.3, has been proposed by ILSCM.

As shown in Figure 25.3, the Logistics City model has constructs such as infrastructure and services. The model captures the possibility that the Logistics City also has connectivity with freight villages, gateway ports and, potentially, another Logistics City.

Singapore sees its pathway of logistics development as the key for meeting future needs that include social value aspects such as education and amenities. For the Logistics City of Dubai, it is argued that economic growth cannot be achieved without social values. The holistic development in Dubai therefore contains a new residential area and a commercial district that includes schools, hospitals, parks, banking and financing, health-care centres,

Table 25.2   **Logistics City value propositions and their categories**

Value Proposition	Economic	Environment	Social
Attractive for new business investment	✓		
Growth of professional business services	✓		
Growth of trade	✓		
Lower unemployment due to growth of trade and industry	✓		✓
Employment opportunities	✓		✓
Improved conditions for travel to work	✓	✓	✓
Training opportunities			✓
Efficient services due to distribution of functionality inland	✓		
Minimal container dwell	✓		
Increased throughput	✓		
On-time logistics services	✓		
Efficient transport utilization	✓	✓	
Reduced congestion		✓	✓
Cutting-edge technology	✓		
Business process enhancement	✓		
Increased uptake, e.g. ICT leading to business efficiencies	✓		
Reduced impact on environment through rail and HPFV via efficient transport corridors			✓
Reduced noise levels			✓
Lower accident rate	✓		✓

Figure 25.3   Data model of a Logistics City

religious facilities, police stations, libraries, university and research centres. Hamburg, a long-established port cluster, focuses on environmental issues, in the cause of sustainability, by arguing that no company or employees would consider relocating to, or living in, a polluted area, which decreases economic growth. Therefore emission and noise has been reduced through the joint efforts of government and industry, and new recreation areas have been developed or are under development. Zaragoza is developing a new logistics cluster, including a research and education facility. To sustain a healthy economic growth, the social and environmental aspect must be considered. Educating the future professionals who will support the Logistics City concept is an important factor and keeping and attracting the highly skilled workforce by ensuring an appropriate quality of life through the provision of social amenities and a clean and pleasant environment is critical to the achievement of regional economic growth.

'International gateways, such as seaports, airports and inland ports, including their logistics facilities, are crucial to participation in the global and regional transport and distribution arena.'

In order to achieve a sustainable global integrated logistics hub, it must be based on a foundation, which is referred to in the conceptual map (shown in Figure 25.3) as 'enablers'. The enablers have been identified as important determinants, and the map is extendable to include others in the future.

Physical, financial and information technology infrastructure are identified as important pillars of the Logistics City. International gateways, such as seaports, airports and inland ports, including their logistics facilities, are crucial to participation in the global and regional transport and distribution arena. However, the quality of the connectivity between these gateways, plus commercial infrastructure and social infrastructure, are the principal factors. Connectivity can be provided by transport infrastructure, such as road and rail, or by information and communication infrastructure. Transport infrastructural excellence on its own does not mean efficient connectivity. Physical transport infrastructure is seen as a necessity for connectivity but on its own is insufficient as a contributor to a Logistics City. The physical flow has to be complemented by information flow provided by an appropriate information and communications infrastructure. As mentioned earlier, Singapore is developing a trade-integrated information 'one-stop' platform that will bring together the different systems to enable seamless information transfer, supporting the high-quality physical infrastructure already in existence.

ACHIEVING DYNAMIC ALIGNMENT IN MELBOURNE

Melbourne strives to benefit from alignment with the efficiencies that may be accrued from acquiring Logistics City 'status'. The challenges are numerous because of the legacy of logistics-intensive 'centres' that have resulted from ad hoc growth in the past. In the study to date, the ILSCM has identified a number of factors to be considered in the project to develop a Logistics City within the established infrastructure.

The Logistics City concept consists of many different stakeholders, each having different aims. Therefore it is crucial to coordinate the efforts of different stakeholders to promote and develop the Logistics City. Lack of clear coordination will produce duplicated actions or opposing activities that adversely affect otherwise efficient physical and virtual connectivity. Different government departments each focus on different policies – for example, road policies, rail policies, land allocation policies and taxation policies. However, those policies do not necessarily align with the wider interests of the Logistics City. Solely investing in road transport infrastructure in order to alleviate congestion does not lead to a sustainable future for the Logistics City. This must be done in conjunction with an aligned information system to provide better coordination and utilization of the road system or introducing policies to promote the movement of freight by rail. The same applies to established industry in different areas of the city.

Melbourne may learn from the example of Singapore which has established a so-called 'champion agency' that acts as the bridge to all the relevant private and public stakeholders involved. Its primary work is to promote, coordinate and develop the logistics industry in Singapore. Identifying developmental needs of private industry, working with governmental departments and agencies to remove unnecessary impediments and aligning regulations are areas of responsibility for the champion agency. There is also the further task of promoting the Logistics City and to attract continued investment by the private sector.

The provision of a 'reference model' will achieve dynamic alignment from the top down and this must be driven as part of the initiative. Figure 25.4 shows a hierarchy of planning toolkits or reference models that provide a set of guidelines and resources to promote re-use and prevent reinvention.

These reference models, as promoted by supportive government policies, provide stakeholders with the necessary references and information to operate and plan within a 'protective' operational envelope. The governance and policy of the Logistics City concept is therefore strongly related to stakeholders. Legislation should be aligned to ease the physical and information flow that allows business growth. In addition, it is important that governance and policy provide stability for the business environment to prosper. Since one of the main functions of the Logistics City concept is a physical trade hub, trade facilitation should be enhanced. The hierarchy of toolkits inherits its generic elements from the parent. This means that generic elements may be defined by the government and tailored at the local level for particular instances. The elements that may be found in the generic toolkit are shown in Figure 25.5.

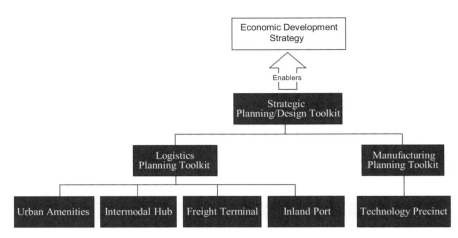

Figure 25.4   Achieving alignment through a hierarchy of planning toolkits

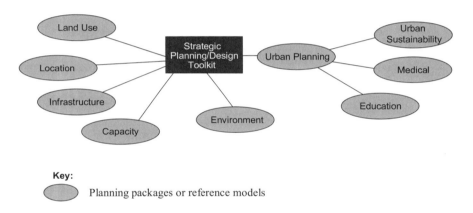

Figure 25.5   Elements of the planning toolkit

Therefore, by defining the 'packages' or reference models at the parent level, specialized toolkits inherit these reference models. These reference models provide a library of solutions and design elements, including methods for capacity planning, land-use planning, and planning for environmentally sound solutions. These supply the 'checklist' of factors that must be considered and key performance indicators that must be met. This in turn provides the roadmap or implementation plan that allows stakeholders to plan and implement their facilities within the government 'envelope' in order to achieve the strategic alignment with a policy for economic growth. The models also allow stakeholders to leverage government planning and legislative packages, which, in some cases, are service offerings provided through expertise from government agencies. In turn, the government, through its champion agency, must review and implement strategy that removes impediments to trade and economic growth.

ACHIEVING A LOGISTICS CITY IN MELBOURNE

The concept of a Logistics City, and achieving the associated status, is becoming recognized as a means of attaining sustained economic growth, as evidenced by a number of current examples around the world. To achieve dynamic alignment in the planning of a Logistics City in Melbourne, this chapter has outlined a hierarchy of planning toolkits that have to be developed by government stakeholders in order to provide an implementation plan which allows for the growth of the logistics services sector within a managed framework. Reference models can provide important insights into how to achieve governance and a sustainable project where there is clearly a symbiotic relationship between economic, urban and environmental factors in and around the location.

ALIGNMENT INSIGHTS

- *To be successful, the Logistics City has to be dynamically aligned within the context of the global supply chain network, providing access to global markets. This enables Australia to benefit from trade, foreign investment, an increase of skilled workforce through immigration and an increase in technology uptake.*

- *Making the concept work in the city of Melbourne requires the alignment of the Logistics City with other ongoing initiatives, such as Transit Cities and other Activity Centres. This brings together urban and industry agglomeration economies.*

- *Different government departments each focus on different policies – for example, road polices, rail policies, land allocation polices taxation policies. Those policies should align with the wider interests of the Logistics City. Solely investing in road transport infrastructure in order to alleviate congestion does not lead to a sustainable future for the Logistics City. This must be done in conjunction with an aligned information system to provide better coordination and utilization of the road system or taking the rail policies into consideration.*

NOTES

1   ILSCM, *A Case for a National Logistics City: Positioning the West for the Future*, Report by the Institute for Logistics and Supply Chain Management, Melbourne, 2007.

2   K.T.K. Toh, C. Sengpiehl, P. Nagel and P. Shi, P., The National Logistics City business and information systems architecture, *Proceedings of the Third International Conference on Innovative Computing Information and Control*, China, 2008.

3   ILSCM, *A Case for a National Logistics City*, op. cit.

4   Cambridge Systematics Inc., *NYMTC Regional Freight Plan – An Element of the Regional Transportation Plan*, Report for the New York Metropolitan Transport Council, New York, 2004.

5   M. Proffitt, M., 2006, 'Dubai World Central: Delivering State-of-the-Art Infrastructure and Logistics Services', Presentation at the Second Trans Middle East Exhibition and Conference, Dubai, 2006; 'Four sign up for Logistics City', *Middle East Economic Digest*, Vol. 50, No. 38 (2006), p. 26; R. Turner, R., 2006, 'Dubai vies to become logistics gateway'. *Shipping Digest*, Vol. 83, No. 4324 (2006), pp. 92–94.

6   P.T. Leach, 'China plans massive logistics city', *Pacific Shipper*, Vol. 83, No. 9 (2006), p. 118; L.H. Harmsen, Y. Guang and S. Pick, 'China's new Logistics City', presentation to the Lingang Group, Shanghai, 2006.

7   S. Tierney, S. 'Welcome to logistics city', Supply Chain Europe, Vol. 13, No. 2 (2004), pp. 25–27.

8   ILSCM, *A Case for a National Logistics City, op. cit.*

9   Y.M. Bontekoning, C. Macharis and J.J. Trip, 'Is a new applied transportation research field emerging? A review of intermodal rail–truck freight transport literature', *Transportation Research Part A: Policy and Practice*, Vol. 38, Iss. 1 (2004), pp. 1–34.

10   C. Sengpiehl, R. Oakden, P. Nagel, K.T.K. Toh and P. Shi, 'The emergence of Logistics Cities: conceptual model', *Journal of Transport and Supply Chain Management*, Vol. 2, Issue 1 (November 2008), pp. 58–77.

11   L.M. Van der Lugt and P.W. de Langen, 'The changing role of ports as locations for logistics activities', *Journal of International Logistics and Trade*, Vol. 3, No. 2 (2005), pp. 59–72.

12   I. Meidute, 'Comparative analysis of the definitions of logistics centres', *Transport*, Vol. 20, No. 3, (2005), pp. 106–110.

13   ILSCM, *A Case for a National Logistics City, op. cit.*

26 The Importance of Intellectual Capital and Knowledge in the Design and Operation of Enterprise Supply Chains

Kate Andrews

In the global knowledge race ... the key driver is the rate at which organizations can transform enterprise knowledge into intellectual capital and products, services and solutions.[1]

There is significant agreement in twenty-first-century management thinking that value is created predominantly from knowledge-based goods, services and solutions. Surprisingly, there has been little research on learning and knowledge transfer associated with successful supply chain management.[2] Whilst a focus on knowledge processes could be expected to improve supply chain performance, benefits have not yet been realized.[3]

In this chapter we apply a *knowledge lens* to supply chain design and operations. We suggest that applying Intellectual Capital (IC) and Knowledge Management (KM) principles can create an inimitable advantage[4] for enterprise supply chains.

Alignment is a critical factor in this topic. Supply chain design begins with a deep understanding of customer requirements and should be operated to maximize responsiveness to customer needs. We will see that the four generic supply chains have distinctively different knowledge personalities that require unique processes. Metaphors of *Factory*, *Test Lab*, *Café* and *Triage* are proposed to describe knowledge priorities for the four generic supply chains.

Finally, we will build on our understanding of cultural capability factors by proposing KM as an essential enabler of supply chain performance.

KNOWLEDGE AND COMPETITIVE ADVANTAGE

Knowledge creation, use, sharing and retention have always been important. What is new is the significant shift towards a focused, strategic approach to managing knowledge, knowledge processes and knowledge products.

Throughout OECD countries, corporate investment in intangibles (research, education and knowledge) is growing at a faster rate than tangible investments.

- *Knowledge management* is the discipline that formalizes approaches to understanding and benefiting from knowledge assets at the firm level. The key contribution of knowledge management is its focus on knowledge as a strategic and competitive resource.

Organizations that manage their knowledge and information resources as strategic assets are advantaged in today's knowledge economy. Maximizing enterprise knowledge potential delivers tangible benefits which are of direct interest to enterprise supply chains. These are:

- operational efficiency;

- opportunities to better service customer and stakeholder needs; and

- a springboard for innovation.

A foundation concept in the field of intangible assets that is important for practice is that there are two dimensions of knowledge, *explicit* and *tacit*. Transferability is the dimension that has emerged as distinguishing between knowledge types.[5]

'Throughout OECD countries, corporate investment in intangibles (research, education and knowledge) is growing at a faster rate than tangible investments.'

- *Explicit knowledge* can be expressed easily and transferred between people without loss of meaning. Explicit knowledge is know-how that has been recorded in some kind of medium such as a document, image, process or tool. Examples include standard operating procedures, manuals, checklists and computer codes.

- *Tacit knowledge* is difficult to articulate and cannot be transferred without close personal contact, demonstration and involvement. Tacit refers to highly personal knowledge that resides in a person's mind and includes physical skills as well as aspects of culture or 'ways of doing things'. Importantly, tacit knowledge cannot be captured, but it can be transferred in discussion or via observation. The tacit dimension is personal, context-specific and experience-dependent. Tacit knowledge is sticky – difficult to transfer and for competitors to replicate.

More specifically, it is the difficult-to-replicate knowledge assets and the manner in which they are deployed that is significant for competitive advantage.

Build the image in your mind of knowledge exchange as a social process. Research confirms that knowledge flows in organizations are mediated by psychosocial factors;[6] where trust is low, knowledge doesn't flow. Knowing and trusting colleagues is an important enabler of knowledge transfer, well expressed colloquially in the aphorism: *to promote knowledge transfer, invest first in travel and beer, and second in information technology.* Also important here is to beware the trap of relying on information systems. McDermott describes this as the great trap: 'If a group of people don't already share knowledge, don't already have plenty of contact, don't already understand what insights and information will be useful to each other, information technology is not likely to create it…'[7]

In summary, here's the checklist for you to judge your existing knowledge maturity. Do you:

- explicitly recognize that knowledge is an important asset requiring management focus?

- have a company-wide shared mindset about what sort of knowledge is most important to you?

- have processes in place to routinely create value from knowledge creation and transfer?

In the next section we develop these ideas further by interleaving intangible and traditional firm assets. Later in the chapter we identify the special knowledge characteristics and priorities for the four generic supply chain types introduced in earlier chapters.

THE INTELLECTUAL CAPITAL APPROACH

The traditional view of 'commercial value' emphasizes tangible or financial resources – those typically found on the balance sheet (cash, property, buildings, machinery and equipment).

Turning to your own company, it's very likely that 'value' is better represented by also understanding intangible resources or intellectual capital. In effect, the intellectual capital approach complements the firm's traditional focus on financial capital by also factoring in valuable expertise, know-how, processes and relationships.

Intellectual capital comprises all non-monetary and non-physical resources that are fully or partly controlled by the organization and contribute to value creation.[8] Figure 26.1 summarizes the three categories of intellectual assets described here:

- *organizational* – know-how that has been converted to something tangible. Examples include databases, processes, methodologies, guides and brands and other formal intellectual property;

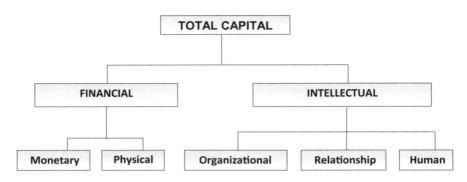

Figure 26.1   The intellectual capital view of company value

- *relationship* – the relationships with customers, supply partners, competitors, research alliances and other stakeholders as well as its market standing and reputation; and

- *human* – the firm's people, their capabilities, expertise and know-how.

The left-hand side of Figure 26.1 is well-known territory. No doubt you have professional teams in your organization who manage, monitor and account for every unit of monetary and physical asset. You track how these assets are acquired by the entity, how they are deployed, and how and when they exit your balance sheet.

In contrast, the intellectual capital component is not so well understood; it is a 'black hole' of strategic analysis.[9] We recognize intuitively that intangibles are important, but their management is problematic. In contrast with financial capital, there is no professional discipline focusing on maximizing the impact and contribution of these assets. Typically, no one in your company stays awake at night wrestling with such questions as: 'What are our key knowledge assets?'; 'Are we combining them to strengthen our competitive position?'; and 'Are we maximizing their use in alignment with our business intent?'

The key challenge in intellectual capital management is transforming intangible assets into something that creates value for the organization. Dynamic capability is the ability to achieve new forms of competitive advantage by appropriately adapting, integrating and reconfiguring intangible assets – organizational skills, resources and competencies.[10]

Putting intangibles and tangibles on the one page offers up new insights about what creates value for your organization. Here's an example: using a traditional lens, we think of customers in terms of the revenue (tangible assets) we earn from them. A knowledge view recognizes that we may also earn *intangible* revenues from our customers.

1. Some customers (capacity-building clients) not only give us revenue, but also build our skills and expertise in ways that set us up to attract new clients. They help us create new human and organizational capital.

2. Some customers (image-building clients) not only give us revenue, but also build our brand or image in the marketplace (if *x* is a client of yours, you must be good!).[11]

Using this perspective, we may choose additional criteria in customer and supplier selection. For example, if 100 per cent of our clients give us dollars but no intangibles, what does this mean for our sustainability?

> *'The intellectual capital component... is a "black hole" of strategic analysis.[9] We recognize intuitively that intangibles are important, but their management is problematic.'*

In summary, understanding intangible assets provides new strategic insights and competitive options for supply chain design and operations. These issues are further developed in the next section.

STRATEGIES TO MANAGE KNOWLEDGE

What's the best way to manage knowledge assets? As you would expect, successful knowledge practices are *aligned* with the firm's strategic intent.

In the late 1990s an influential article by Hansen, Nohria and Tierney in the *Harvard Business Review*[12] suggested that there are two fundamental approaches to knowledge management, with their appropriateness dependent on the firm's business strategy. No doubt you can see that the type of knowledge to be transferred is influential here: we know that explicit knowledge can be readily expressed and transferred and hence is the appropriate focus for a codification strategy. Conversely, tacit knowledge cannot be readily expressed and transferred, and, therefore, a personalization strategy would be appropriate.

The authors contrast firms in the same industries (consulting, health and IT) for which either a personalization or codification strategy may be appropriate. That is, the appropriate knowledge strategy is firm-specific, rather than industry-specific.

Hansen et al.'s article remains highly significant for its emphasis on aligning knowledge strategy with business strategy. We will reshape the concepts slightly to emphasize the types of customers being serviced; this is a foundation for later discussions that will identify knowledge priorities for the four generic supply chains.

Model 1: Operational Excellence.

Do your customers expect highly standardized products and services? Systematic management of reliability, efficiency and timeliness are key features of the operational excellence business driver. Standardization is achieved when the enterprise consistently applies its best practices system-wide. For the customer, there is high consistency and predictability; variation is unwanted. The key performance indicators for Model 1 organizations are items such as consistency, reliability, timeliness and productivity. You will recognize that *lean* supply chains respond directly to operational excellence imperatives.

Turning to the knowledge impact, for organizations whose business model is founded on offering standard products and services, the appropriate knowledge management focus is knowledge re-use. Documenting knowledge (codification) to make it transferable should be the emphasis here. Our aim is to rapidly identify excellent practices, consolidate them into replicable procedures and get them into use.

In intellectual capital terms, converting human capital into organizational capital allows best practices to be applied flawlessly by everyone in the organization. We make the knowledge independent of those who created it and open up the possibility of achieving benefits of scale.

Model 2: Design Excellence

Your clients may have expectations that are quite different from those outlined in the previous section. If your clients come to you for innovative, highly customized products and services, key performance indicators such as innovation, agility, responsiveness and customer intimacy will be significant. The aim is new standards and breakthrough service, rather than consistency. The *fully flexible* supply chain responds directly to this type of driver.

Given the design excellence characteristics, a knowledge re-use model will not be appropriate for these firms. There will be relatively little emphasis on standardization and more focus on creating new knowledge. In intellectual capital terms, fostering human and relationship capital are our key levers for servicing this customer type. We will transform expertise to create service breakthroughs.

Identifying our experts and making it easy for them to connect is a priority. Knowledge will be transferred person-to-person (personalization) and through networks, rather than documented. Benefits flow when the organization encourages, identifies, uses and repurposes value created from its own experience, informal innovation, formal research and development, and emerging customer and stakeholder needs.

GENERIC SUPPLY CHAIN MODELS AND THEIR DISTINCTIVE KNOWLEDGE PRIORITIES

This section builds on the operational excellence and design excellence discussion to propose distinctive knowledge profiles for the four generic supply chain models. Understanding the generic models' unique knowledge personalities allows us to commit resources to high pay-off areas. A clear understanding of *what* knowledge creates commercial value allows us to craft initiatives to support the creation and transfer of knowledge that is most significant to our supply chain (see Figure 26.2).

The starting-point for each model is understanding customers' needs. This provides the basis for deriving distinctive knowledge priorities.

Lean Supply Chains: Rock-solid Core Business

With its unambiguous focus on efficiency and low relationship requirements, the lean supply chain is a pure operational excellence example.

The knowledge metaphor for the lean supply chain is the *Factory*, with its image of consistency, standardization and production focus. In lean supply chains, efforts are focused on four areas:

1. rapid identification of excellent practices;

2. replicating best practices in procedures, guides and methodologies (organizational capital);

3. promoting the consistent take-up and application of organizational capital throughout the supply chain; and

4. focusing on continuous improvement – how can we learn from our experience to get better at what we do every day?

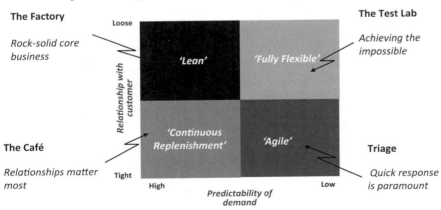

Figure 26.2   The four generic supply chains and their intellectual capital demands

Source: Adapted from John Gattorna, *Living Supply Chains*, FT Prentice Hall, Harlow, 2006.

Fully Flexible: Where Nothing is Impossible

Fully flexible supply chains are, of course, very different. Here, the focus is on solving the unsolvable. The metaphor is the *Test Lab*, where what's possible is continuously challenged. Key points for the Test Lab are as follows:

1. We don't apply the rules, we redefine them.

2. We have a strong focus on external scanning, formal and informal R&D, and creative people.

3. Building knowledge networks, providing access to experts and a high-trust culture will fuel the Test Lab.

4. In combination, this means that organizational capital is relatively less important. Instead, our focus in on human capital and relationship capital (including alliances, research partners and thought-leaders).

> *'We need to build organizational memory... about the customer and their particular requirements. If customer relationships are tied up primarily with particular staff, we risk losing the client if key staff... depart.'*

Continuous Replenishment: Where Relationships Matter Most

Continuous replenishment supply chains have very a predictable demand from known customers. With a focus on customer retention, the appropriate metaphor is the *Café*, denoting a collaborative, high-relationship zone. Key points for the *Café* are as follows:

1. Our knowledge efforts emphasize creating and deploying information and knowledge about the customer's particular requirements.

2. To mitigate risk, we need to build organizational memory (rather than individual knowledge) about the customer and their particular requirements. If customer relationships are tied up primarily with particular staff, we risk losing the client if key staff belonging to either party depart.

3. The challenge is to build the 'trust zone' and a wide and deep relationship between ourselves and the client.

4. Converting relationship capital into organizational capital is the focus in continuous replenishment supply chains.

Agile: Where Quick Response is Paramount

Agile supply chains also have a distinct knowledge personality. With its emphasis on responding instantly to the unforeseen, the knowledge metaphor for the agile supply chain is that of *Triage*.[13] The key connotation is not the 'battlefield' (although it may sometimes feel as though it is) but the rapid diagnosis and identification of priorities as the basis for offering an instantaneous and appropriate response. Key points are as follows:

1. Competitive advantage will be derived from making the fine-grade distinctions in diagnosis that allow well-honed responses to be provided.

2. Agile supply chains need to invest in learning from their experience – specifically, drawing evidence-based conclusions on what works best for *this* type of customer in *this* situation. Robust *lessons learned* processes will be important.

3. The knowledge focus is on developing corporate memory (organizational capital) around diagnosis and response patterns.

ALIGNMENT INSIGHTS

*   *Different customer needs drive particular supply chains, which in turn make distinctively different demands of your body of knowledge.*

*   *Your high-impact knowledge and key knowledge challenges are determined by your particular supply chain model.*

*   *Knowledge management is a critical cultural capability in enterprise supply chain design and operations, and runs across all four generic supply chain models.*

*   *Viewing supply chains through a knowledge lens creates new insights into, and opportunities for, maximizing customer alignment and value.*

NOTES

1   R. Chase, 'Examining Global Knowledge Trends', *Knowledge Management Review*, (January–February 2007), pp. 20–23 at p. 22.

2   Two recent articles have considered knowledge and learning in relation to supplier development: M. Giannakis, 'Facilitating learning and knowledge transfer through supplier development', *Supply Chain Management: An International Journal*, Vol. 13, No. 1 (2008), pp. 62–72; K.J. Mason, and S. Leek, 'Learning to build a supply network: an exploration of dynamic business models', *Journal of Management Studies*, Vol. 45, No. 4 (2008), pp. 774–799.

3   Giannakis, 'Facilitating learning and knowledge transfer', *op. cit.*

4   Defying or surpassing imitation, matchless. In intellectual capital terms, inimitability is the extent to which the strategic asset is resistant to imitation. See, for example, G. Roos, S. Pike and L. Fernstrom, *Managing Intellectual Capital in Practice*, Elsevier/Butterworth-Heinemann, Oxford, 2005.

5   I. Nonaka, 'The knowledge creating company', *Harvard Business Review* (November–December 1991), pp. 96–104.

6   K. Andrews and B. Delahaye, 'Influences on knowledge processes in organisational learning: the psychosocial filter', *Journal of Management Studies*, Vol. 37, No. 6 (2000), pp. 797–810.

7   R. McDermott, 'Why information technology inspired but cannot deliver knowledge management', in E.L. Lesser, M.A. Fontaine and J.A. Slusher (eds), *Knowledge and Communities*, Butterworth Heinemann, Boston, 2000, pp. 21–35.

8   Adapted from Roos, Pike and Fernstrom, *Managing Intellectual Capital in Practice, op. cit.*

9   J.C. Spender and R.M. Grant, 'Knowledge and the firm: overview', *Strategic Management Journal*, Vol. 17, Special Issue (Winter 1996), pp. 5–9.

10   Roos, Pike, and Fernstrom, *Managing Intellectual Capital in Practice, op. cit.*

11   See K.E. Sveiby, *The New Organizational Wealth: Managing and Measuring Knowledge-based Assets*, Berret Koehler Inc., San Francisco, 1997.

12   M.T. Hansen, N. Nohria and T. Tierney, 'What's your strategy for managing knowledge?', *Harvard Business Review* (March–April 1999), pp. 106–116.

13   Triage: the determination of priorities for action in an emergency.

27 China and India: The Future Giants of Supply Chain Developments in the Twenty-first Century

Paul W. Bradley

As the new century unfolds, it is clear that future supply chain developments will be led from Asia. This is a dramatic difference from the last few decades when the USA and Europe were defining almost all the trends, innovative processes and cutting-edge technologies. The rapid expansion of China as the world's leading manufacturing centre and Asia's growing consumer market power has created historical shifts in economic development and consequent changes in supply chain networks. The rise of India as a new economic powerhouse will further propel these changes and, at the same time, introduce new models in the supply chain by combining innovative technologies and virtual networks to meet the country's growing consumer demand. If properly leveraged, the complex challenges presented by the Indian market today can create unique opportunities for the future. As a direct consequence of this new environment, dynamic supply chain networks will become a core competitive advantage for the leading companies across Asia.

LOGISTICS' HISTORICAL TRANSFORMATION

The concept of logistics evolved as a vital military tool and played a hidden role in the success of many military campaigns. From Genghis Khan to Alexander the Great, ancient history witnessed the movement of armies across massive land masses and effective distribution channels of food, materials and other critical supplies were essential to success on the battlefield. The weaknesses of Napoleon's supply chain in the Russian campaigns was repeated a century later by Hitler in the Second World War with similar disastrous results. In contrast, perhaps the best recent example of how logistics has redefined itself in a military environment is the first Gulf War when forward-staging of food, water and military supplies were positioned in the middle of the desert in a matter of weeks to support over 500,000 troops. The power of military logistics as a hidden tactical advantage is equally relevant in the global business world where dynamic movement of products comprising components sourced from multiple countries needs to reach the individual consumer. Today, global supply chain architecture creates the invisible tools that control the arteries of international commerce.

THE EVOLUTION OF LOGISTICS TO DEMAND CHAIN

There are many stages in the evolution of logistics, but most companies are still at the very foundation of development. By simple definition, logistics is the process of efficiently moving product between two points. The art of logistics, with its core components of warehousing, drayage, freight forwarding, customs clearance, and ocean and air transport, is the specific technical skill in effectively coordinating the movement of physical product between a specific origin and destination point, while simultaneously executing the entire shipping process within given time constraints. Total logistics companies are currently working to transcend their role in the logistics process to a more proactive integrative approach: linking technology and infrastructure to their core shipping services, providing them with better control of shipments and closer interaction with their customers.

'The supply chain manager plays a more neutral and transparent role as the lead "orchestrator", coordinating all activities across the entire chain, while outsourcing to other service providers as necessary.'

However, supply chain management evolves to a different definition in which the entire chain is creatively connected and optimized, linking the raw materials feeding the manufacturing plant, assessing minimum-order quantity planning, reviewing forecast accuracy, and potentially utilizing hubs and sub-hubs which, when properly implemented, will ultimately feed product to meet consumer demand and prevent lost sales opportunities.

By definition, the supply chain manager plays a more neutral and transparent role as the lead 'orchestrator', coordinating all activities across the entire chain, while outsourcing to other service providers as necessary to maximize efficiency and cost savings.

Demand chain management, if well executed, flips the model further by utilizing dynamic networks across the chain to rapidly fulfil consumer demand at the store shelf level with automatic replenishment, and without being constrained by the manufacturing plants Minimum-Order Quantities (MOQs). Innovative technology becomes a critical factor for success, and the use of hubs, sub-hubs and 'virtual infrastructure' further facilitates efficiency and competitive advantage.

SUPPLY CHAIN TRANSFERENCE FROM THE WEST TO ASIA

In the last century the USA and Europe have led the development of supply chain centers of excellence; this was due to leading edge technologies, state-of-the-art infrastructure and a highly sophisticated consumer market. As we move into the twenty-first century, Asia will assume a wider leadership role in developing and implementing new supply chain solutions and will ultimately contribute towards the design of new business models. This shift will continue to grow, based on several fundamental economic changes.

- In the coming decades, the Asian consumer market will grow to become much larger than the combined consumer markets of the USA and Europe. The best-practice supply chain solutions of the West will be transferred to Asia, while new supply chain solutions unique to Asia will also be developed locally and successfully deployed.

- Investment in new logistics infrastructure in the West has been in steady decline for some time. Logistics facilities are starting to age, and funding for upgrades is limited. At the same time, Asia has been aggressively investing in new infrastructure, and many of the newest and most modern airport and ocean port facilities are now located in this region. This trend will continue and in fact accelerate further, allowing Asia to more creatively leverage its infrastructure and ideas to develop new supply chain models.

- Intra-Asia trade volume will continue to dramatically expand.

- Many of the world's most modern manufacturing plants are now located in China and Southeast Asia.

- Technology, especially software development and business process outsourcing, are being driven from India.

The combination of these events will lead to Asia becoming the centre of excellence for new innovative supply chain solutions, especially when combining the force of global manufacturing, innovative technologies, new infrastructure and a rising consumer market.

THE EVOLUTION OF MANUFACTURING FACILITIES TO VIRTUAL MANUFACTURING

These unique evolutionary events shaping logistics practices are also tied to the recent transformation in manufacturing as depicted in Figure 27.1.

Originally, manufacturing facilities were located near the consumer target market or in the country of demand for that product. Eventually, manufacturing centres of excellence developed where, as an example, a plant in Indonesia might produce soaps for all of Asia and a plant in the Philippines might produce toothpaste for Asia. These centres of excellence now feed the entire region, specifically because the sophistication of the logistics model allows the product to move rapidly from a central production point. However, as regional SCM hubbing and sub-hubbing continues to evolve (with Singapore being the ideal model), product can now be moved through a dynamic supply

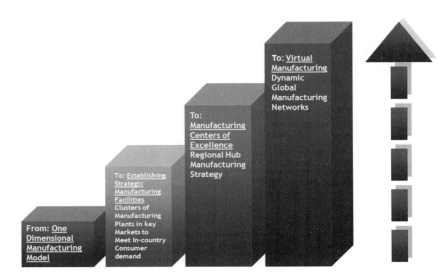

Figure 27.1   Global manufacturing's evolutionary path

chain network with single product visibility across the entire chain. This creates the potential to create 'virtual manufacturing' through dynamic supply chain networks. Thus, the consumer product company can focus on product design, testing and marketing while leveraging non-owned manufacturing plants to produce their product with hubs and sub-hubs strategically located across the globe to rapidly move product in response to changing consumer demand. This trend dramatically broadens the frontier of how the supply chain model can be exploited for unique competitive advantage.

The Rise of China (East meets West): Li & Fung Defines a New Global Supply Chain Model

As China emerges as the largest manufacturing centre in the world, Hong Kong, as the Special Administrative Region of China, has played an increasingly important role in bridging the link between China and the West. As the largest Hong Kong-based multilateral trading company, Li & Fung has simultaneously risen as a creator of radical new supply chain business models combining cutting-edge logistics processes with 'dispersed' (virtual) manufacturing.

Since the reform era of Deng Xiao Ping, China has encouraged direct foreign investment, constructed new production plants based on the newest production technologies, and matched this with highly talented and cost-efficient Chinese labour. China focused its exports on the mature US and European consumer markets which, in return, created revenue to cover fixed costs and, over time, contributed to rising profits and the largest national trade surplus in history. As the standard of living dramatically improves, China can now focus the same manufacturing assets to meet the growing needs of its own consumers and the wider Asia consumer market as well. Since the global consumer has primarily contributed to fixed costs, the domestic market can be supplied by variable costs, resulting in significantly lower costs for the Chinese consumer while creating a potential market entry barrier to foreign manufactured products. With the Chinese consumer retail market expected to overtake that of the USA within the next 10–15 years, this will become a dramatic achievement, which will also have a profound impact on the global economy.

Evolving from within this historic Chinese environment, the Li & Fung Group has been recognized in various forums as one of the leading global supply chain companies. The company is a hybrid entity, combining three generations of history as a Chinese trading company with a uniquely global culture as an innovative thought-leader. Li & Fung started out in 1937 as a Chinese trading company in Canton, then moved to Hong Kong and eventually began a rapid transformation in the 1970s under the leadership of Dr Victor Fung and his brother William. Victor, a former professor at Harvard Business School, had a vision to change the family business by leveraging the best ideas from the West and the East. Today, the Li & Fung Group has an annual revenue over US$14 billion, with business entities spanning more than 10,000 'virtual manufacturing plants' which feed both US and European consumers. The Li & Fung Group also owns international retail franchises in Asia and a logistics distribution entity designed to feed products to the rising Asian consumers. Many of the top universities, including Harvard, have written case studies on the Li & Fung model.

Today Li & Fung is one of the largest trading companies of consumer products, yet it does not own any assets and is neutral in this space. The company has built dynamic supply chain networks spanning more than 10,000 independent production plants by aggregating the capacity and capability of each facility. Li & Fung has separate divisions of experts in product design (working collaboratively with their customers), product sourcing and logistics. They even aggregate the purchase of raw material, feed it to predesignated plants, determine the quality specifications and can thereby deliver the same product from completely unrelated manufacturing facilities spanning more than 40 countries. Today, Li & Fung produces product for many Fortune 500 companies, playing the role of global orchestrator across the entire supply chain.

In one example, Li & Fung was sourcing shirts in Asia for several leading brands. When the West Coast strike occurred in the USA several years ago, before the Christmas holiday season, Li & Fung simply shifted the raw materials to predesignated facilities in Central America, bringing the product into the US East Coast in time for Christmas sales. The American consumer was unaware that the production process had shifted across the world in a matter of weeks. When the West Coast strike ended, production shifted back to Asia because of its more competitive costs. This creative use of a dynamic supply chain network was flawlessly executed and is often repeated across many commodities in response to changing labour costs, currency fluctuations, political risks and the determination of optimal production facilities. Today Li & Fung sources product from more than 40 nations. Whilst China is still the largest production centre, the Li & Fung model will continuously shift and adapt according to what is determined to be the most optimal production point for a specific product at that specific time.

Another entity in the Li & Fung Group, the IDS Group, created 'regional SCM hubbing' solutions for Fortune 500 companies through its facilities in China, Hong Kong and Singapore. One leading consumer company was sourcing product destined for the Asian consumer market from Europe with a long lead-time. Its competitors sourced similar product in Asia. The challenge was that each country had to purchase a small quantity of different SKUs of product, but the minimum-order quantity was much higher than their domestic market need. This meant that some countries had to hold potentially more than six to eight months of product, also entailing an immediate impact on cash flow from duty payments and storage costs because of the minimum-order quantity and lead-time requirements mandated from the European plant. Different types of SKUs were trapped in different countries, resulting in potential lost sales as well. The solution was to establish a regional SCM hub in Singapore. IDS played the role of neutral orchestrator on behalf of the company. Each country placed its orders based on actual demand; then IDS aggregated the orders and converted them into a single super-order exceeding the minimum-order quantity of the plant in Europe. In essence, Asia became one single sourcing point, which allowed the plant to optimize production runs and each country to pull product on a just-in-time basis matched against actual sales demand. Product moving on the water from Europe to the hub was tracked down to the carton and piece level, creating a 'floating warehouse concept'. The regional SCM hub made all products in Singapore visible to each country on a real-time basis, proactively shipping product by SKU in the required quantity. Repackaging and relabelling could rapidly adapt individual product to the specific market and language required, including promotion kits linked to specific sales campaigns. Singapore became the 'virtual factory', feeding product to each market as needed in the exact form and quantity based on each particular market's demand. Lead-time to market was drastically reduced, and customer sales surged as a result. The same model was then extended to other Fortune 500 companies and is still today expanding in scope and impact.

The Li & Fung Group provides many unique examples where the concept of 'virtual manufacturing' and 'regional SCM hubbing' have been launched, refined and, ultimately, creatively leveraged to provide powerful competitive advantages for themselves as dynamic service providers and, most importantly, to deliver benefit to their global customers and the individual consumer.

The Rise of India: Arshiya International Launches a New Value Chain Model Leveraging a Network of FTWZ Hubs

The transformation of another economic superpower is just commencing; and India is now adapting by creating new business models of its own, intentionally fusing global best practices with unique knowledge of the local market. One leading example, Arshiya International, was created in the past few years to build a new business model for India that could rapidly adapt to the changing economic environment by developing a multidimensional business structure providing different entry points to its customers through distinctly separate business entities under a 'value chain umbrella' of services (see Figure 27.2).

| Global Integrated Supply Chain Technology | 3PL Logistics Network | Neutral 4PL Supply/Demand Chain Solutions | Infrastructure FTWZ Regional Hubs & Sub Hubs | Rail Infrastructure Network | Other Value Added Services | Knowledge Center |

Figure 27.2   Integrated value chain

Source: Arshiya International Ltd.

These services are ultimately integrated through a common IT platform. This visionary company was created by Ajay Mittal, a member of one of India's leading business families. Arshiya, through a combination of acquisitions, joint ventures and start-up companies, is building an 'Indian value chain network'. Constituent entities include: global freight forwarding and 3PL logistics companies connected to major countries throughout the world; supply chain and demand chain management services through a separate 4PL entity; a fully-owned IT company with a fully integrated web-enabled SCM software platform; logistics infrastructure, which is creating a network of massive FTWZ (free trade warehousing zone) logistics parks across India; a national railroad service (the company having recently acquired one of the special national rail licences); and additional entities currently being planned to further extend the breadth of the value network to its growing customer base.

THE INDIAN ENVIRONMENT

Over the past few years, India has launched its break-out to connect to the world as a rising economic superpower of the future. The transformation is already evident. Foreign direct investment in FY2007-08 has risen to over US$24.5 billion, and economic growth for the fiscal year 2007–08 reached 9 per cent – among the highest in the world. Entrepreneurial leadership is also evident. According to *Forbes Magazine*, India has 20 billionaires compared to 15 billionaires in mainland China (excluding Hong Kong).

'The organized retail market in India is currently estimated to represent around 2–3 per cent of consumer spending... Within the next ten years, according to the latest projections, organized retail is anticipated to climb to more than 20 per cent of domestic retail consumption.'

Although the current logistics infrastructure remains a key barrier to efficiency, the rise of the Indian consumer is placing enormous pressure on the government and private markets to move faster to meet accelerating demands, and to ultimately obtain the economic benefits that will result. According to recent studies, the organized retail market in India is currently estimated to represent around 2–3 per cent of consumer spending, with the majority of purchases still conducted through small, niche, owner-operated shops. Within the next ten years, according to the latest projections, organized retail is anticipated to climb to more than 20 per cent of domestic retail consumption, potentially making India the third largest retail market in the world after China and the USA. In order to reach its full potential, India must launch a bold logistics strategy. With the world's largest youth population, India is uniquely positioned to convert investment in logistics infrastructure into dynamic economic growth.

Whereas China's competitive advantage has been manufacturing, India's advantage is technology. In a sense, China has been building highways while India has been building 'virtual highways'. India should now utilize its unique technological advantage to create entirely new models of dynamic supply chain networks to break through existing barriers and ensure sustained economic growth. The government has recently committed to new investments in ports, airports and highways, and this is creating an environment of future opportunity, but new strategies also need to rapidly evolve to meet rising consumer expectations.

TACTICAL VERSUS STRATEGIC ASSETS

While traditional logistics companies in India build warehouse facilities to meet rising consumer demand, Arshiya (a new publicly listed company) has opted for a strategy of differentiation. In addition to its 3PL logistics business, Arshiya has created a distinctly new 4PL company through a joint venture with a leading US logistics company. Through this new business entity, Arshiya is gaining entry to Indian retailers by providing full mapping and redesign of customer's logistics processes. Thereafter, it is envisioned that its consulting team will insert themselves into the customer's organizational structures as a neutral coordinator for the full scope of supply chain activities, playing the role of lead orchestrating manager for all entities touching the customer's supply chains. This allows the team to analyse existing processes and design solutions, and be responsible for executing the operations within an open book style of commercial arrangement plus a management fee and gain-sharing. Since Arshiya also has its own IT company and software (Cyberlog), the 4PL entity can absorb warehouse facilities across India without owning any of these tactical assets, but can control them with its own fully integrated software and with its own managers on-site. This means that the company can provide a wide range of warehouse options across India, with full product visibility, direct control of the operating processes and standardized KPIs, all without any asset ownership (see Figure 27.3).

Arshiya can therefore provide rapidly adaptable solutions to its customers as the business environment changes, without being constrained or biased by

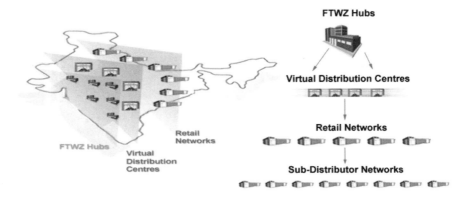

Figure 27.3   Retail distribution

Source: Arshiya International Ltd.

traditional logistics infrastructure. This is the first stage in creating a dynamic supply chain network for India; Arshiya has already begun creating initial case studies for distributing product across the country for several Indian retailers through a virtual warehouse network and plans to extend the same model to eventually encompass other commodities and industries.

While small and mid-sized warehouse assets can be viewed as 'tactical assets' because their value will change constantly as roads and zoning regulations shift, retail markets disburse and product distribution points change, 'strategic assets', in contrast, have long-term value as part of a permanent architecture in the supply chain network and can provide a unique role in value creation, both immediate and long-term. Following this logic, it is optimal to control, but not own 'virtual assets', but to own and directly control 'strategic assets', such as FTWZ supply chain hubs.

FTWZ HUBBING

In addition to leveraging the unique power of controlling virtual warehousing networks across India, Arshiya is gaining early-mover advantage by launching a new strategy for FTWZ hubbing (see Figure 27.4).

Through new government regulations, FTWZ (free trade warehousing zones) can be created in specific cases if large tracts of land can be purchased in specially identified locations within the country, and if they can meet very high standards and legal requirements. Within this context, Arshiya has designed a strategy to create massive FTWZ logistics parks (estimated between 100 and 200 acres or more) and will potentially place at least five of these FTWZ facilities in optimal locations dispersed across India, creating regional super-hubs for product distribution across each region. This will also provide the potential for just-in-time inventory-holding and dynamic product distribution across the expanding retail networks within the country. This is in stark contrast to the current highly inefficient operating environment where huge inventories are stored in small warehouses scattered in different states, without product visibility and standardized processes.

In addition to the dynamic product dispersion benefits, major tax incentives can potentially be derived by companies for products within the FTWZ, providing multiple financial benefits for both products that feed domestic consumption and products that are exported to overseas markets. Within each facility, product can move through value-enhancement processes, such as repackaging, relabelling, kitting activities and so on. In addition to planning its own buildings within the FTWZ hubs, Arshiya intends to allow key customers to build customized facilities and will also develop potential partnerships with major global shipping lines linked through the CY and CFS facilities. Each planned facility will be located close to major ocean ports and airport facilities, and all of the FTWZ facilities will be linked through a

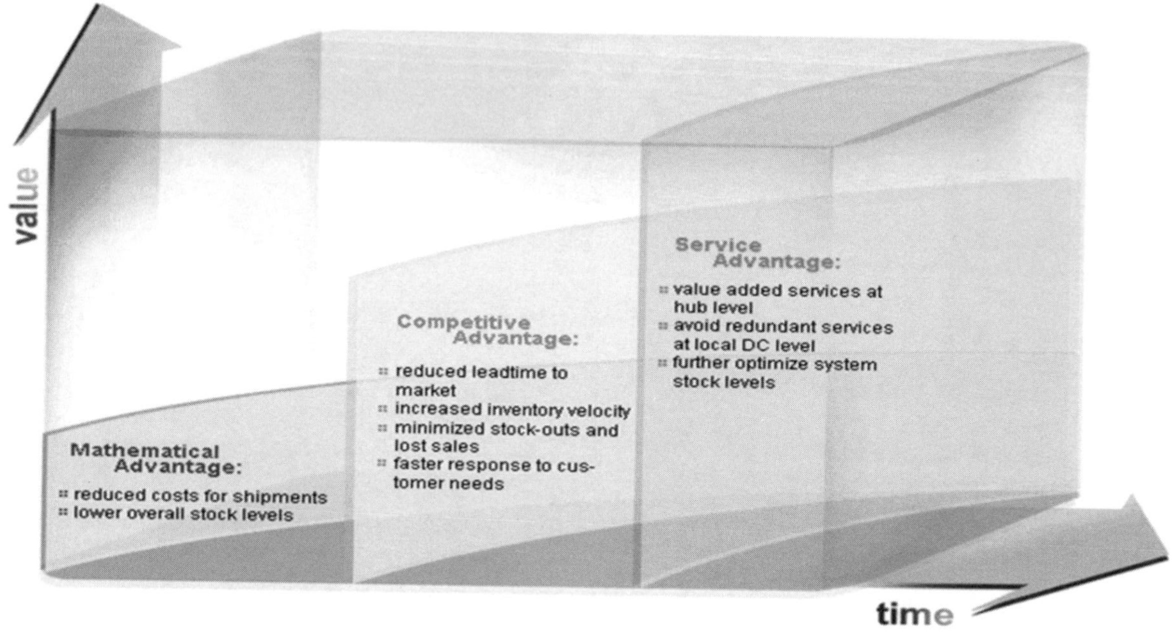
value
time
Mathematical Advantage:
reduced costs for shipments
lower overall stock levels
Competitive Advantage:
reduced leadtime to market
increased inventory velocity
minimized stock-outs and lost sales
faster response to customer needs
Service Advantage:
value added services at hub level
avoid redundant services at local DC level
further optimize system stock levels

Source: Paul W. Bradley, All Rights Reserved.

Figure 27.4 Impact of regional SCM hubbing

national rail network in the future, allowing product to shift rapidly across India and between the strategically located FTWZ facilities (see Figure 27.5).

These facilities are also anticipated to have their own support infrastructure, such as power plants, within the compound. The FTWZ facilities near port locations, such as (JNPT), will also serve as hubs for product distribution not only within India, but also to the Middle East and the Indian subcontinent region as well. In fact, Arshiya is planning extended investments in the Middle East, especially the Gulf region, to extend the adjacency benefits of the hubbing model.

Arshiya has already acquired land in a number of key areas within India, including land near the JNPT port facility in Mumbai. It has also placed orders for dedicated trains and supporting equipment linked through its national rail licence to operate its own trains across the country in dedicated corridors. Overall, Arshiya is anticipated to spend more than several billion dollars in long-term FTWZ and rail infrastructure investments. Through this strategy, Arshiya will own strategic assets, such as value chain hubs and sub-hubs within the country, connected to non-asset-based 'virtual warehouses' at the lower level to act as cross-docking touch points if needed, depending on each customer's specific requirements.

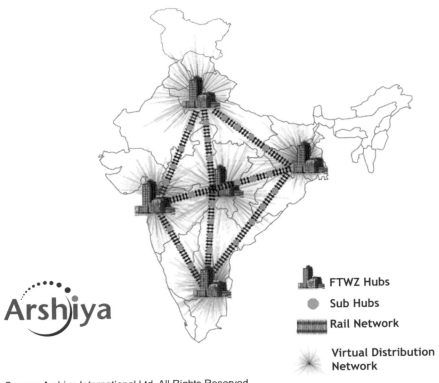

Source: Arshiya International Ltd, All Rights Reserved.

Figure 27.5   Arshiya's project diamond

VALUE-CHAIN UMBRELLA ARCHITECTURE

Arshiya International is creating a unique supply chain model for the future in which a customer can enter through any of its core business entities, such as freight forwarding for air, sea and project logistics; IT supply chain software; or even neutral 4PL supply chain management services. However, the strategic assets, such as FTWZ hubs, sub-hubs ,and rail infrastructure, will be owned and operated, and the lower-value tactical warehouse assets will be 'virtualized'. Ultimately, all distinct entities within the Arshiya umbrella will be connected through one integrated Cyberlog IT platform, with no traditional software restrictions. Despite the many infrastructure and logistics obstacles currently in India, Arshiya is creating an entirely new supply chain model for disbursed logistics architecture through its value-chain umbrella concept. In essence, Arshiya can control the entire supply–demand chain transparently for its customers, while creating a dynamic supply chain network that can continuously adapt to changing market conditions.

SINGAPORE AS THE VIRTUAL COORDINATION CENTRE FOR THE 'REVERSE L'

Since its independence, Singapore has been a leading country in terms of creative innovation and thought leadership. As China and India both rise as global economic powers, Singapore has uniquely positioned itself as the virtual enhancement center of Asia, connecting to both China and India, and integrating the ASEAN region as the 'reverse L' integrator on the map of Asia (see Figure 27.6).

Singapore has already achieved status as one of the major banking and financial centres in the region and currently operates the largest port in the world – the birthplace of regional hubbing. It is also a preferred location for many multinational companies' Asian regional headquarters. Combining its leading role as an ocean and air hub with its link to global companies and quick access to financial capital, Singapore has positioned itself as a centre for assisting the development of China and rise of India by providing multidimensional support as an island of thought-leadership connected to both Asian economic powers, plus the USA, Europe and Japan. The government has led the way in defining new models of regional hubbing and value-creation centres, as well as providing funding support for innovative technology development. One recent example is the Singapore Trade Exchange, an Internet portal through which product can be sourced, financed, shipped and tracked worldwide, linked to leading financial institutions, freight forwarders, shipping lines and air carriers. These are just some of the ways in which Singapore has creatively adapted as a nation to enhance the speed of development in China and India as a supporting centre of innovation connected to both rising economic powers.

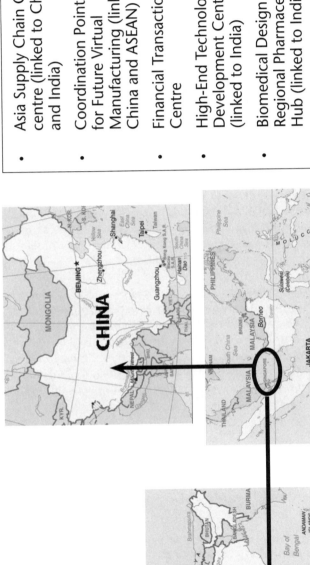

- Asia Supply Chain Control centre (linked to China and India)

- Coordination Point for Future Virtual Manufacturing (linked to China and ASEAN)

- Financial Transaction Centre

- High-End Technology Development Centre (linked to India)

- Biomedical Design & Regional Pharmaceutical Hub (linked to India)

CHINA

ASEAN

INDIA

Figure 27.6 **Singapore as a pivot point leveraging the 'reverse L' for strategic advantage**

ASIA'S DYNAMIC SUPPLY CHAIN MODELS OF THE FUTURE

The supply chain market continues to evolve in terms of technology and innovative concepts. China's dominant position in global manufacturing has created new concepts for dynamic manufacturing centres of excellence in which global brands can leverage the power of 'virtual manufacturing networks', converting fixed costs into variable costs and aggregating competing volumes through shared infrastructure.

India's leading role in technology development, combined with logistics infrastructure challenges, will provide the impetus for new models in virtual logistics networks to be created, including the value chain umbrella and FTWZ hubbing, while simultaneously enabling more rapid implementation of supply chain solutions.

In an age of knowledge empowerment, each market can learn from the mistakes and successes of other countries and regions, while also defining new concepts for the future. As China continues its growth momentum and India begins an exciting new phase as a rising economic power, they can merge the best practices of the world with new concepts and technology unique to their own environment, creating unlimited possibilities.

In summary, leading Asian supply chain companies view the obstacles confronting their business environment today as exciting opportunities, which can be creatively exploited to create competitive advantage. Ultimately, when human talent is unleashed, supported by a passion for knowledge and innovative technology, new possibilities will be defined. China and India are now beginning that journey! The twenty-first century will look to Asia as the transformation point for new and exciting dynamic supply chain business models to define the future.

ALIGNMENT INSIGHTS

- *Li & Fung's unique business model of virtual manufacturing and integrated global supply chain networks connecting sourcing points from more than 40 countries and feeding the world's retailers in a seamless delivery mode is perhaps the best example of constructing dynamic supply chain networks. The IDS logistics model targets a unique niche with 'regional SCM hubbing' utilizing Singapore and China as connecting points to feed the Asian consumer. Through its various entities, the Li & Fung Group continues to refine and adapt the way in which product can feed complex consumer networks.*

- *Arshiya International is starting to create a new model specifically for India. Its vision of building regional FTWZ hubs in key strategic areas of India, in close proximity to key ocean and airport facilities, and ultimately to be linked with a national rail network, will, once completed, dramatically change the way product feeds into and out of India just as the Indian consumer market begins significant expansion in the coming decade. This is another example of planning to create a dynamic supply chain network in a rising new economy market with significant room for manoeuvre to shift product flow within the Indian subcontinent as this market and business model further evolve.*

- *Singapore, as a visionary country, has creatively adapted to the realities of the changing Asian market and rising powers of China and India, but has created a unique niche as the 'Reverse L' connecting the two major economic powers and ASEAN markets with the global markets of the USA and Europe as well. As one of the largest centres of regional corporate headquarters, the largest port in Asia, a leading global financial centre and a driver of new creative ideas, such as the Trade Exchange and knowledge centres for logistics, Singapore is ultimately playing a unique role as a connection centre for dynamic supply chains across Asia.*

- *The combination of China and India as rising economic and consumer markets and the visionary adaptation of countries like Singapore will further enhance the evolution of dynamic supply chain networks in the twenty-first century.*

28 The Supply Chains of 2030

John Gattorna and Deborah Ellis

Where a calculator on the ENIAC is equipped with 18,000 vacuum tubes and weighs 30 tons, computers in the future may have only 1,000 vacuum tubes and perhaps weigh 1.5 tons.[1]

This book has explored many aspects of the current state of play of enterprise supply chains and the opportunities emerging to improve the effectiveness of their operations. It often helps to gain perspective on these opportunities and on the present paradigm by looking further ahead – to a future beyond the edge of our usual planning horizon. So let us speculate on what the supply chains of 2030 might look like.

The most logical way to project forward is by considering the forces that will shape supply chain configurations in the next two decades. These 'forces of change' can be categorized under three headings as follows, and are depicted diagrammatically in Figure 28.1:

1. **Changes emanating from the operating environment**. These are the factors in the local, regional and global economy, society, government and the natural environment, which could potentially impact on operations.

2. **The continuing development of enablers**. The changes to information availability and management have been critical to the development of enterprise supply chains over the last two decades. The indication is that the progression of systems capability will continue at an exponential rate going forward, and this progression will be a key driver in the advancement of supply and logistics operations.

3. **The evolution of logistics/supply chain understanding and associated models**. Over the last 25 years industry has developed a more sophisticated appreciation of the role and potential of supply chains and logistics systems. A much wider view has emerged, as indicated by the shifting everyday terminology: from distribution

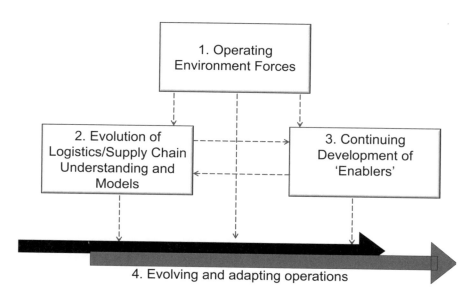

Figure 28.1   Supply chain evolution – influences

management to logistics management to supply chain management and now with increasing use of even broader terms, such as demand chain and value chain management.[2] In any event, call it what you will, the next phases of this evolution will shape any operation that emerges over the next 20–25 years, just as the models will themselves be shaped by the changing environment and the progression of technological capability.

THE OPERATING ENVIRONMENT

By 2030 environmental considerations will be completely integrated into the organizational mindset. Strategic planning and capital decision-making will automatically factor in the cost of carbon, and the reporting structure will monitor and report emissions in established and audited formats. Significant resources will have been deployed to dramatically reduce the impact of the major emitting areas of power and fuel. In the period leading up to 2030 the businesses producing high levels of greenhouse gas that have not taken significant action to minimize their impact will have disappeared, either under the weight of the cost of carbon passed on via government-legislated schemes, or because of the impact on share price from sustained attacks by consumers and investment houses.

The most apparent impact on the supply chain when carbon emissions are integrated into decision-making is that of the network of facilities that support manufacturing and distribution. Although sourcing across borders and centralization of distribution facilities will still exist, any 'before' and 'after' snapshot of the network to support a given level of sales is likely to see higher proportions of localized sourcing, more postponement and more consolidation as the impact of the additional 'real' costs of freight are factored into the pipeline.

'In the period leading up to 2030 the businesses producing high levels of greenhouse gas that have not taken significant action to minimize their impact will have disappeared.'

Freight evaluations will also inevitably lead to a reassessment of rail and sea transportation because of their carbon efficiency relative to road. In countries such as Australia, with long distances between major population centres, the changing economics of freight should, by 2030, have driven a dramatically improved network of rail links and more sophisticated interchanges between rail and road at major nodes.

Delivery formats will also have evolved, with the consolidation of deliveries into CBD areas to minimize both emissions and time lost due to congestion. Night deliveries will be the 'norm' rather than the exception, even though there is a social cost offsetting the natural efficiency gains of this arrangement.

The other notable change to supply chain networks will be the increase in the levels of materials flowing back (reverse logistics). This will be driven by two forces. First, manufacturers will be expected to take on a *life-cycle responsibility* for the products they produce, and in many countries this will, by 2030, be embedded in various pieces of legislation similar to those currently in place in Japan and some European countries. Established channels (many in business-model formats that hardly exist today) will optimize the end-of-life consumer durable products through 're-use, recycling and disposal' options. The attractiveness of re-using materials will also have been significantly enhanced by the cost of carbon associated with smelting, refining and forming from original materials. The concept of a broad-brush building demolition, for example, is even now beginning to be replaced by a retrieval of major inputs including concrete, glass, steel and timber with the advent of new forms of reprocessing into materials for next-generation projects.

Second, *oil volatility* will continue to be a major force in the changing face of logistics. Even many of the more pessimistic forecasters suggest that 'peak oil' will have occurred by 2030, and as demand in China and India grows and supply tightens the price will inevitably increase exponentially. The supply and price impacts will eventually drive the development of alternative fuels, but in the first decade there are no indicators to give confidence that this will have been achieved to a fully commercial level by the third decade. We must assume therefore that, combined with some form of levy on emissions the rising cost of oil will have created significant pressure to minimize transport miles, improve capacity utilization, and shift the preferred transport mode towards rail and sea.

China and India's economic development will continue to change the *patterns of trade* across the world. As China's wage levels and experience increases, it will move along the industrial upgrading path that Japan and Taiwan have forged before it, producing more sophisticated value-added products and leveraging its expertise in new sectors, while supporting larger middle classes. By 2030 the next generation of low-cost producers (such as Vietnam and Sri Lanka) will be well established and starting to generate their own higher levels of domestic demand. The flows that, early in the century, were predominantly *out* of Asia appear destined to be much more interwoven by 2030 with the rebalancing of trade and the influence of the localization forces of emissions and transport cost, creating much more complex flows which will capture optimal combinations of cost and capabilities.

The global financial crisis of 2008 that abruptly ended the long period of sustained growth changed many of the assumptions that supply chains had been built on, in particular global sourcing. Failure of the global financial system also has implications for the smooth operation of supply chains at best, and the disappearance of major firms at worst, for credit and cash flow reasons. For instance, if General Motors disappeared from the automotive industry, consider what havoc this would play on the established supply chain network in that industry. The potential for future disruptions in supply chains has increased exponentially due to this latest crisis,[3] and firms would do well to spend a lot more time developing risk management regimes in the years to come. However, this crisis also brings with it new opportunities for financial institutions to more deeply embed themselves in enterprise supply chains through innovative trade financing and off-balance-sheet financing of inventories – all designed to make supply chains more cost-effective.

THE CONTINUING DEVELOPMENT OF SUPPLY CHAIN ENABLERS

The internet has fundamentally enabled the connective concept of supply chain management to move towards reality over the past two decades and it appears set to underpin the next generation of developments. The interconnection within and between geographically dispersed operations and between organizations will evolve to new levels.

The key partners in stable supply chains will have *real-time visibility* of the key information they rely on, across organizational boundaries – from sales off-take downstream to production schedules, inventory holdings and dispatch delays with upstream partners. Sophisticated 'Chinese walls' will be used to enable sharing of the relevant data while protecting more sensitive data. Many decisions, such as sourcing decisions and ordering from suppliers, will become automatic responses to a pre-prescribed set of rules using data from both ordering and supplying organizations. The shift from forecast-driven supply to demand-driven supply will continue, but improved IT capability will allow a much smoother and quicker response, with less need for human intervention.

Greatly improved *tracking and remote management capability* will eventually result from the widespread utilization of RFID, Smart containers and GPS (although each of these formats has considerable refinement and cost barriers to address before they can fully support global supply chains). By 2030 the capacity of these sensor telemetry tools will extend beyond collecting information on the progress of goods in transit and the performance of equipment, and will include two-way communication to pre-empt and respond to problems.

Whereas ERP systems have enabled organizations to develop standardized operations and exchange data, and move transactions readily across sites and countries, they have also become a straitjacket for the development of contemporary supply chains. They are built around functional modules which tend to reinforce the silos that usually lead to sub-optimal supply chain performance, and both ERP systems and specialist packaged software tend to result in the operation adapting to fit the technology. This conformance can minimize the ability of organizations to compete through business processes.

> *'The global financial crisis of 2008 that abruptly ended the long period of sustained growth changed many of the assumptions that supply chains had been built on, in particular global sourcing.'*

The next generation of system developments, based around *Service-Oriented Architecture (SOA)* and *web services*, holds promise for much more innovation and flexibility in the way software supports business processes. SOA structures large applications as a collection of smaller modules put together in a 'mix and match' format to more closely reflect the specific needs of the business. The concept of *business content libraries* of workflows and solutions that incorporate best practice processes usually accompanies any discussion of SOA.

These developments suggest a future in which software is much more tailored to an organization or a group of collaborating organizations, and a situation where both business processes and the supporting technology can more quickly adapt to new opportunities and changes in the market.

Beyond the technology gains, a picture is also painted of a much more resilient supply chain *knowledge management capability* by 2030. The process becomes a basic and interchangeable unit of management. The technology company i2 captures best-practice workflows in its business content library.[4] Workflows are presented in a graphical form similar to a Visio or PowerPoint flowchart. Embedded within the flowchart graphic is the logic that supports the execution of the workflow. This more intuitive approach to managing systems opens the door for the human and system components of business processes to be captured and maintained together in a more cohesive and durable format.

The consideration of enablers would not be complete without recognizing that, by 2030, our supply chains will be more intelligent! With increasing computing power, the optimization engines that until the early 2000s could feasibly only support strategic and tactical decisions using 'offline' historic data sets, will be used in real time for most everyday complex operational trade-offs, such as scheduling, expediting, pick sequencing and transport routing. More sophisticated analytics and layers of decision support (including simulation models, optimization models and even alternative reality games) will be used by planning groups directing fluid networks that weekly or monthly optimize the global sourcing and distribution patterns that are now reviewed annually at best.

MATURING OF THE SUPPLY CHAIN BUSINESS MODEL

Many commentators look to a future of *demand-driven supply chains*, in which close collaborative relationships between trading partners allow the true demand signals (sales) to be captured and automatically transmitted upstream to supplying organizations that respond quickly with appropriate stock fulfillment. While this vision of less reliance on forecasting and inventory buffers against forecast error is part of the story, it cannot be the complete picture. A mature version of market-responsive supply chains recognizes that customers are not homogeneous and that a single version of an operation is unlikely to either be cost-effective or satisfy all customers.

The current trends suggest that the operations of 2030 will have recognized the need for truly *differentiated service offerings and a supporting portfolio of supply chain types*. There will be a group of customers for whom the full advantages of visibility and exchange of information described above are exploited, but customers who are transitory or who operate in highly competitive marketplaces and chase price by using multiple suppliers will not be interested in the long-term commitments needed for sharing data or building relationships. Similarly, sourcing arrangements with suppliers can be seen to benefit from improved connectivity, but for one group this might mean sharing databases, combined processes and automatic replenishment systems to support the stable path in the supply chain, whereas for another group it will translate into e-sourcing, auctions and standardized trading arrangements in support of a volatile/agile path.

Not only will the arrangements with customers and suppliers evolve, but in two decades the business model in the middle may well be quite different. Outsourcing as a practice will be entering its third or fourth generation, and the early thrust to outsource everything will be well behind us. By 2030 companies will know much better which parts of their business to outsource to third parties and which to keep in-house. Essentially, if speed and agility to service a fast-changing market is needed, outsourcing from long-distance locations will not work. Indeed, there is already evidence that some companies have realized this and are withdrawing parts of their product range from overseas manufacture and accepting the higher local costs of production as the premium they must pay for greater speed and responsiveness to their markets. *Capacity all along the supply chain is going to be a key ingredient of success.*

Some business models, however, will be based entirely on networks of dispersed facilities that the market-facing company does not own. Some of these facilities may be positioned locally as noted above, and others spread across countries that have a particular competitive price or quality advantage for selected lines. Some of the big brand owners such as Adidas and Nike and one of the most successful sourcing companies of the late 1990s–early 2000s, Li & Fung, have successfully forged this path to support their customers. The model of *'orchestrating' networks of diverse manufacturing and distribution facilities* to provide responsive types and levels of capacity is particularly suited to the vagaries of the fashion and accessories markets and is likely to be the mainstay of these industries by 2030.

One of the drivers of new business models in logistics and supply chains has always been the quest for scale. In smaller markets, such as Australia, the only realistic way to achieve that scale for many product categories is with *industry-level arrangements*. Industry-level logistics consortiums, where the majority of competitors in an industry use a single industry-owned logistics entity to undertake all the physical activities, can provide major cost advantages where companies are willing to cooperate. Aggregated logistics operations also increase transport utilization, in the process taking pressure off the environment through correspondingly less emissions. The traditional barriers to industry-level arrangements in the past have been perceived as the competition regulators, but in recent years the distinction between competing in the marketplace

'Many commentators look to a future of a demand-driven supply chain, in which close collaborative relationships between trading partners allow the true demand signals (sales) to be captured and automatically transmitted upstream to supplying organizations.'

on price, product range, brand and associated dimensions while collaborating to provide a more economically efficient use of capacity has been supported, with examples already in place in the resources and cash-management industries. Over the coming years this model is expected to extend into industries such as pharmaceuticals, FMCG, electronic high-tech, oil and gas and building materials as well as other industrial sectors.

Similarly, *regional aggregations* of complementary manufacturers are expected to combine their logistics operations to overcome the disadvantages of locations remote to major markets (in parallel with the development of clustering approaches to other opportunities such as R&D and IT development).

One of the aspects of sound business planning that has been underrepresented in supply chain decision-making until the last few years is *risk management*. Logistics networks have been designed to minimize operating cost at a given service level, and capacities and inventories have been fine-tuned and driven by lean mindsets. In the first part of the new century, though, perhaps one of the biggest issues on the minds of business executives is the potential impact of disruption to their corporate supply chains, irrespective whether the cause is terrorism, natural disasters, delays in supply or systems failures. Already we are seeing that such disruptions can have up to a 30 per cent negative impact on a firm's share price, and the effects can last for up to three years![5]

Planning approaches that incorporate risk into all tactical and strategic plans is more likely to be the norm by 2030. This will also reflect the more sophisticated methods of planning which use hard-edge analytics and modelling combined with intuition and experience in techniques such as 'real options' and scenario planning. The complexity of the alternatives and trade-offs available across the systems, multiple participants and multiple supply chains of 2030 will demand *highly developed planning formats* and highly trained management.

AND FINALLY...

The biggest change affecting the formation, operation and performance of supply chains by 2030 is that enterprises will regard them as central to the health and well-being of the business, rather than just a specialist functional activity. This change in philosophy will open up new areas of value extraction across the entire business, as well as up and down the supply chains that a given business is involved in.

Inside the firm, executives of every discipline will recognize that they all have a contribution to make towards the performance of the firm's supply chains, because, after all, these provide the real-time linkages to suppliers and customers alike, both of which are the life-blood of the business.

And this realization will not be limited to product organizations. By 2030 service organizations across many industries will be actively using supply chain principles to drive performance. Organizations such as banks, insurance companies, tourist organizations, hospitals and education establishments will be forced to apply supply chain principles in search of the optimum cost-service zone to perform in. There is simply no other way.

ALIGNMENT INSIGHTS

- *The future operating environment will be more hostile and far less forgiving than that which we have experienced for the last 15 years. Managing in times of growth is made easier by the sheer scale of demand; managing in extremely volatile times when business and consumer confidence is all over the place is something else.*

- *Given that there is never any change unless there is pressure for such change, the next two decades should see many breakthroughs in all areas of the supply chain, from technology to the greater understanding of human behaviour. So out of the gloom of difficult market conditions will rise the 'phoenix' in the form of innovation and creativity as we humans endeavour to find new, sophisticated ways to get ahead of fast-rising complexity. If we fail, a lot of people will be hurt. It is a must-do, a life-or-death race, but one which we can win and must win.*

- *In light of the above comments, we need to break away from the conventions of the past and find fundamentally new business models that better 'fit' the new operating conditions. This means collaborating more with external parties in our supply chains when it's appropriate and finding superior ways of organizing our people on the inside of the firm. We need to align both the inside and outside worlds.*

NOTES

1   *Popular Mechanics*, March 1949.
2   We are not in favour of all this terminology change and take the position that we should now stick with the 'supply chain' term, as imperfect as it is, and simply redefine its boundaries as our thinking develops in this area.
3   See Chapter 22 for a more detailed treatment of this topic.
4   'i2 business content library', i2, 2008, http://www.i2.com/solutions/business_content_library.cfm.
5   See Chapter 22 for a more detailed treatment of this topic.

Last Word

John Gattorna

If readers get to this point in the book, they will be under no misconception about the key messages it contains. Hopefully readers, especially industry professionals, will try some of the recipes recommended in these pages. One thing is for sure: we cannot, in the type of uncertain world we are heading into, after the financial meltdown of 2008–09, continue with the same old conventional ways of doing things. We need a new business model for the business as a whole and for the supply chains of which they are part. There have to be fundamental changes in mindset and corresponding practice just to survive, let alone thrive. The new business model suggested in this book is 'dynamic alignment' in all its variants. Indeed, 'alignment' principles will be at the core of any new model. 'Alignment' is everywhere – in the way top golfers like Tiger Woods plays his golf, in the day-to-day work of orthopaedic surgeons and, indeed, embedded in nature and natural systems as depicted on the jacket of this book. It is inexorably woven into our lives, and we must recognize this fact and adopt its principles to design our enterprise supply chains for peak performance in the tough years ahead. The 'game' rules have changed, and it is time for inspired leadership – not a retreat into short-term cost-cutting. Adherence to the 'alignment' principles detailed in this book will show us better ways to achieve more by way of cost reductions, and growing the top line through enhanced customer satisfaction.

Here are the ten 'must dos' for supply chain designers and business practitioners going forward:

1. Always start with the customer, because customers ultimately drive supply chains through the very way in which they prefer to buy products and services.

2. Recognize that we are setting ourselves up to fail by the way we continue to design and operate our organizational structures. The internal structure of the enterprise must more accurately mirror the structure of the marketplace being served, and care should be taken in the way we position our people in these structures.

3. We must find ways to 'join all the dots' so that what is happening on the outside will be more easily read and interpreted by people on the inside of the enterprise.

For now, there is too much guessing and second-guessing going on; those in market-facing positions have the responsibility of interpreting market signals and passing

'We are setting ourselves up to fail by the way we continue to design and operate our organizational structures.'

this information on to non-market-facing personnel inside the firm.

4. Procurement strategies on the supply side of the chain are just as important to success as sales and distribution strategies on the demand side; both sides must be in synch, irrespective of the particular combinations of supply chain types being invoked. This situation is depicted in Figure LW.1.

5. By building organizational 'clusters' on the inside of the enterprise we are likely to get better alignment with both functional departments *and* external customer segments; good working relationships in each case are vital for peak performance.

6. In the end, as first demonstrated by Toyota in the automotive industry, the best results come from buyers and sellers working together against waste in the chain; in this way, *both* parties benefit.

7. Sustainability of enterprise supply chains in the face of increased probability of disruptions is going to be a major consideration in the next two decades, and risk-management regimes will be essential to mitigate potential losses and system failures. The inevitable rise in oil prices is going to drive new disciplines in enterprise supply chains.

8. Corporate social responsibility will also play a bigger role in the way enterprises behave, because consumers are deadly serious about the need for this – and they will vote with their feet if they see contrary behaviour, no matter how big the organization or how powerful the brand.

9. New growth opportunities will emerge as the concept of globalization comes under pressure, and customers and consumers alike once again warm to products and services that are designed and made in the region or closer to home, in the immediate locality.

10. Overall, the outstanding challenge is more of a mental rather than a physical one. In the next generation we need leaders to emerge, who understand that ultimately supply chains connecting buyers and sellers the world over are in effect 'human systems'. As such, we need

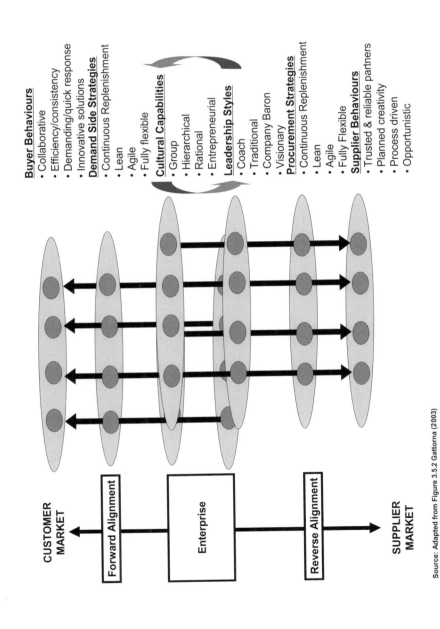

Buyer Behaviours
· Collaborative
· Efficiency/consistency
· Demanding/quick response
· Innovative solutions

Demand Side Strategies
· Continuous Replenishment
· Lean
· Agile
· Fully flexible

Cultural Capabilities
· Group
· Hierarchical
· Rational
· Entrepreneurial

Leadership Styles
· Coach
· Traditional
· Company Baron
· Visionary

Procurement Strategies
· Continuous Replenishment
· Lean
· Agile
· Fully Flexible

Supplier Behaviours
· Trusted & reliable partners
· Planned creativity
· Process driven
· Opportunistic

CUSTOMER
MARKET

Forward Alignment

Enterprise

Reverse Alignment

SUPPLIER
MARKET

Source: Adapted from Figure 3.5.2 Gattorna (2003)

Figure LW.1   Supply-side alignment: the mirror image of the customer side

a more multidisciplinary approach to designing and operating the supply chains of the future, and a retraction of the sins of the past: for example, overemphasis on IT; paranoia about competitors; and a preoccupation with hard assets at the expense of softer assets such as humans and their behaviour, knowledge and intellectual capital. Those enterprises that achieve this vital change in mindset will be those at the top of the performance tree in 2030.

Select Bibliography

A Business and ICT Architecture for a Logistics City, accepted for publication in 2008, *International Journal of Production Economics: Interlocking of Information Systems for International Supply and Demand Chains Management.*

Epstein, M.J. (2008), *Making Sustainability Work: Best Practices in Managing and Measuring Corporate Social, Environmental and Economic Impacts*, Berrett-Koehler.

Esty, D.C. and Winston, A.S. (2006), *Green to Gold; How Smart Companies Use Environmental Strategy to Innovate, Create Value and Build Competitive Advantage*, Yale University Press.

Flapper, S.D., Nunen, J. van and Wassenhove, L. Van (eds) (2005), *Managing Closed-Loop Supply Chains*, Springer, Berlin and Heidelberg.

Gattorna, J.L. (ed.) (2003), *Gower Handbook of Supply Chain Management* (5th edn), Gower Publishing, Aldershot.

Gattorna, J.L. (2006), *Living Supply Chains*, FT Prentice Hall, Harlow.

Giannakis, M. (2008). Facilitating learning and knowledge transfer through supplier development. *Supply Chain Management: An International Journal* 13/1, pp. 62–72.

Hirsch, R.L., Bezdek, R.H. and Wendling, R.M. (2007), 'Peaking of World Oil Production: Recent Forecasts', US Department of Energy/National Energy Technology Lab, NETL-2007/1263, 5 February, http://www.fraw.org.uk/library/peakoil/hirsch_2007.pdf.

Humphries, A.S. and Wilding, R. (2003), 'Sustained Monopolistic Business Relationships: An Interdisciplinarity Case', *British Journal of Management*, Vol. 14, pp. 323–338.

Humphries, A.S. and Wilding, R. (2004), 'Long Term Collaborative Business Relationships: The Impact of Trust and C3 Behaviour', *Journal of Marketing Management*, Vol. 20, pp. 1107–1122.

Kong, C.C. (2005), 'Petrochemicals – 5: Profit Improvement', Report, July–August, *Hydrocarbon Asia*, hcasia.safan.com.

Kopczak, L.R. and Thomas, A. (2005), *From Logistics to Supply Chain Management: The Path Forward in the Humanitarian Sector*, White paper, Fritz Institute, San Francisco, CA.

Marn, M.V., Roegner, E.V. and Zawada, C.C. (2005), *The Price Advantage*, John Wiley, Hoboken, NJ.

Nagle, T.T. and Hogan, J.E. (2002), *The Strategy and Tactics of Pricing: A Guide to Growing More Profitably*, Prentice Hall/Pearson Education, Upper Saddle River, NJ.

Plambeck, E.L. (2007), 'The Greening of Wal-Mart's Supply Chain', *Supply Chain Management Review*, Vol. 5, No. 11, p. 18.

Robeson, J.F. and Copacino, W.C. (1994), *The Logistics Handbook*, The Free Press, New York.

Rogers, D.S. and Tibben-Lembke, R.S. (1998), *Going Backwards: Reverse Logistics Trends and Practices*, Reverse Logistics Executive Council, RLEC Press, Pittsburgh, PA.

Roos, G., Pike, S., and Fernstrom, L. (2006), *Managing Intellectual Capital in Practice*, Butterworth-Heinemann.

Ryals, L. and Humphries, A.S. (2007), 'Seeing Eye to Eye', *Chief Purchasing Officers Agenda*, Vol. 3, No. 4, pp. 53–57.

Sengpiehl, C., Oakden, R., Nagel, P., Toh, K.T.K. and Shi, P. (2008), 'The Emergence of Logistics Cities: Conceptual Model', Journal of Transport and Supply Chain Management, Vol. 2, Issue 1, (November), pp. 58–77.

Shapiro, J.F. (2002), 'Modelling Approaches for Supply Chain Decisions', *ASCET Journal, Achieving Supply Chain Excellence through Technology*, Montgomery Research, San Francisco.

Shapiro, J.F. (2006), *Modeling the Supply Chain* (2nd edn), Southwestern Press, Carlsbad, CA.

Shapiro, J.F. and Wagner, S.N. in association with Arriaga, F.G. and Marenco, S. (2008), 'Strategic Inventory Optimisation', unpublished paper, February 2008.

Simchi-Levi, D., Kaminsky, P, and Simchi-Levi, E. (2000), *Designing and Managing the Supply Chain*, Irwin McGraw-Hill, New York.

About John Gattorna

Dr John L. Gattorna, BE (Melb), MBA (Monash), PhD (Cranfield), was born in a country town in rural New South Wales, Australia. He attended boarding school, and took his Engineering degree at Melbourne University. He then worked as a young engineer for several years, building roads and bridges for the Victorian State Highway Construction Authority, and later branched out into oilfield equipment with FMC Corp. Following this he spent four years at the Vickers Detroit Hydraulics division of Sperry Rand. It was while working for the latter organization that he undertook MBA studies on a part-time basis. He says these were the hardest years of his life, working and studying as if full-time in both! It was while he was studying for his MBA at Monash that he met Dr Mark Doctoroff, a visiting Fulbright Scholar, who first introduced John to the 'Distribution Management' topic, which later morphed into Logistics, and finally Supply Chain Management.

John became so interested in this burgeoning field that he decided to swap careers and, as a direct consequence of this decision, he headed for the UK to study for his doctorate at the renowned Cranfield School of Management, Cranfield University. John spent four years at Cranfield and a year at Oxford in the late 1970s, before deciding to return to Australia with his young family in 1980. He started teaching at the University of New South Wales that same year, and subsequently moved to Macquarie University in 1984, both located in Sydney, but full-time academic life was not what he ultimately wanted to do.

In 1985, John founded his own consulting firm, specializing in marketing and logistics, and this grew into a high-prolife consultancy, with clients spread across the world. In 1994, Andersen Consulting (now Accenture) approached John about joining forces with them and, after a year of discussions, John joined Andersen in 1995, taking parts of his previous business with him and started Andersen Consulting's Logistics Strategy Practice in the Asia Pacific region. John subsequently became Managing Partner of the Accenture Supply Chain Practice in Australia and Southern Asia and developed the business over a period of 7 years, before retiring in December 2002.

However John, like Charles Handy, doesn't believe in the 'R' word and since then has become an acknowledged 'Thought Leader' in the global supply chain field. Today he continues to write and publish at a prolific rate and acts in an advisory capacity to many organizations around the world. He is much sought after on the international conference circuit and each year he appears at over 20 conferences and seminars.

John's passion is the 'dynamic' alignment framework which he co-developed in the 1990s and has made continual refinements through field use ever since. It is this framework that provides much of the inspiration for his 'thought leadership' and involves taking a unique multi-disciplinary view of the way supply chains work within and between enterprises. As John often says, 'it is people that propel supply chains, not technology or hard assets'.

In parallel with his speaking, writing and advisory work, John holds Adjunct Professorships at several universities including: Macquarie Graduate School of Management, Macquarie University, Sydney; Victoria University, Melbourne, where his is Chair of the Industry Advisory Board at the Institute of Logistics and Supply Chain Management (ILSCM); and he teaches at the Le Havre and Caen campuses of Normandy Business School, France each year.

Every two years, John leads a major Supply Chain Business Summit, which attracts panelists and delegates from all over the world to discuss and debate topic issues. In February 2010, the theme of the Summit will be: *Fix Your Supply Chains and You'll Fix Your Enterprise (and the Economy)*.

John has several new books in the pipeline and interested parties should visit his website for more details: www.johngattorna.com. He always welcomes dialogue, and can be contacted at any time at the following email address: john@johngattorna.com.

Notes on Contributors

John Gattorna

Dr John Gattorna is an acknowledged 'thought-leader' on the global supply chain scene. For over two decades he has researched, consulted and worked in various capacities in and around enterprise supply chains. He established and led the Australian and South Asian Accenture supply chain practice, 1995–2002 and has since focused on advising boards and senior management on how to improve the 'alignment' of their enterprise supply chains with customers, suppliers and third-party providers. John's most recent book, *Living Supply Chains* (FT Prentice Hall, Harlow, 2006) is receiving wide acclaim for its innovative content which cuts across all disciplines in the enterprise. He is also much sought after as a speaker on the international conference circuit, and holds a number of visiting professorships at universities in Australia, the UK, Asia and Europe. John always welcomes contact from interested parties in the global supply chain community and can be contacted at: john@johngattorna.com; www. johngattorna.com.

Kate Andrews

Kate Andrews is Professor, Faculty of Information Technology, QUT and Principal of specialist knowledge asset consultancy KNOWABLE. She is an organizational psychologist who, for her doctorate, investigated knowledge processes in a pre-eminent biomedical research consortium. Her research on psychosocial influences on knowledge transfer is influential. In her consulting role, Kate has particular interests in knowledge creation and transfer within and across companies and mitigating knowledge loss as key staff exit. Maximizing learning from major projects, partnerships and alliance is a further specialization. Kate teaches at postgraduate level and delivers knowledge master classes in Australia, Hong Kong, Malaysia, Singapore and India. E-mail: kate.andrews@knowable.com.au.

Carlos Aravechia

Carlos Aravechia is an industrial engineer from the Federal University of Sao Carlos and holds a Master of Science degree in supply chain management from Methodist University of Piracicaba, both in Brazil. He is CPIM-certified by APICS. A former teacher and researcher, he currently leads supply chain management transformation projects at Axia Consulting. E-mail: carlos. aravechia@axiaconsulting.com.br.

Mike Bernon

Mike Bernon is an academic at Cranfield School of Management (UK) and specializes in supply chain management. His research focuses on supply chain sustainability, carbon footprint measurement, reverse logistics and global supply chain design. He has been the principal investigator for a number of recent major research programmes, including the World Bank; the UK Department for Transport (DfT); UK Department for the Environment; Food and Rural Affairs (DEFRA); and the EPSRC UK. Along with his lecturing duties at Cranfield, he is also visiting professor at a number of academic institutions worldwide and speaks at numerous conferences on subjects relating to environmental and ethical supply chain management issues. E-Mail: m.p.bernon@Cranfield.ac.uk.

Leeora Black

Leeora D. Black, PhD, is founder and Managing Director of the Australian Centre for Corporate Social Responsibility. Leeora's work focuses on analysing and solving complex CSR issues and problems, building organizational CSR capacity and strategy, stakeholder engagement and research, and CSR measurement. She advises global firms, government businesses and social sector organizations on the integration of CSR into business operations and strategies, stakeholder engagement and communications, issues management and reputation. Her doctorate pioneered new methods of CSR measurement. Leeora is a widely published author and speaker on corporate social responsibility. E-mail: leeorablack@accsr.com.au.

Paul W. Bradley

Paul W. Bradley has held key positions in international business for more than two decades. He is currently involved in several entrepreneurial ventures and serves on various international boards and advisory committees. Mr. Bradley previously served as President of Arshiya International, a leading Indian multinational company listed on the Bombay Stock Exchange and as Managing Director of IDS Logistics International and IDS Logistics Singapore (a member of the Li & Fung Group of Companies), as well as other leadership positions in the logistics industry. He received his MBA Degree in International Management from Thunderbird, School of Global Management. Mr. Bradley was selected by the World Economic Forum as one of the 'New Asian Leaders' and was also recognized as the 'Asian Supply Chain Manager of the Year' by Lloyds FTB Publications in 2004. He currently serves as Vice Chairman of Supply Chain Asia and is a Fellow of the Chartered Institute of Logistics and Transport. Prior to the logistics industry, Mr. Bradley worked in various political assignments including the United States Senate and the British House of Commons. E-mail: pwbradley@pacific.net.sg.

Carlos Frederico Bremer

Carlos Bremer holds a PhD in Industrial Engineering from University of Sao Paulo, Brazil, as well as a post-doctoral degree from RWTH Aachen University in Germany. He is certified CPIM and CSCP by APICS. He has had 15 years' academic experience with more than 50 publications in the SCM knowledge domain. In his practical career, he has worked for companies such as Siemens in Germany and, since 2001, has been working as a SCM consultant. Currently, he is Executive Partner at Axia Consulting, Brazil. E-mail: carlos.bremer@axiaconsulting.com.br.

Rodrigo Cambiaghi Azevedo

Rodrigo Cambiaghi Azevedo is a Master of Science and Bachelor in Industrial Engineering from the University of Sao Paulo, Brazil. He is currently pursuing his PhD in Supply Chain Management at Université Laval, Quebec, Canada. He is a certified CPIM by APICS. His experience as a supply chain management consultant spans several countries including Brazil, Italy and Slovakia. He has also worked in the automotive industry for companies such as Volkswagen and Daimler-Benz, in Germany. He currently heads the innovation process at Axia Consulting. E-mail: rodrigo.cambiaghi@axiaconsulting.com.br.

Brett Campbell

Brett Campbell has over 20 years' experience of operations performance improvement, including 13 years in senior operations management and eight years of supply chain strategic consulting and operational design in resources, manufacturing and FMCG industries throughout Australia, Europe and Asia. Brett was the lead partner for Deloitte's Asia Pacific Supply Chain Practice prior to joining Grays Online – Australia's largest B2C online auctioneer and retailer as at Octoner 2008 – as their Chief Operating Officer. He is a recognized international expert in supply chain and operational improvement, procurement and strategic sourcing, and inbound and outbound channel strategies. He has published various procurement and logistics papers, including 'Achieving Immediate Value from eSourcing', one of the chapters in the *Handbook of Supply Chain Management* (Gower 2003). E-mail: brett.campbell@grays.com.au.

Jeremy Clarke

Jeremy Clarke heads LLC Law, a niche UK logistics and MHE law firm providing industry-specific legal support to PLC and SME companies on 3PL, 4PL and collaborative service arrangements; automated MHE procurement, sales and distribution; and corporate joint ventures, investments, acquisitions and disposals. Jeremy is known for his strategic approach, bringing fresh and highly commercial thinking to the legal process and enabling the law to be used as an effective tool for business. He writes and lectures widely across the UK, Europe, Australasia and the Far East. E-mail: jclarke@llc-law.co.uk.

Deborah Ellis

Deborah Ellis is a supply chain consultant based in Sydney. She has conducted projects in Australia and Asia since 1990 in a wide range of industries including industrial, FMCG, retail, resources and banking. Her consulting practice, Carpenter Ellis, has, in recent years, undertaken logistics reviews, network modeling and other ground-breaking projects for major banks, applying supply chain principles to the distribution of cash. She has also collaborated with Dr John Gattorna on industry-level engagements for the Australian coal industry and for the Australian textiles, clothing and footwear Industry. Earlier in her career Deborah held line responsibility for logistics operations with Master Foods (Mars Corporation) and in third-party perishable distribution with Frigmobile (Swire). Deborah has presented at conferences in Australia, South Africa and the USA on supply chain topics including network optimization modelling, her specialization. E-mail: debellis@carpenterellis.com.

Anna Game-Lopata

Anna Game-Lopata has been Editor of *Logistics* and *Packaging* magazines since 2006 and 2008 respectively. She is not only responsible for content, but also the two associated website businesses and industry awards programmes. Anna's background in the media spans radio, TV and publishing, including 10 years as a talk-back radio producer for commercial, community and ABC radio in Melbourne. She has also held a variety of roles with ABC TV including script editor for the first series of MDA (Medical Defence Australia), researcher for *The Arts Show* and assistant for the first series of *Kath and Kim* and *The Einstein Factor*. Prior to joining RBI, Australia's largest B2B publisher, Anna worked as Features Editor for the successful online magazine, *The Australian Investor*. E-mail:Anna.Game-Lopata@ReedBusiness.com.au.

Scott Githens

Scott Githens is the National Supply Chain Planning Manager for OneSteel Distribution in Australia, with responsibility for the implementation and improvement of supply chain strategy, planning (including S&OP) and inventory management capabilities across the business. Before joining OnsSteel, Scott was a Senior Manager in Accenture's supply chain practice, specializing in supply chain strategy and operating model development, S&OP and supply chain planning, and inventory management, as well as organizational change management and human performance aspects of supply chain transformation programmes. Scott has a BA in Logistics Engineering and Management and Human Resources Management from The University of NSW and is an APICS CPIM. E-mail: GithensS@onesteel.com.

Janet Godsell

Dr Janet Godsell is a Senior Research Fellow at the Supply Chain Research Centre at Cranfield University. For the last eight years she has been conducting a range of research, teaching and independent consultancy activities in her specialist area of customer-driven supply chain strategy.

Janet's motivation is to turn 'good research into good practice', an ambition fuelled by her industrial roots. She has worked for ICI, Sumitomo Heavy Industries Ltd, Shell, Astra Zeneca and Dyson in the UK and Japan, gaining practical experience in all aspects of supply chain strategy. She is a chartered engineer, with a Masters in Mechanical Engineering, Manufacture and Management from the University of Birmingham. She also has an MBA and PhD from Cranfield University. E-mail: janet.godsell@cranfield.ac.uk.

Kevin B. Hendricks

Kevin Hendricks is a Professor of Operations Management and Information Technology at the Wilfrid Laurier University, Ontario, Canada. He has a Bachelor and Masters degree in Electrical Engineering and a PhD (1990) in Operations Management, all from Cornell University. His research and teaching interests are in the areas of stochastic modeling of manufacturing systems, the relation between operations management and accounting, and stock price performance. E-mail: khendricks@wlu.ca.

Lucas Cley da Horta

Lucas Horta holds Bachelor and Master of Science degrees in Mechanical Engineering from the University of Sao Paulo, Brazil, and is CPIM, CIRM and CSCP certified by APICS and PMP certified by PMI. Since 2001 he has worked in SCM Consulting, and he currently holds an executive account managerial position at Axia Consulting. E-mail: lucas.horta@axiaconsulting.com.br.

Kate Hughes

Kate Hughes is a supply chain consultant in Australia and South-East Asia, based in Sydney. She specializes in industry studies, behavioural segmentation and supply chain alignment. Before building her own business, Kate worked in retail with IKEA (Australia), commencing in store sales and finishing in supply chain management at the Australian head office. Her passion is in understanding and improving deployment and performance of humanitarian supply chains. Kate holds a first-class BSc in Geography and Botany, a Masters in Applied Science in remote sensing and geographic information systems (GIS), and an MBA. She is currently a PhD student at Macquarie Graduate School of Management (MGSM), completing her studies in humanitarian response and supply chain alignment. E-mail: kate.hughes@hughes-scm.com.

Andrew Humphries

Andrew is Chairman and CEO of SCCI Ltd. He has over 35 years' experience as a practical military logistics manager and director. He obtained his PhD from Cranfield School of Management, and his expertise lies in performance improvement within complex, commercial relationships. Andrew has applied his innovative techniques to assisting managers to understand the complexity and the bottom-line relationship issues in a wide variety of national and international organizations in the public and private sectors. He is a well-known speaker and has published widely. His latest book, co-authored with

Dr Andrew Gibbs, is titled *Strategic Alliances and Marketing Partnerships* (Kogan Page, 2009). E-mail: andrew.humphries@sccindex.com.

Nigel Jones

Nigel Jones is General Manager Group Supply Chain Strategy and Best Practice, Fonterra Cooperative Group, New Zealand. He is responsible for developing the supply chain strategy for Fonterra, the world's largest dairy exporter; Nigel joined the dairy industry with 18 years' experience in leading international companies within the logistics industry. Since joining Fonterra Nigel has developed and led a series of major initiatives that have delivered significant financial and environmental benefits. In addition to a comprehensive operational background and seagoing qualifications, Nigel is a Fellow of the Chartered Institute of Logistics and Transport and holds Bachelor degrees in Accountancy and Business Finance, and an MSc in Supply Chain and Logistics from Cranfield University in the UK. E-mail: Nigel.Jones@fonterra.com.

Chung Chee Kong

Chung Chee Kong is the founder and Managing Director of Acceval, a Singapore-based pricing and profit optimization software company, providing advisory services on pricing excellence. Chung's area of expertise is pricing and supply chain management, especially for the manufacturing industries. He has a pricing research certification from the Professional Pricing Society (PPS) and is CPIM (APICS) certified. Chung is competent in both management and technology consulting and has helped various companies in the Asia Pacific region embark on various transformation initiatives in the area of pricing management. His experience includes engagements with companies such as Sumitomo Chemical; The Polyolefin Company (Shell Chemical Joint Venture), Becton Dickinson, Petronas, Ranbaxy, Akzo Nobel, ExxonMobil, Siam Cement Chemical Company, among others. At Acceval, he developed a fully-fledged Margin Optimization model which aligns pricing, customer strategy and the supply chain in order to optimize margin. This capability is enabled through PriXLence™, Acceval's pricing and profit optimization software which received the 'Best Customer ROI' award from SAP. Chung has written a number of articles on pricing management and, in addition to being a regular speaker on the topics of pricing management and supply chain management at regional forums, has delivered speeches as a guest lecturer at regional universities. Prior to founding Acceval, Chung Chee Kong worked for Shell Eastern Petroleum before becoming a Senior Manager at Accenture and Deloitte Consulting respectively. E-mail: ck.chung@acceval-intl.com.

Pieter Nagel

Pieter is the Director of the Institute for Logistics and Supply Chain Management at Victoria University, Melbourne, Australia. After commencing his career in his native South Africa, he developed an international reputation as a leader in supply chain strategy. He was appointed as the first occupant of an industry-sponsored Chair in Logistics at the University of Pretoria in South

Africa in 1985, which then evolved to become the Centre for Supply Chain Management. He also established the Centre for Logistics Management at the Johannesburg University. He moved to Australia in 1998. Pieter has worked on all major continents delivering logistics expertise to the petrochemical, defence, banking and finance, and retail sectors. Among his significant achievements has been his pivotal role in the establishment of three key research and learning institutes. His areas of interest include: the future development of supply chains into dynamic value networks; the strategic logistics environment; effective strategic procurement as a prime business tool; and developing Melbourne Australia as a national Logistics City. E-mail: Pieter.Nagel@vu.edu.au.

Linda Nuthall

Linda Nuthall is an independent Management Consultant based in Sydney. Previously, she was a Strategy Manager in Accenture's Australia and New Zealand supply chain practice. She has experience working across a broad range of industries in such areas as demand and inventory management, network and organization structure design, customer segmentation, strategic alignment and performance management. Her publications include 'Supply Chain Network Optimization Modelling' and 'Supply Chain Performance Measures and Systems', chapters in the *Handbook of Supply Chain Management* (Gower, 2003); the 'Supply Chain Management Tools' chapter in *Strategic Supply Chain Alignment* (Gower, 1998) and she also conducted much of the research for *Supply Chain Cybermastery* (Gower, 2001) and *Smart Things to Know About Six Sigma* (Capstone, 2003). Linda holds a Bachelor of Applied Science (Industrial Mathematics and Computing) degree from Charles Sturt University, NSW, and an MSc in Supply Chain Management from Cranfield University, UK. E-mail: lindanuthall@yahoo.com.au.

Roger Oakden

Roger Oakden gained many years of industrial management and ERP applications experience prior to his appointment as Associate Director at a major consulting firm where he and his team assisted clients to improve their operations systems, logistics and strategic procurement. He then built up the Masters programme in Logistics Management at a major Australian university into the largest in the Asia-Pacific region. Roger now provides advice and education on improving logistics systems and processes to businesses throughout Australia and Asia and is an Associate of the Institute for Logistics and Supply Chain Management at Victoria University. E-mail: Roger.Oakden@vu.edu.au.

Michael Proffitt

Michael Proffitt has been involved with the logistics and supply chain sector for over 25 years. He has held board positions with Danzas in Switzerland and Hays in the UK, and has held a number of senior management positions within Deutsche Post. His most recent position was CEO of Dubai Logistics City – a key element within the 140-km² Dubai World Central development, which includes the new Al Maktoum International Airport. When fully completed, DWC will house between

900,000 and 1 million people, and the airport will have an annual capacity of approximately 160 million passengers and 12 million tons of air cargo. Michael has gained significant global experience and is now a Strategic Advisor to several high-profile companies across a number of different continents. E-mail: mproffitt@hotmail.co.uk.

Mark Reynolds

Mark Reynolds is a passionate advocate of corporate responsibility and sustainability for supply chain businesses. His role as Associate Director Sustainability with the Australian supply chain consultancy, the Portland Group, builds on his 25 years' experience of team leadership in engineering, manufacturing, logistics and supply chain projects. Mark's interests extend from strategic planning down to detailed analysis, communications and culture change. He has wide-ranging industry knowledge and exposure across food and beverages, supermarket and general retailing, logistics, building products, chemicals, industrial gases, agriculture, automotive, telecommunications, electronics, aerospace, basic metals, pharmaceuticals and electrical products. Mark holds Bachelor of Engineering (Mechanical) and Master of Engineering (Electrical) degrees from the University of Auckland, New Zealand. E-mail: markreynolds@iinet.net.au or mreynolds@portlandgroup.com.

Alyson Rodi

Alyson Rodi is a partner in the Deloitte International and Corporate Tax team in Sydney. She has over 15 years' experience of advising clients in this area. In addition to her extensive Australian experience, Alyson also has experience working in the international tax groups of Deloitte's London and Dublin offices, and working for a major London law firm. Alyson has worked across a wide range of industries on cross-border transactions, including tax structuring and transaction support for major IPO, infrastructure and private equity transactions, as well as advising on inbound and outbound investment structures. E-mail: ARodi@deloitte.com.au.

Vinod R. Singhal

Vinod Singhal is the Dr Alfred F. and Patricia L. Knoll Professor of Operations Management at the College of Management at Georgia Institute of Technology. He is the Associate Dean for MBA programmes, Area Coordinator for Operations Management, and the Associate Director for the Center for Paper Business and Industry Studies, an industry centre funded by the Sloan Foundation. He has an MSc in Operations Research and a PhD in Operations Management from the Simon School of Business, University of Rochester. His research and teaching interests are in the area of the relationship between operations management and accounting and stock price performance. He has served on the Board of Examiners of the Georgia Oglethorpe Award, Bell South's President Quality Award, and is currently on the Baldrige Board of Examiners. He is frequent presenter at various academic and practitioner conferences and at universities. E-mail: Vinod. Singhal@mgt.gatech.edu.

Keith Toh

Keith joined the Institute for Logistics and Supply Chain Management (ILSCM) from the Logistics Institute (Asia Pacific), Singapore, where he worked on research projects involving supply chain and risk management, uptake of RFID technology amongst supply chain partners, and return on investment (ROI) studies in supply chains. Prior to his affiliation with the Logistics Institute (Asia Pacific), Keith worked for Fujitsu Services in the UK and was involved with software life-cycle and application services. He has a PhD in enterprise modeling, retains a keen interest in enterprise architectures (EA) and is involved with the development of the Logistics City EA. E-mail: Keith.Toh@vu.edu.au.

Michael Whiting

Mike is currently Visiting Lecturer in Humanitarian Logistics at Cranfield University, UK. He lectures on the Defence Acquisition Management Course and at the Resilience Centre, and is a founder member of the Cardiff and Cranfield Universities' Humanitarian Logistics Initiative (CCHLI). Michael is also a Chartered Member of the Chartered Institute of Logistics and Transport (CILT) Humanitarian and Emergency Logistics Professionals (HELP) Steering Committee. Mike's 44 years of experience in logistics encompasses several post-conflict situations, including Angola, Bosnia-Herzegovina and Kosovo, as well as work in East and Central Africa, the Middle East, Cyprus, Turkey and Indonesia. Most recently, Mike was in Thailand and Myanmar for DfID where he was responsible for tasking fixed-wing and rotary aircraft engaged in delivering humanitarian aid to the victims of Cyclone Nargis. E-mail: michael4335@aol.com.

Stuart Whiting

Stuart Whiting has recently been appointed as the Global Head for DHL's global and multinational customers based at DHL's global headquarters in Bonn, Germany. Prior to this appointment Stuart held numerous commercial and logistics management positions across Asia Pacific for DHL, including; Country General Manager – Taiwan; Vice President Commercial Supply Chains – Asia Pacific; Director Global and Multinational Customers and Logistics – Japan; and Commercial Manager – Singapore. Prior to his DHL appointment, Stuart worked for TNT both in the USA and Asia, building and implementing supply chain and logistics management solutions for North American companies across the Pacific and within Asia Pacific. Stuart is a Fellow of the Chartered Institute of Logistics and Transport and holds a Global MSc in Logistics and Supply Chain Management from Cranfield University, UK. E-mail: stuart.whiting@dhl.com.

Richard Wilding

Richard is Director of SCCI Ltd. and Professor of Supply Chain Risk Management at the Centre for Logistics and Supply Chain Management, Cranfield School of Management, UK. He works with European and international companies on logistics and supply chain projects in all sectors, including pharmaceutical, retail, automotive, high-technology, food, drink and professional services to name a few. He is a highly acclaimed presenter and regular speaker at industry conferences and has undertaken lecture tours of Europe and Asia. His special areas of interest include the creation of collaborative business environments, reducing supply chain vulnerability and risk, time compression and techniques for aligning supply chains to maximize customer value and reduce cost. E-mail: r.d.wilding@cranfield.ac.uk.

Kim Winter
Kim Winter is founder and Managing Director of global specialists Logistics Executive Recruitment and is an acknowledged expert in the logistics and supply chain human resourcing field. With business units throughout Australia, Asia, Middle East and Europe, his company is the largest specialist organization of its kind delivering search, executive recruitment and recruitment outsource/project management solutions. He has held a number of senior executive positions within tier 1 supply chain organizations, regularly speaks at international conferences/forums and provides thought leadership on issues such as talent strategy, attraction, acquisition, development and retention. Kim has initiated, and is involved with, a number of humanitarian supply chain initiatives in East Africa and is co-founder of Oasis Africa Australia (www.oasisafrica.net), a thriving humanitarian organization which operates an acclaimed not-for-profit business model based out of the Kibera slum community school for 850 orphaned children in Nairobi, Kenya. E-mail: kimw@lrs.net.au.

Index